NOCHE ROJA

VERTIGO CRIME

PRAISE FOR SIMON OLIVER'S *THE EXTERMINATORS*

"Audacious. Simon Oliver knows his way around a story, and I'm impressed."

—JOSH OLSON,
SCREENWRITER, *A HISTORY OF VIOLENCE*

"Creepy, crass, head-shaking fun."

—ENTERTAINMENT WEEKLY

"A cunning, provocative slab of graphic fiction."

—BRIAN AZZARELLO,
WRITER, *100 BULLETS*

"More intriguing plot twists than *Lost*."

—WIZARD MAGAZINE

"Outstanding! Vertigo is the HBO of the comic-book world.
It proves this with THE EXTERMINATORS."

—WASHINGTON EXAMINER

"Hilariously black. Puts the creepy back in crawly."

—RUE MORGUE MAGAZINE

WRITER
SIMON OLIVER

ART
JASON LATOUR

LETTERS
CLEM ROBINS

NOCHE ROJA

Karen Berger SVP – Executive Editor
Jonathan Vankin Editor
Sarah Litt Asst. Editor
Robbin Brosterman Design Director – Books
Louis Prandi Art Director

DC COMICS
Diane Nelson President
Dan DiDio and Jim Lee Co-Publishers
Geoff Johns Chief Creative Officer
Patrick Caldon EVP – Finance and Administration
John Rood EVP – Sales, Marketing and Business Development
Amy Genkins SVP – Business and Legal Affairs
Steve Rotterdam SVP – Sales and Marketing
John Cunningham VP – Marketing
Terri Cunningham VP – Managing Editor
Alison Gill VP – Manufacturing
David Hyde VP – Publicity
Sue Pohja VP – Book Trade Sales
Alysse Soll VP – Advertising and Custom Publishing
Bob Wayne VP – Sales
Mark Chiarello Art Director

NOCHE ROJA
VERTIGO CRIME

SUSTAINABLE FORESTRY INITIATIVE   Certified Chain of Custody
60% Certified Fiber Sourcing and
40% Post-Consumer Recycled
www.sfiprogram.org

NSF-SFICOC-C0001801

This label applies to the text stock.

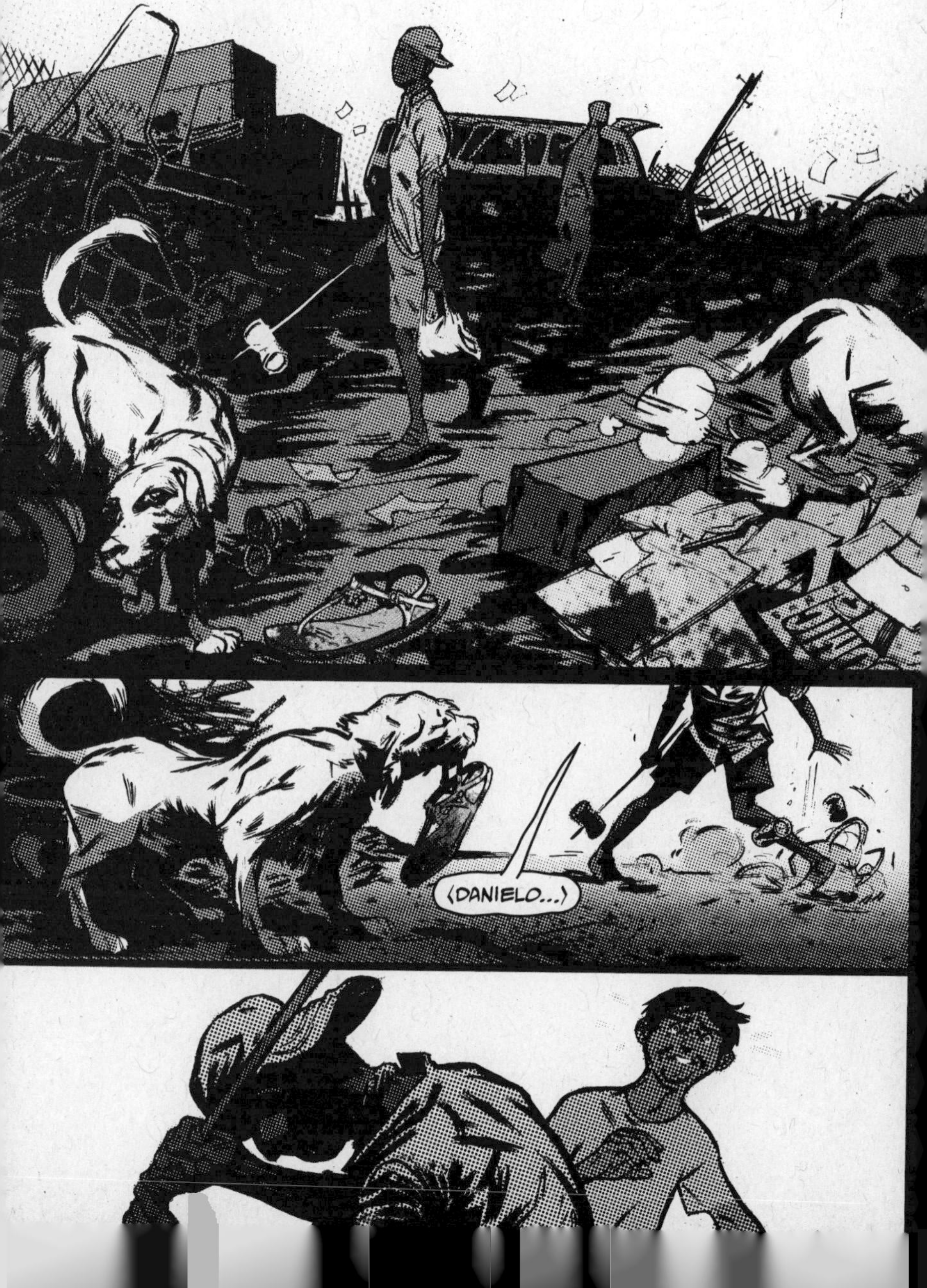
⟨DANIELO...⟩

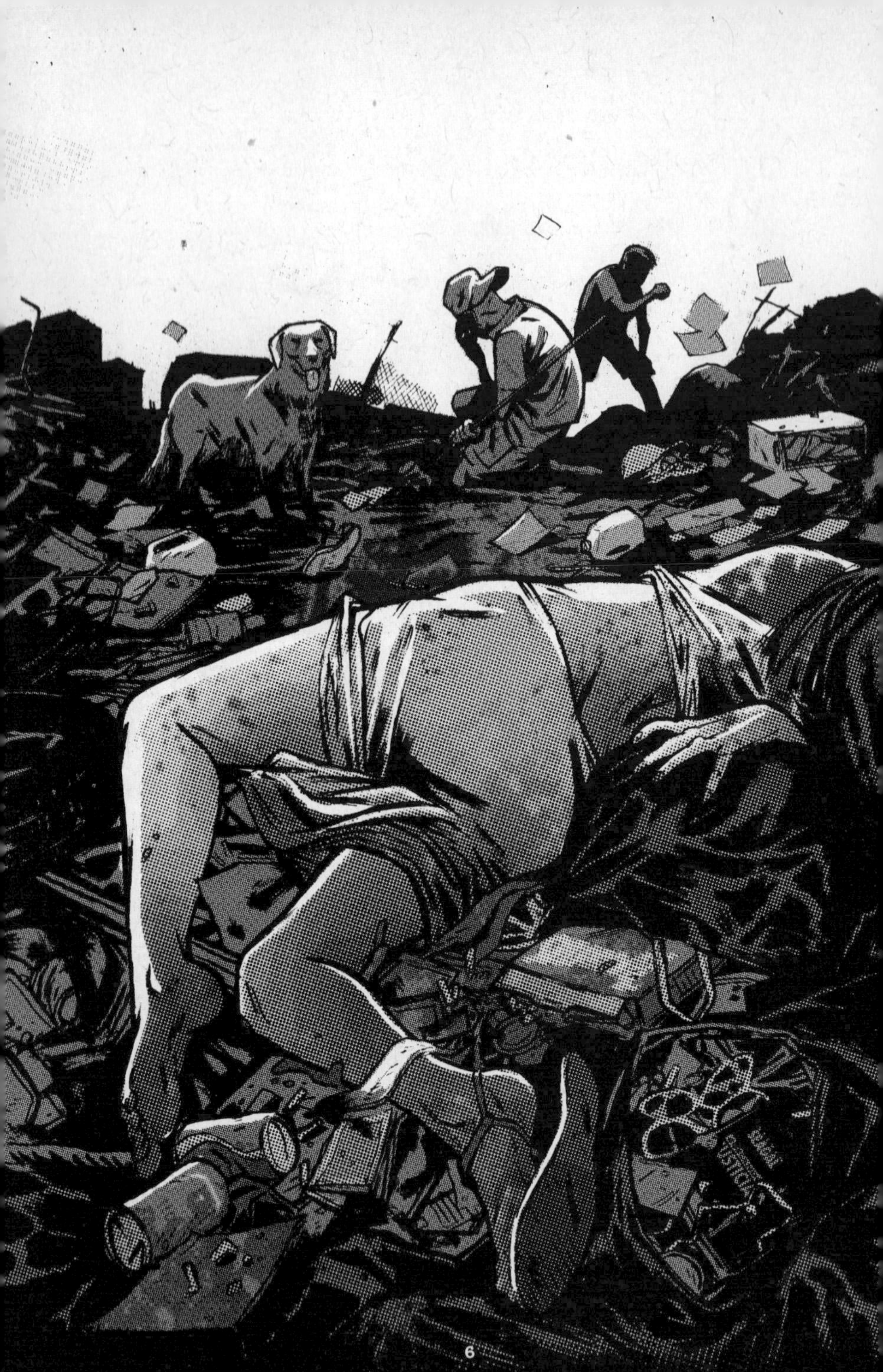

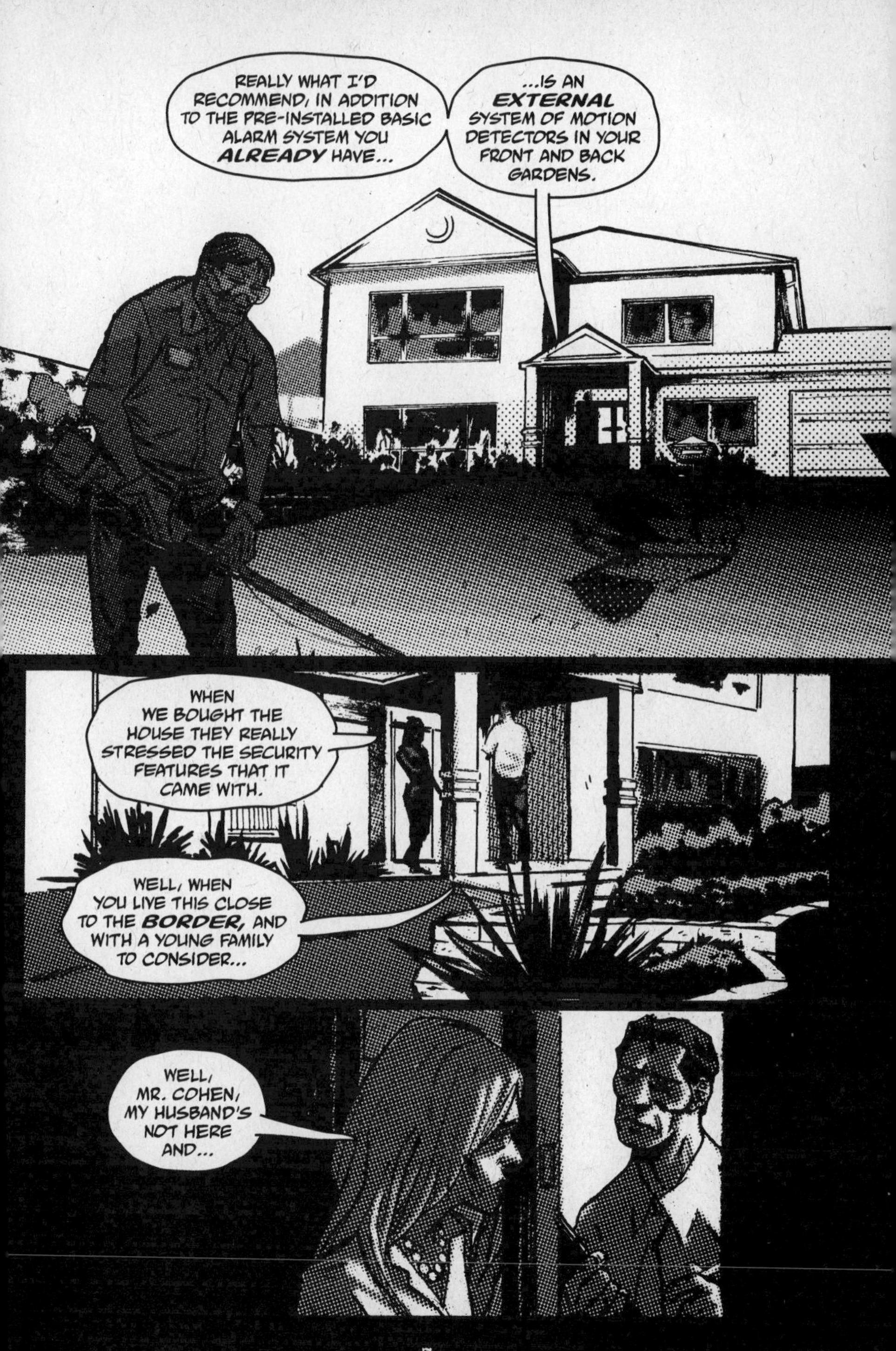
REALLY WHAT I'D RECOMMEND, IN ADDITION TO THE PRE-INSTALLED BASIC ALARM SYSTEM YOU ALREADY HAVE...
...IS AN EXTERNAL SYSTEM OF MOTION DETECTORS IN YOUR FRONT AND BACK GARDENS.
WHEN WE BOUGHT THE HOUSE THEY REALLY STRESSED THE SECURITY FEATURES THAT IT CAME WITH.
WELL, WHEN YOU LIVE THIS CLOSE TO THE BORDER, AND WITH A YOUNG FAMILY TO CONSIDER...
WELL, MR. COHEN, MY HUSBAND'S NOT HERE AND...

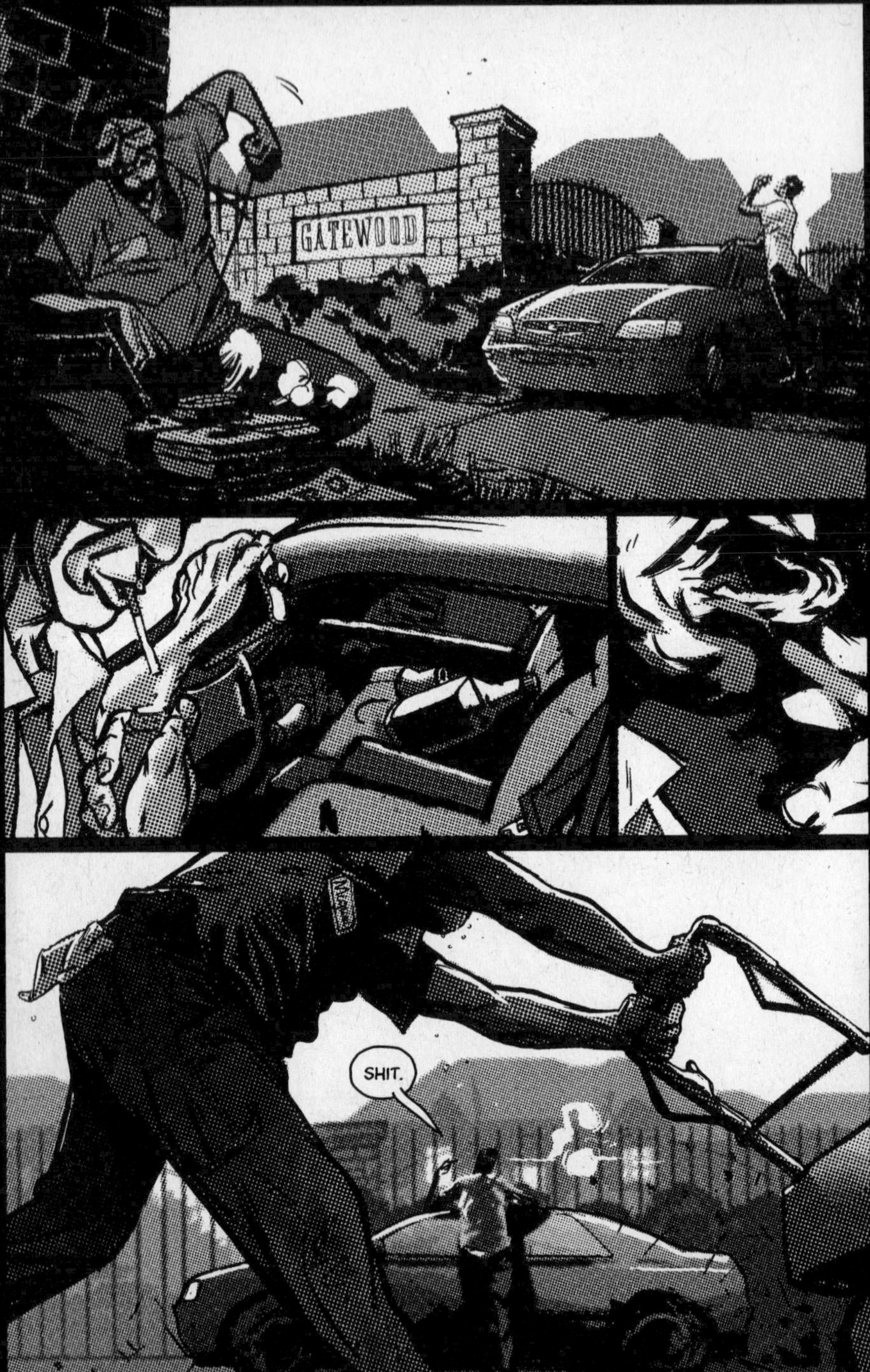
GATEWOOD
SHIT.

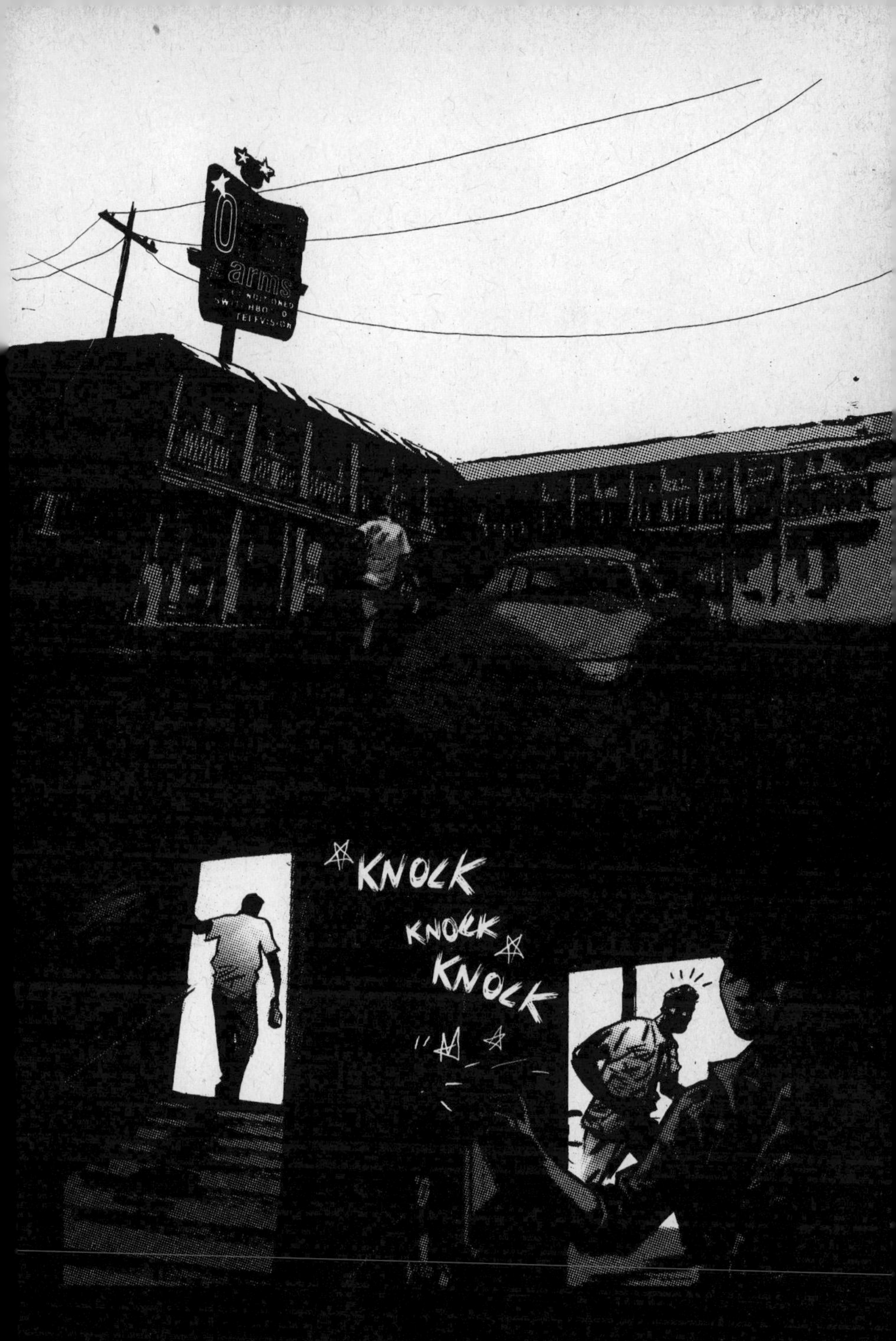
arms
KNOCK
KNOCK
KNOCK

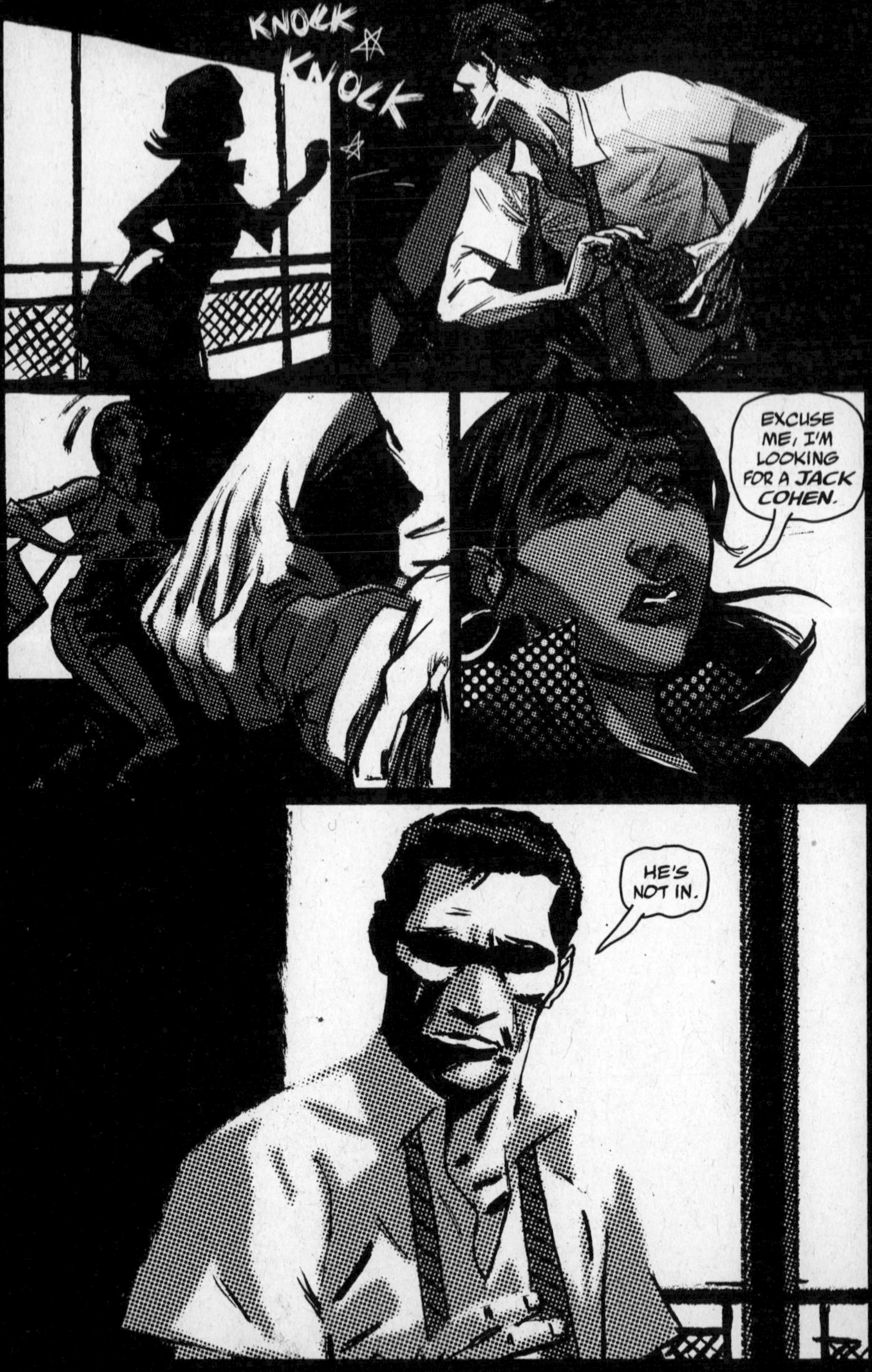
KNOCK KNOCK
EXCUSE ME, I'M LOOKING FOR A JACK COHEN.
HE'S NOT IN.

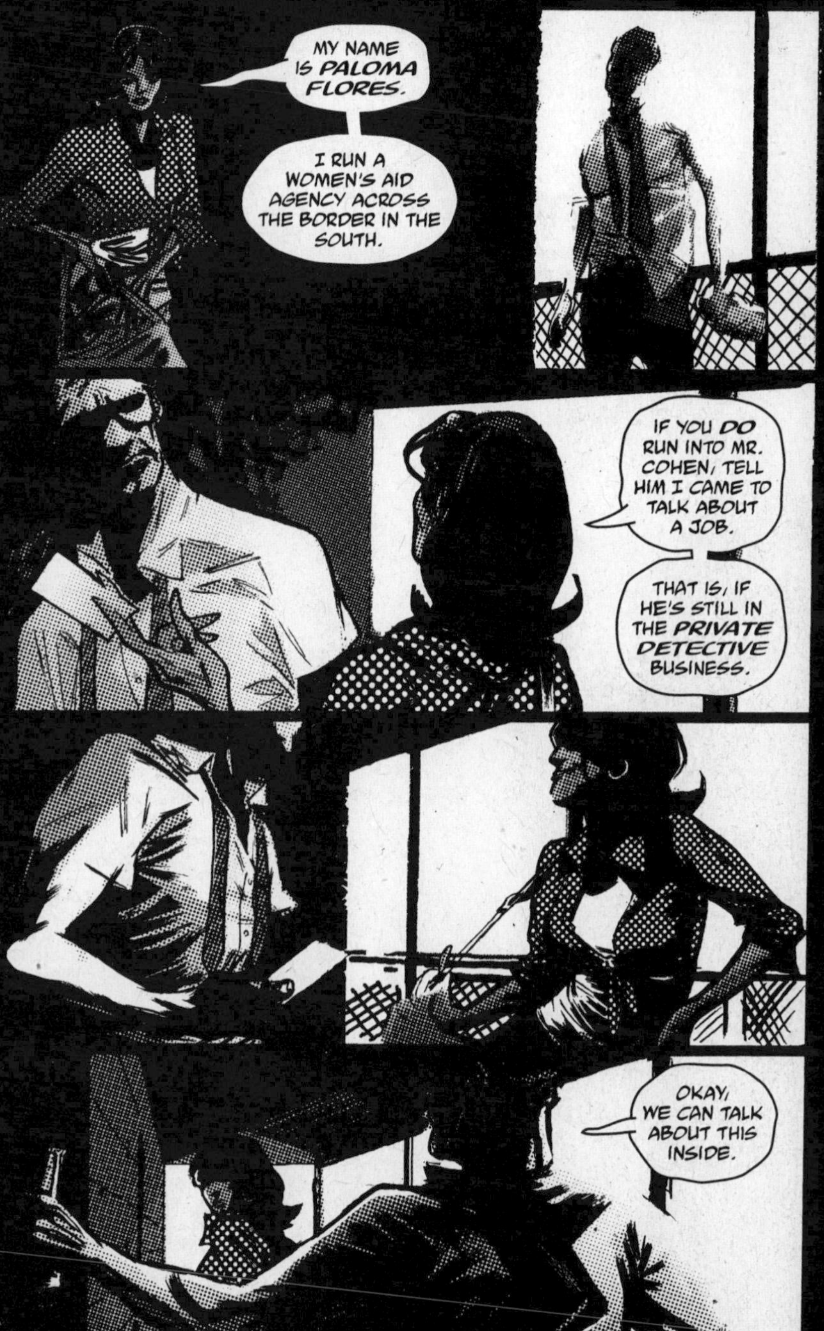
MY NAME IS *PALOMA FLORES.*
I RUN A WOMEN'S AID AGENCY ACROSS THE BORDER IN THE SOUTH.
IF YOU *DO* RUN INTO MR. COHEN, TELL HIM I CAME TO TALK ABOUT A JOB.
THAT IS, IF HE'S STILL IN THE *PRIVATE DETECTIVE* BUSINESS.
OKAY, WE CAN TALK ABOUT THIS INSIDE.

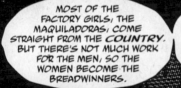

MOST OF THE FACTORY GIRLS, THE *MAQUILADORAS*, COME STRAIGHT FROM THE *COUNTRY*. BUT THERE'S NOT MUCH WORK FOR THE MEN, SO THE WOMEN BECOME THE BREADWINNERS.

THERE'S A LOT OF RESENTMENT TOWARDS THESE WOMEN. RAPE, VIOLENT ASSAULT. WE'RE TALKING SOMETHING LIKE 300 MURDERS OVER THE LAST TWO YEARS.

BUT THIS CASE IS SOMETHING DIFFERENT.

OVER THE PAST 18 MONTHS, THE MUTILATED BODIES OF SIX FACTORY GIRLS HAVE TURNED UP IN THE WASTE-LAND ALONG THE EDGE OF TOWN.

AND THOSE ARE JUST THE ONES WE'RE *AWARE* OF.

I'VE PUT TOGETHER A FILE ON THE VICTIMS.

?

LOOK, MISS FLORES, BEFORE WE GO ANY FURTHER YOU SHOULD *KNOW*, I DON'T TAKE ANY JOBS SOUTH OF THE BORDER.

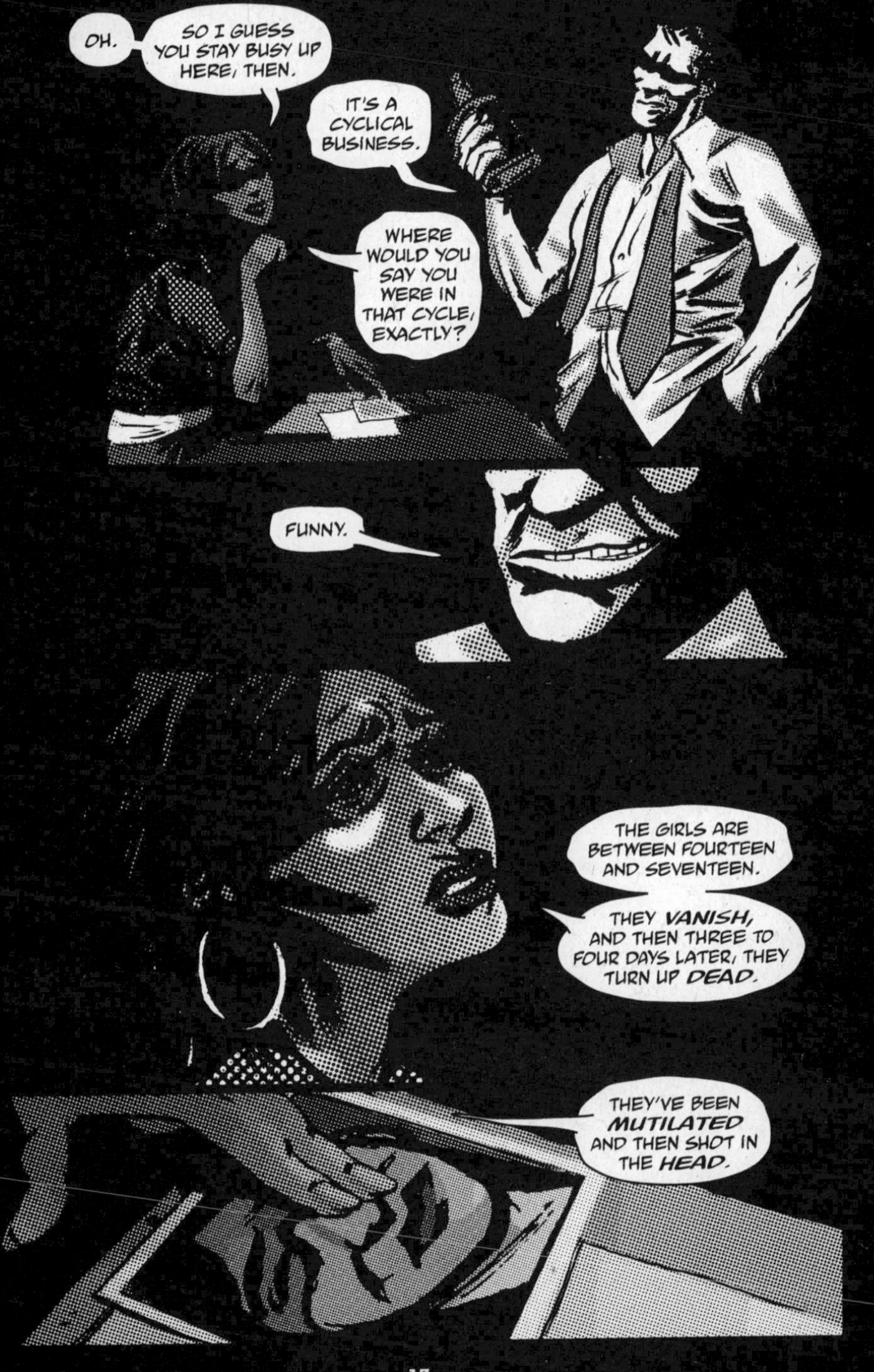
OH.
SO I GUESS YOU STAY BUSY UP HERE, THEN.
IT'S A CYCLICAL BUSINESS.
WHERE WOULD YOU SAY YOU WERE IN THAT CYCLE, EXACTLY?
FUNNY.
THE GIRLS ARE BETWEEN FOURTEEN AND SEVENTEEN.
THEY VANISH, AND THEN THREE TO FOUR DAYS LATER, THEY TURN UP DEAD.
THEY'VE BEEN MUTILATED AND THEN SHOT IN THE HEAD.

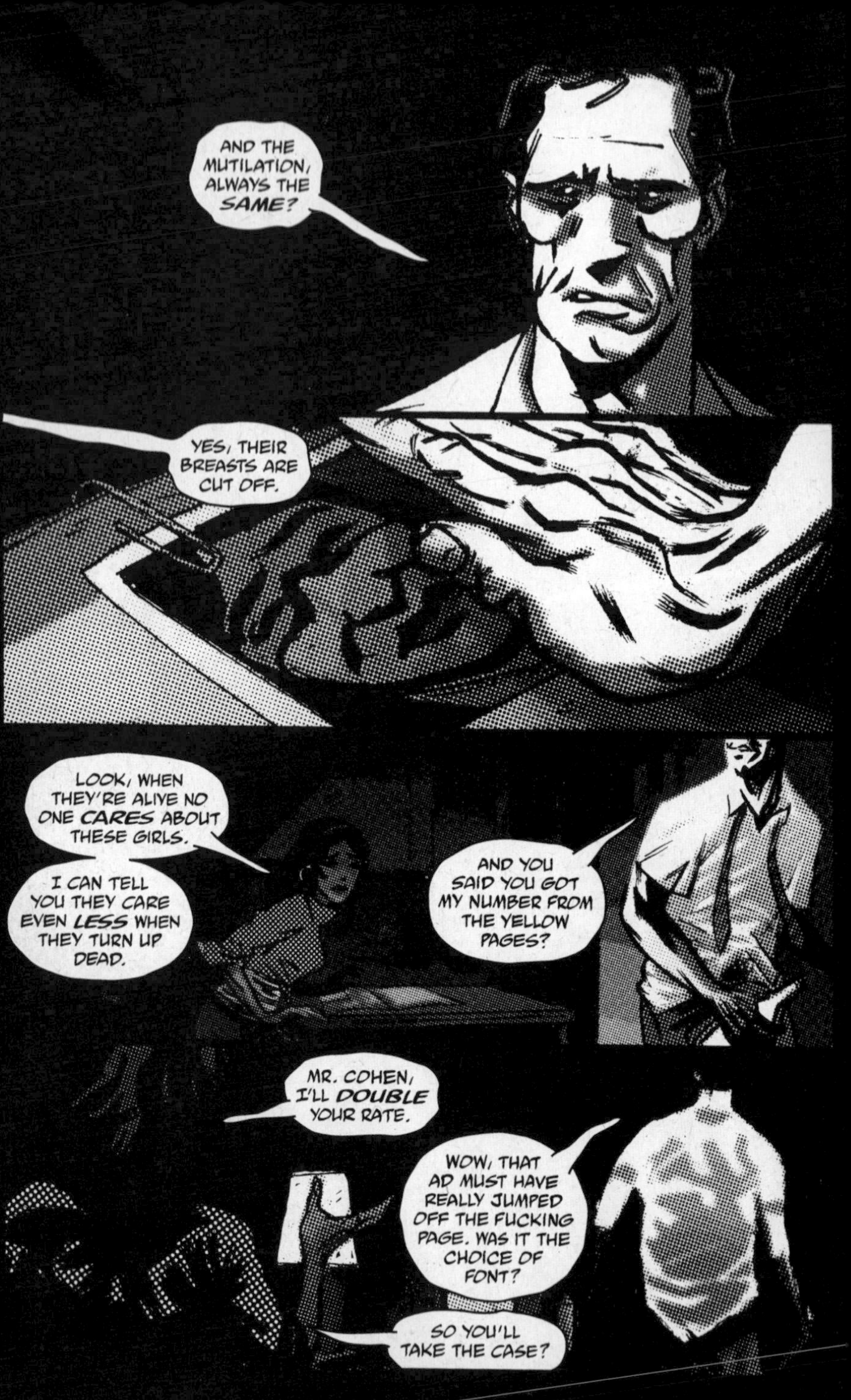
AND THE MUTILATION, ALWAYS THE SAME?
YES, THEIR BREASTS ARE CUT OFF.
LOOK, WHEN THEY'RE ALIVE NO ONE CARES ABOUT THESE GIRLS.
I CAN TELL YOU THEY CARE EVEN LESS WHEN THEY TURN UP DEAD.
AND YOU SAID YOU GOT MY NUMBER FROM THE YELLOW PAGES?
MR. COHEN, I'LL DOUBLE YOUR RATE.
WOW, THAT AD MUST HAVE REALLY JUMPED OFF THE FUCKING PAGE. WAS IT THE CHOICE OF FONT?
SO YOU'LL TAKE THE CASE?

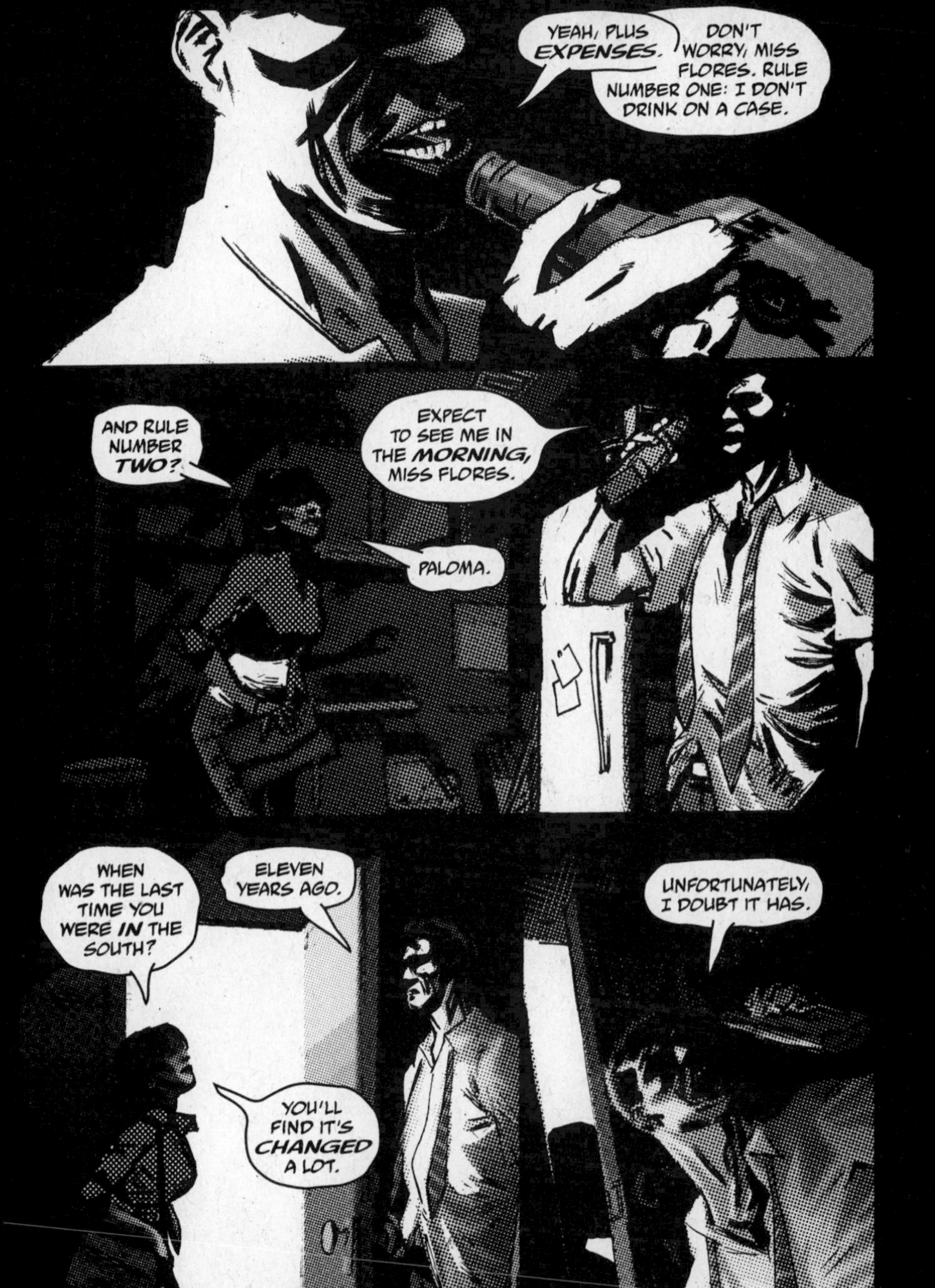
YEAH, PLUS EXPENSES.
DON'T WORRY, MISS FLORES. RULE NUMBER ONE: I DON'T DRINK ON A CASE.
AND RULE NUMBER TWO?
EXPECT TO SEE ME IN THE MORNING, MISS FLORES.
PALOMA.
WHEN WAS THE LAST TIME YOU WERE IN THE SOUTH?
ELEVEN YEARS AGO.
YOU'LL FIND IT'S CHANGED A LOT.
UNFORTUNATELY, I DOUBT IT HAS.

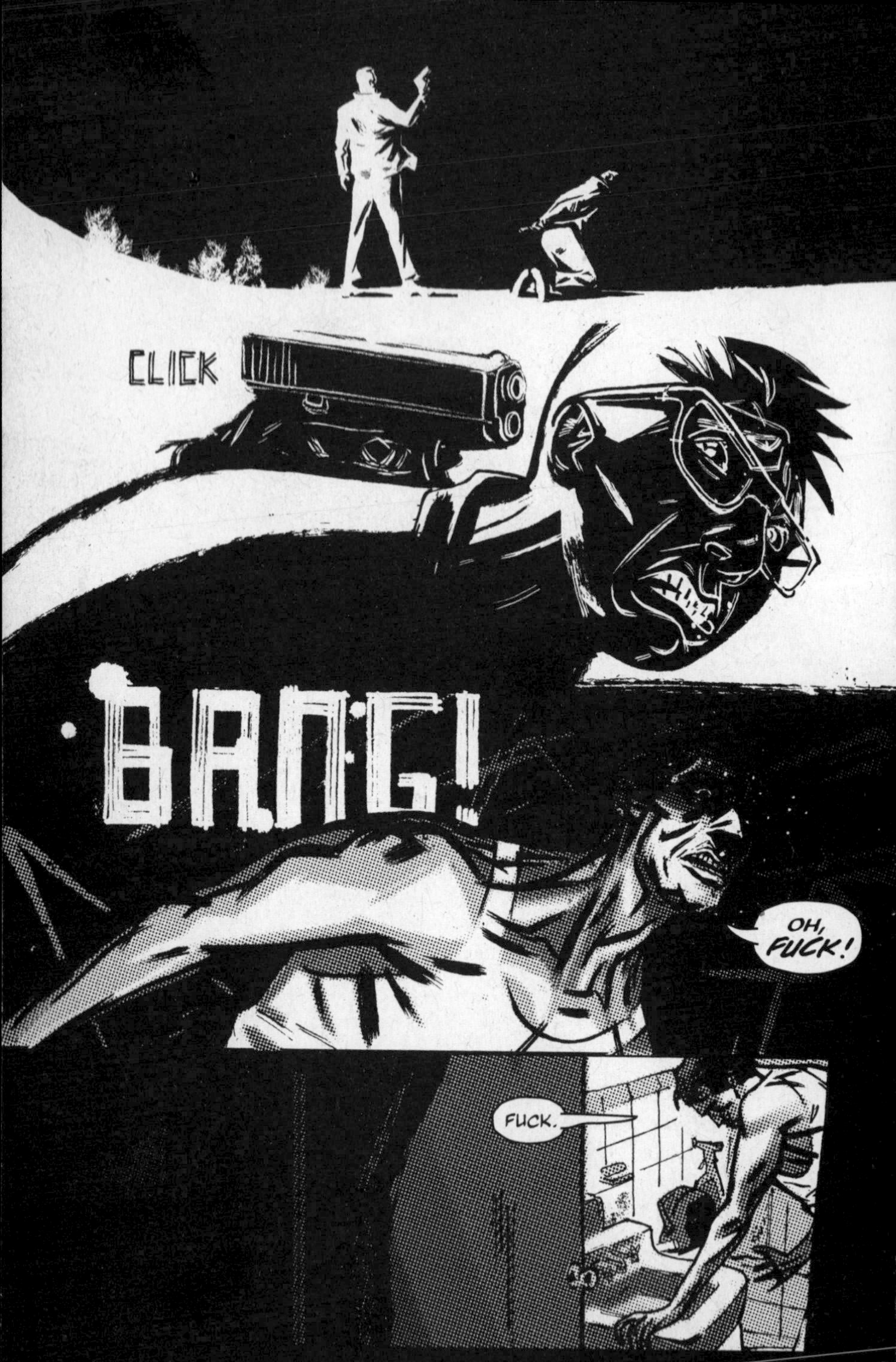
CLICK
BANG!
OH, FUCK!
FUCK.

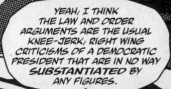

MEXICO

YEAH, I THINK THE LAW AND ORDER ARGUMENTS ARE THE USUAL KNEE-JERK, RIGHT WING CRITICISMS OF A DEMOCRATIC PRESIDENT THAT ARE IN NO WAY *SUBSTANTIATED* BY ANY FIGURES.

FIGURES THAT IF YOU TAKE THE TIME TO REALLY EXAMINE IN ANY DEPTH SHOW A VERY TOUGH STAND ON CRIME AND A RESULTING *DROP* IN OVERALL NATIONAL CRIME FIGURES.

THIS IS PUBLIC RADIO, AND I'M SPEAKING WITH THIS MORNING'S GUEST, *SENATOR JOHN WILSON.*

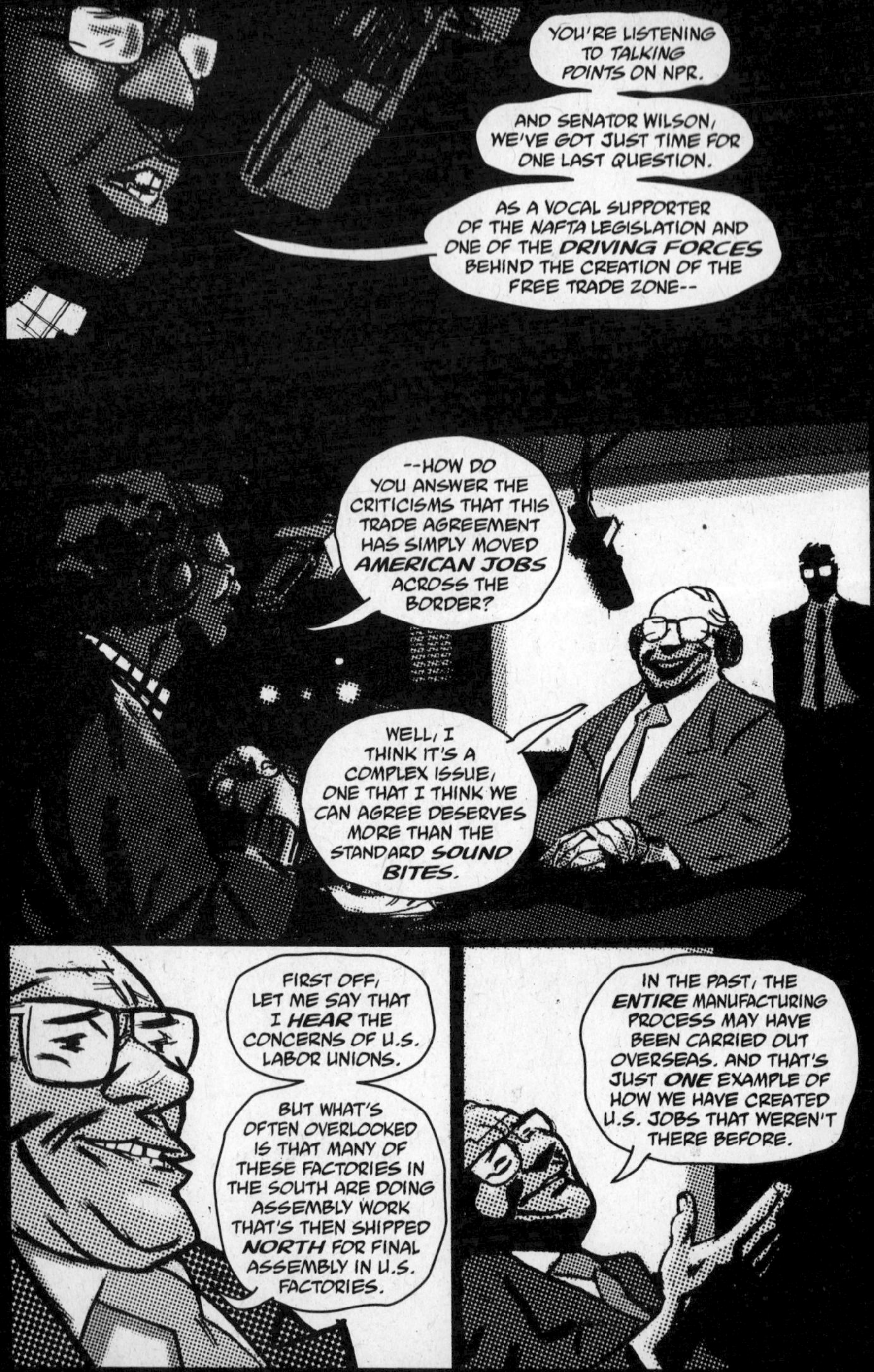
YOU'RE LISTENING TO TALKING POINTS ON NPR.
AND SENATOR WILSON, WE'VE GOT JUST TIME FOR ONE LAST QUESTION.
AS A VOCAL SUPPORTER OF THE NAFTA LEGISLATION AND ONE OF THE DRIVING FORCES BEHIND THE CREATION OF THE FREE TRADE ZONE--
--HOW DO YOU ANSWER THE CRITICISMS THAT THIS TRADE AGREEMENT HAS SIMPLY MOVED AMERICAN JOBS ACROSS THE BORDER?
WELL, I THINK IT'S A COMPLEX ISSUE, ONE THAT I THINK WE CAN AGREE DESERVES MORE THAN THE STANDARD SOUND BITES.
FIRST OFF, LET ME SAY THAT I HEAR THE CONCERNS OF U.S. LABOR UNIONS.
BUT WHAT'S OFTEN OVERLOOKED IS THAT MANY OF THESE FACTORIES IN THE SOUTH ARE DOING ASSEMBLY WORK THAT'S THEN SHIPPED NORTH FOR FINAL ASSEMBLY IN U.S. FACTORIES.
IN THE PAST, THE ENTIRE MANUFACTURING PROCESS MAY HAVE BEEN CARRIED OUT OVERSEAS. AND THAT'S JUST ONE EXAMPLE OF HOW WE HAVE CREATED U.S. JOBS THAT WEREN'T THERE BEFORE.

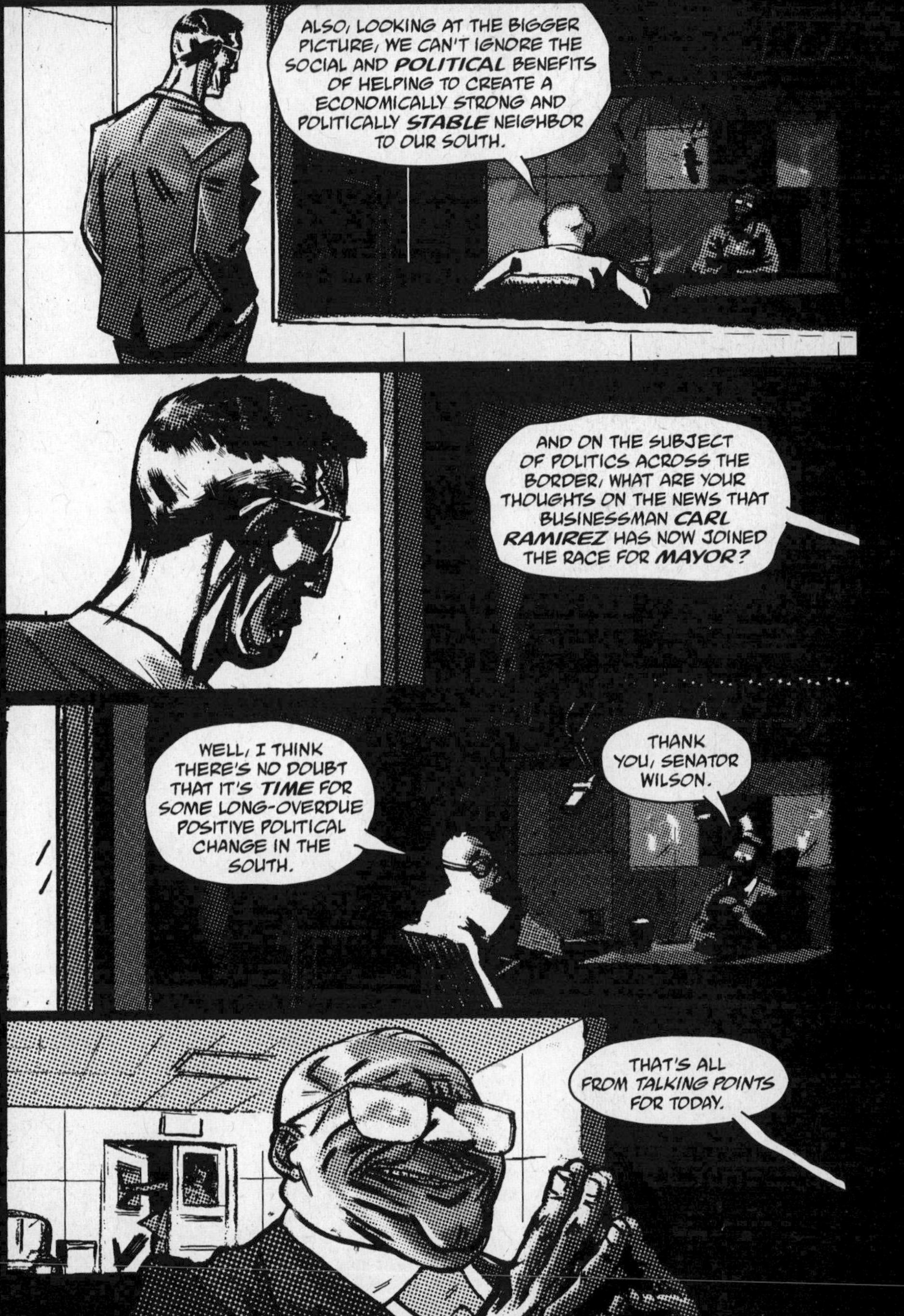
ALSO, LOOKING AT THE BIGGER PICTURE, WE CAN'T IGNORE THE SOCIAL AND POLITICAL BENEFITS OF HELPING TO CREATE A ECONOMICALLY STRONG AND POLITICALLY STABLE NEIGHBOR TO OUR SOUTH.
AND ON THE SUBJECT OF POLITICS ACROSS THE BORDER, WHAT ARE YOUR THOUGHTS ON THE NEWS THAT BUSINESSMAN CARL RAMIREZ HAS NOW JOINED THE RACE FOR MAYOR?
WELL, I THINK THERE'S NO DOUBT THAT IT'S TIME FOR SOME LONG-OVERDUE POSITIVE POLITICAL CHANGE IN THE SOUTH.
THANK YOU, SENATOR WILSON.
THAT'S ALL FROM TALKING POINTS FOR TODAY.

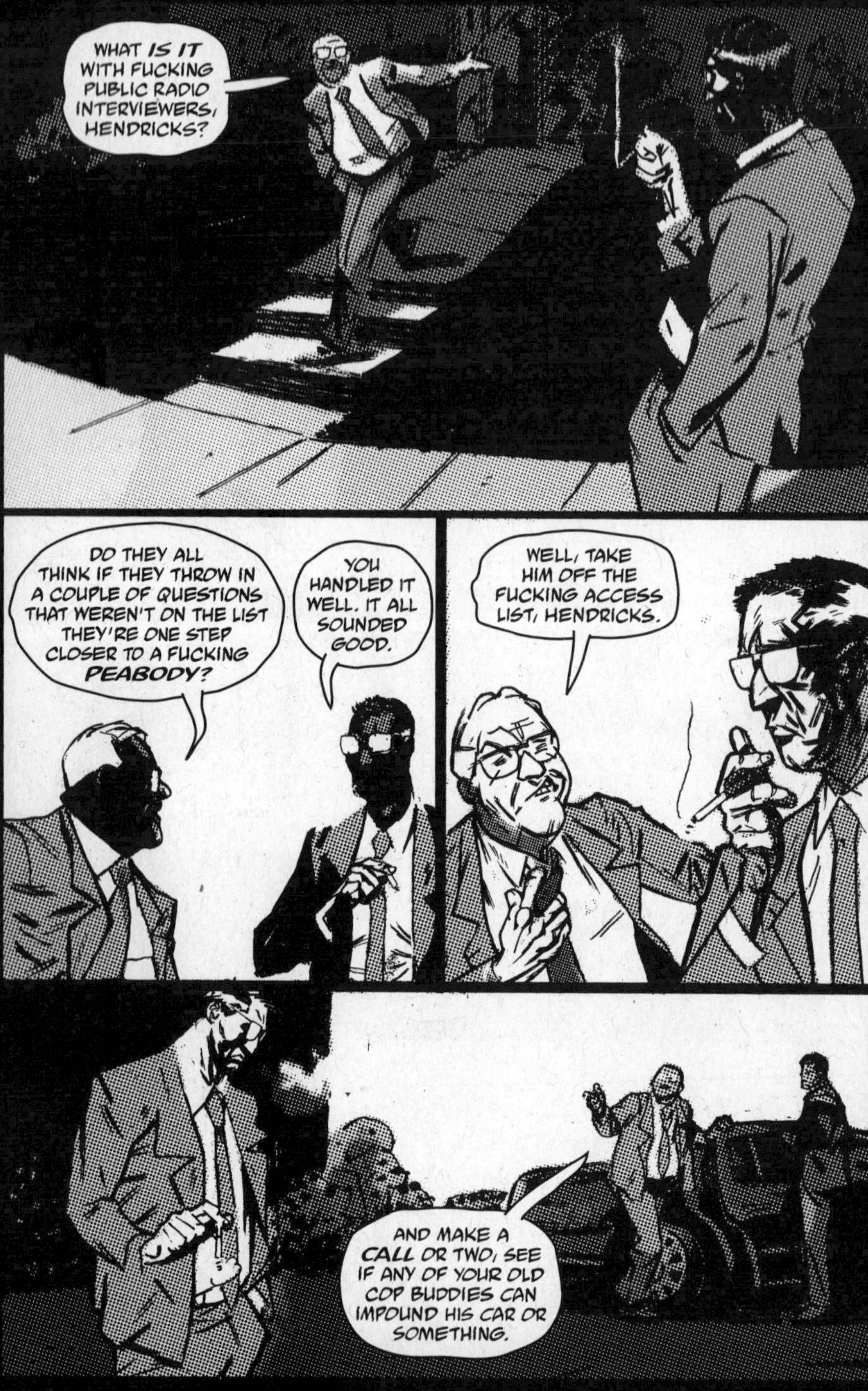
WHAT IS IT WITH FUCKING PUBLIC RADIO INTERVIEWERS, HENDRICKS?
DO THEY ALL THINK IF THEY THROW IN A COUPLE OF QUESTIONS THAT WEREN'T ON THE LIST THEY'RE ONE STEP CLOSER TO A FUCKING PEABODY?
YOU HANDLED IT WELL. IT ALL SOUNDED GOOD.
WELL, TAKE HIM OFF THE FUCKING ACCESS LIST, HENDRICKS.
AND MAKE A CALL OR TWO, SEE IF ANY OF YOUR OLD COP BUDDIES CAN IMPOUND HIS CAR OR SOMETHING.

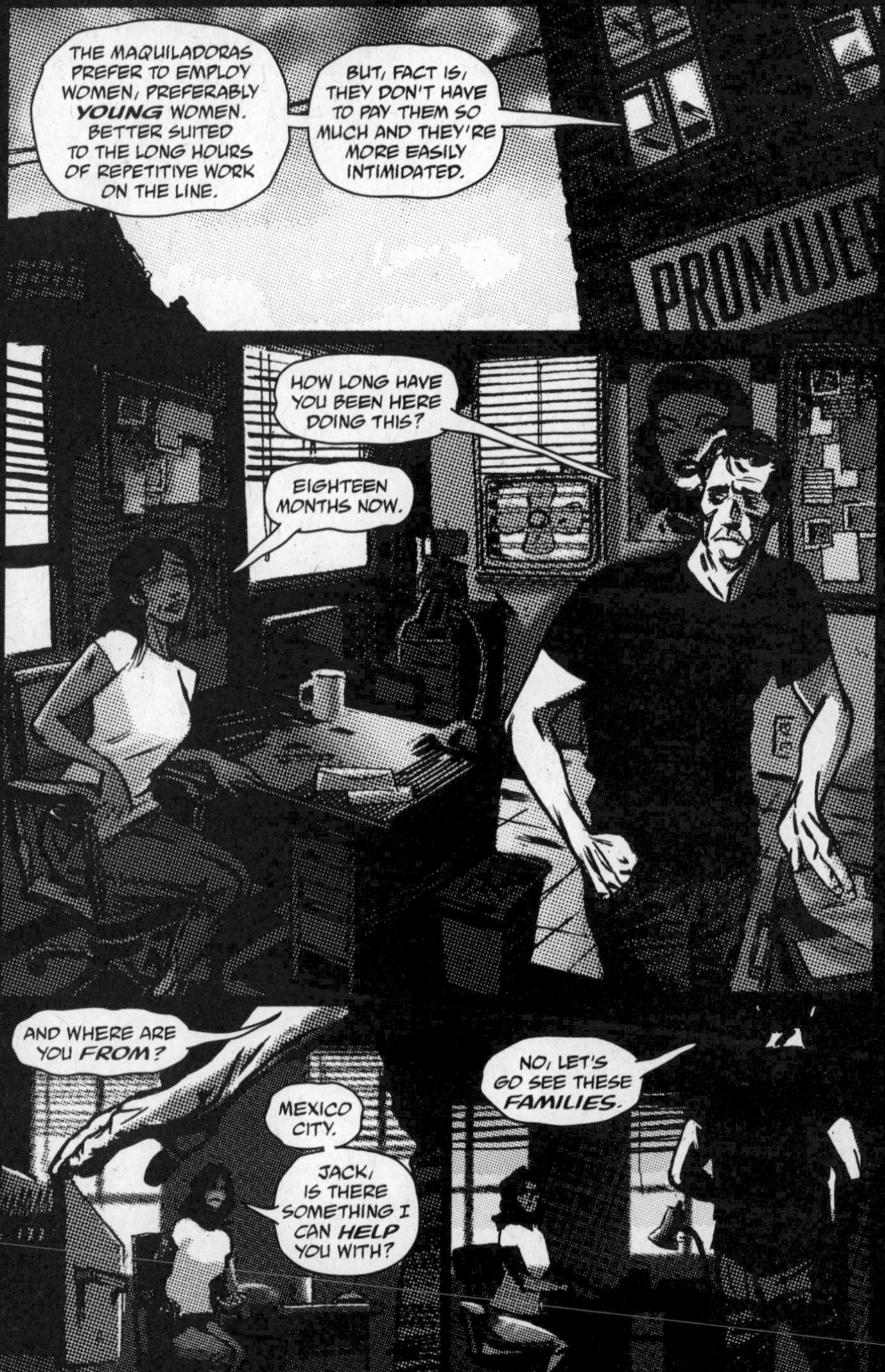
THE MAQUILADORAS PREFER TO EMPLOY WOMEN, PREFERABLY YOUNG WOMEN. BETTER SUITED TO THE LONG HOURS OF REPETITIVE WORK ON THE LINE.
BUT, FACT IS, THEY DON'T HAVE TO PAY THEM SO MUCH AND THEY'RE MORE EASILY INTIMIDATED.
PROMUJE
HOW LONG HAVE YOU BEEN HERE DOING THIS?
EIGHTEEN MONTHS NOW.
AND WHERE ARE YOU FROM?
MEXICO CITY.
JACK, IS THERE SOMETHING I CAN HELP YOU WITH?
NO, LET'S GO SEE THESE FAMILIES.

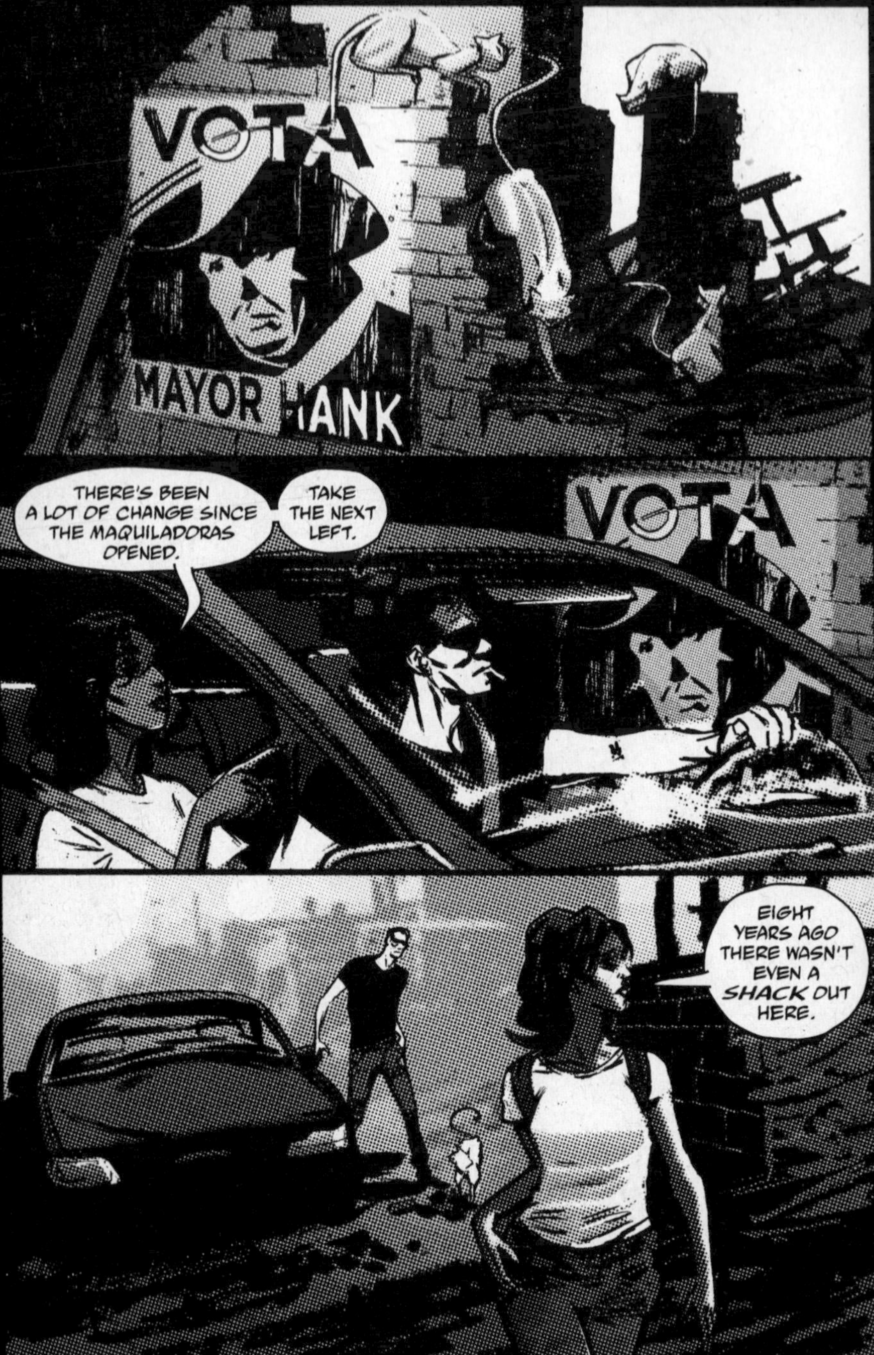
VOTA
MAYOR HANK
VOTA
THERE'S BEEN A LOT OF CHANGE SINCE THE MAQUILADORAS OPENED.
TAKE THE NEXT LEFT.
EIGHT YEARS AGO THERE WASN'T EVEN A SHACK OUT HERE.

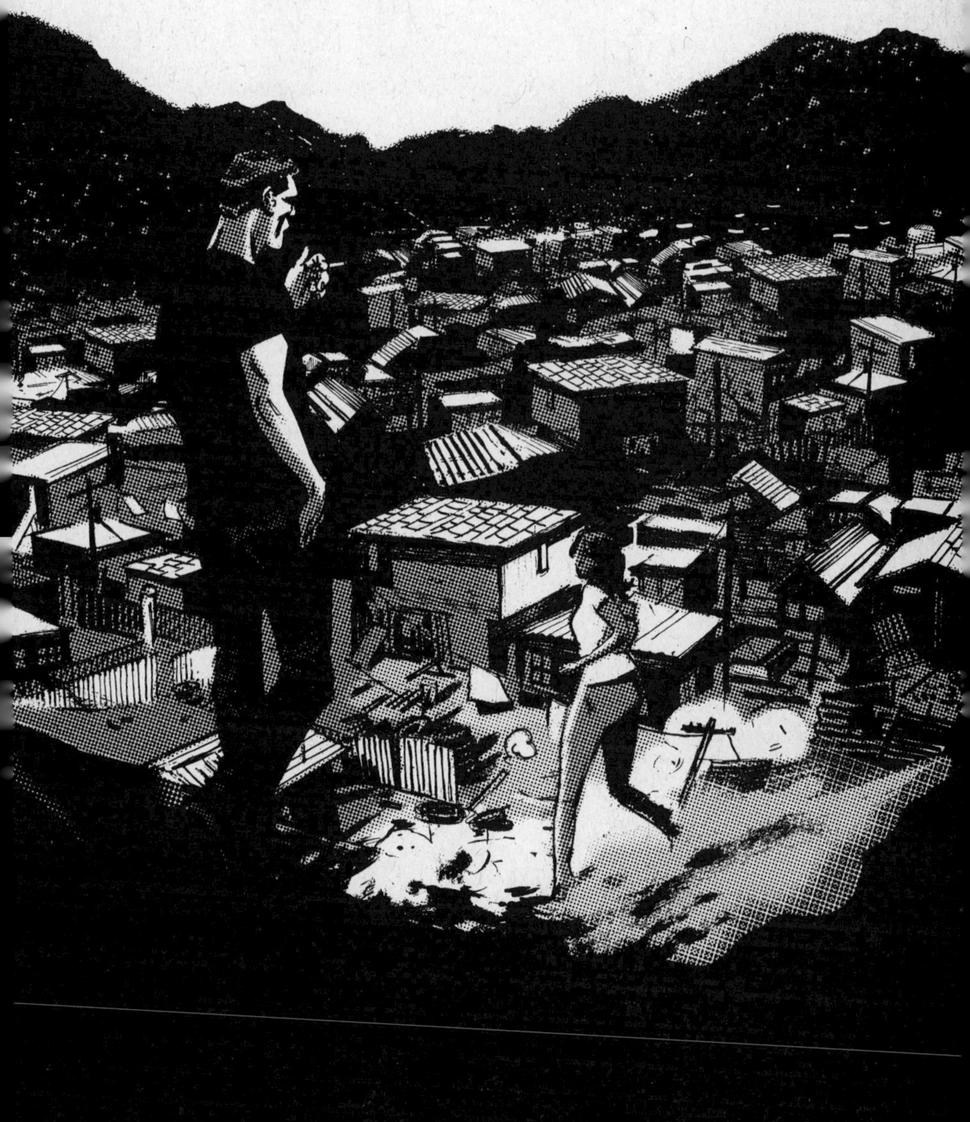

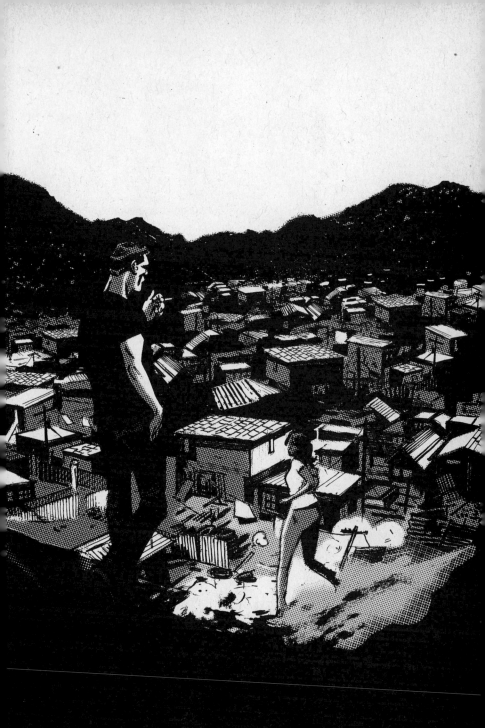

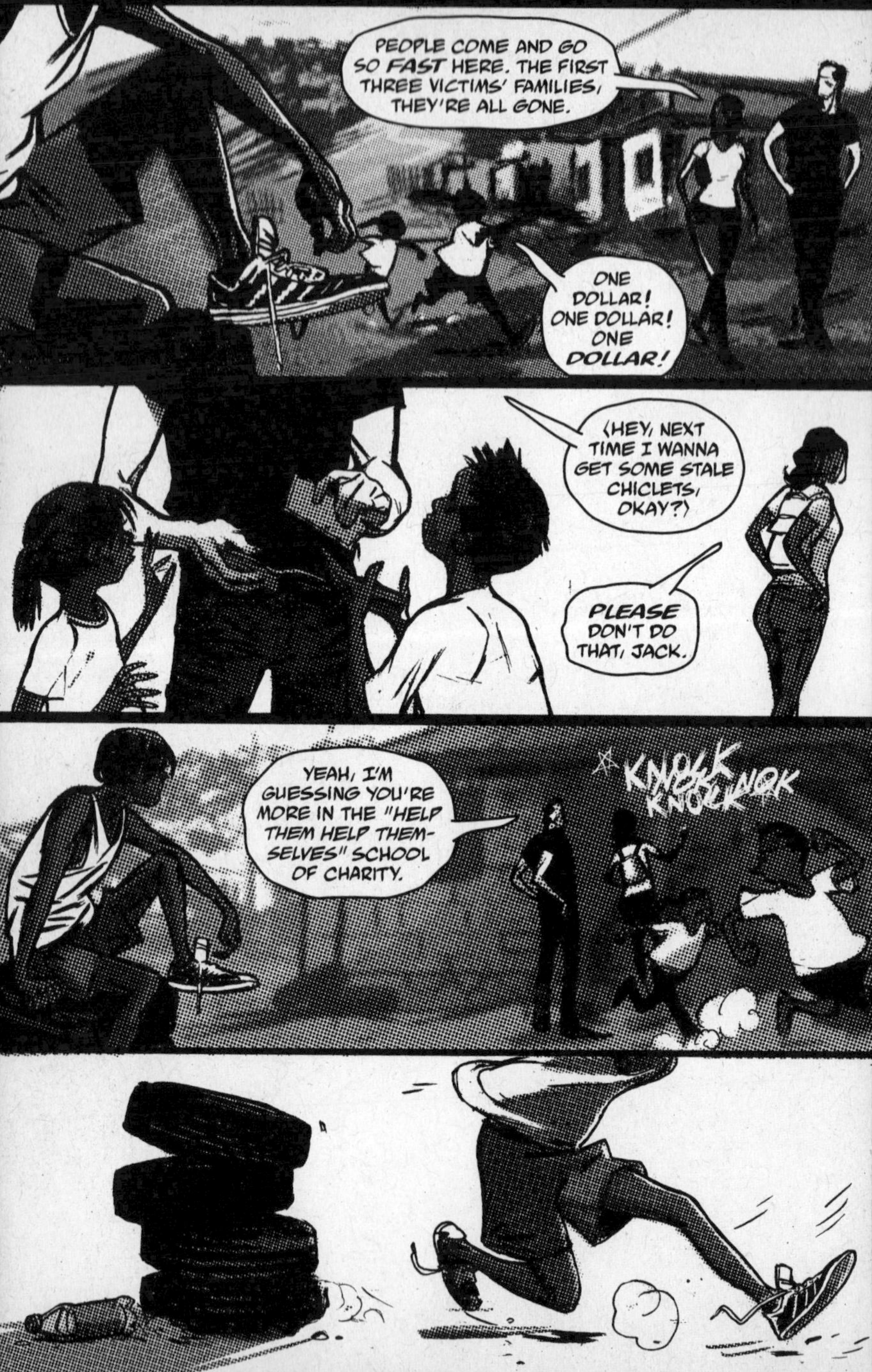
PEOPLE COME AND GO SO FAST HERE. THE FIRST THREE VICTIMS' FAMILIES, THEY'RE ALL GONE.
ONE DOLLAR! ONE DOLLAR! ONE DOLLAR!
(HEY, NEXT TIME I WANNA GET SOME STALE CHICLETS, OKAY?)
PLEASE DON'T DO THAT, JACK.
YEAH, I'M GUESSING YOU'RE MORE IN THE "HELP THEM HELP THEMSELVES" SCHOOL OF CHARITY.
KNOCK KNOCK KNOCK KNOCK

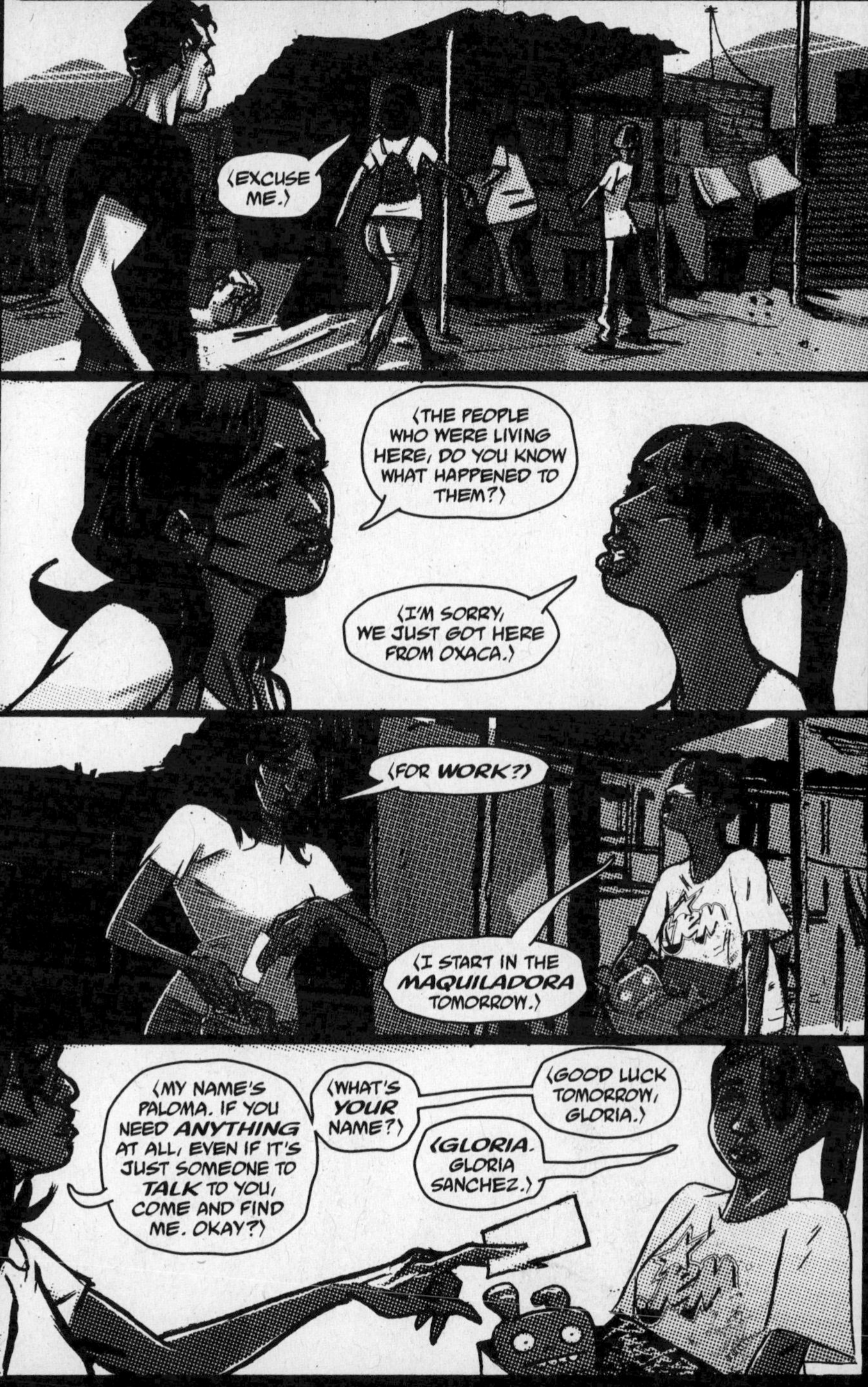

⟨EXCUSE ME.⟩
⟨THE PEOPLE WHO WERE LIVING HERE, DO YOU KNOW WHAT HAPPENED TO THEM?⟩
⟨I'M SORRY, WE JUST GOT HERE FROM OXACA.⟩
⟨FOR WORK?⟩
⟨I START IN THE MAQUILADORA TOMORROW.⟩
⟨MY NAME'S PALOMA. IF YOU NEED ANYTHING AT ALL, EVEN IF IT'S JUST SOMEONE TO TALK TO YOU, COME AND FIND ME. OKAY?⟩
⟨WHAT'S YOUR NAME?⟩
⟨GLORIA. GLORIA SANCHEZ.⟩
⟨GOOD LUCK TOMORROW, GLORIA.⟩

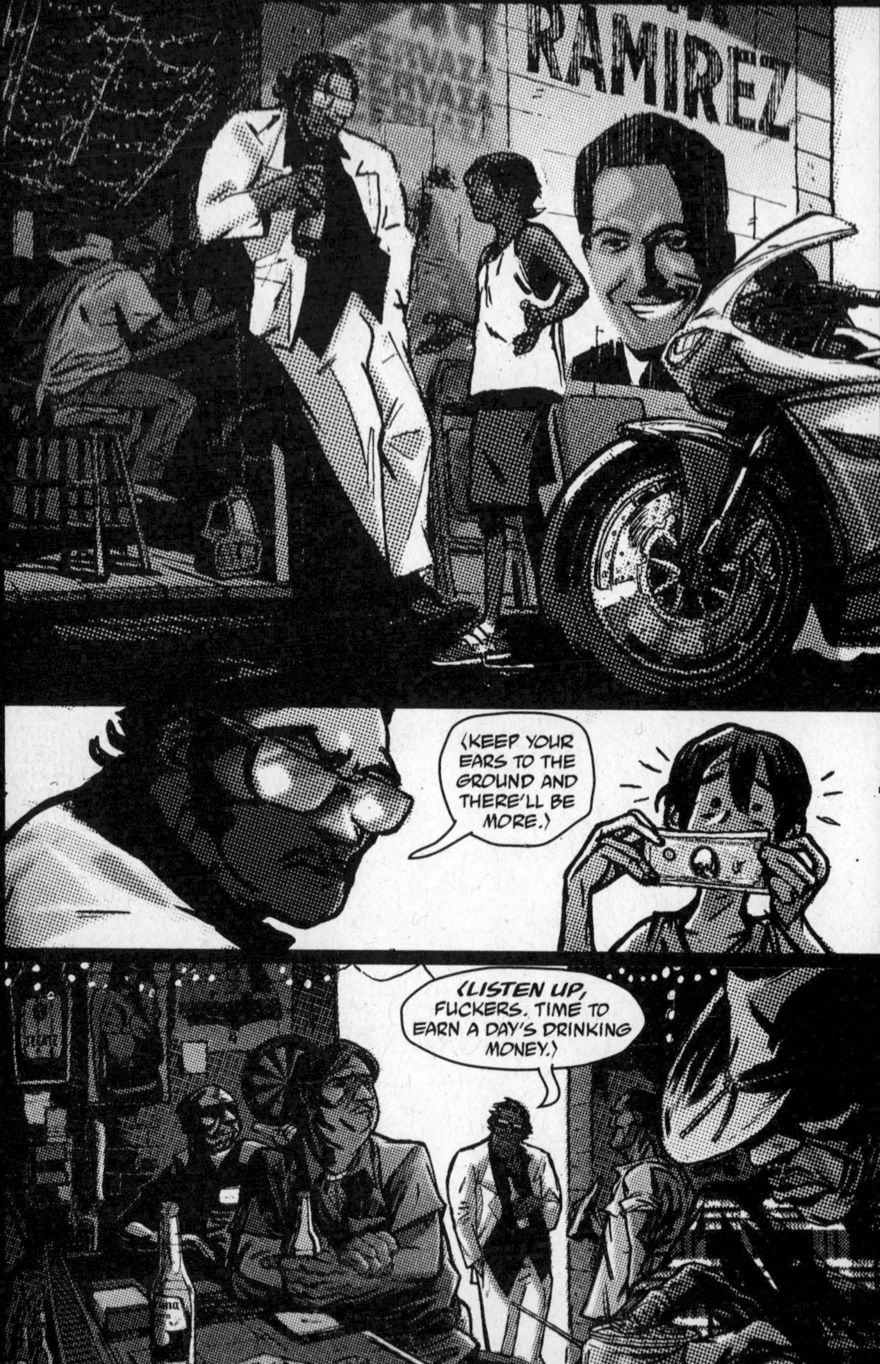
RAMIREZ
‹KEEP YOUR EARS TO THE GROUND AND THERE'LL BE MORE.›
‹LISTEN UP, FUCKERS. TIME TO EARN A DAY'S DRINKING MONEY.›

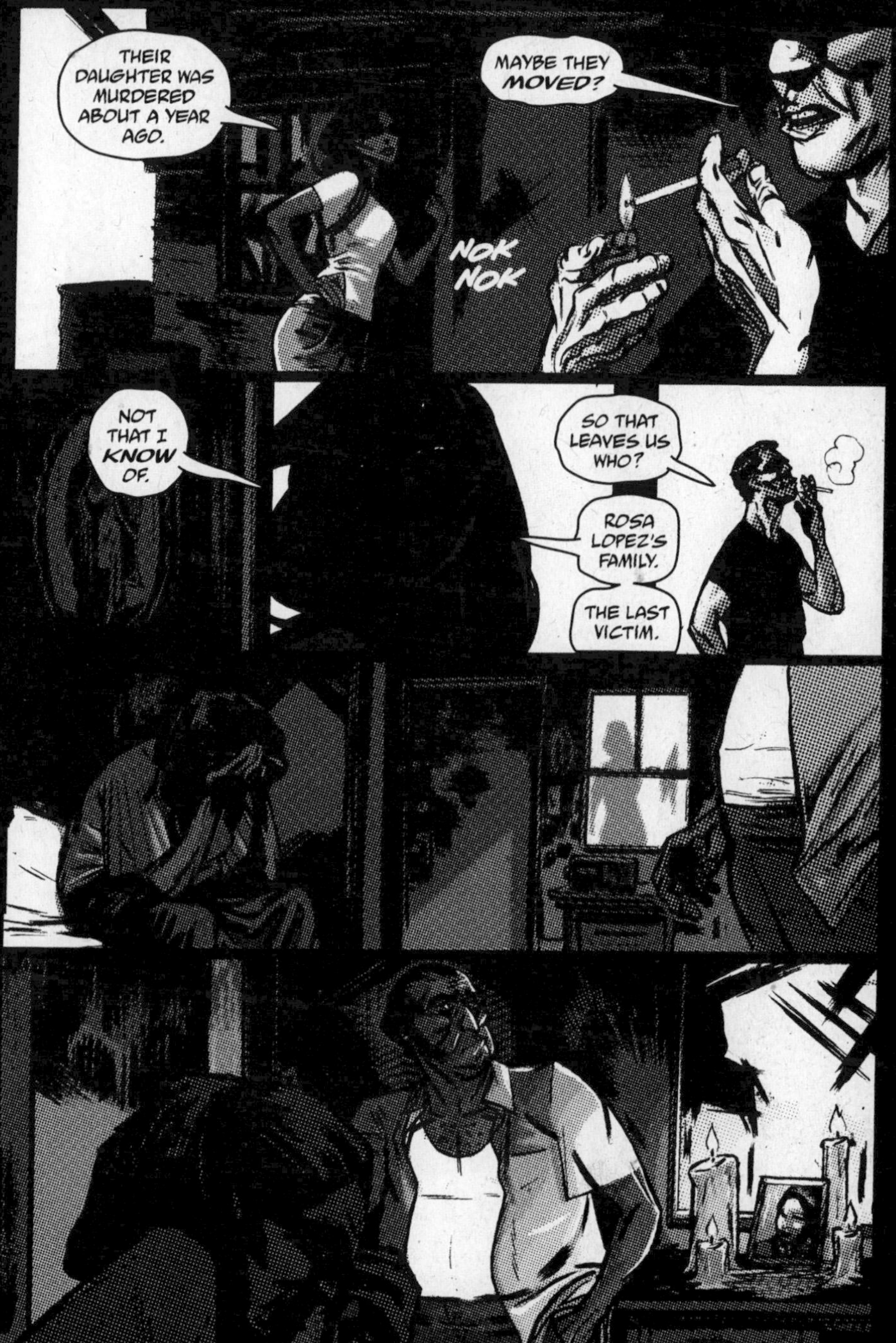
THEIR DAUGHTER WAS MURDERED ABOUT A YEAR AGO.
MAYBE THEY MOVED?
NOK NOK
NOT THAT I KNOW OF.
SO THAT LEAVES US WHO?
ROSA LOPEZ'S FAMILY.
THE LAST VICTIM.

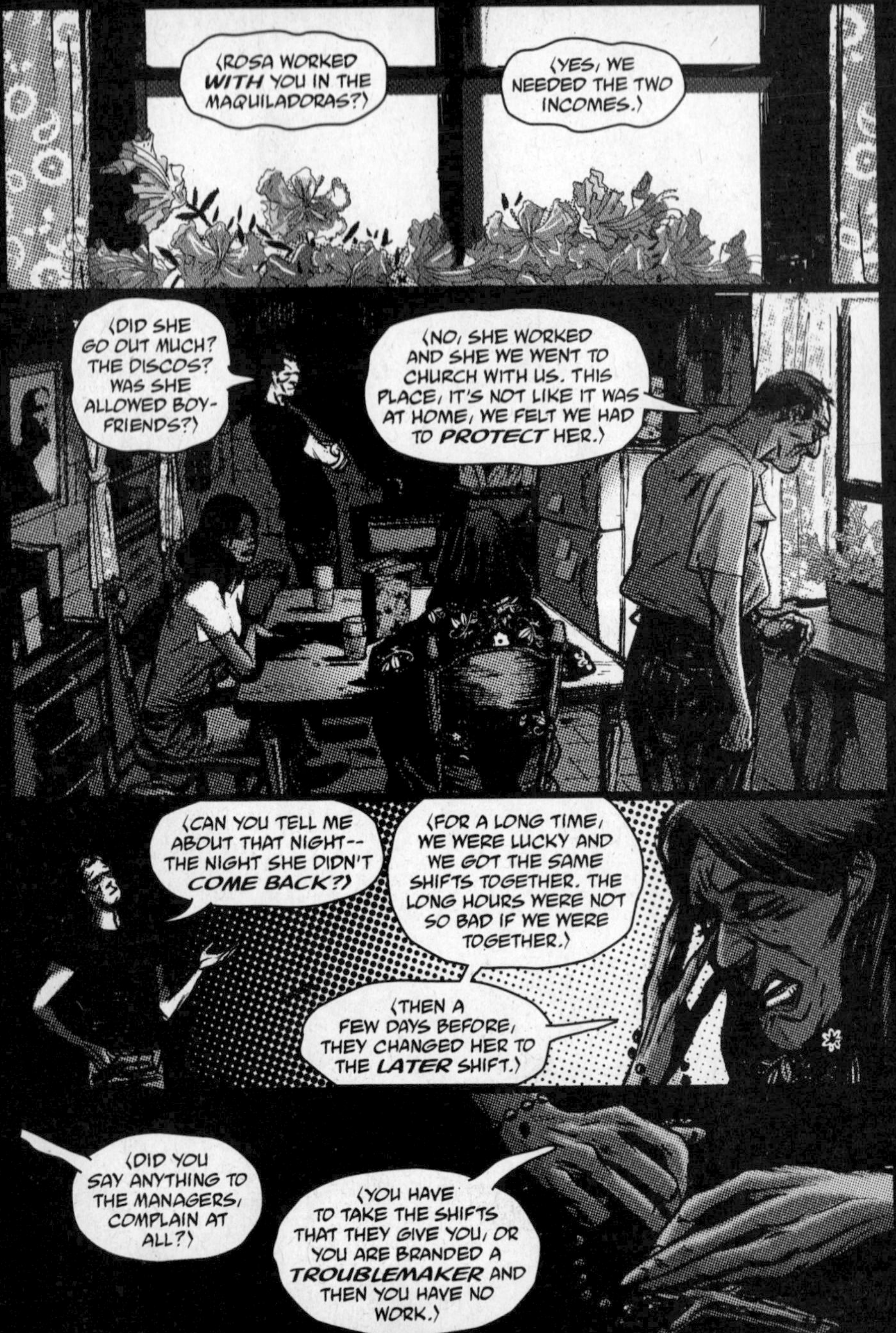
⟨ROSA WORKED WITH YOU IN THE MAQUILADORAS?⟩
⟨YES, WE NEEDED THE TWO INCOMES.⟩
⟨DID SHE GO OUT MUCH? THE DISCOS? WAS SHE ALLOWED BOY-FRIENDS?⟩
⟨NO, SHE WORKED AND SHE WE WENT TO CHURCH WITH US. THIS PLACE, IT'S NOT LIKE IT WAS AT HOME, WE FELT WE HAD TO PROTECT HER.⟩
⟨CAN YOU TELL ME ABOUT THAT NIGHT-- THE NIGHT SHE DIDN'T COME BACK?⟩
⟨FOR A LONG TIME, WE WERE LUCKY AND WE GOT THE SAME SHIFTS TOGETHER. THE LONG HOURS WERE NOT SO BAD IF WE WERE TOGETHER.⟩
⟨THEN A FEW DAYS BEFORE, THEY CHANGED HER TO THE LATER SHIFT.⟩
⟨DID YOU SAY ANYTHING TO THE MANAGERS, COMPLAIN AT ALL?⟩
⟨YOU HAVE TO TAKE THE SHIFTS THAT THEY GIVE YOU, OR YOU ARE BRANDED A TROUBLEMAKER AND THEN YOU HAVE NO WORK.⟩

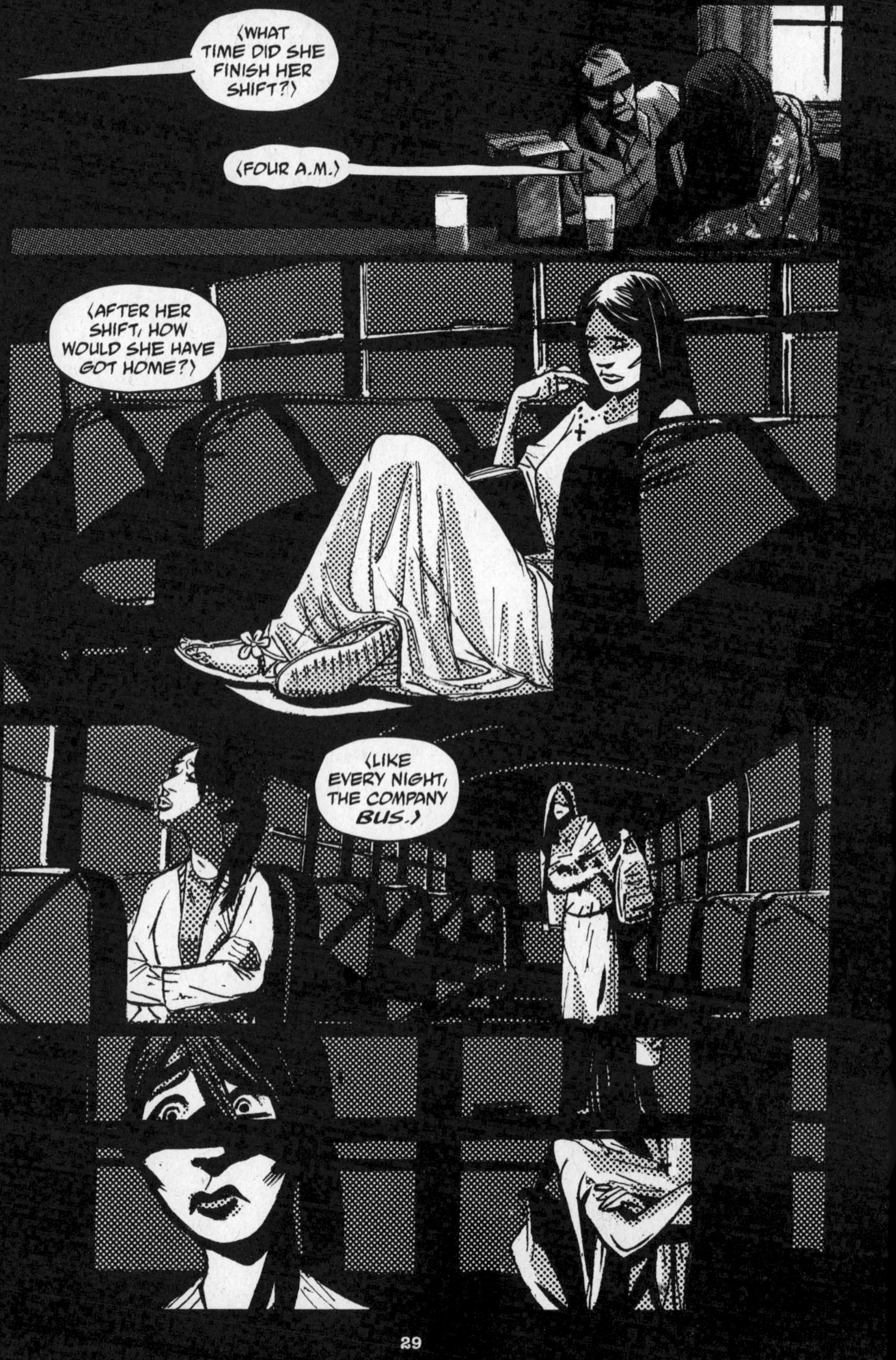
⟨WHAT TIME DID SHE FINISH HER SHIFT?⟩
⟨FOUR A.M.⟩
⟨AFTER HER SHIFT, HOW WOULD SHE HAVE GOT HOME?⟩
⟨LIKE EVERY NIGHT, THE COMPANY BUS.⟩

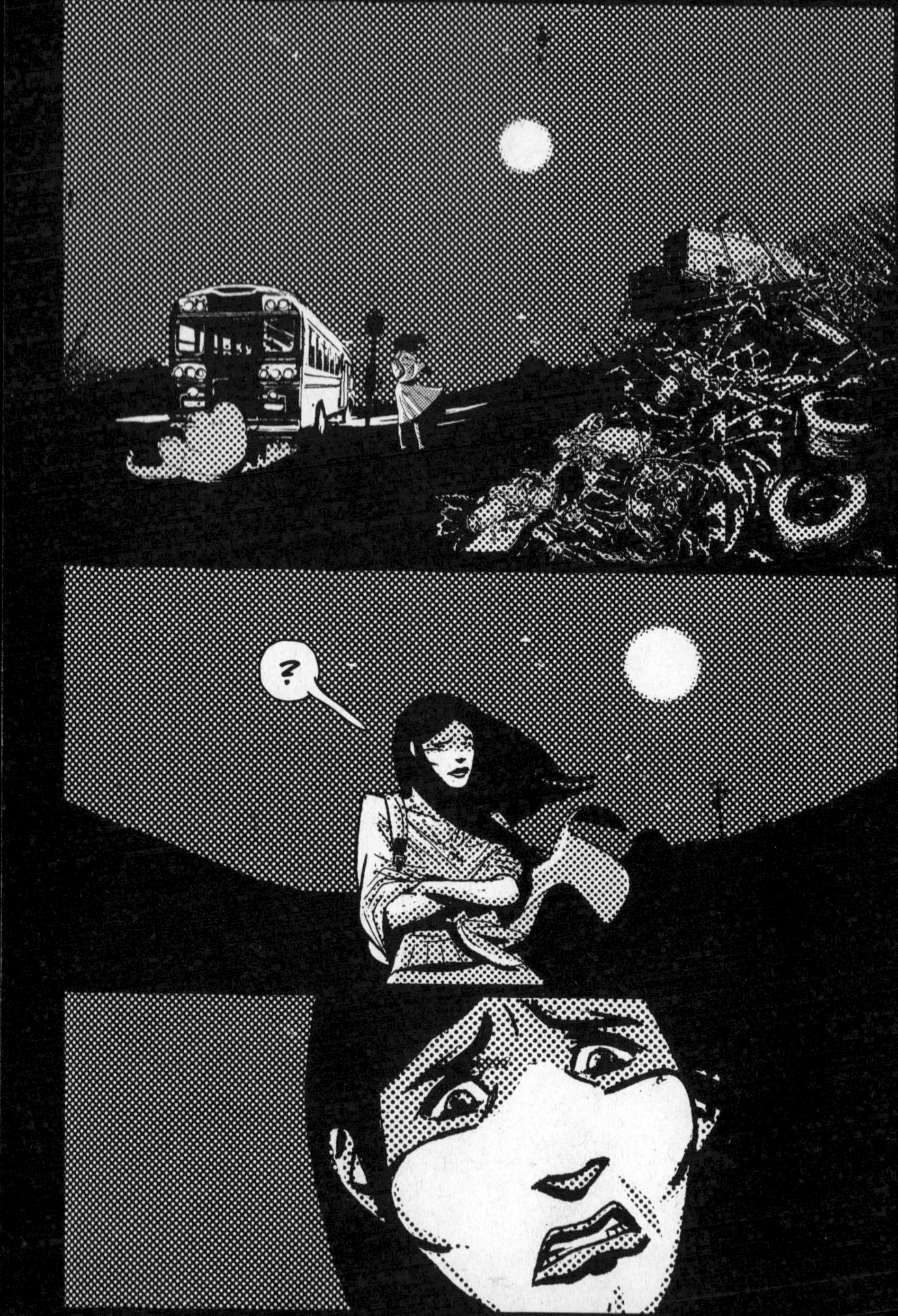
?

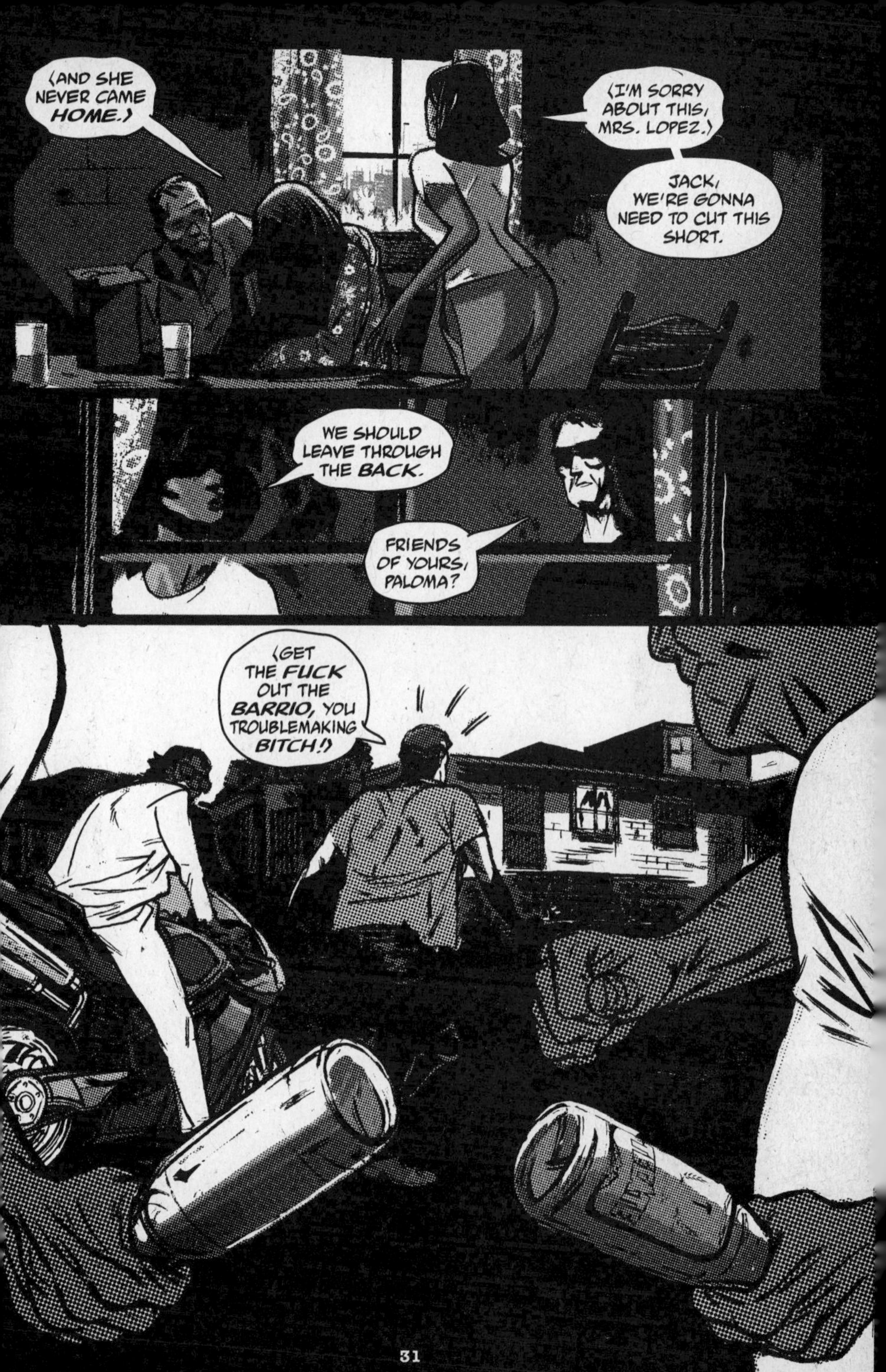
⟨AND SHE NEVER CAME HOME.⟩
⟨I'M SORRY ABOUT THIS, MRS. LOPEZ.⟩
JACK, WE'RE GONNA NEED TO CUT THIS SHORT.
WE SHOULD LEAVE THROUGH THE BACK.
FRIENDS OF YOURS, PALOMA?
⟨GET THE FUCK OUT THE BARRIO, YOU TROUBLEMAKING BITCH!⟩

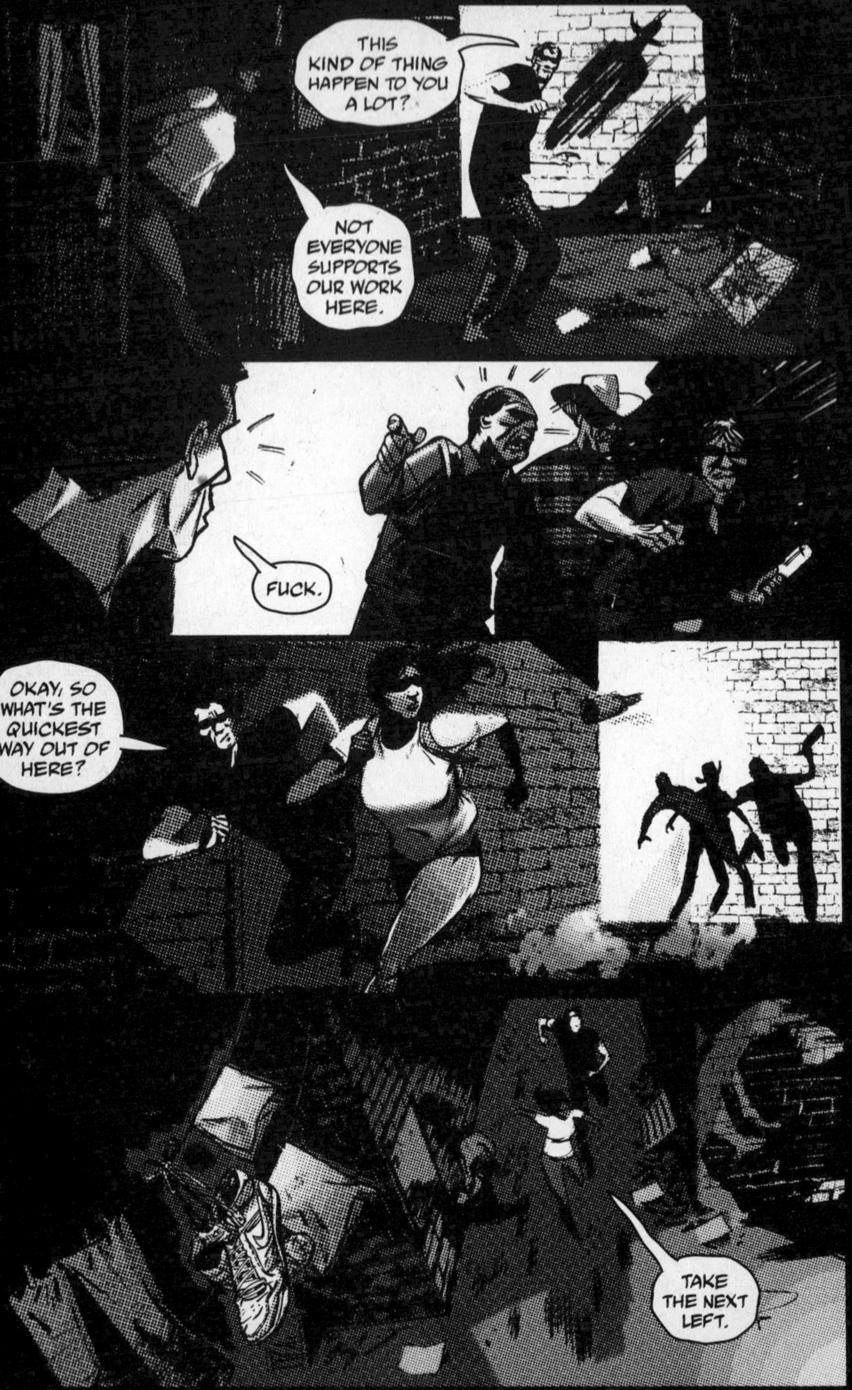
THIS KIND OF THING HAPPEN TO YOU A LOT?
NOT EVERYONE SUPPORTS OUR WORK HERE.
FUCK.
OKAY, SO WHAT'S THE QUICKEST WAY OUT OF HERE?
TAKE THE NEXT LEFT.

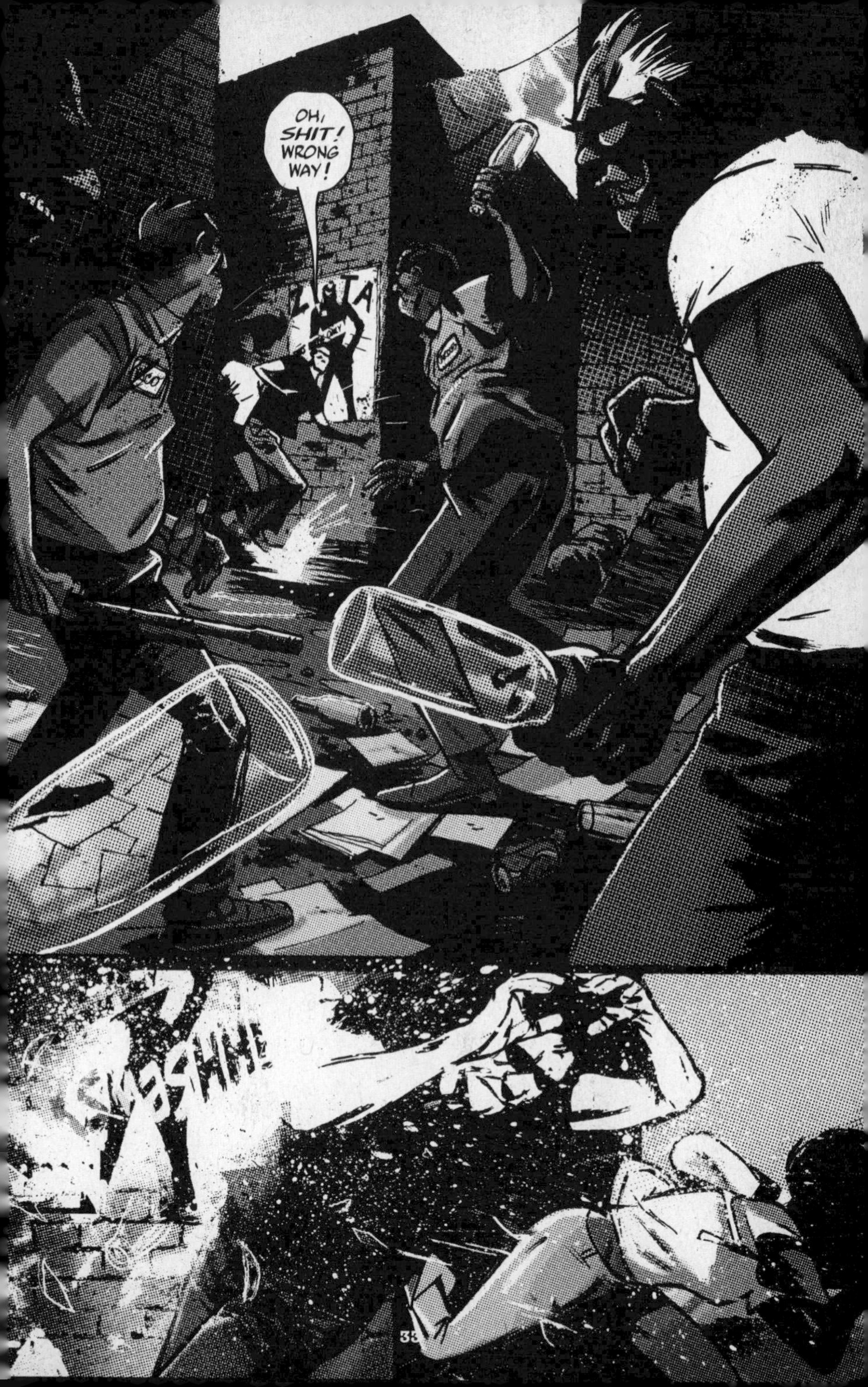
OH, SHIT! WRONG WAY!

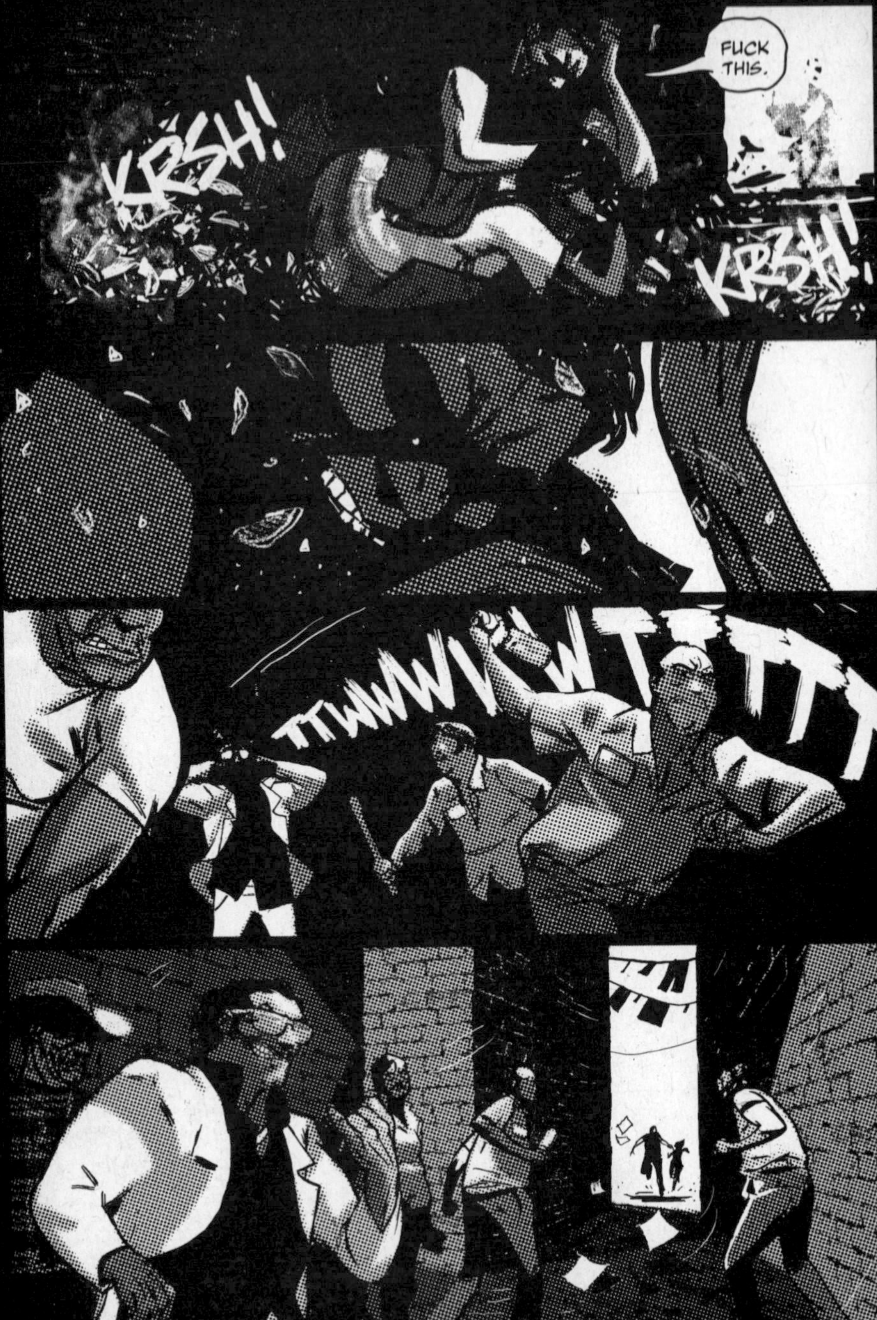
FUCK THIS.
KRSH!
KRSH!
TTWWWWWWTTTTT

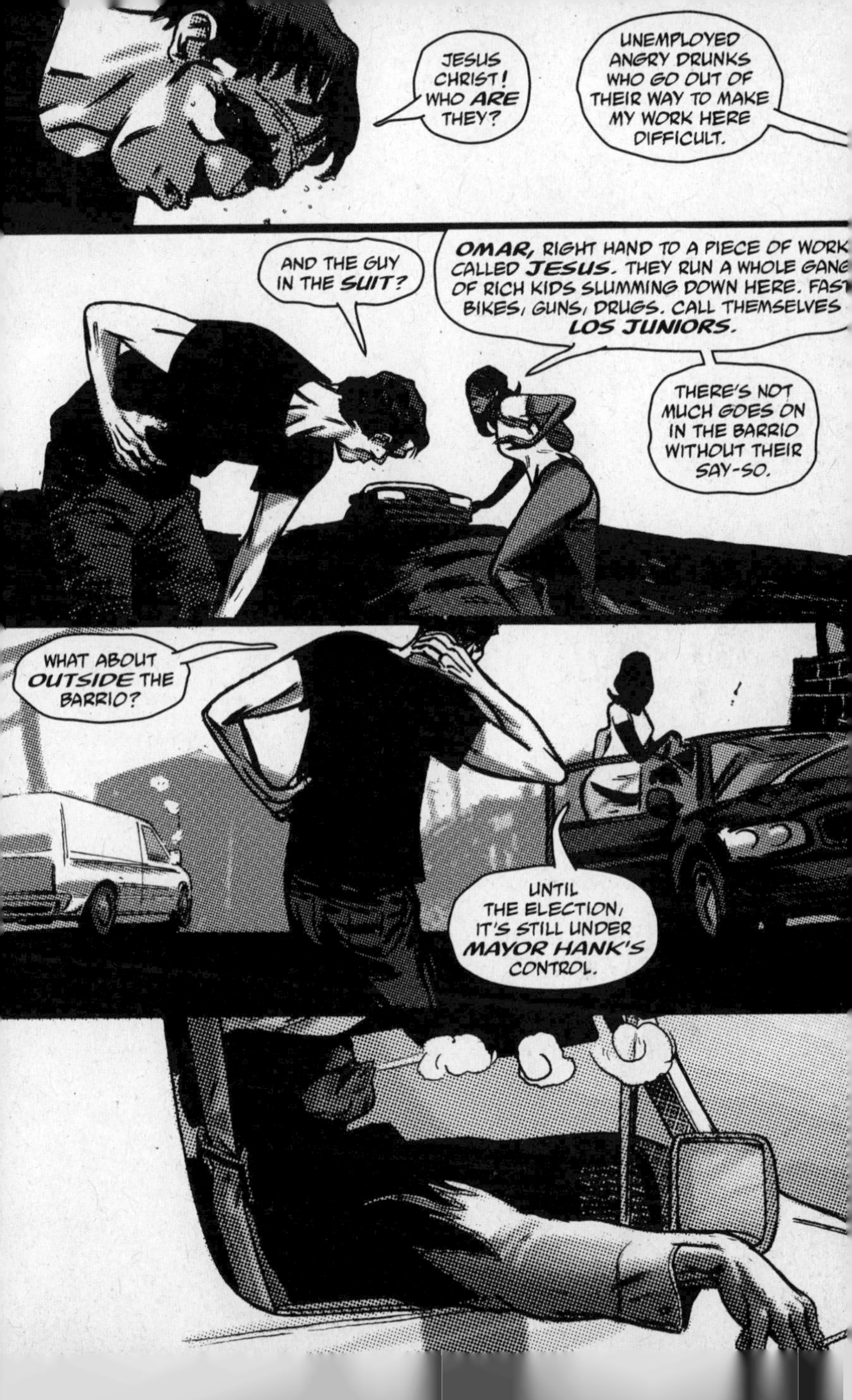
JESUS CHRIST! WHO ARE THEY?
UNEMPLOYED ANGRY DRUNKS WHO GO OUT OF THEIR WAY TO MAKE MY WORK HERE DIFFICULT.
AND THE GUY IN THE SUIT?
OMAR, RIGHT HAND TO A PIECE OF WORK CALLED JESUS. THEY RUN A WHOLE GANG OF RICH KIDS SLUMMING DOWN HERE. FAST BIKES, GUNS, DRUGS. CALL THEMSELVES LOS JUNIORS.
THERE'S NOT MUCH GOES ON IN THE BARRIO WITHOUT THEIR SAY-SO.
WHAT ABOUT OUTSIDE THE BARRIO?
UNTIL THE ELECTION, IT'S STILL UNDER MAYOR HANK'S CONTROL.

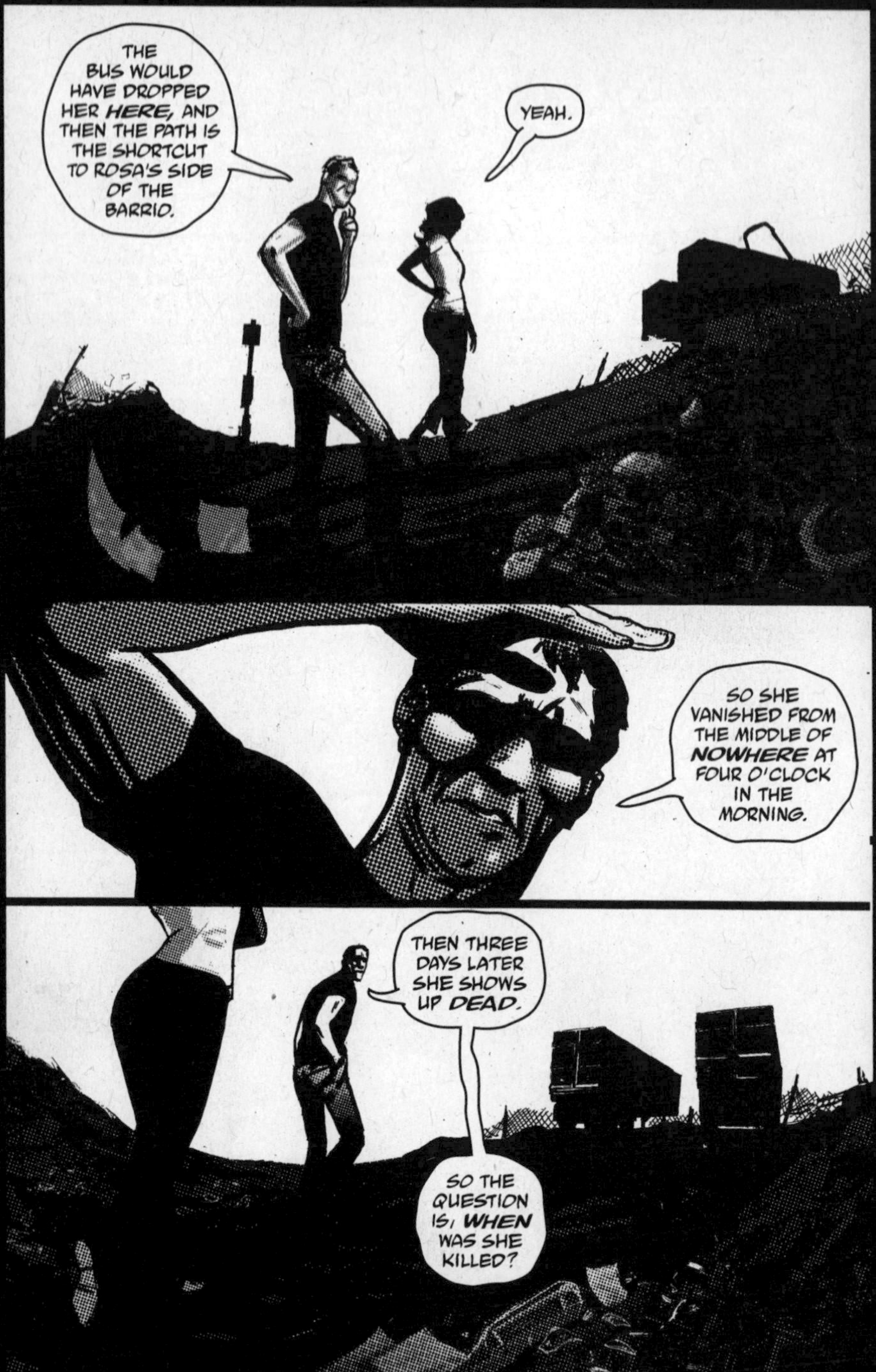
THE BUS WOULD HAVE DROPPED HER HERE, AND THEN THE PATH IS THE SHORTCUT TO ROSA'S SIDE OF THE BARRIO.
YEAH.
SO SHE VANISHED FROM THE MIDDLE OF NOWHERE AT FOUR O'CLOCK IN THE MORNING.
THEN THREE DAYS LATER SHE SHOWS UP DEAD.
SO THE QUESTION IS, WHEN WAS SHE KILLED?

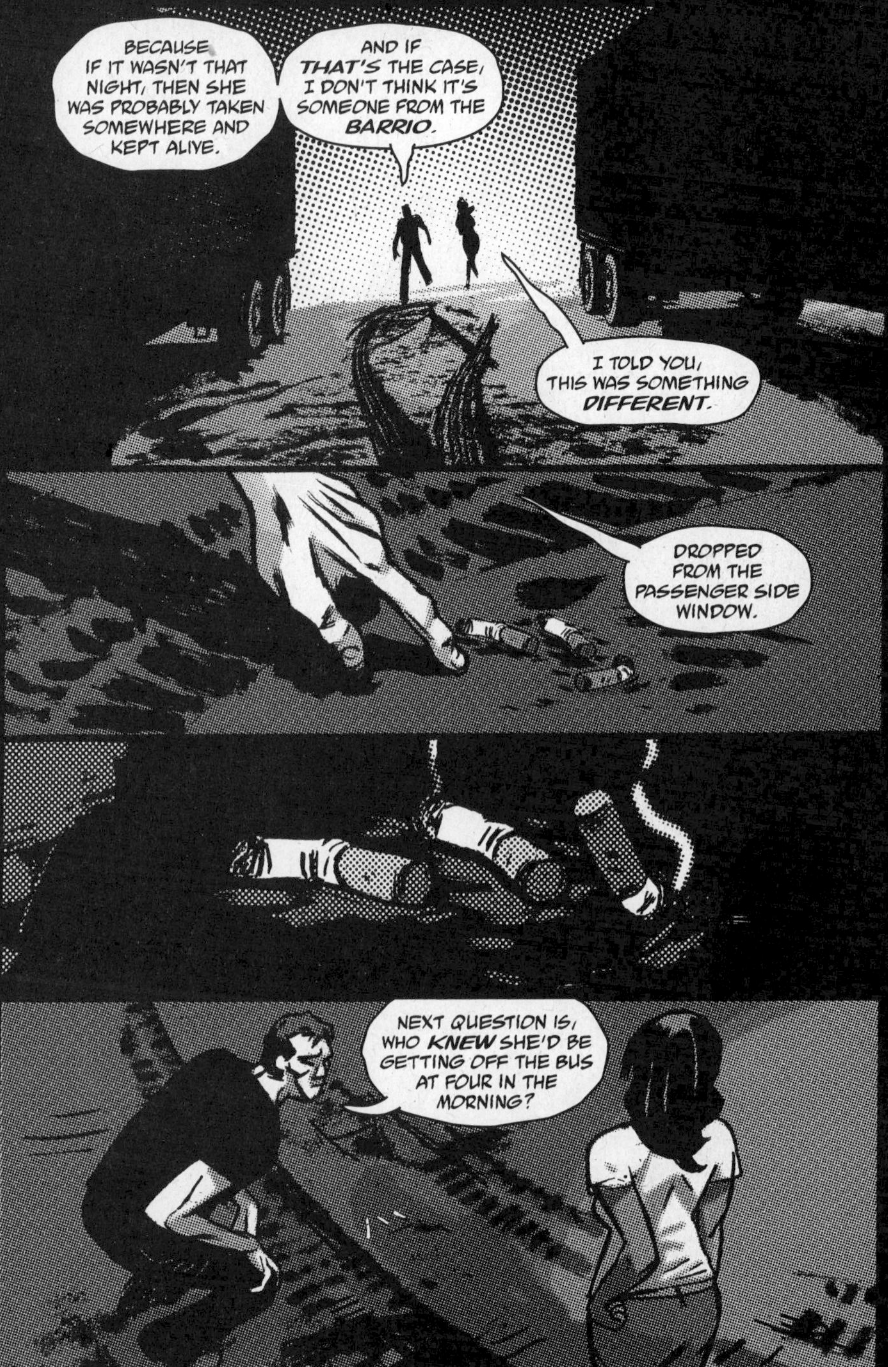
BECAUSE IF IT WASN'T THAT NIGHT, THEN SHE WAS PROBABLY TAKEN SOMEWHERE AND KEPT ALIVE.
AND IF *THAT'S* THE CASE, I DON'T THINK IT'S SOMEONE FROM THE *BARRIO*.
I TOLD YOU, THIS WAS SOMETHING *DIFFERENT*.
DROPPED FROM THE PASSENGER SIDE WINDOW.
NEXT QUESTION IS, WHO *KNEW* SHE'D BE GETTING OFF THE BUS AT FOUR IN THE MORNING?

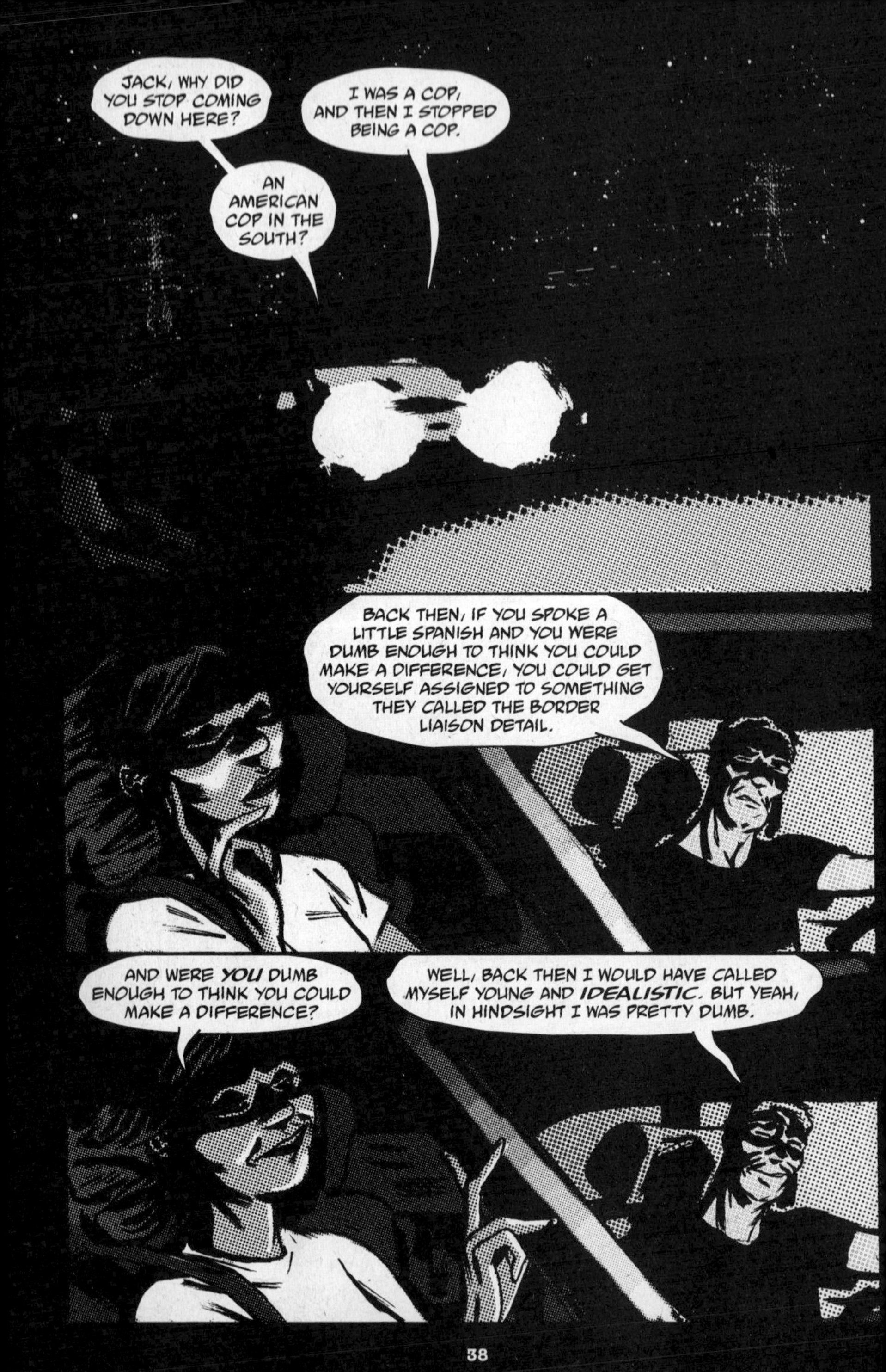
JACK, WHY DID YOU STOP COMING DOWN HERE?
AN AMERICAN COP IN THE SOUTH?
I WAS A COP, AND THEN I STOPPED BEING A COP.
BACK THEN, IF YOU SPOKE A LITTLE SPANISH AND YOU WERE DUMB ENOUGH TO THINK YOU COULD MAKE A DIFFERENCE, YOU COULD GET YOURSELF ASSIGNED TO SOMETHING THEY CALLED THE BORDER LIAISON DETAIL.
AND WERE **YOU** DUMB ENOUGH TO THINK YOU COULD MAKE A DIFFERENCE?
WELL, BACK THEN I WOULD HAVE CALLED MYSELF YOUNG AND ***IDEALISTIC***. BUT YEAH, IN HINDSIGHT I WAS PRETTY DUMB.

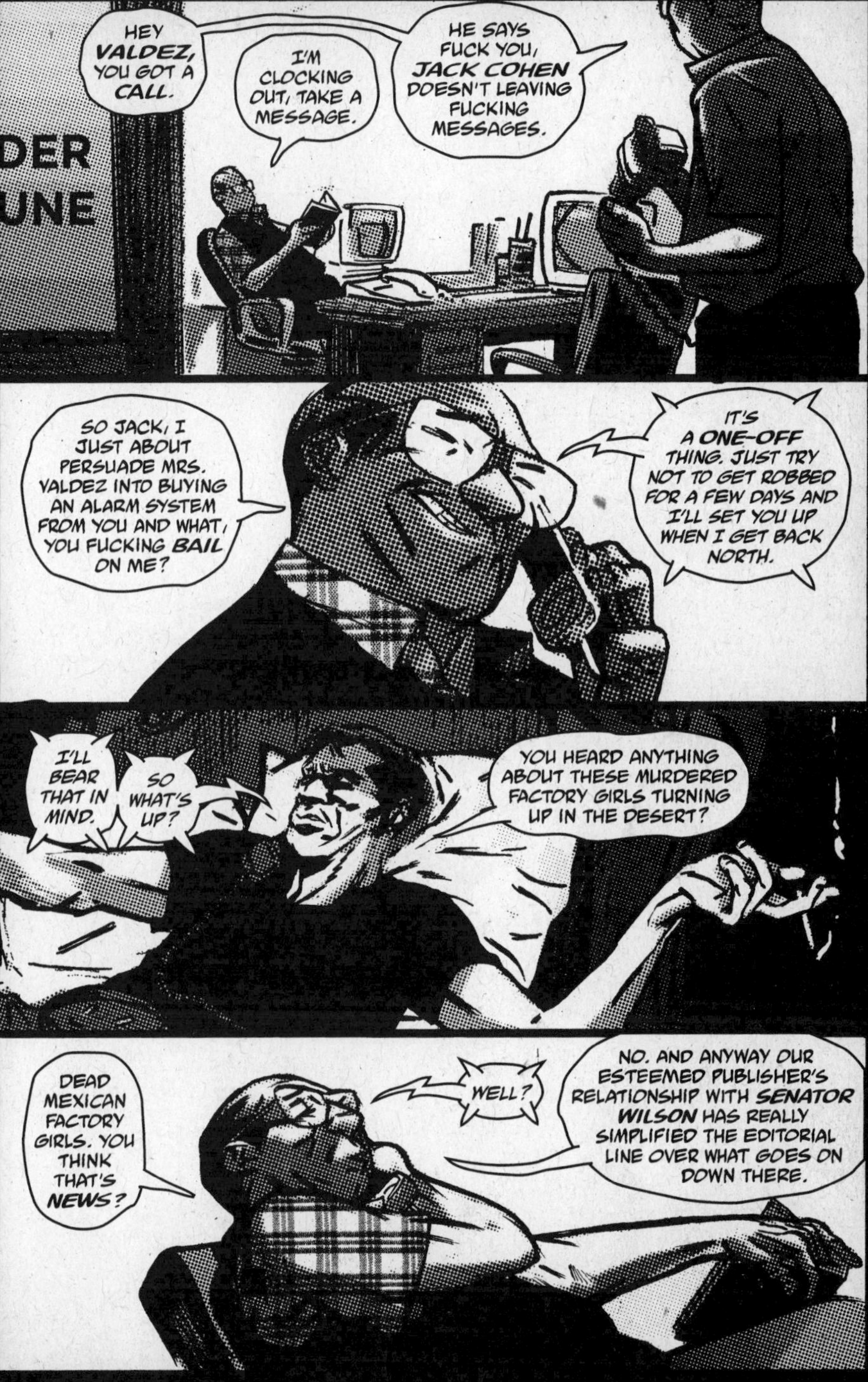
HEY **VALDEZ,** YOU GOT A **CALL.**
I'M CLOCKING OUT, TAKE A MESSAGE.
HE SAYS FUCK YOU, **JACK COHEN** DOESN'T LEAVING FUCKING MESSAGES.
DER
UNE
SO JACK, I JUST ABOUT PERSUADE MRS. VALDEZ INTO BUYING AN ALARM SYSTEM FROM YOU AND WHAT, YOU FUCKING **BAIL** ON ME?
IT'S A **ONE-OFF** THING. JUST TRY NOT TO GET ROBBED FOR A FEW DAYS AND I'LL SET YOU UP WHEN I GET BACK NORTH.
I'LL BEAR THAT IN MIND.
SO WHAT'S UP?
YOU HEARD ANYTHING ABOUT THESE MURDERED FACTORY GIRLS TURNING UP IN THE DESERT?
DEAD MEXICAN FACTORY GIRLS. YOU THINK THAT'S **NEWS?**
WELL?
NO. AND ANYWAY OUR ESTEEMED PUBLISHER'S RELATIONSHIP WITH **SENATOR WILSON** HAS REALLY SIMPLIFIED THE EDITORIAL LINE OVER WHAT GOES ON DOWN THERE.

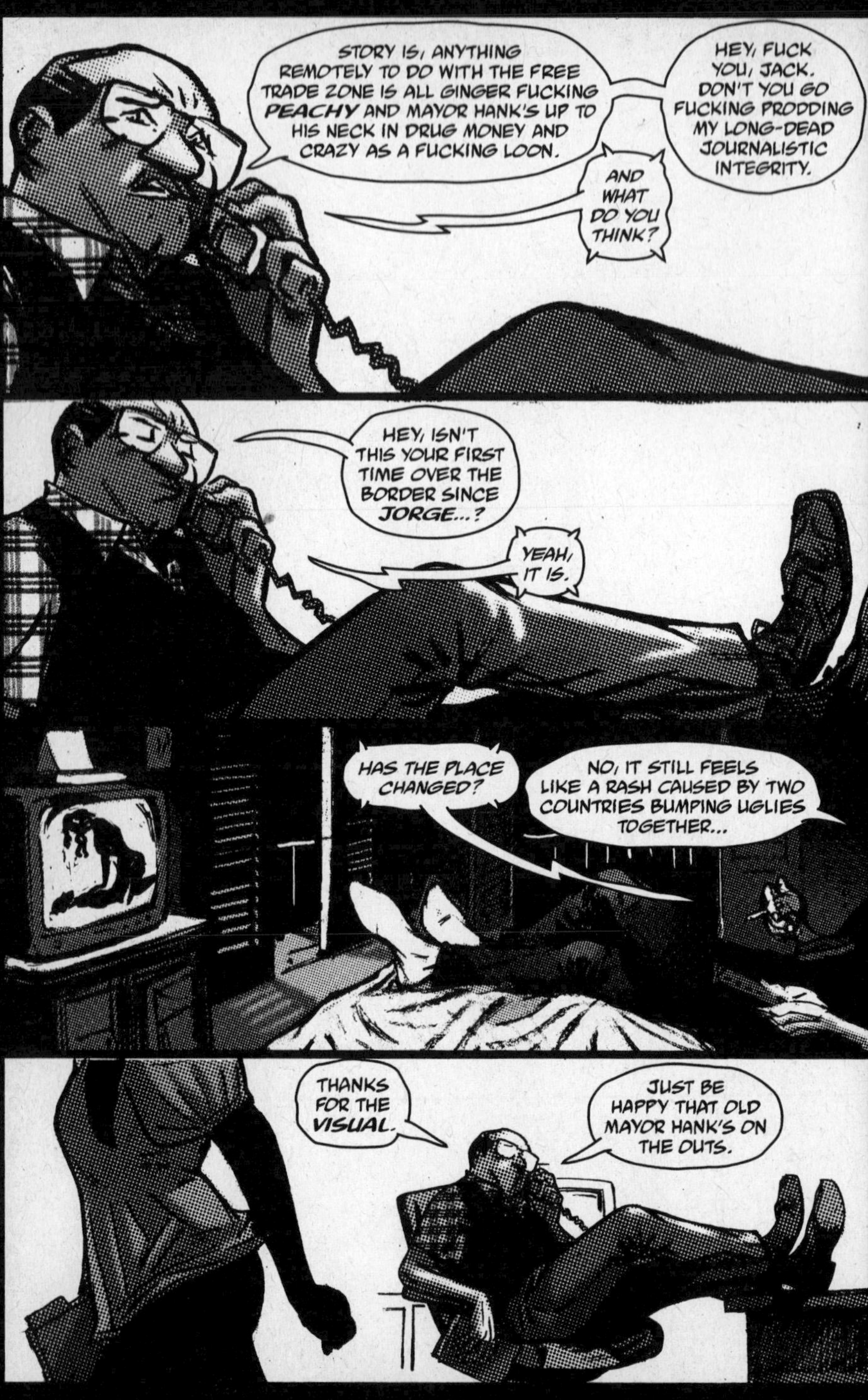
STORY IS, ANYTHING REMOTELY TO DO WITH THE FREE TRADE ZONE IS ALL GINGER FUCKING PEACHY AND MAYOR HANK'S UP TO HIS NECK IN DRUG MONEY AND CRAZY AS A FUCKING LOON.
HEY, FUCK YOU, JACK. DON'T YOU GO FUCKING PRODDING MY LONG-DEAD JOURNALISTIC INTEGRITY.
AND WHAT DO YOU THINK?
HEY, ISN'T THIS YOUR FIRST TIME OVER THE BORDER SINCE JORGE...?
YEAH, IT IS.
HAS THE PLACE CHANGED?
NO, IT STILL FEELS LIKE A RASH CAUSED BY TWO COUNTRIES BUMPING UGLIES TOGETHER...
THANKS FOR THE VISUAL.
JUST BE HAPPY THAT OLD MAYOR HANK'S ON THE OUTS.

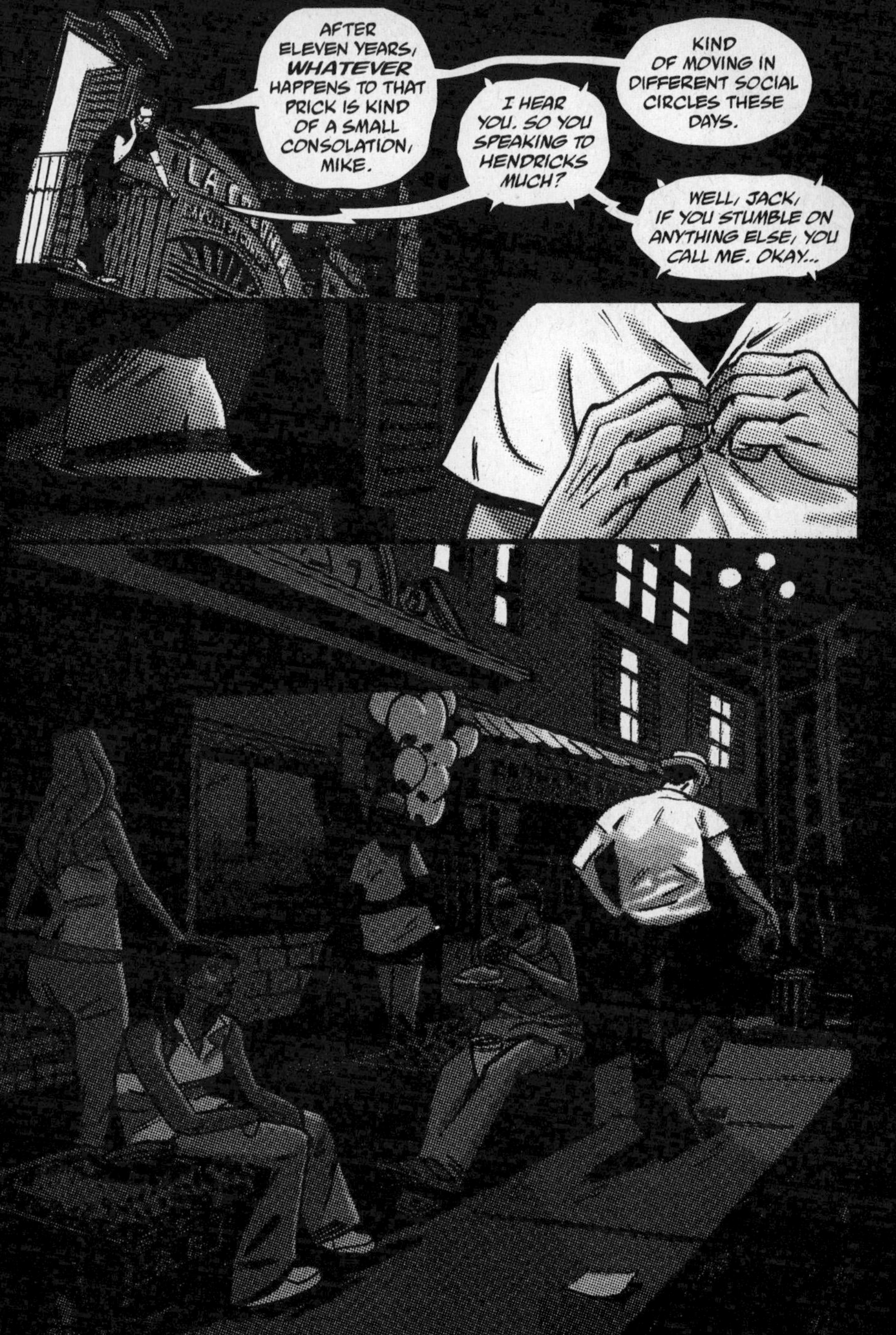
AFTER ELEVEN YEARS, WHATEVER HAPPENS TO THAT PRICK IS KIND OF A SMALL CONSOLATION, MIKE.
I HEAR YOU. SO YOU SPEAKING TO HENDRICKS MUCH?
KIND OF MOVING IN DIFFERENT SOCIAL CIRCLES THESE DAYS.
WELL, JACK, IF YOU STUMBLE ON ANYTHING ELSE, YOU CALL ME. OKAY...

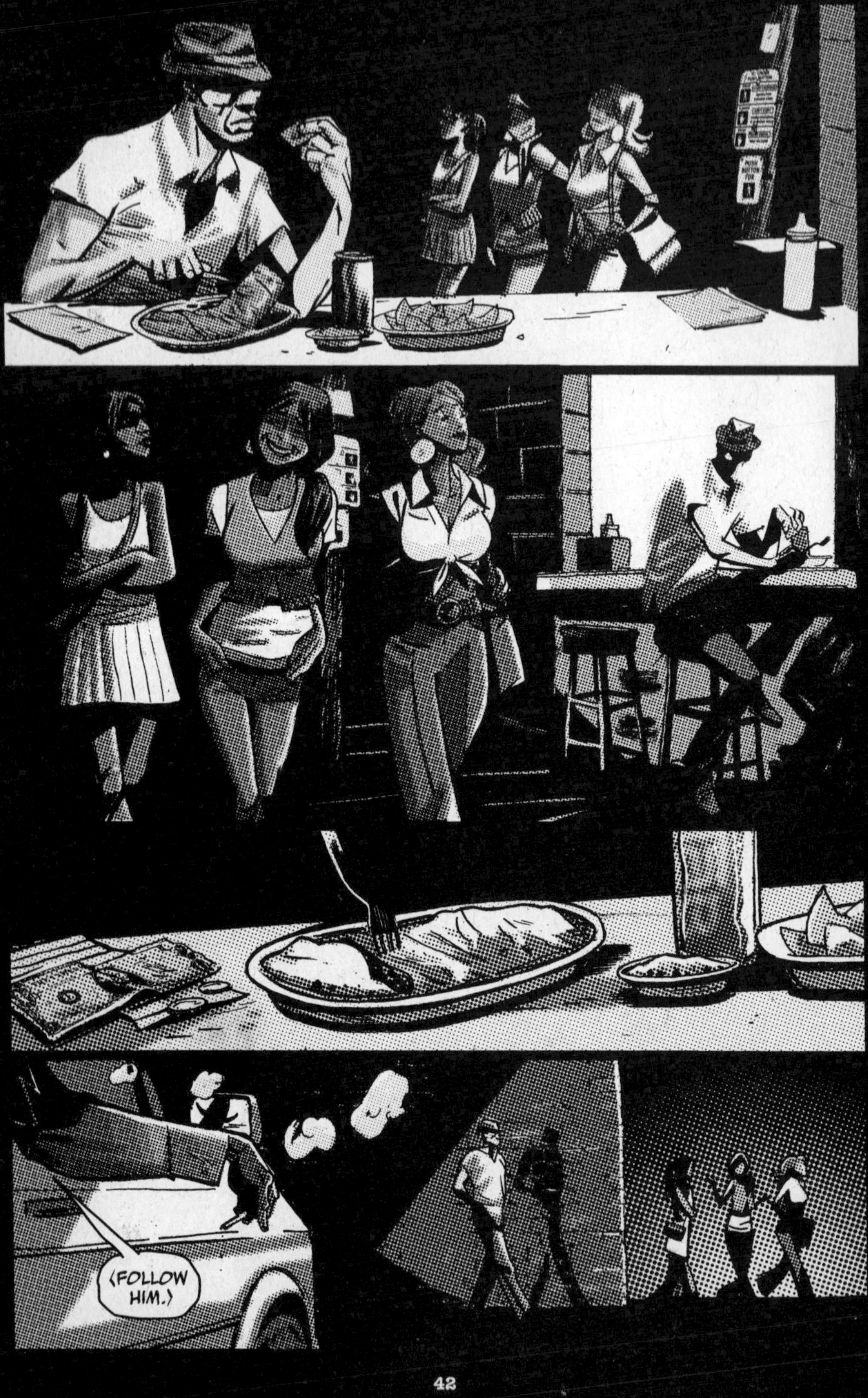
⟨FOLLOW HIM.⟩

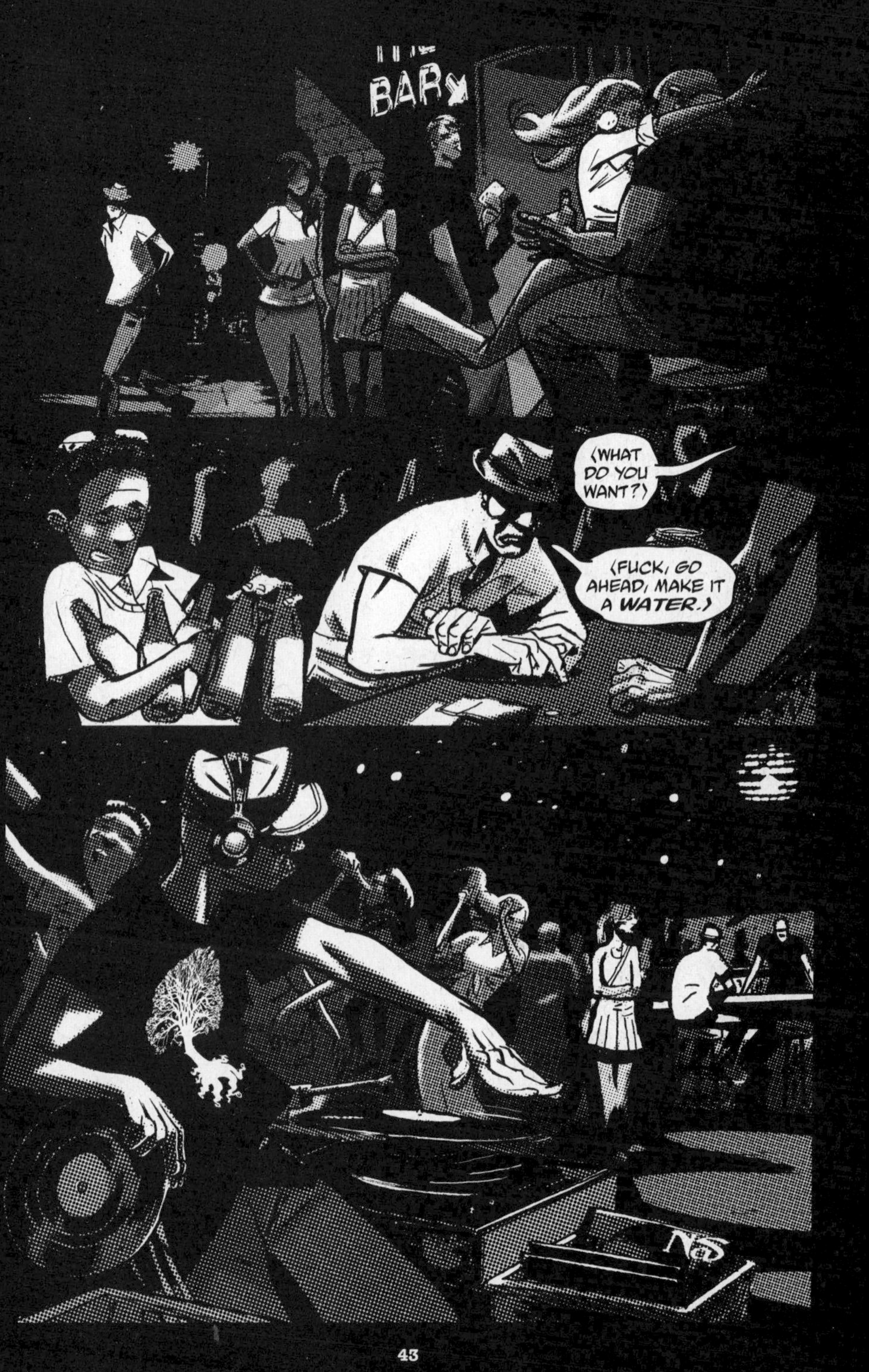
BAR
‹WHAT DO YOU WANT?›
‹FUCK, GO AHEAD, MAKE IT A **WATER**.›

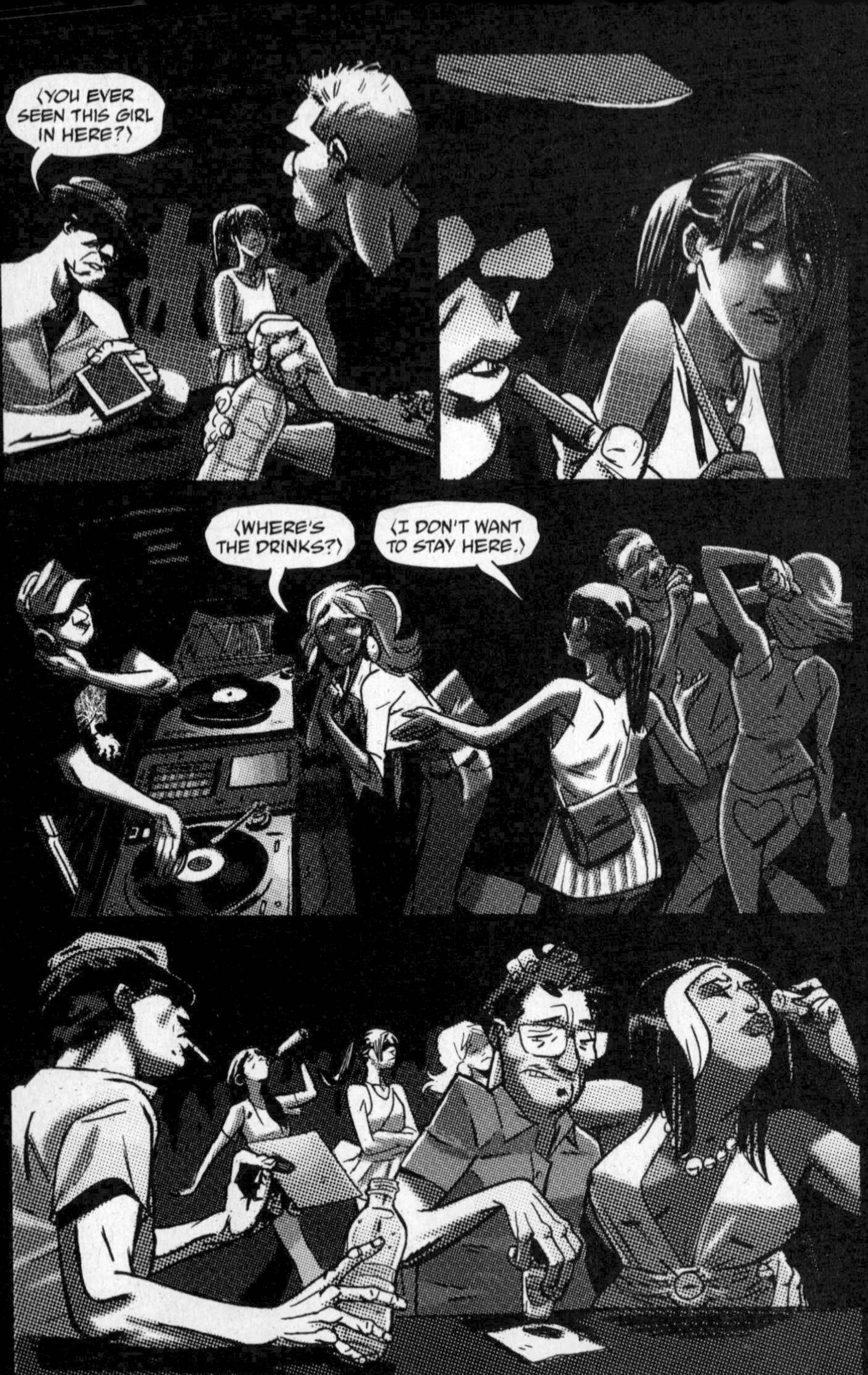
(YOU EVER SEEN THIS GIRL IN HERE?)
(WHERE'S THE DRINKS?)
(I DON'T WANT TO STAY HERE.)

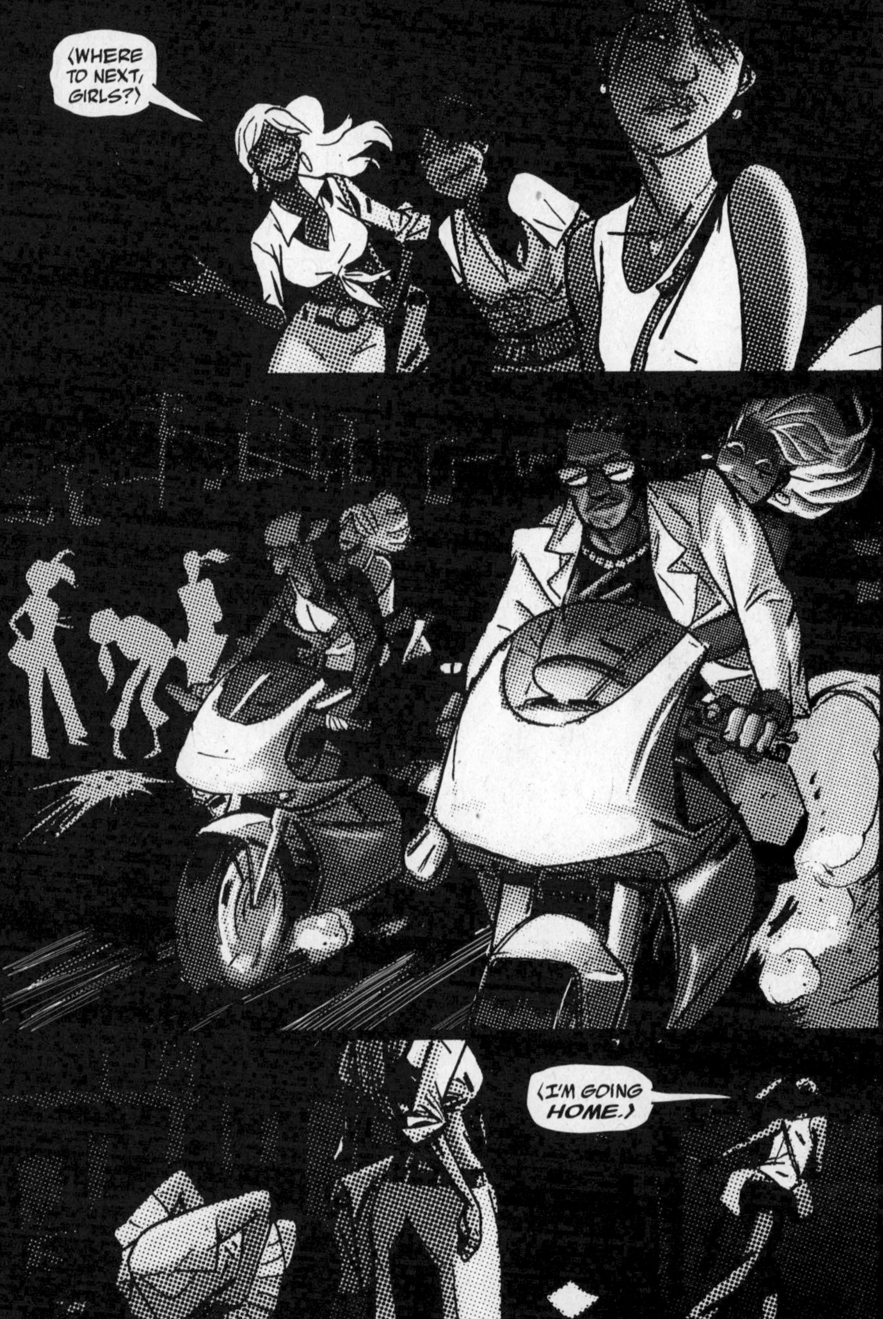
⟨WHERE TO NEXT, GIRLS?⟩
⟨I'M GOING HOME.⟩

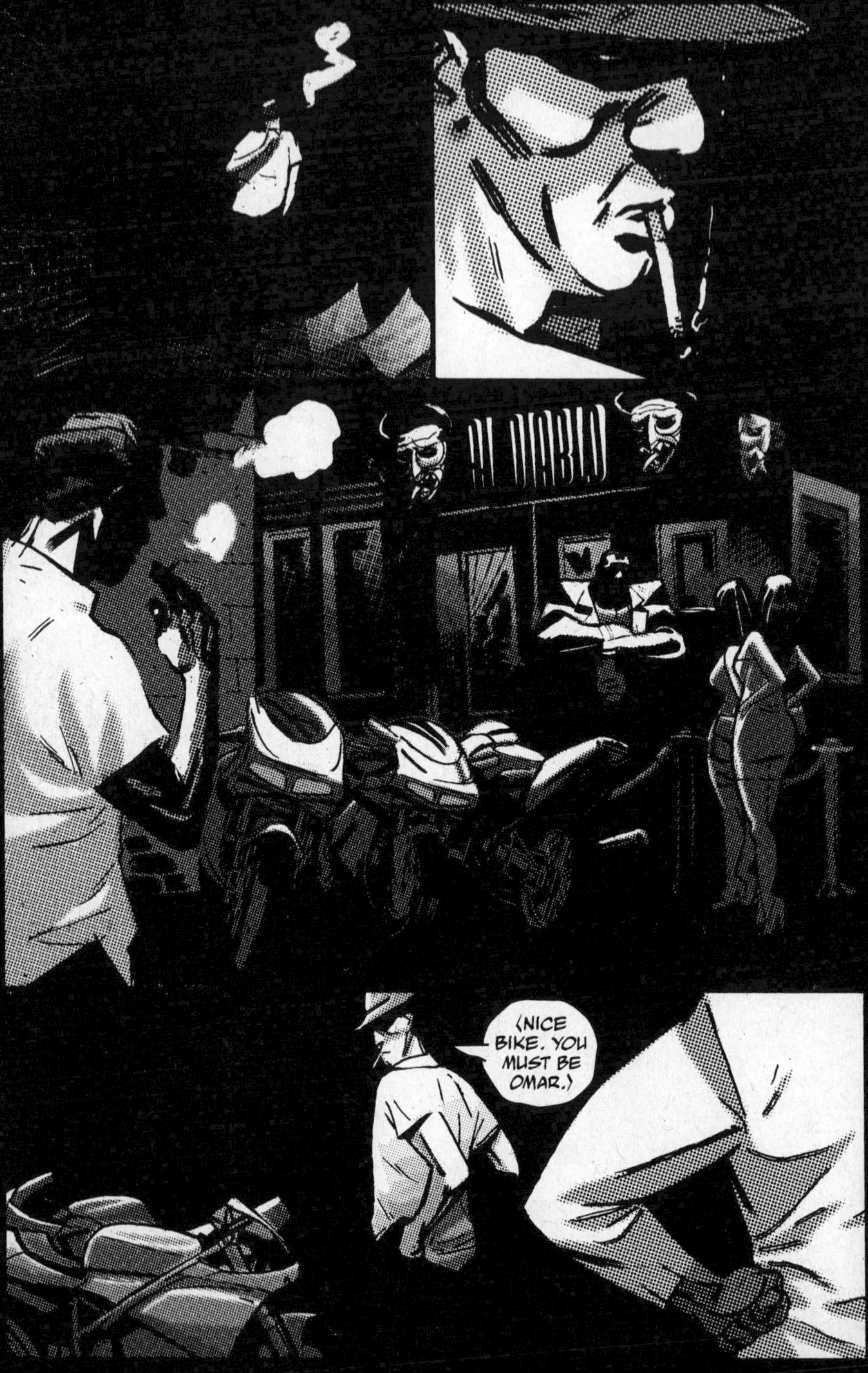
AL DIABLO
(NICE BIKE. YOU MUST BE OMAR.)

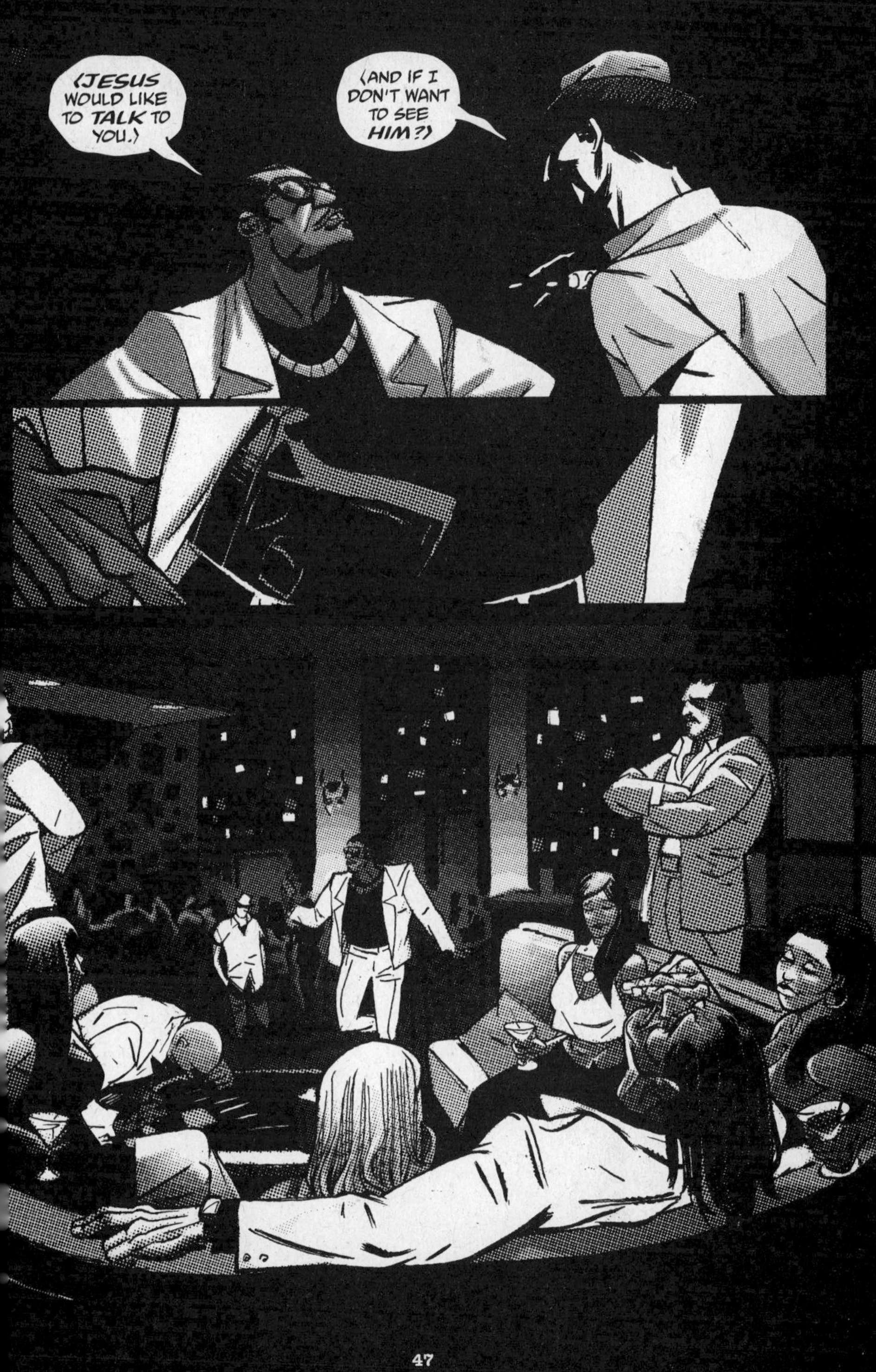
‹JESUS WOULD LIKE TO TALK TO YOU.›
‹AND IF I DON'T WANT TO SEE HIM?›

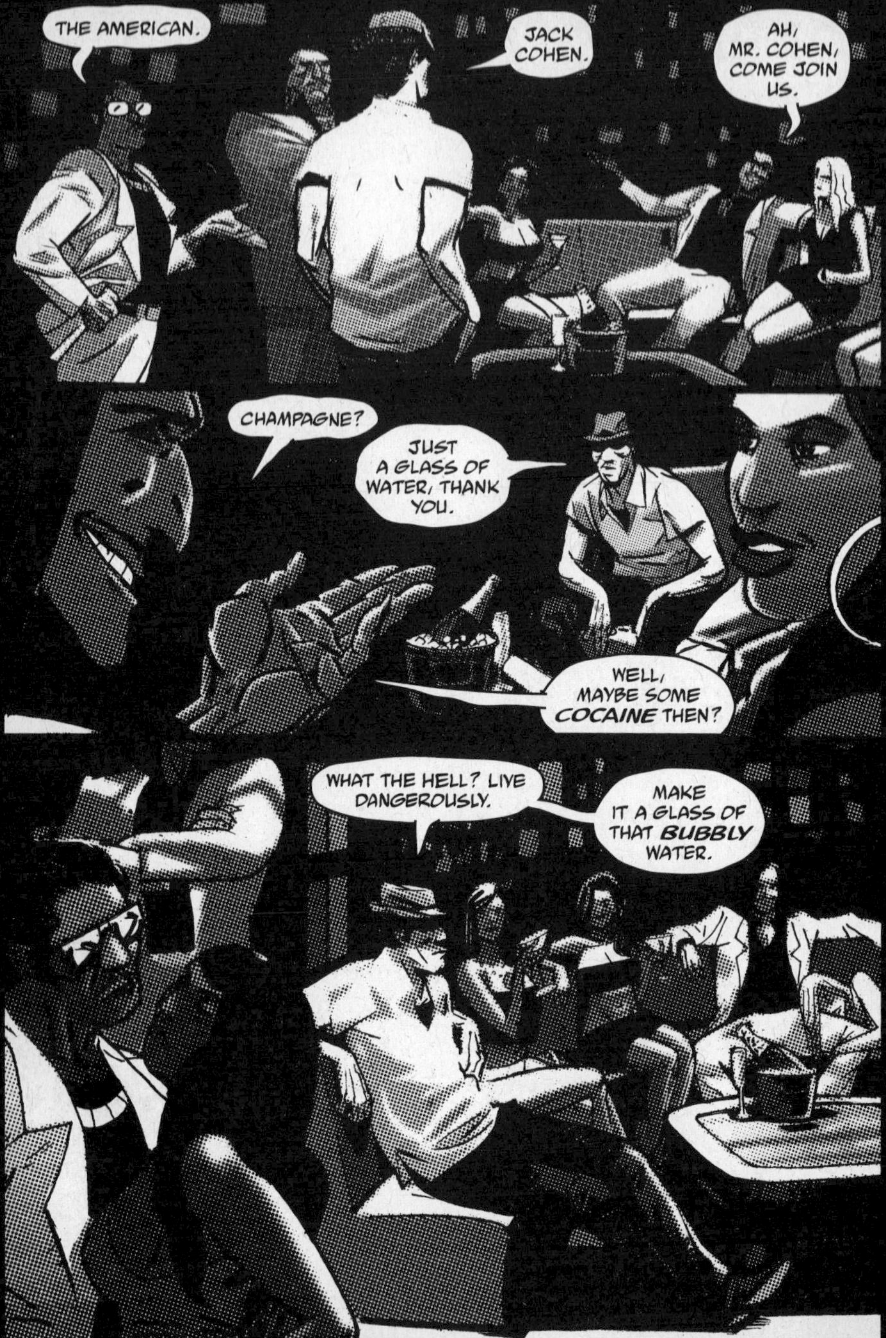
THE AMERICAN.
JACK COHEN.
AH, MR. COHEN, COME JOIN US.
CHAMPAGNE?
JUST A GLASS OF WATER, THANK YOU.
WELL, MAYBE SOME *COCAINE* THEN?
WHAT THE HELL? LIVE DANGEROUSLY.
MAKE IT A GLASS OF THAT *BUBBLY* WATER.

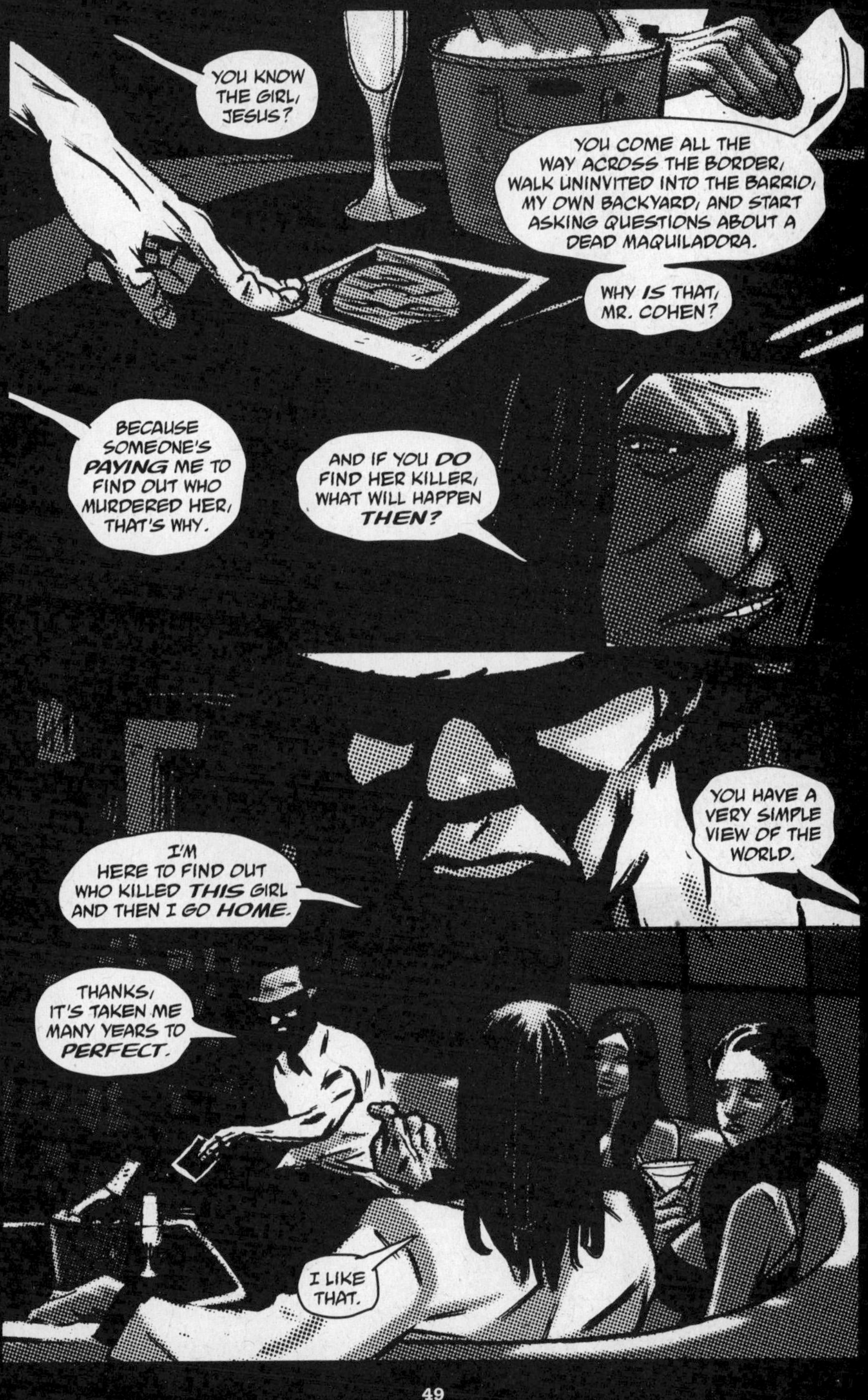

YOU KNOW THE GIRL, JESUS?
YOU COME ALL THE WAY ACROSS THE BORDER, WALK UNINVITED INTO THE BARRIO, MY OWN BACKYARD, AND START ASKING QUESTIONS ABOUT A DEAD MAQUILADORA.
WHY IS THAT, MR. COHEN?
BECAUSE SOMEONE'S PAYING ME TO FIND OUT WHO MURDERED HER, THAT'S WHY.
AND IF YOU DO FIND HER KILLER, WHAT WILL HAPPEN THEN?
YOU HAVE A VERY SIMPLE VIEW OF THE WORLD.
I'M HERE TO FIND OUT WHO KILLED THIS GIRL AND THEN I GO HOME.
THANKS, IT'S TAKEN ME MANY YEARS TO PERFECT.
I LIKE THAT.

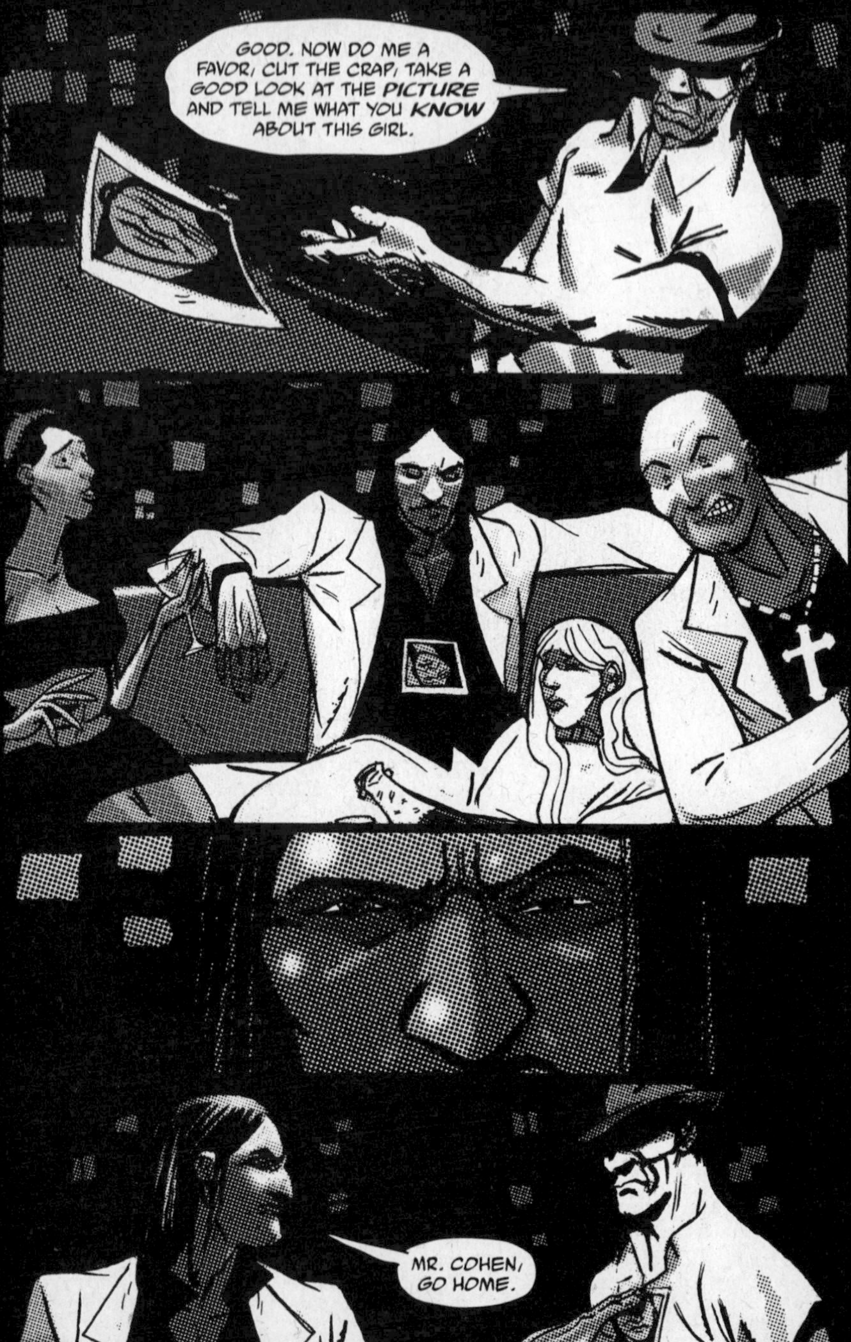
GOOD. NOW DO ME A FAVOR, CUT THE CRAP, TAKE A GOOD LOOK AT THE PICTURE AND TELL ME WHAT YOU KNOW ABOUT THIS GIRL.
MR. COHEN, GO HOME.

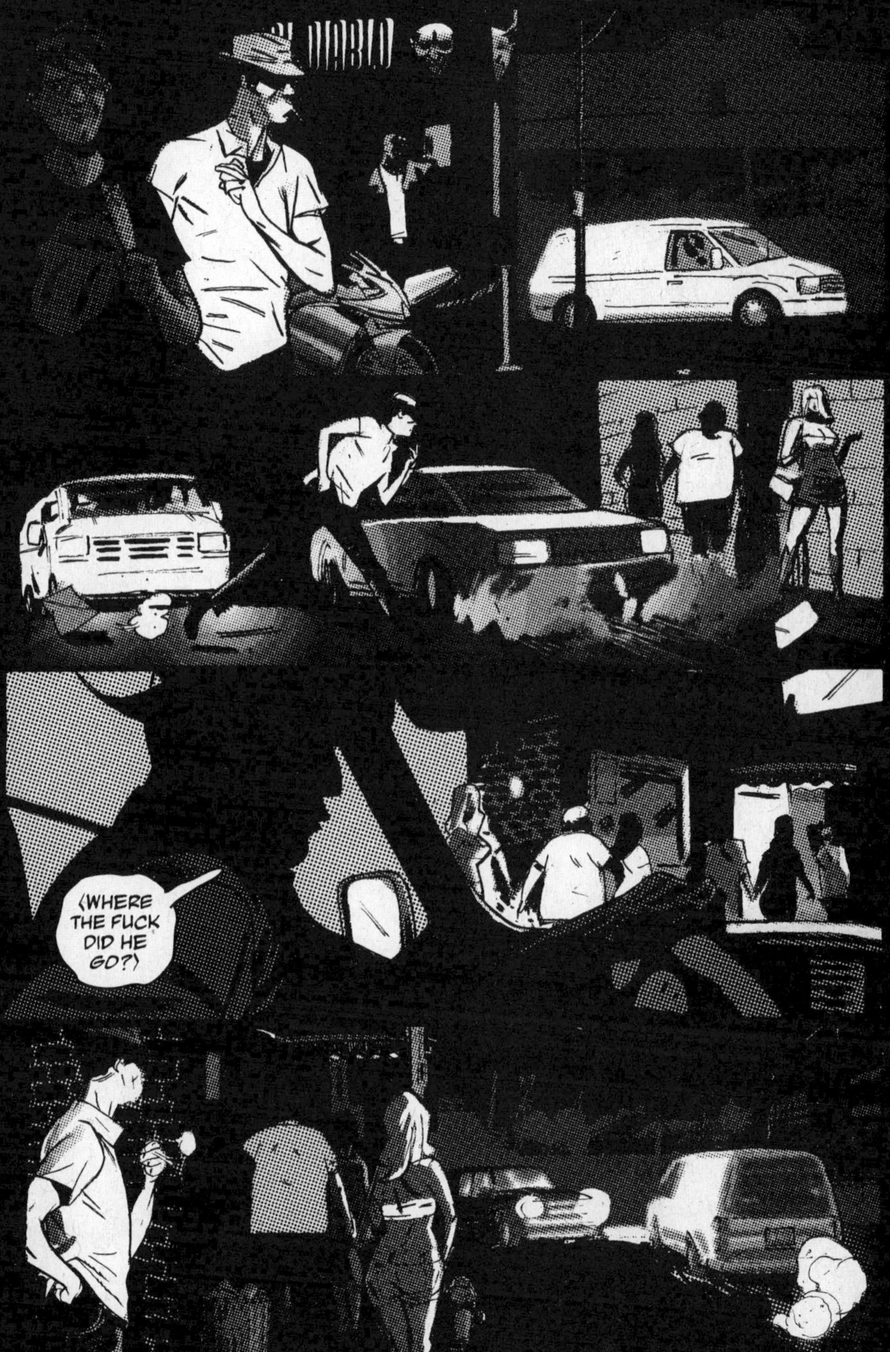
EL DIABLO
⟨WHERE THE FUCK DID HE GO?⟩

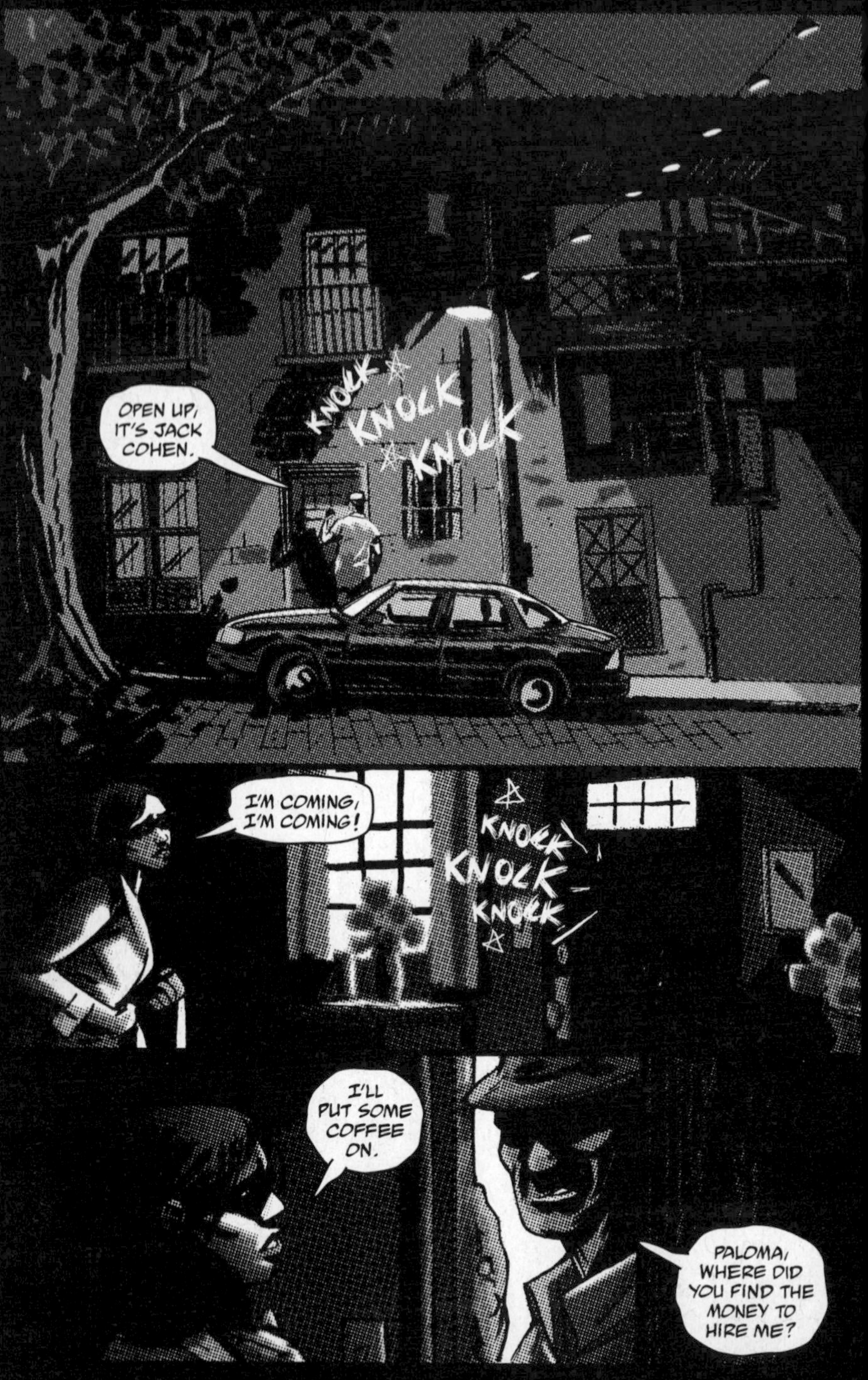
OPEN UP, IT'S JACK COHEN.
KNOCK KNOCK KNOCK
I'M COMING, I'M COMING!
KNOCK KNOCK KNOCK
I'LL PUT SOME COFFEE ON.
PALOMA, WHERE DID YOU FIND THE MONEY TO HIRE ME?

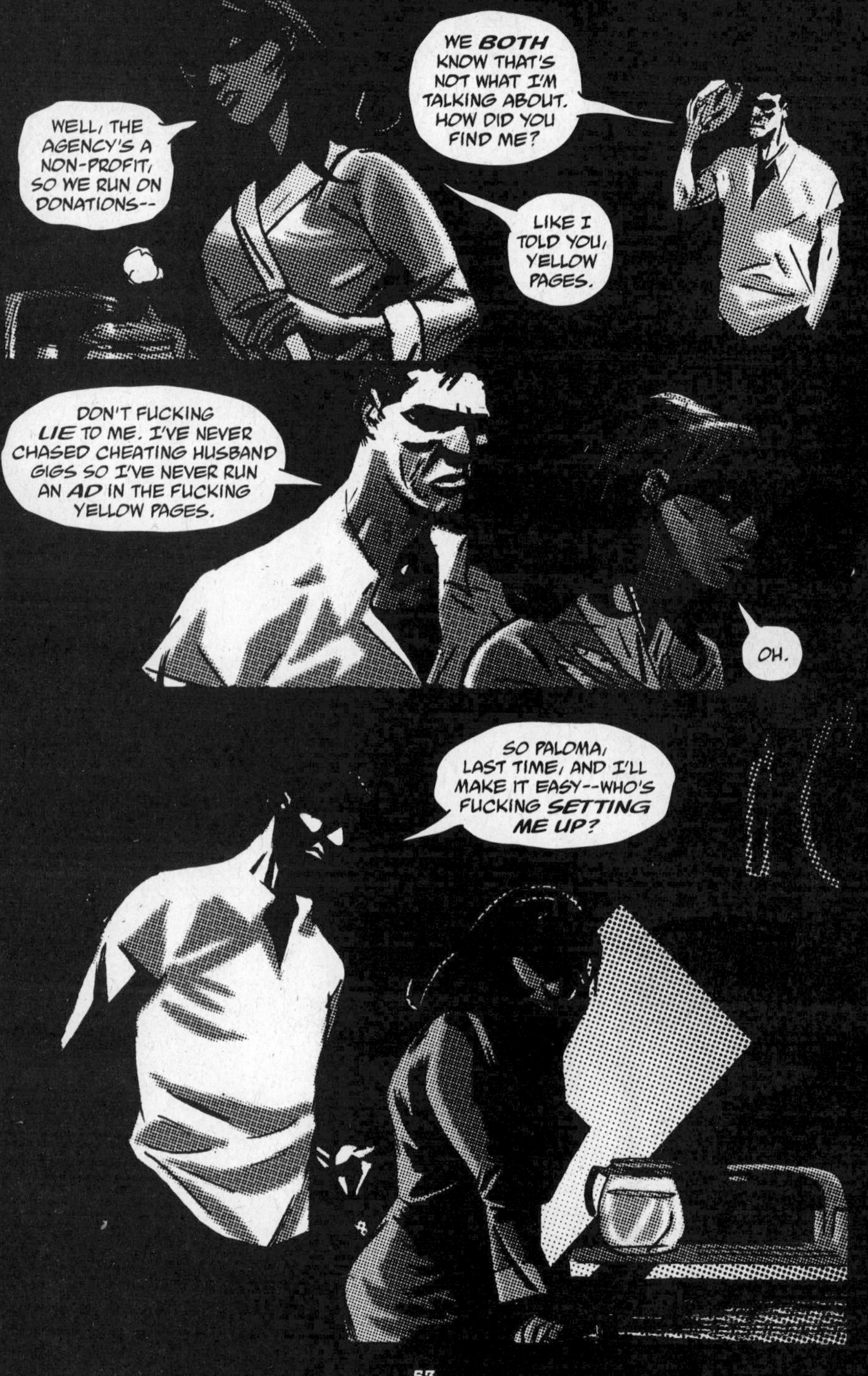
WELL, THE AGENCY'S A NON-PROFIT, SO WE RUN ON DONATIONS--
WE BOTH KNOW THAT'S NOT WHAT I'M TALKING ABOUT. HOW DID YOU FIND ME?
LIKE I TOLD YOU, YELLOW PAGES.
DON'T FUCKING LIE TO ME. I'VE NEVER CHASED CHEATING HUSBAND GIGS SO I'VE NEVER RUN AN AD IN THE FUCKING YELLOW PAGES.
OH.
SO PALOMA, LAST TIME, AND I'LL MAKE IT EASY--WHO'S FUCKING SETTING ME UP?

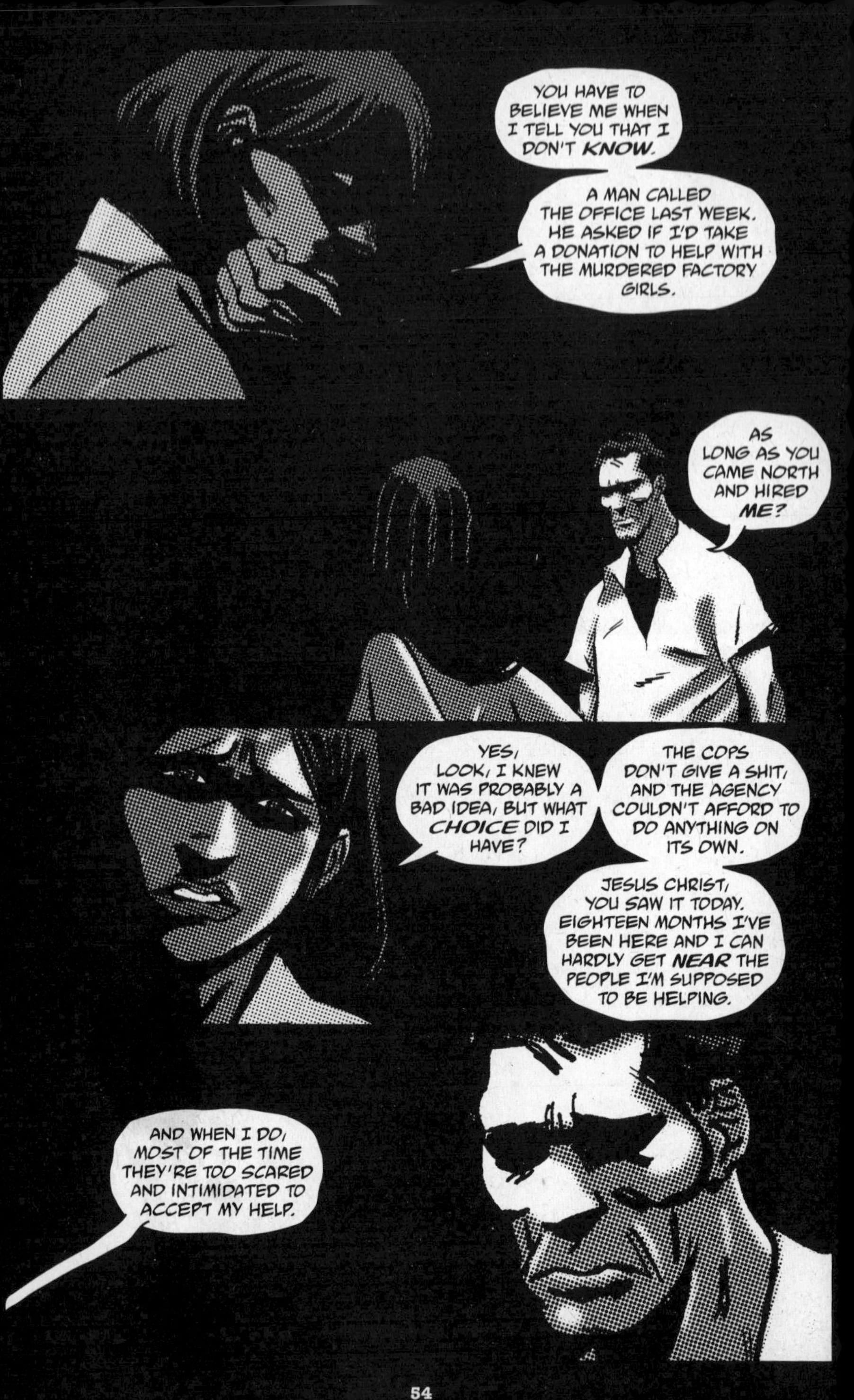
YOU HAVE TO BELIEVE ME WHEN I TELL YOU THAT I DON'T **KNOW**.
A MAN CALLED THE OFFICE LAST WEEK. HE ASKED IF I'D TAKE A DONATION TO HELP WITH THE MURDERED FACTORY GIRLS.
AS LONG AS YOU CAME NORTH AND HIRED **ME**?
YES, LOOK, I KNEW IT WAS PROBABLY A BAD IDEA, BUT WHAT **CHOICE** DID I HAVE?
THE COPS DON'T GIVE A SHIT, AND THE AGENCY COULDN'T AFFORD TO DO ANYTHING ON ITS OWN.
JESUS CHRIST, YOU SAW IT TODAY. EIGHTEEN MONTHS I'VE BEEN HERE AND I CAN HARDLY GET **NEAR** THE PEOPLE I'M SUPPOSED TO BE HELPING.
AND WHEN I DO, MOST OF THE TIME THEY'RE TOO SCARED AND INTIMIDATED TO ACCEPT MY HELP.

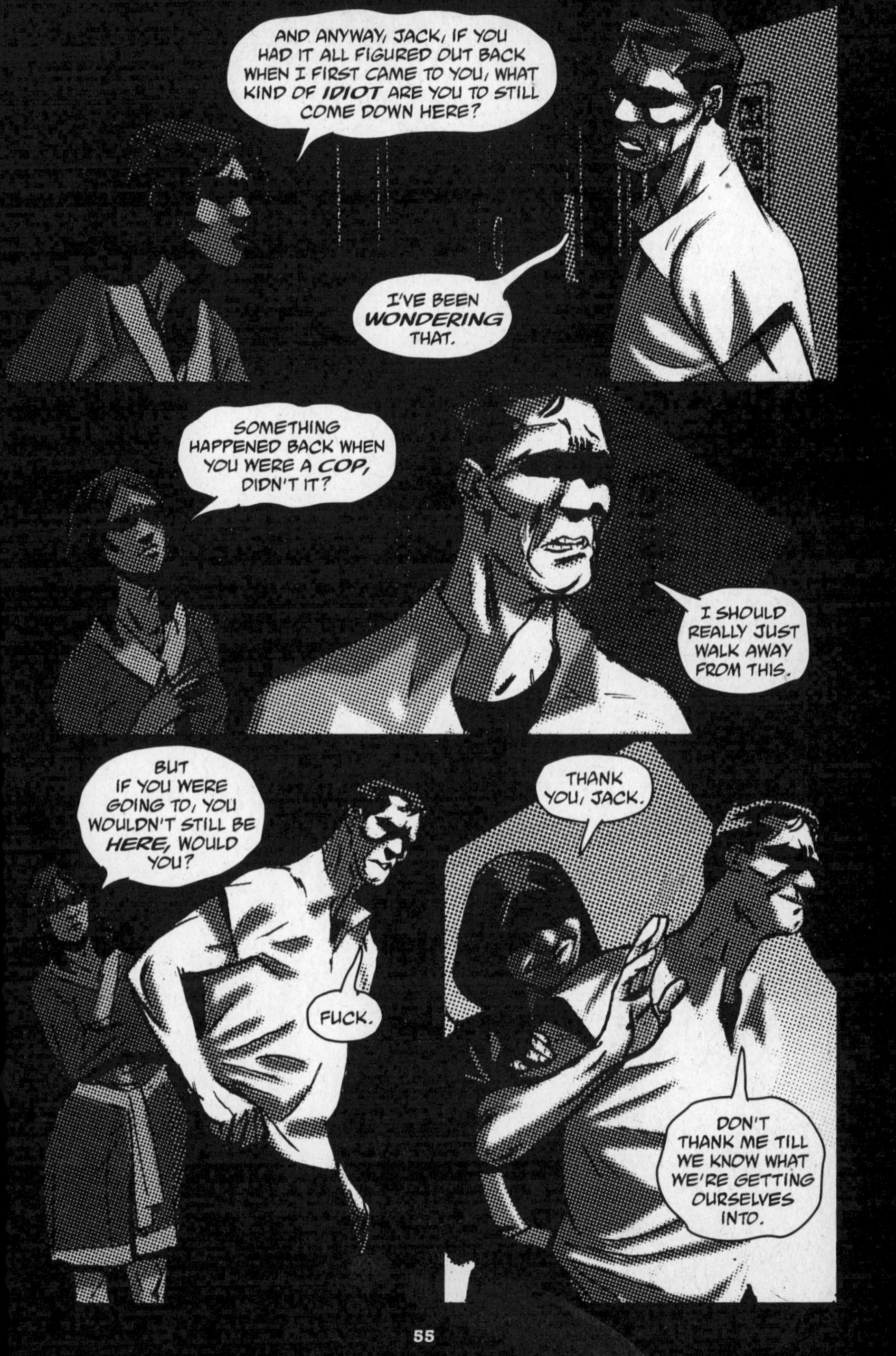
AND ANYWAY, JACK, IF YOU HAD IT ALL FIGURED OUT BACK WHEN I FIRST CAME TO YOU, WHAT KIND OF *IDIOT* ARE YOU TO STILL COME DOWN HERE?
I'VE BEEN *WONDERING* THAT.
SOMETHING HAPPENED BACK WHEN YOU WERE A *COP*, DIDN'T IT?
I SHOULD REALLY JUST WALK AWAY FROM THIS.
BUT IF YOU WERE GOING TO, YOU WOULDN'T STILL BE *HERE*, WOULD YOU?
FUCK.
THANK YOU, JACK.
DON'T THANK ME TILL WE KNOW WHAT WE'RE GETTING OURSELVES INTO.

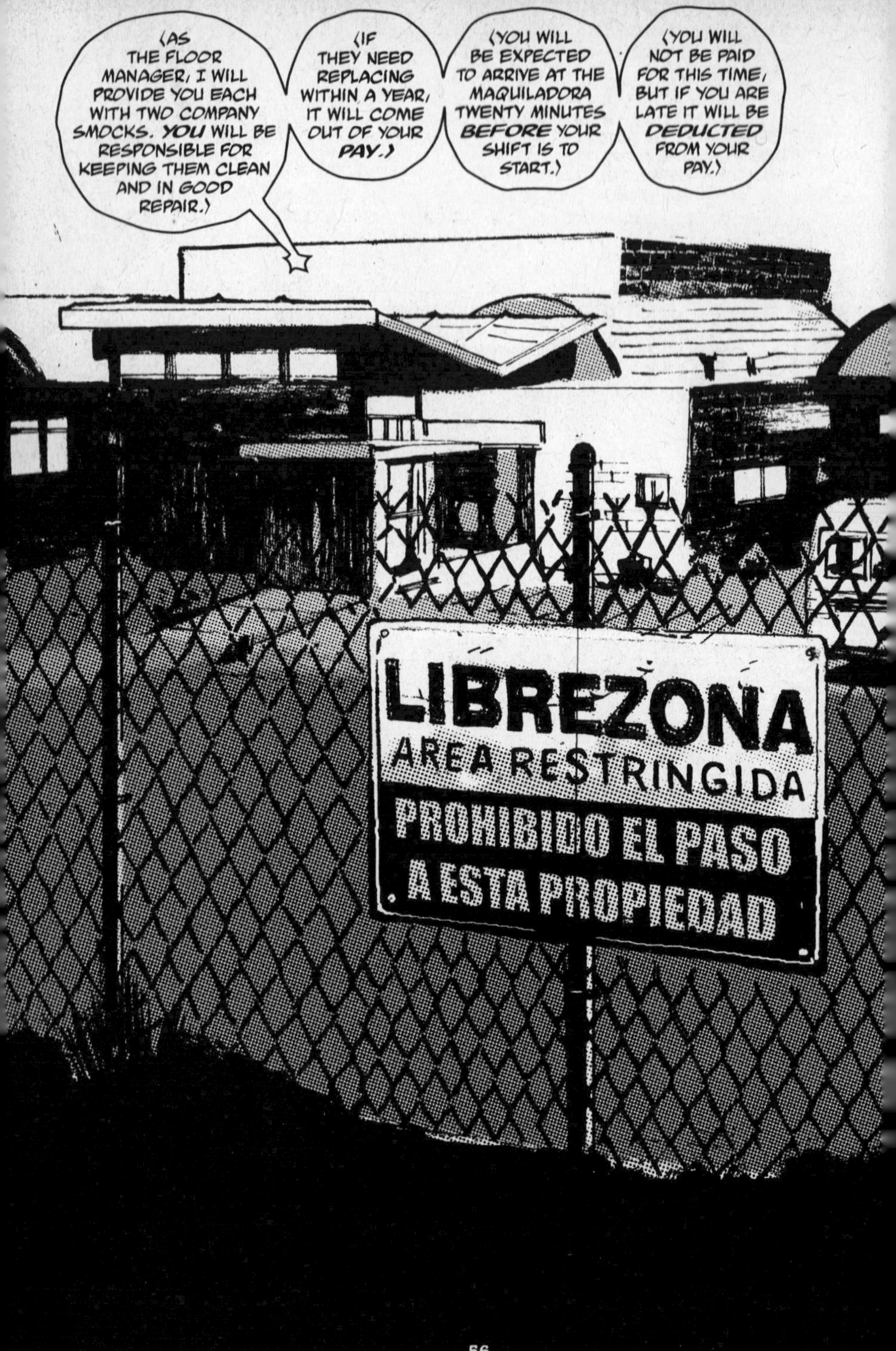
⟨AS THE FLOOR MANAGER, I WILL PROVIDE YOU EACH WITH TWO COMPANY SMOCKS. *YOU* WILL BE RESPONSIBLE FOR KEEPING THEM CLEAN AND IN GOOD REPAIR.⟩
⟨IF THEY NEED REPLACING WITHIN A YEAR, IT WILL COME OUT OF YOUR *PAY*.⟩
⟨YOU WILL BE EXPECTED TO ARRIVE AT THE MAQUILADORA TWENTY MINUTES *BEFORE* YOUR SHIFT IS TO START.⟩
⟨YOU WILL NOT BE PAID FOR THIS TIME, BUT IF YOU ARE LATE IT WILL BE *DEDUCTED* FROM YOUR PAY.⟩
LIBREZONA
AREA RESTRINGIDA
PROHIBIDO EL PASO
A ESTA PROPIEDAD

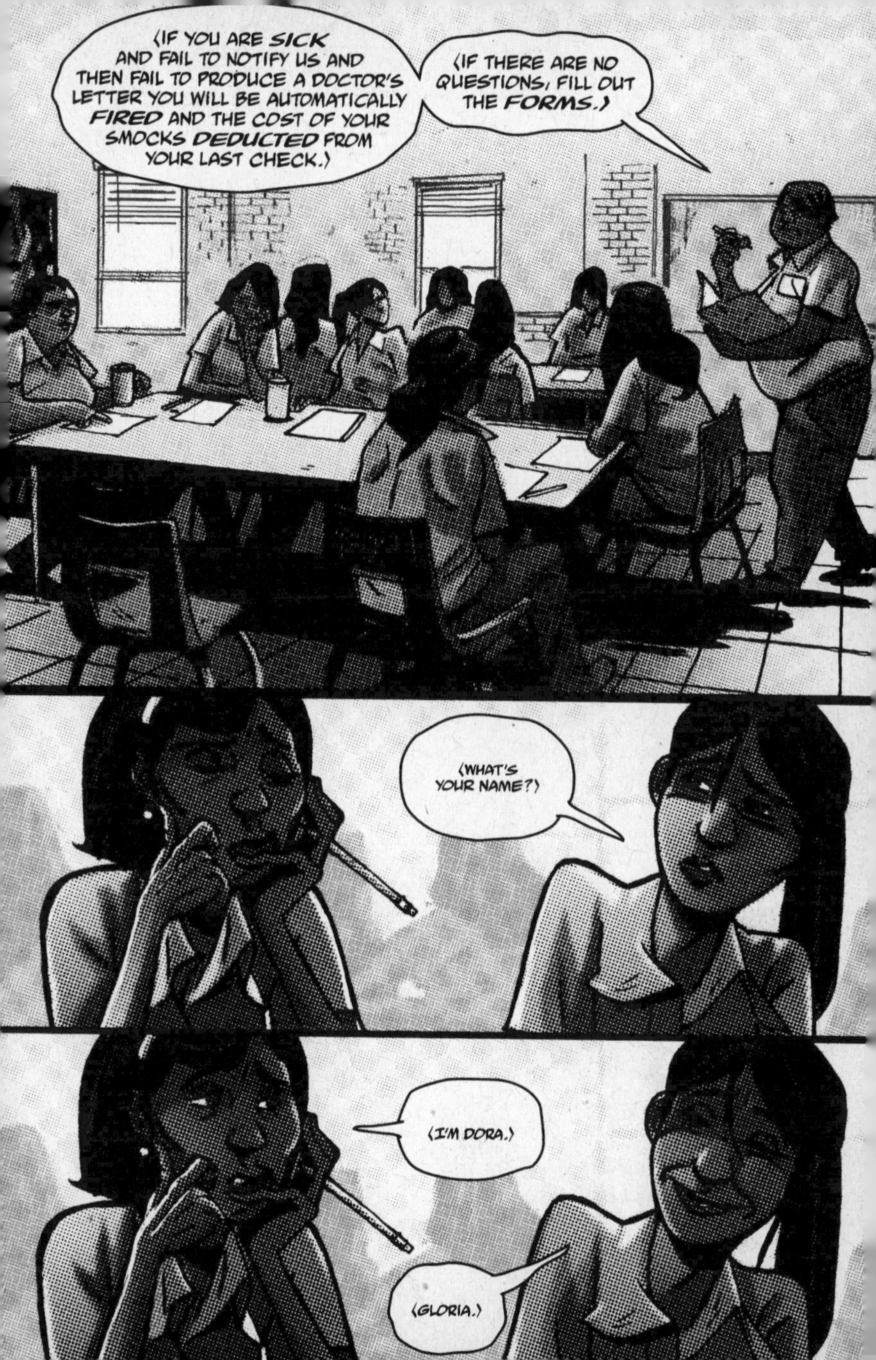
(IF YOU ARE SICK AND FAIL TO NOTIFY US AND THEN FAIL TO PRODUCE A DOCTOR'S LETTER YOU WILL BE AUTOMATICALLY FIRED AND THE COST OF YOUR SMOCKS DEDUCTED FROM YOUR LAST CHECK.)
(IF THERE ARE NO QUESTIONS, FILL OUT THE FORMS.)
(WHAT'S YOUR NAME?)
(I'M DORA.)
(GLORIA.)

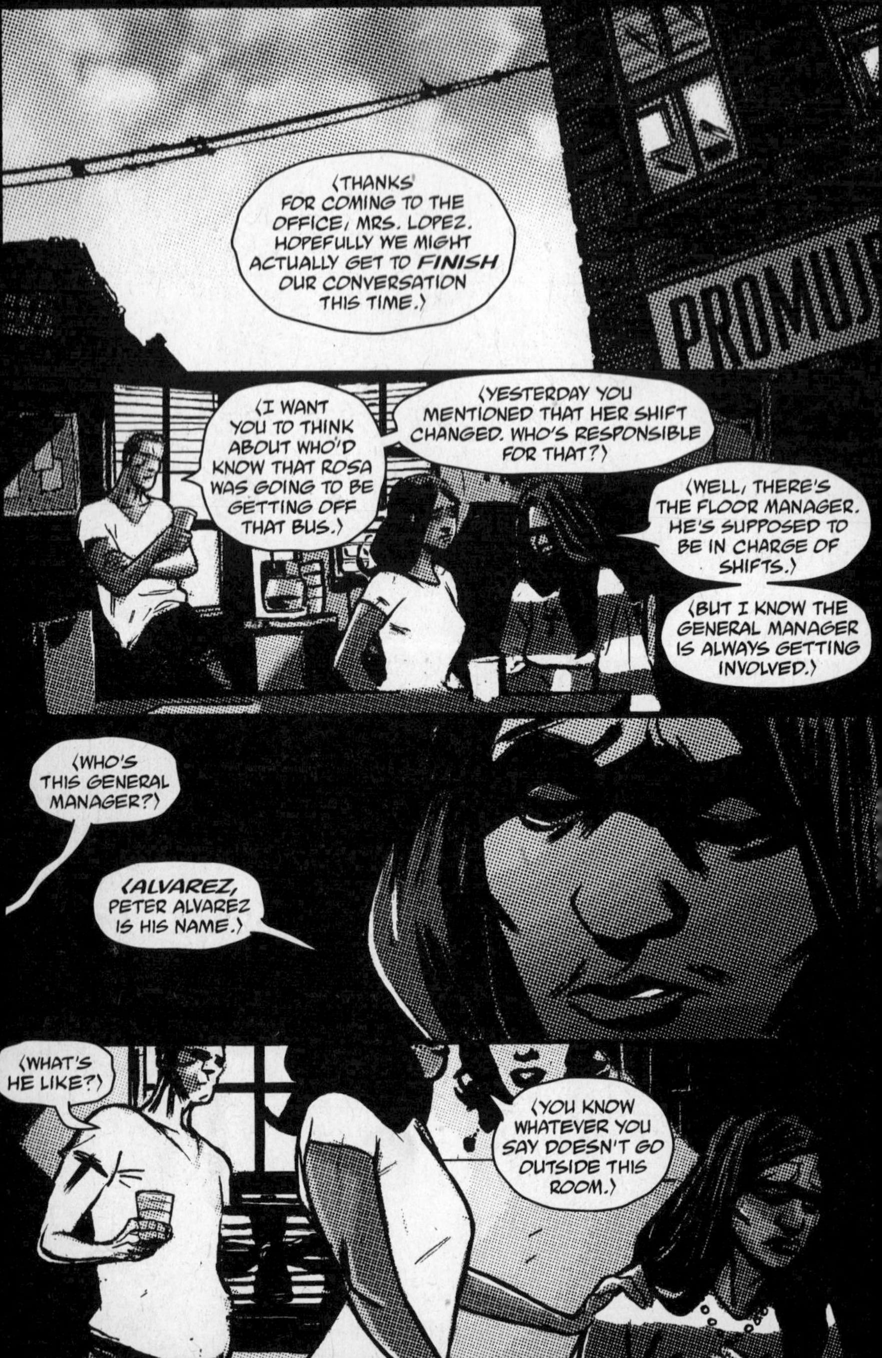
‹THANKS FOR COMING TO THE OFFICE, MRS. LOPEZ. HOPEFULLY WE MIGHT ACTUALLY GET TO FINISH OUR CONVERSATION THIS TIME.›
PROMU
‹I WANT YOU TO THINK ABOUT WHO'D KNOW THAT ROSA WAS GOING TO BE GETTING OFF THAT BUS.›
‹YESTERDAY YOU MENTIONED THAT HER SHIFT CHANGED. WHO'S RESPONSIBLE FOR THAT?›
‹WELL, THERE'S THE FLOOR MANAGER. HE'S SUPPOSED TO BE IN CHARGE OF SHIFTS.›
‹BUT I KNOW THE GENERAL MANAGER IS ALWAYS GETTING INVOLVED.›
‹WHO'S THIS GENERAL MANAGER?›
‹ALVAREZ, PETER ALVAREZ IS HIS NAME.›
‹WHAT'S HE LIKE?›
‹YOU KNOW WHATEVER YOU SAY DOESN'T GO OUTSIDE THIS ROOM.›

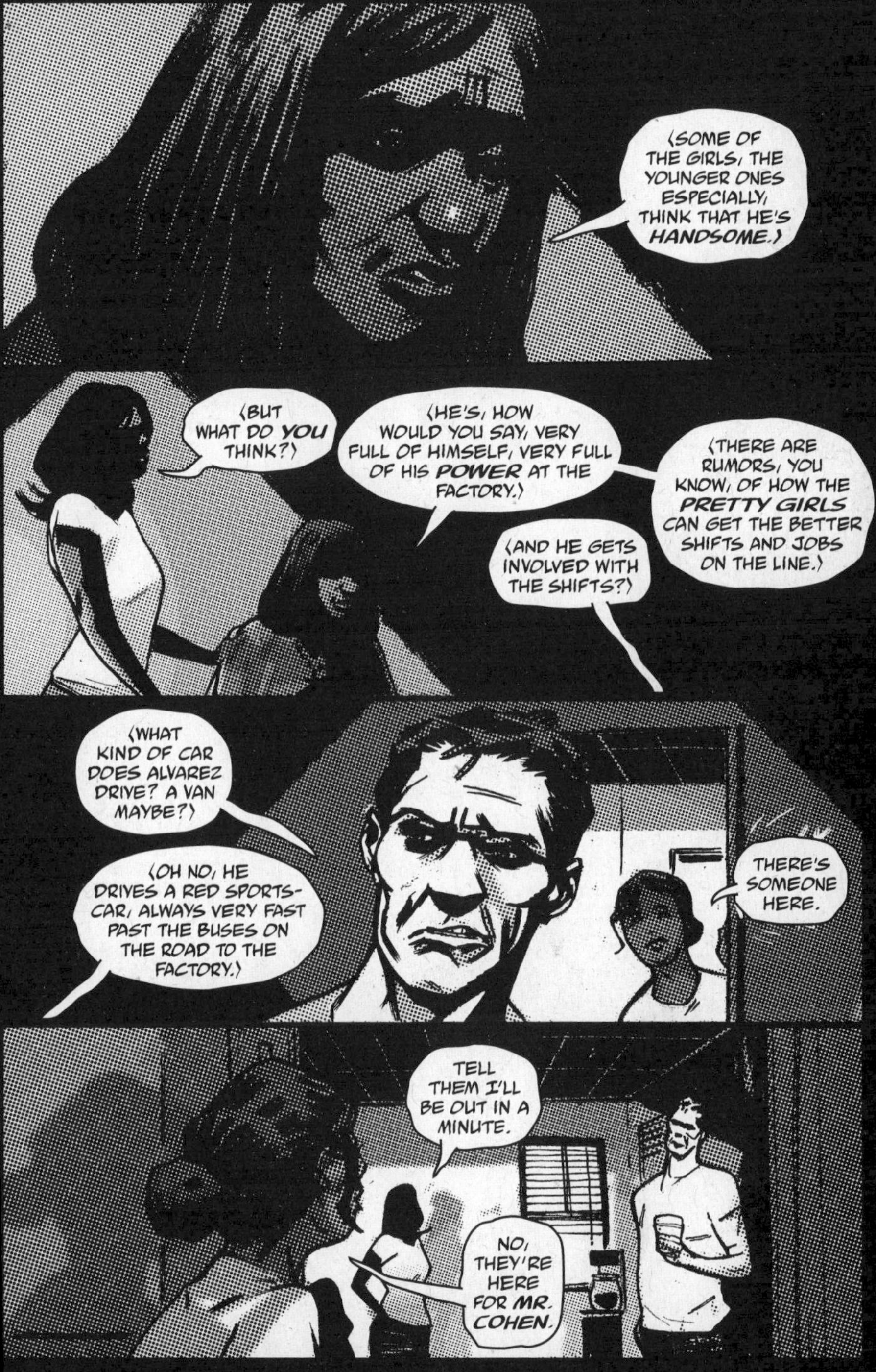
⟨SOME OF THE GIRLS, THE YOUNGER ONES ESPECIALLY, THINK THAT HE'S HANDSOME.⟩
⟨BUT WHAT DO YOU THINK?⟩
⟨HE'S, HOW WOULD YOU SAY, VERY FULL OF HIMSELF, VERY FULL OF HIS POWER AT THE FACTORY.⟩
⟨THERE ARE RUMORS, YOU KNOW, OF HOW THE PRETTY GIRLS CAN GET THE BETTER SHIFTS AND JOBS ON THE LINE.⟩
⟨AND HE GETS INVOLVED WITH THE SHIFTS?⟩
⟨WHAT KIND OF CAR DOES ALVAREZ DRIVE? A VAN MAYBE?⟩
⟨OH NO, HE DRIVES A RED SPORTS-CAR, ALWAYS VERY FAST PAST THE BUSES ON THE ROAD TO THE FACTORY.⟩
THERE'S SOMEONE HERE.
TELL THEM I'LL BE OUT IN A MINUTE.
NO, THEY'RE HERE FOR MR. COHEN.

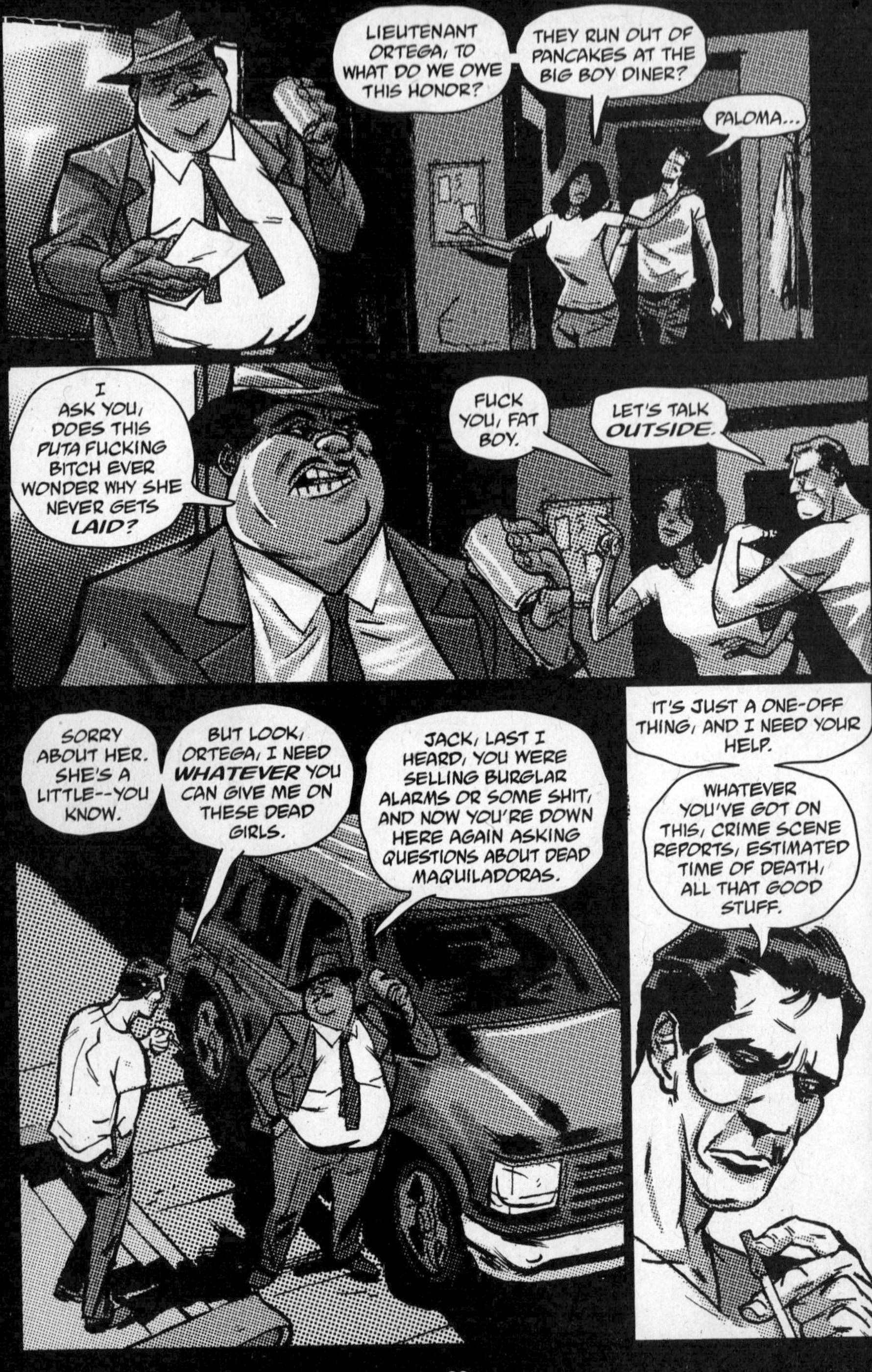
LIEUTENANT ORTEGA, TO WHAT DO WE OWE THIS HONOR?
THEY RUN OUT OF PANCAKES AT THE BIG BOY DINER?
PALOMA...
I ASK YOU, DOES THIS PUTA FUCKING BITCH EVER WONDER WHY SHE NEVER GETS LAID?
FUCK YOU, FAT BOY.
LET'S TALK OUTSIDE.
SORRY ABOUT HER. SHE'S A LITTLE--YOU KNOW.
BUT LOOK, ORTEGA, I NEED WHATEVER YOU CAN GIVE ME ON THESE DEAD GIRLS.
JACK, LAST I HEARD, YOU WERE SELLING BURGLAR ALARMS OR SOME SHIT, AND NOW YOU'RE DOWN HERE AGAIN ASKING QUESTIONS ABOUT DEAD MAQUILADORAS.
IT'S JUST A ONE-OFF THING, AND I NEED YOUR HELP.
WHATEVER YOU'VE GOT ON THIS, CRIME SCENE REPORTS, ESTIMATED TIME OF DEATH, ALL THAT GOOD STUFF.

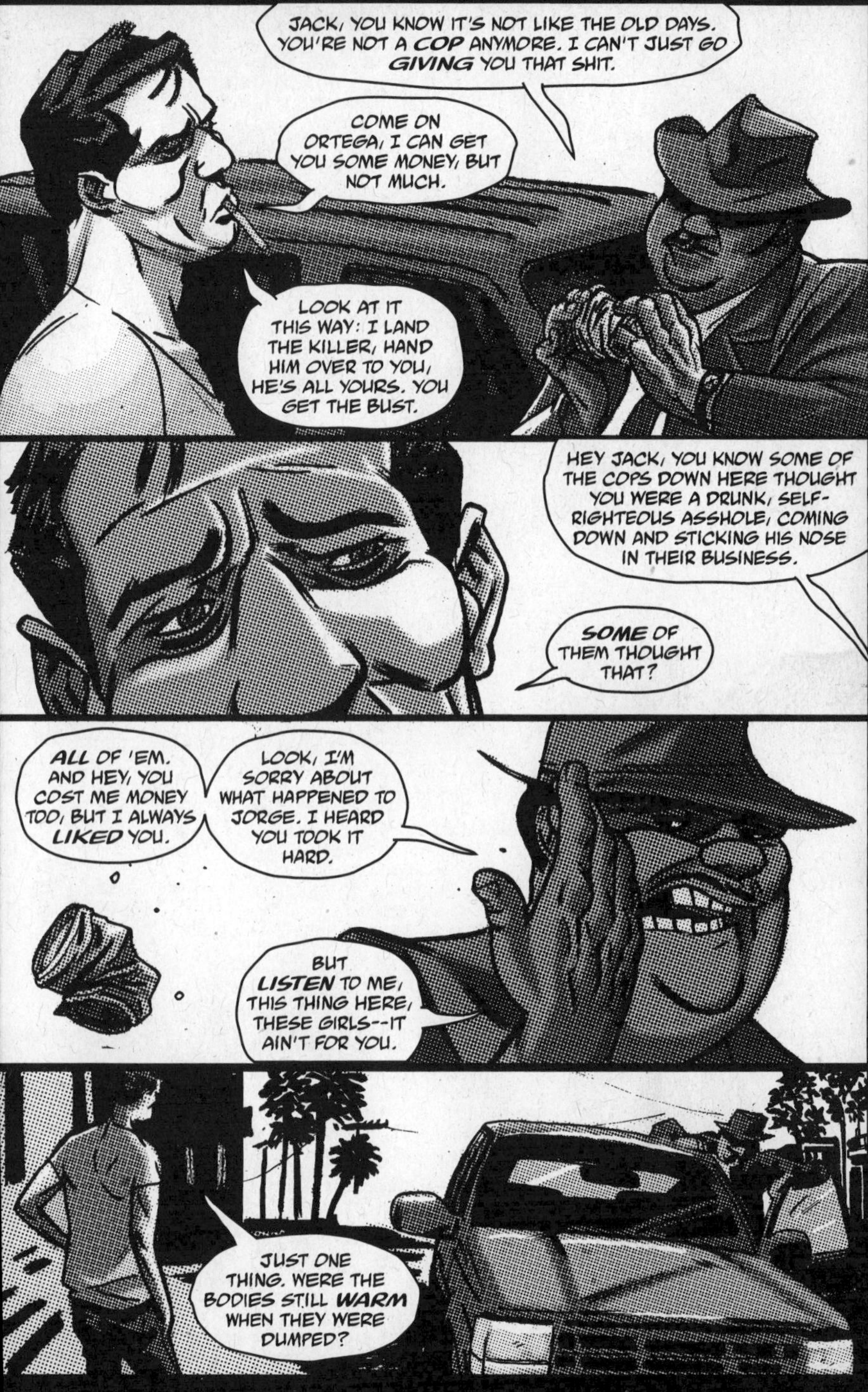
JACK, YOU KNOW IT'S NOT LIKE THE OLD DAYS. YOU'RE NOT A COP ANYMORE. I CAN'T JUST GO GIVING YOU THAT SHIT.
COME ON ORTEGA, I CAN GET YOU SOME MONEY, BUT NOT MUCH.
LOOK AT IT THIS WAY: I LAND THE KILLER, HAND HIM OVER TO YOU, HE'S ALL YOURS. YOU GET THE BUST.
HEY JACK, YOU KNOW SOME OF THE COPS DOWN HERE THOUGHT YOU WERE A DRUNK, SELF-RIGHTEOUS ASSHOLE, COMING DOWN AND STICKING HIS NOSE IN THEIR BUSINESS.
SOME OF THEM THOUGHT THAT?
ALL OF 'EM. AND HEY, YOU COST ME MONEY TOO, BUT I ALWAYS LIKED YOU.
LOOK, I'M SORRY ABOUT WHAT HAPPENED TO JORGE. I HEARD YOU TOOK IT HARD.
BUT LISTEN TO ME, THIS THING HERE, THESE GIRLS--IT AIN'T FOR YOU.
JUST ONE THING. WERE THE BODIES STILL WARM WHEN THEY WERE DUMPED?

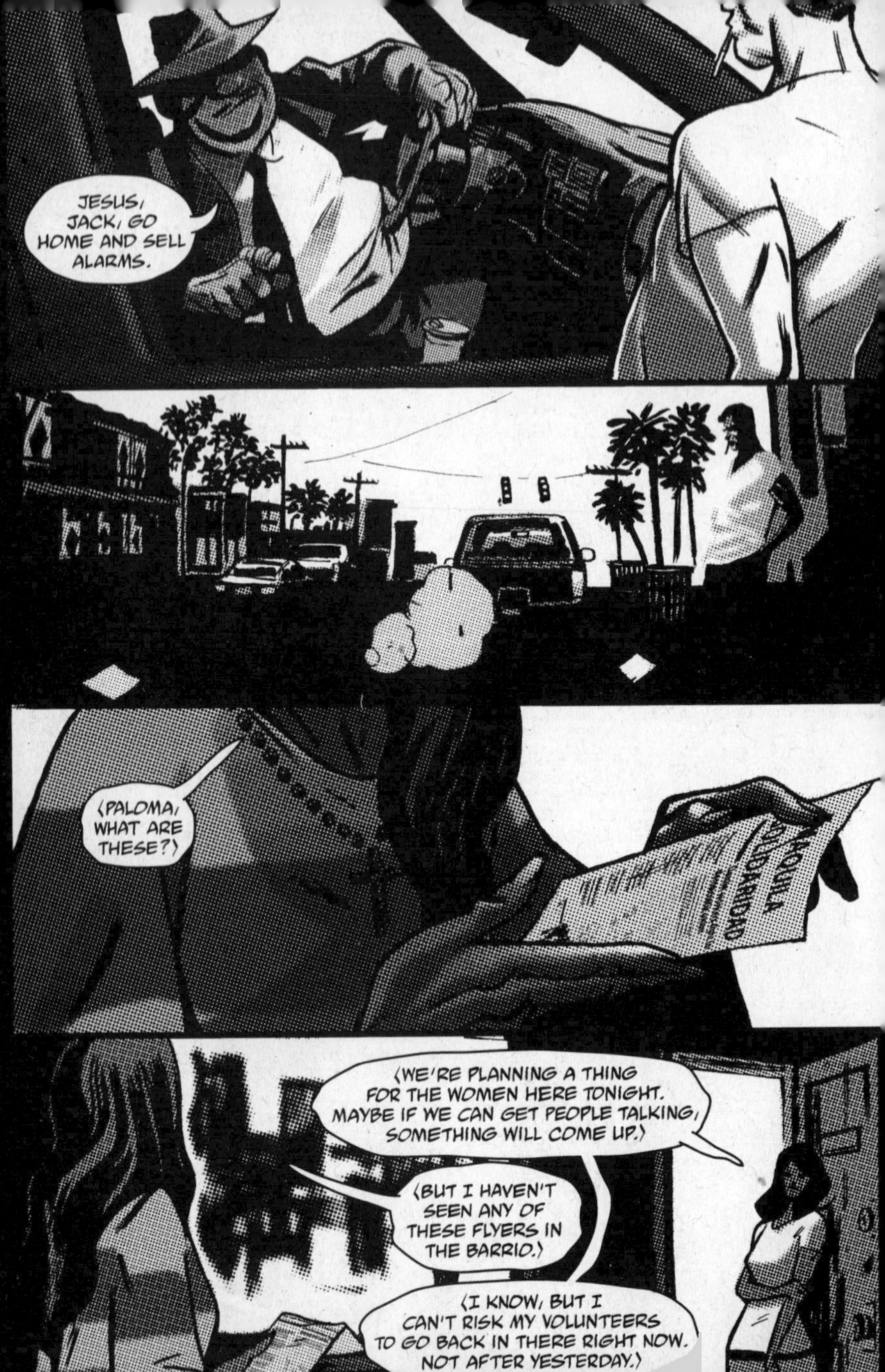
JESUS, JACK, GO HOME AND SELL ALARMS.
⟨PALOMA, WHAT ARE THESE?⟩
⟨WE'RE PLANNING A THING FOR THE WOMEN HERE TONIGHT. MAYBE IF WE CAN GET PEOPLE TALKING, SOMETHING WILL COME UP.⟩
⟨BUT I HAVEN'T SEEN ANY OF THESE FLYERS IN THE BARRIO.⟩
⟨I KNOW, BUT I CAN'T RISK MY VOLUNTEERS TO GO BACK IN THERE RIGHT NOW. NOT AFTER YESTERDAY.⟩

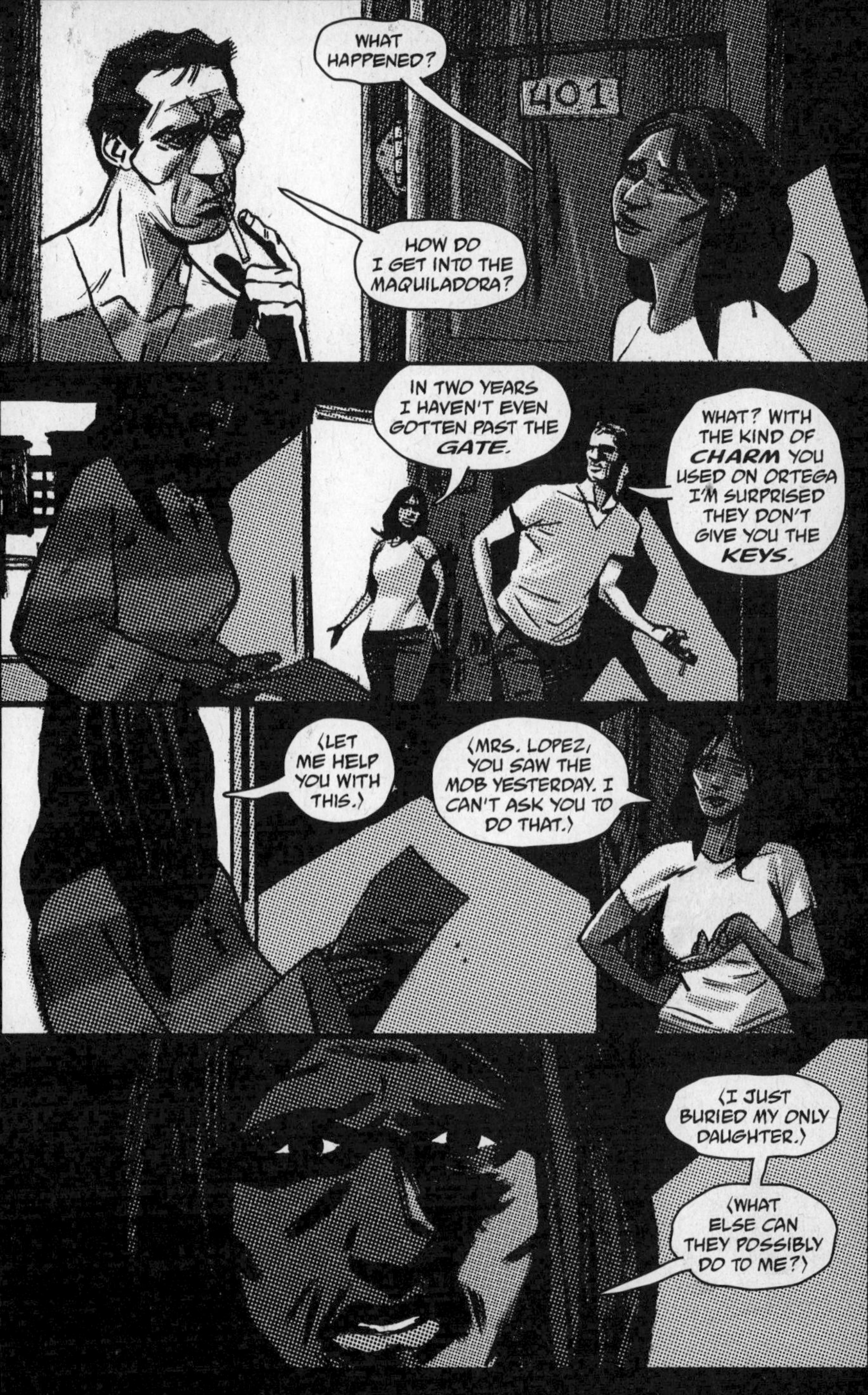
WHAT HAPPENED?
HOW DO I GET INTO THE MAQUILADORA?
401
IN TWO YEARS I HAVEN'T EVEN GOTTEN PAST THE GATE.
WHAT? WITH THE KIND OF CHARM YOU USED ON ORTEGA I'M SURPRISED THEY DON'T GIVE YOU THE KEYS.
⟨LET ME HELP YOU WITH THIS.⟩
⟨MRS. LOPEZ, YOU SAW THE MOB YESTERDAY. I CAN'T ASK YOU TO DO THAT.⟩
⟨I JUST BURIED MY ONLY DAUGHTER.⟩
⟨WHAT ELSE CAN THEY POSSIBLY DO TO ME?⟩

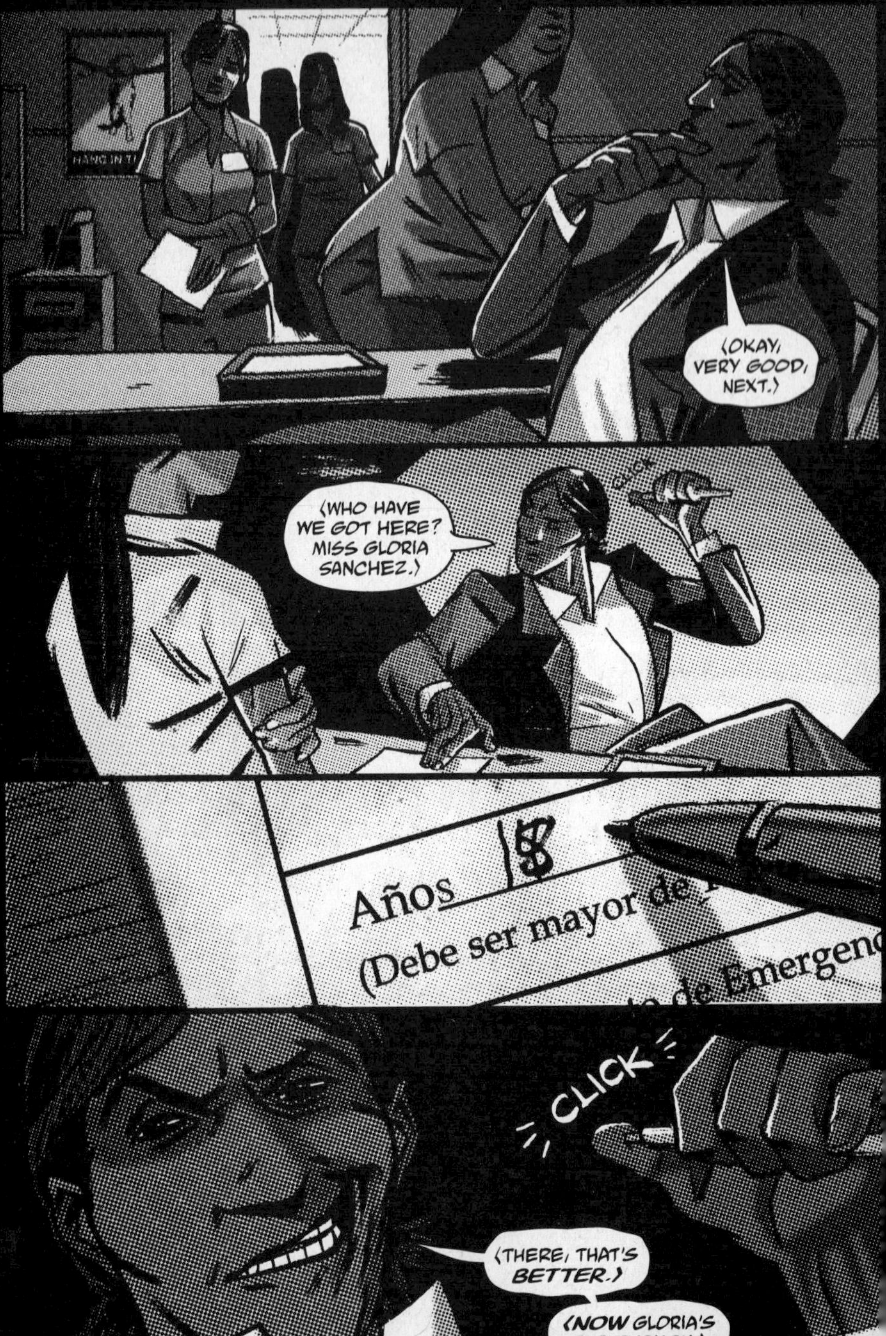
⟨OKAY, VERY GOOD, NEXT.⟩
⟨WHO HAVE WE GOT HERE? MISS GLORIA SANCHEZ.⟩
CLICK
Años
(Debe ser mayor de
CLICK
⟨THERE, THAT'S BETTER.⟩
⟨NOW GLORIA'S OLD ENOUGH.⟩

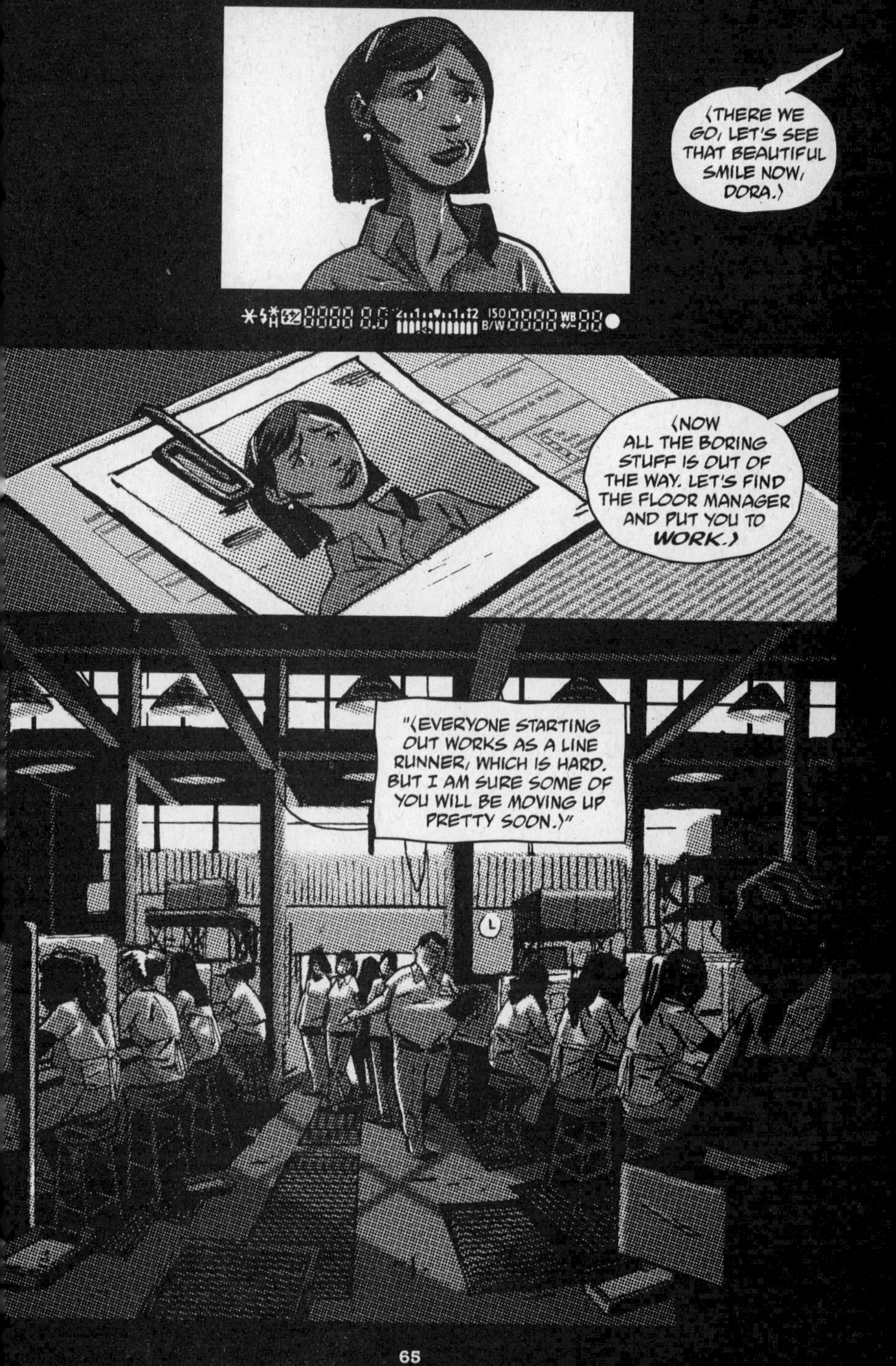
⟨THERE WE GO, LET'S SEE THAT BEAUTIFUL SMILE NOW, DORA.⟩
⟨NOW ALL THE BORING STUFF IS OUT OF THE WAY. LET'S FIND THE FLOOR MANAGER AND PUT YOU TO **WORK.**⟩
"⟨EVERYONE STARTING OUT WORKS AS A LINE RUNNER, WHICH IS HARD. BUT I AM SURE SOME OF YOU WILL BE MOVING UP PRETTY SOON.⟩"

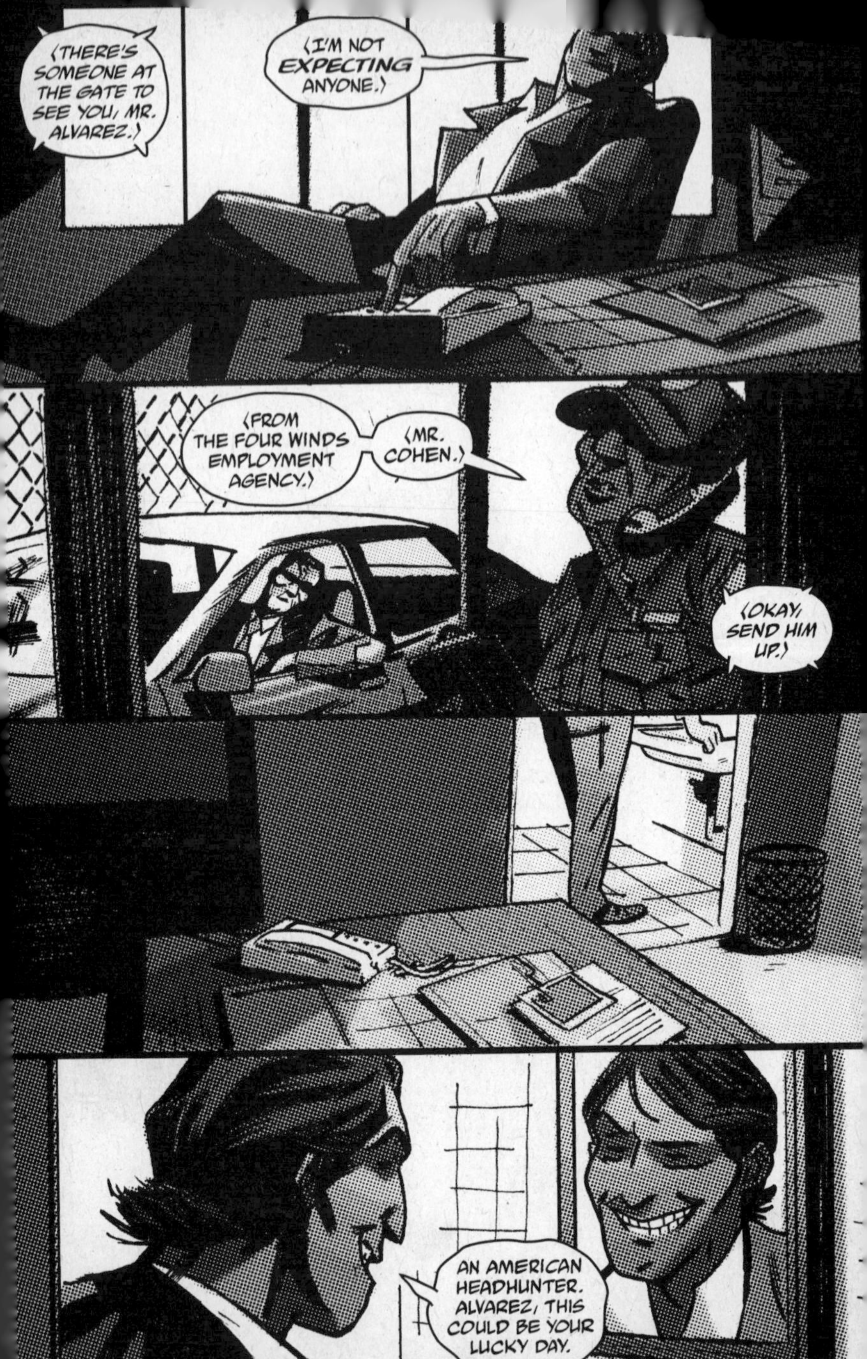
⟨THERE'S SOMEONE AT THE GATE TO SEE YOU, MR. ALVAREZ.⟩
⟨I'M NOT *EXPECTING* ANYONE.⟩
⟨FROM THE FOUR WINDS EMPLOYMENT AGENCY.⟩
⟨MR. COHEN.⟩
⟨OKAY, SEND HIM UP.⟩
AN AMERICAN HEADHUNTER. ALVAREZ, THIS COULD BE YOUR LUCKY DAY.

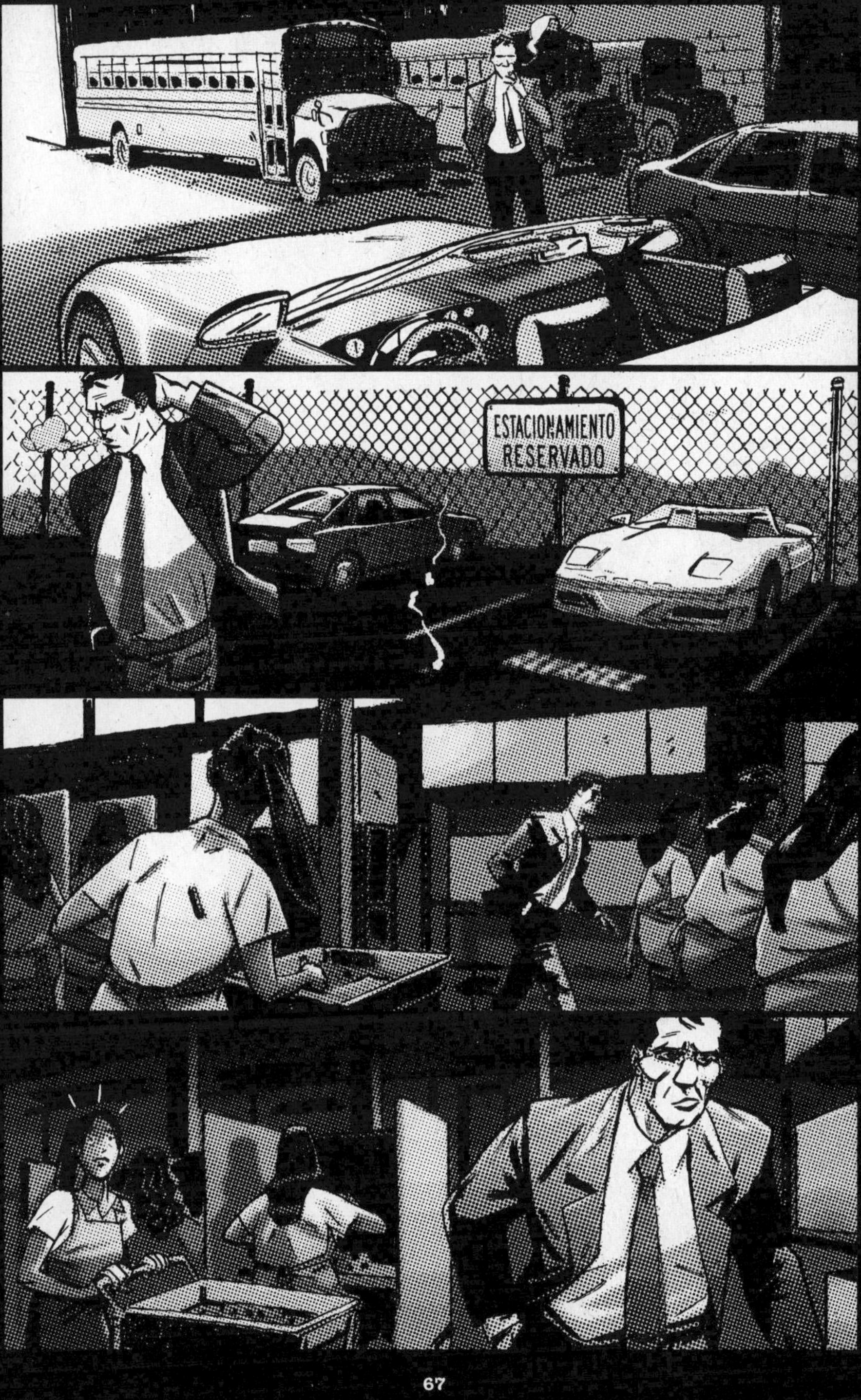
ESTACIONAMIENTO RESERVADO

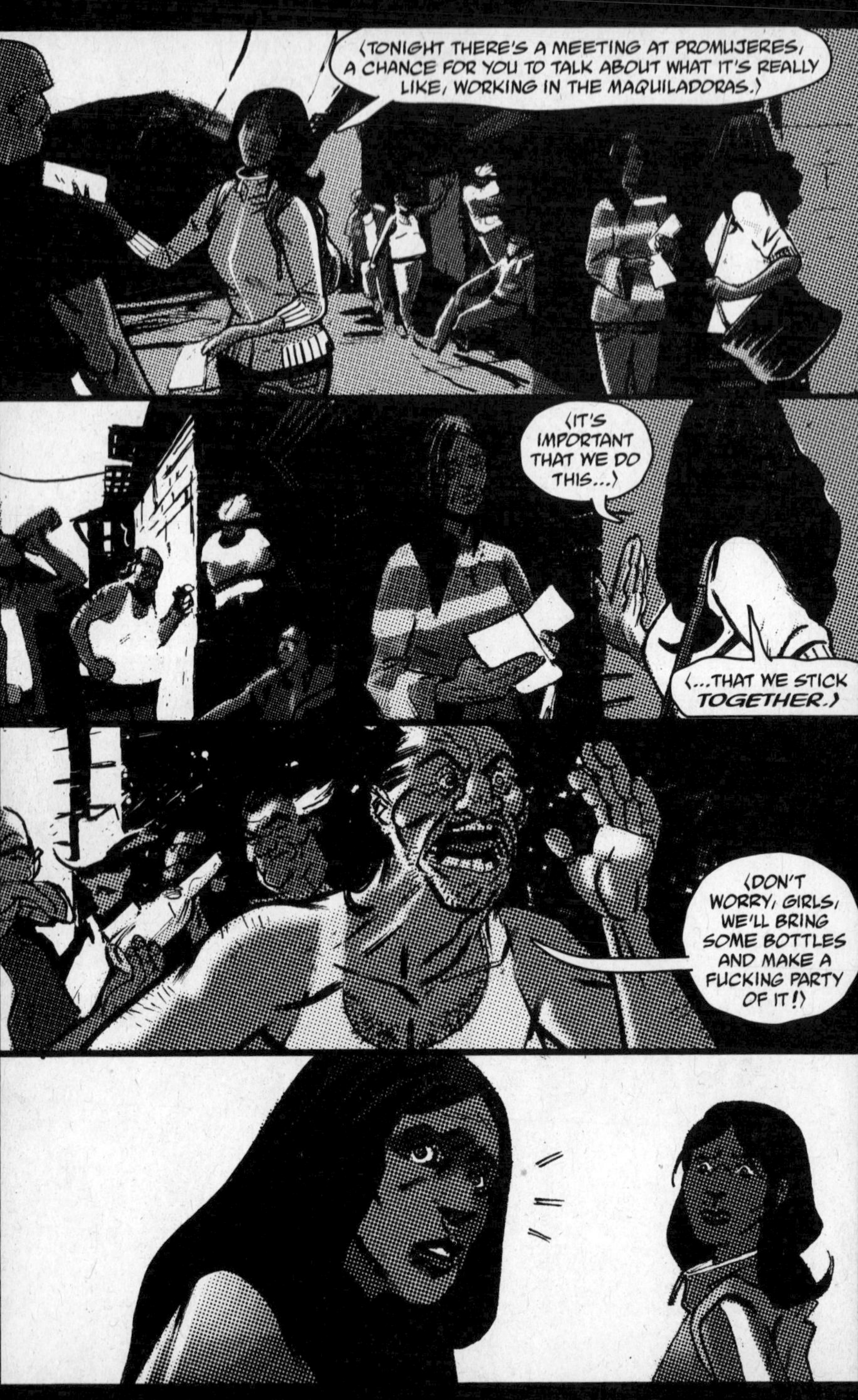

‹TONIGHT THERE'S A MEETING AT PROMUJERES, A CHANCE FOR YOU TO TALK ABOUT WHAT IT'S REALLY LIKE, WORKING IN THE MAQUILADORAS.›
‹IT'S IMPORTANT THAT WE DO THIS...›
‹...THAT WE STICK *TOGETHER.*›
‹DON'T WORRY, GIRLS, WE'LL BRING SOME BOTTLES AND MAKE A FUCKING PARTY OF IT!›

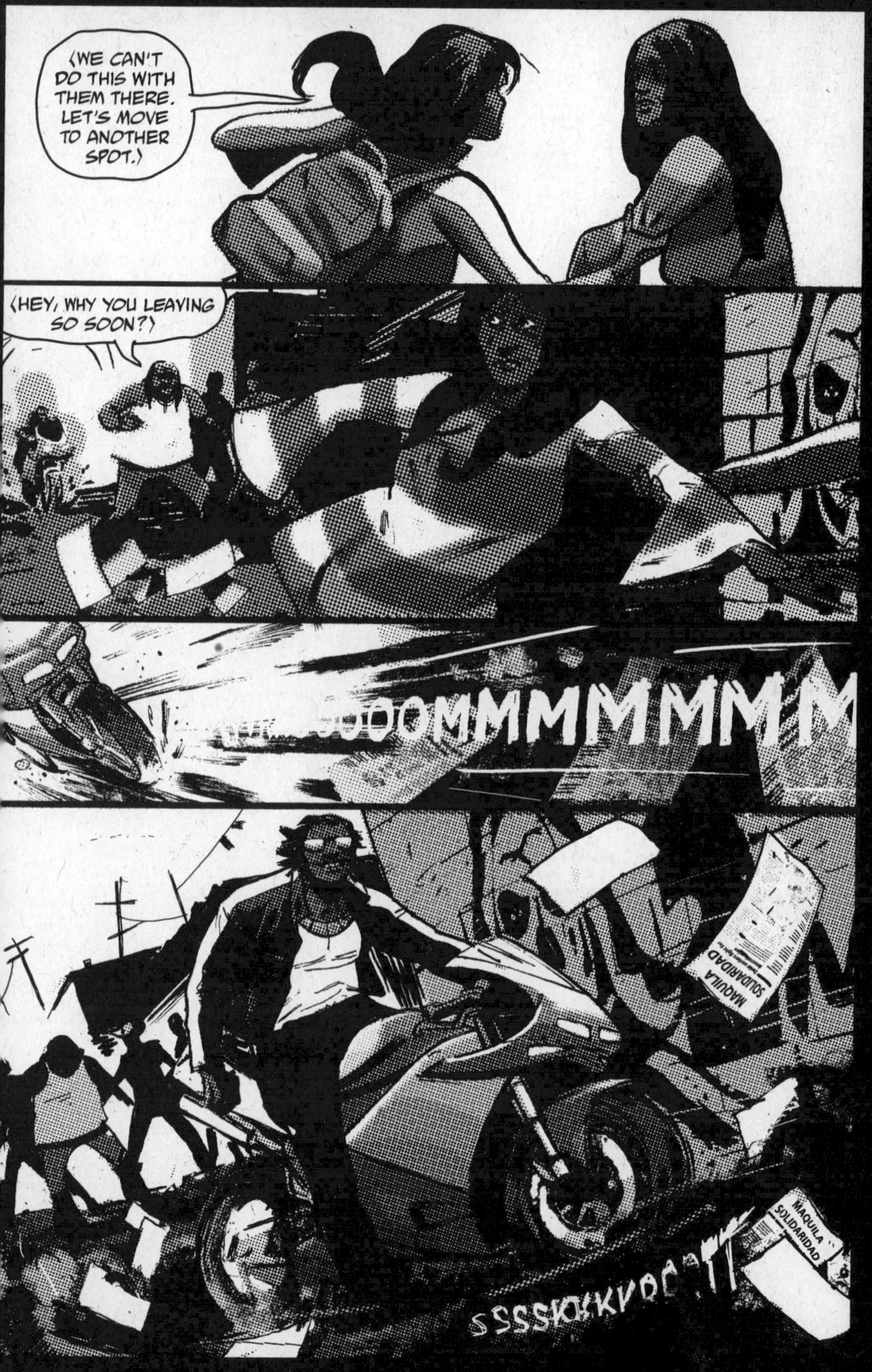
‹WE CAN'T DO THIS WITH THEM THERE. LET'S MOVE TO ANOTHER SPOT.›
‹HEY, WHY YOU LEAVING SO SOON?›
OOOMMMMMMMMM
MAQUILA SOLIDARIDAD
MAQUILA SOLIDARIDAD
SSSSKKKRR

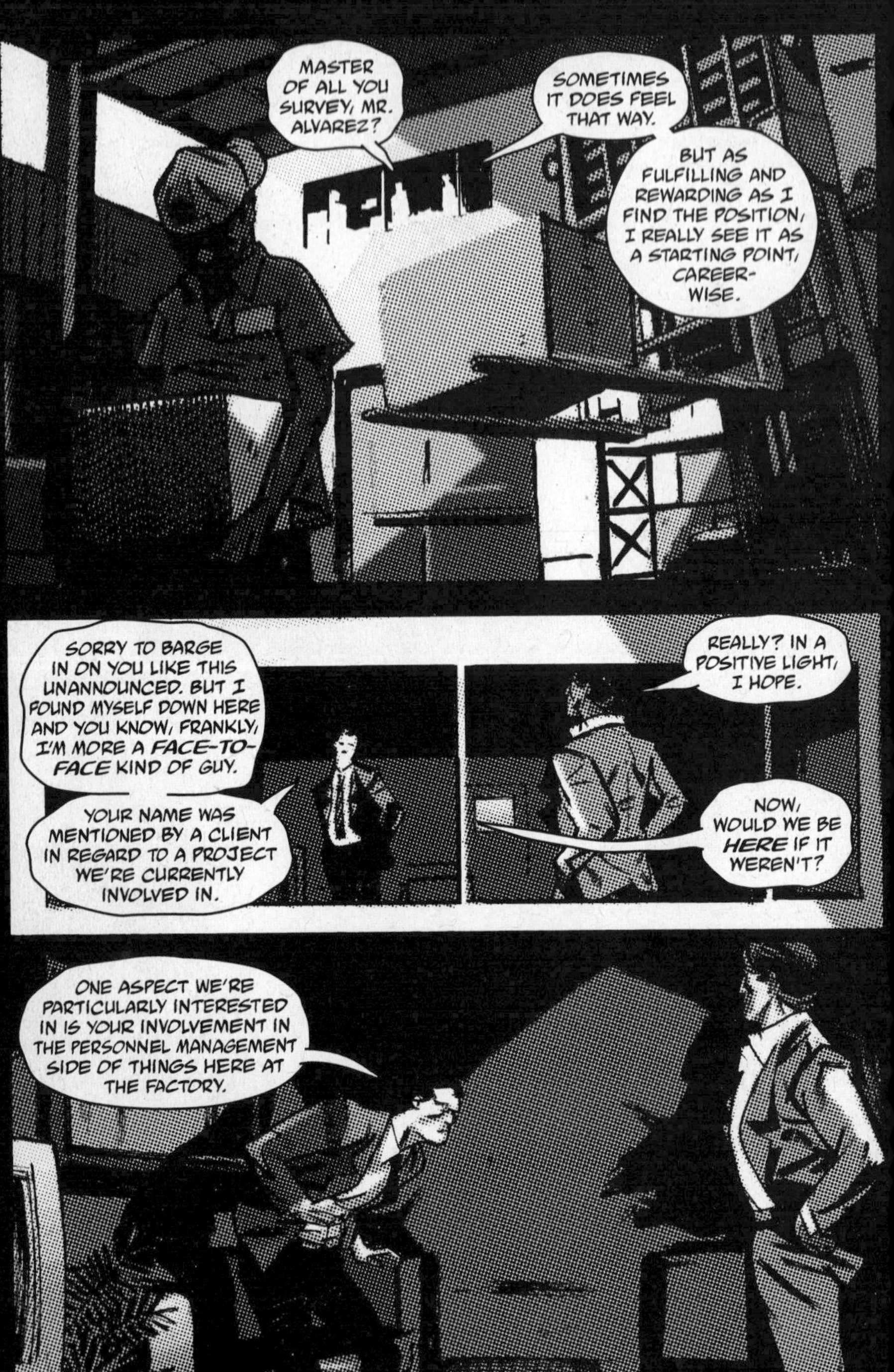

MASTER OF ALL YOU SURVEY, MR. ALVAREZ?
SOMETIMES IT DOES FEEL THAT WAY.
BUT AS FULFILLING AND REWARDING AS I FIND THE POSITION, I REALLY SEE IT AS A STARTING POINT, CAREER-WISE.
SORRY TO BARGE IN ON YOU LIKE THIS UNANNOUNCED. BUT I FOUND MYSELF DOWN HERE AND YOU KNOW, FRANKLY, I'M MORE A *FACE-TO-FACE* KIND OF GUY.
YOUR NAME WAS MENTIONED BY A CLIENT IN REGARD TO A PROJECT WE'RE CURRENTLY INVOLVED IN.
REALLY? IN A POSITIVE LIGHT, I HOPE.
NOW, WOULD WE BE *HERE* IF IT WEREN'T?
ONE ASPECT WE'RE PARTICULARLY INTERESTED IN IS YOUR INVOLVEMENT IN THE PERSONNEL MANAGEMENT SIDE OF THINGS HERE AT THE FACTORY.

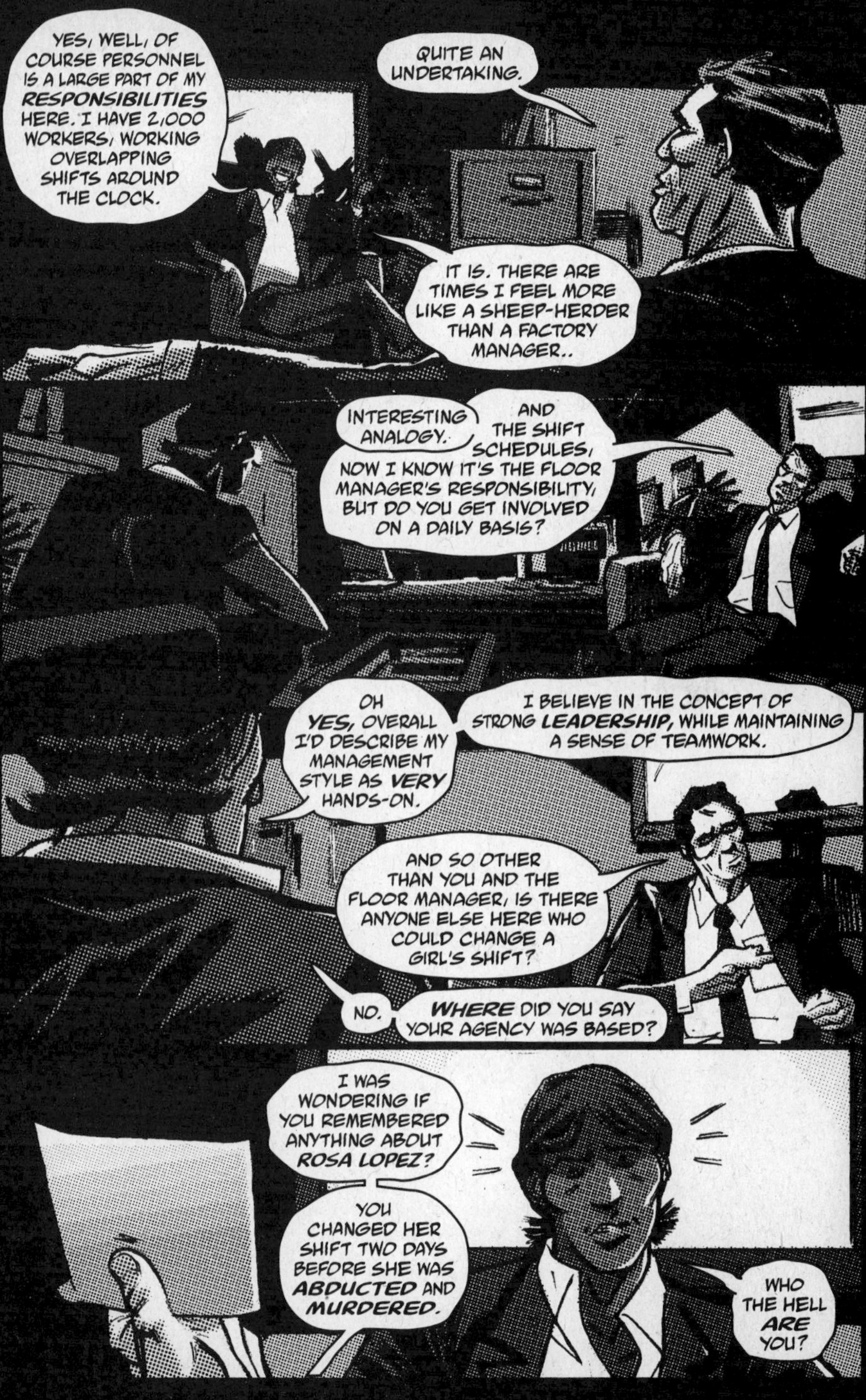
YES, WELL, OF COURSE PERSONNEL IS A LARGE PART OF MY RESPONSIBILITIES HERE. I HAVE 2,000 WORKERS, WORKING OVERLAPPING SHIFTS AROUND THE CLOCK.
QUITE AN UNDERTAKING.
IT IS. THERE ARE TIMES I FEEL MORE LIKE A SHEEP-HERDER THAN A FACTORY MANAGER..
INTERESTING ANALOGY.
AND THE SHIFT SCHEDULES, NOW I KNOW IT'S THE FLOOR MANAGER'S RESPONSIBILITY, BUT DO YOU GET INVOLVED ON A DAILY BASIS?
OH YES, OVERALL I'D DESCRIBE MY MANAGEMENT STYLE AS VERY HANDS-ON.
I BELIEVE IN THE CONCEPT OF STRONG LEADERSHIP, WHILE MAINTAINING A SENSE OF TEAMWORK.
AND SO OTHER THAN YOU AND THE FLOOR MANAGER, IS THERE ANYONE ELSE HERE WHO COULD CHANGE A GIRL'S SHIFT?
NO.
WHERE DID YOU SAY YOUR AGENCY WAS BASED?
I WAS WONDERING IF YOU REMEMBERED ANYTHING ABOUT ROSA LOPEZ?
YOU CHANGED HER SHIFT TWO DAYS BEFORE SHE WAS ABDUCTED AND MURDERED.
WHO THE HELL ARE YOU?

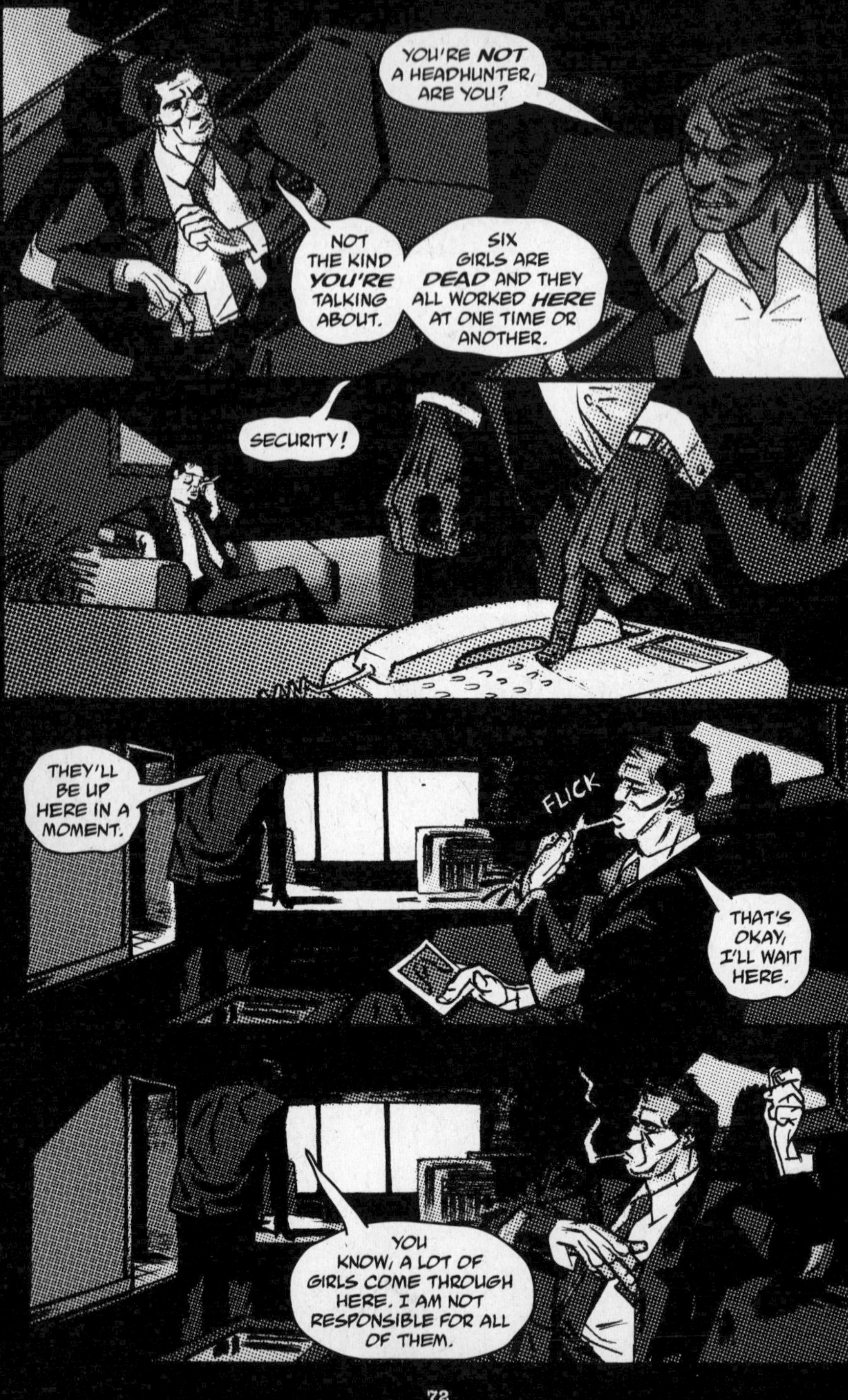
YOU'RE NOT A HEADHUNTER, ARE YOU?
NOT THE KIND YOU'RE TALKING ABOUT.
SIX GIRLS ARE DEAD AND THEY ALL WORKED HERE AT ONE TIME OR ANOTHER.
SECURITY!
THEY'LL BE UP HERE IN A MOMENT.
FLICK
THAT'S OKAY, I'LL WAIT HERE.
YOU KNOW, A LOT OF GIRLS COME THROUGH HERE. I AM NOT RESPONSIBLE FOR ALL OF THEM.

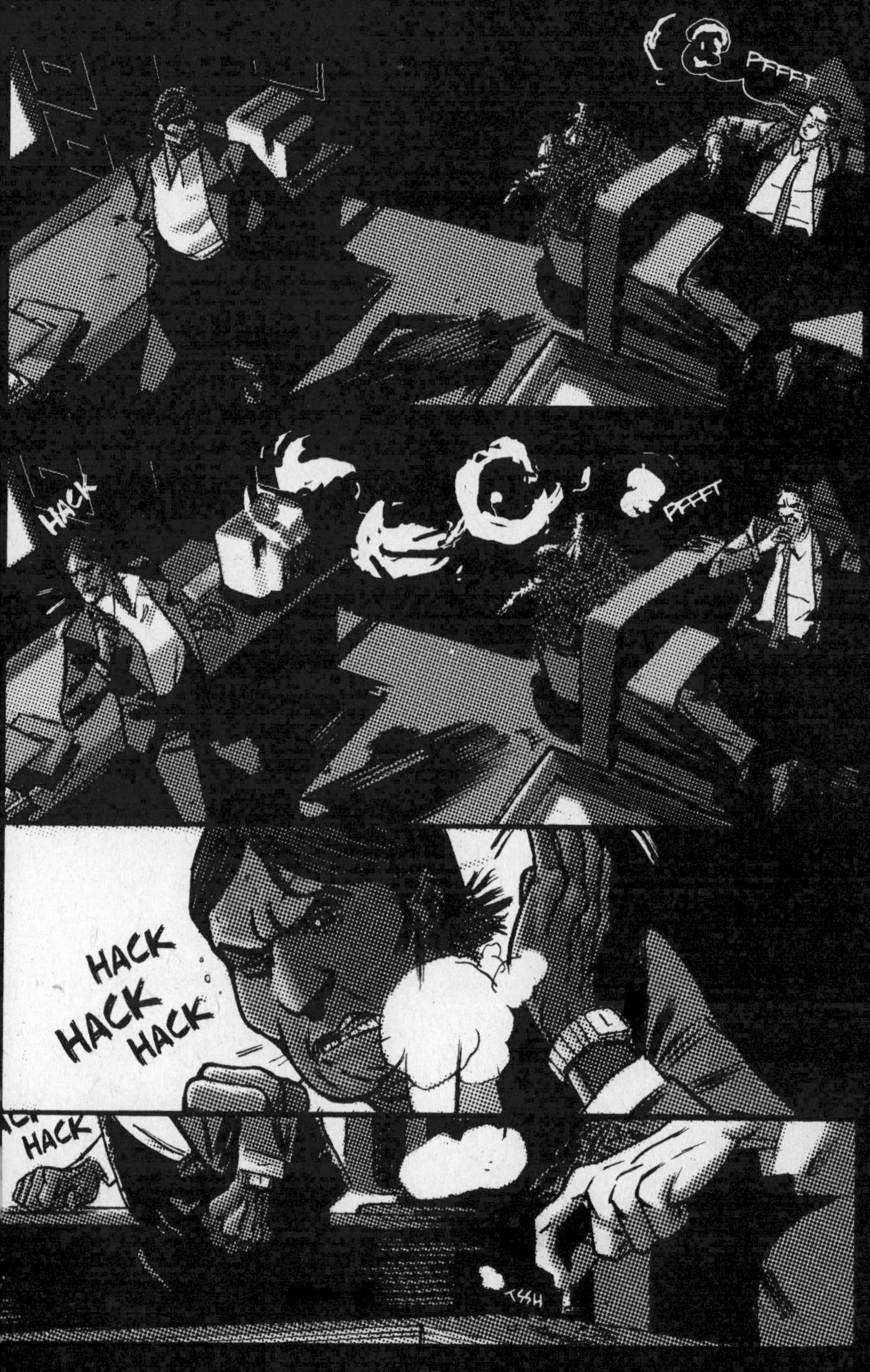
PFFFT
HACK
PFFFT
HACK
HACK
HACK
HACK
TSSH

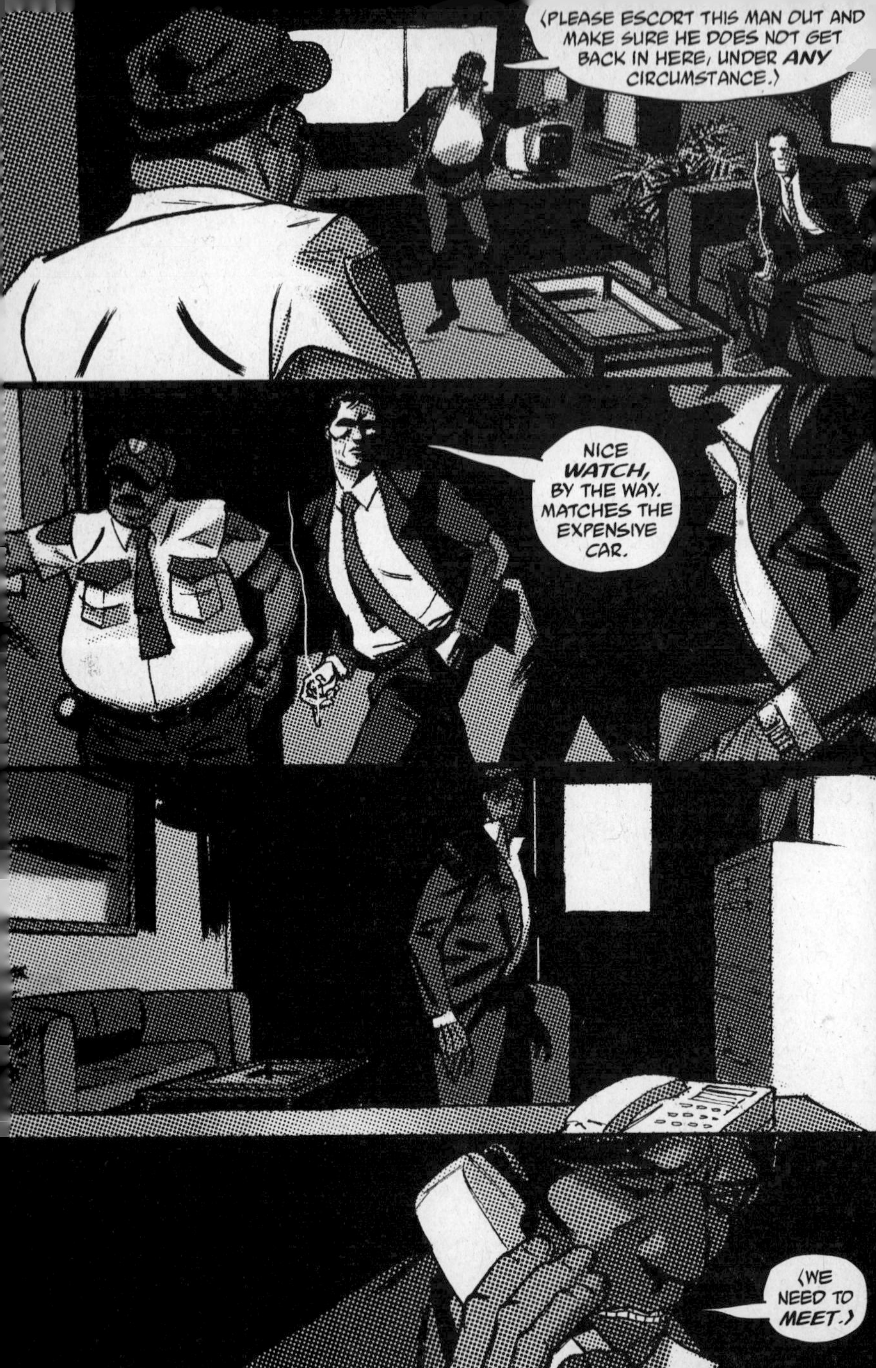
⟨PLEASE ESCORT THIS MAN OUT AND MAKE SURE HE DOES NOT GET BACK IN HERE, UNDER ANY CIRCUMSTANCE.⟩
NICE WATCH, BY THE WAY. MATCHES THE EXPENSIVE CAR.
⟨WE NEED TO MEET.⟩

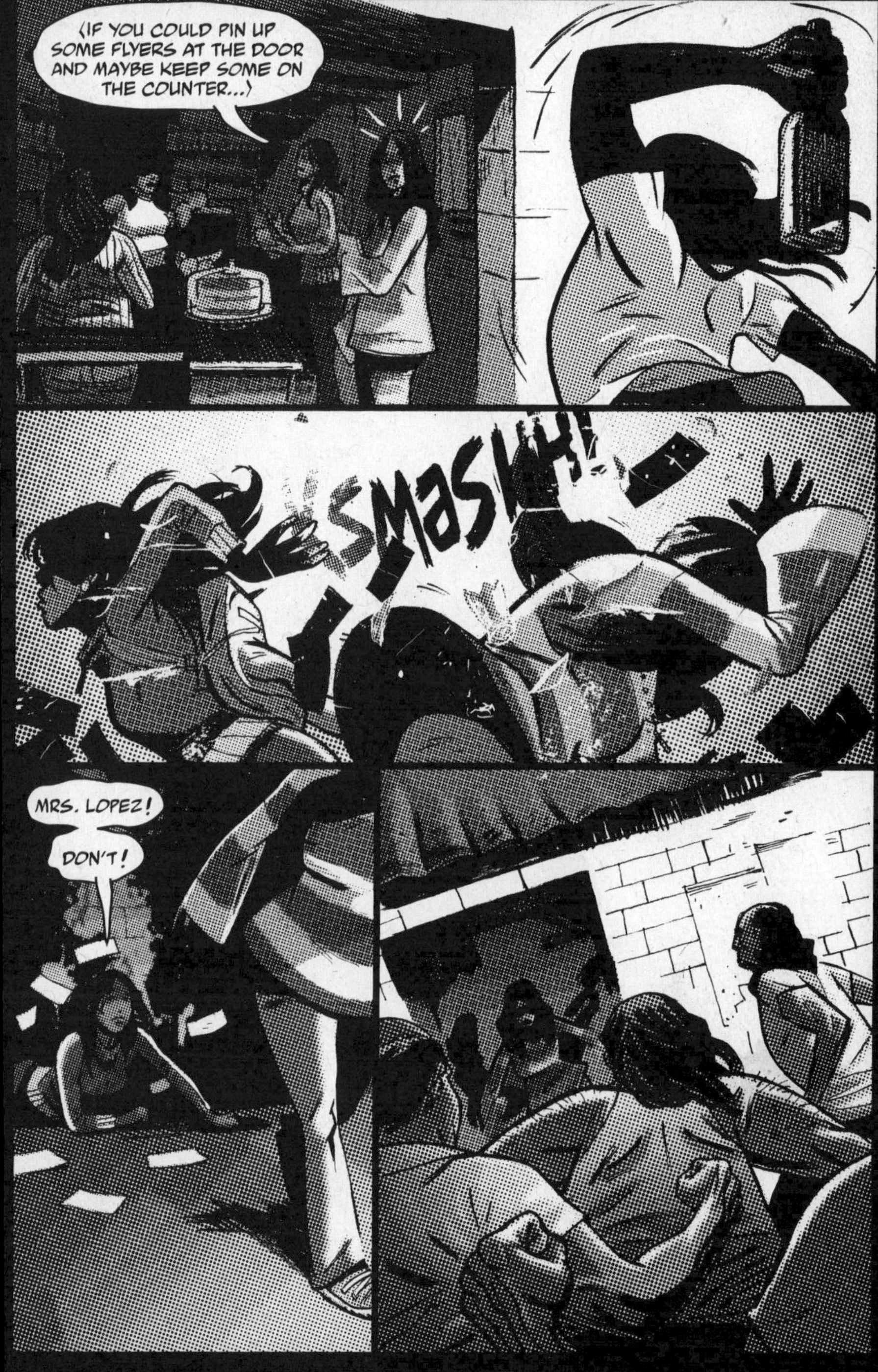
⟨IF YOU COULD PIN UP SOME FLYERS AT THE DOOR AND MAYBE KEEP SOME ON THE COUNTER...⟩
SMASH!
MRS. LOPEZ!
DON'T!

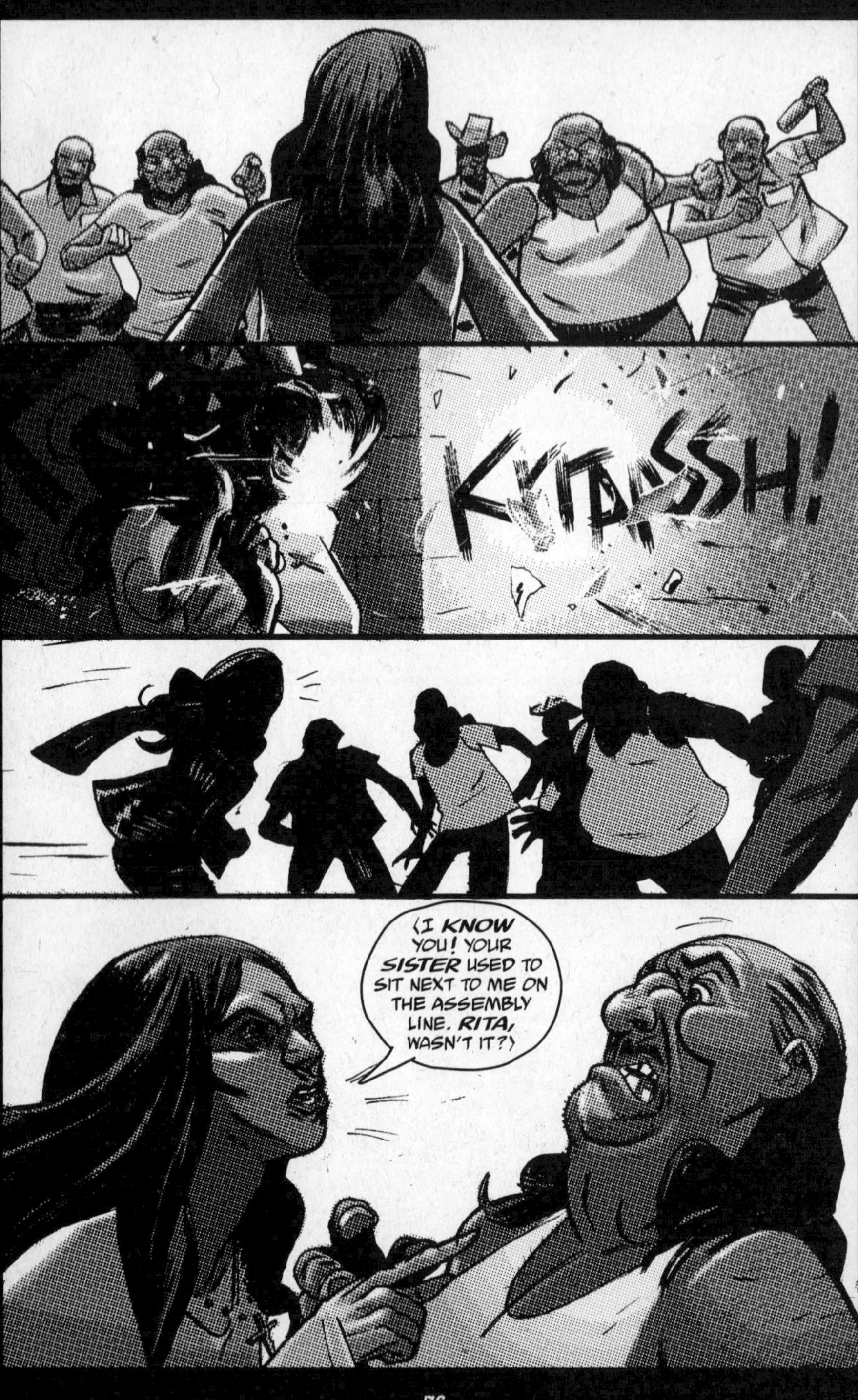
KTTASSH!
⟨I KNOW YOU! YOUR SISTER USED TO SIT NEXT TO ME ON THE ASSEMBLY LINE. RITA, WASN'T IT?⟩

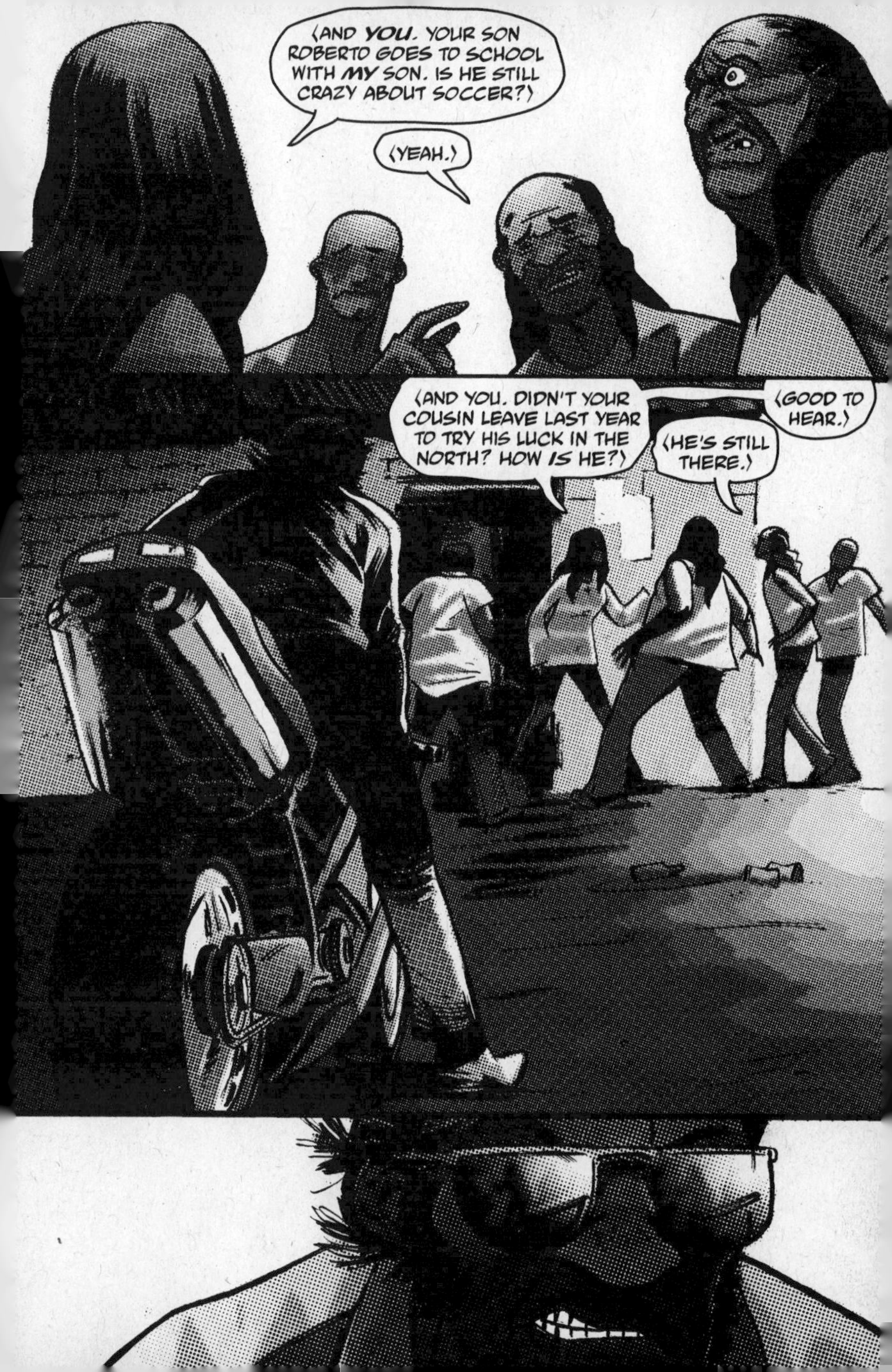
⟨AND YOU. YOUR SON ROBERTO GOES TO SCHOOL WITH MY SON. IS HE STILL CRAZY ABOUT SOCCER?⟩
⟨YEAH.⟩
⟨GOOD TO HEAR.⟩
⟨AND YOU. DIDN'T YOUR COUSIN LEAVE LAST YEAR TO TRY HIS LUCK IN THE NORTH? HOW IS HE?⟩
⟨HE'S STILL THERE.⟩

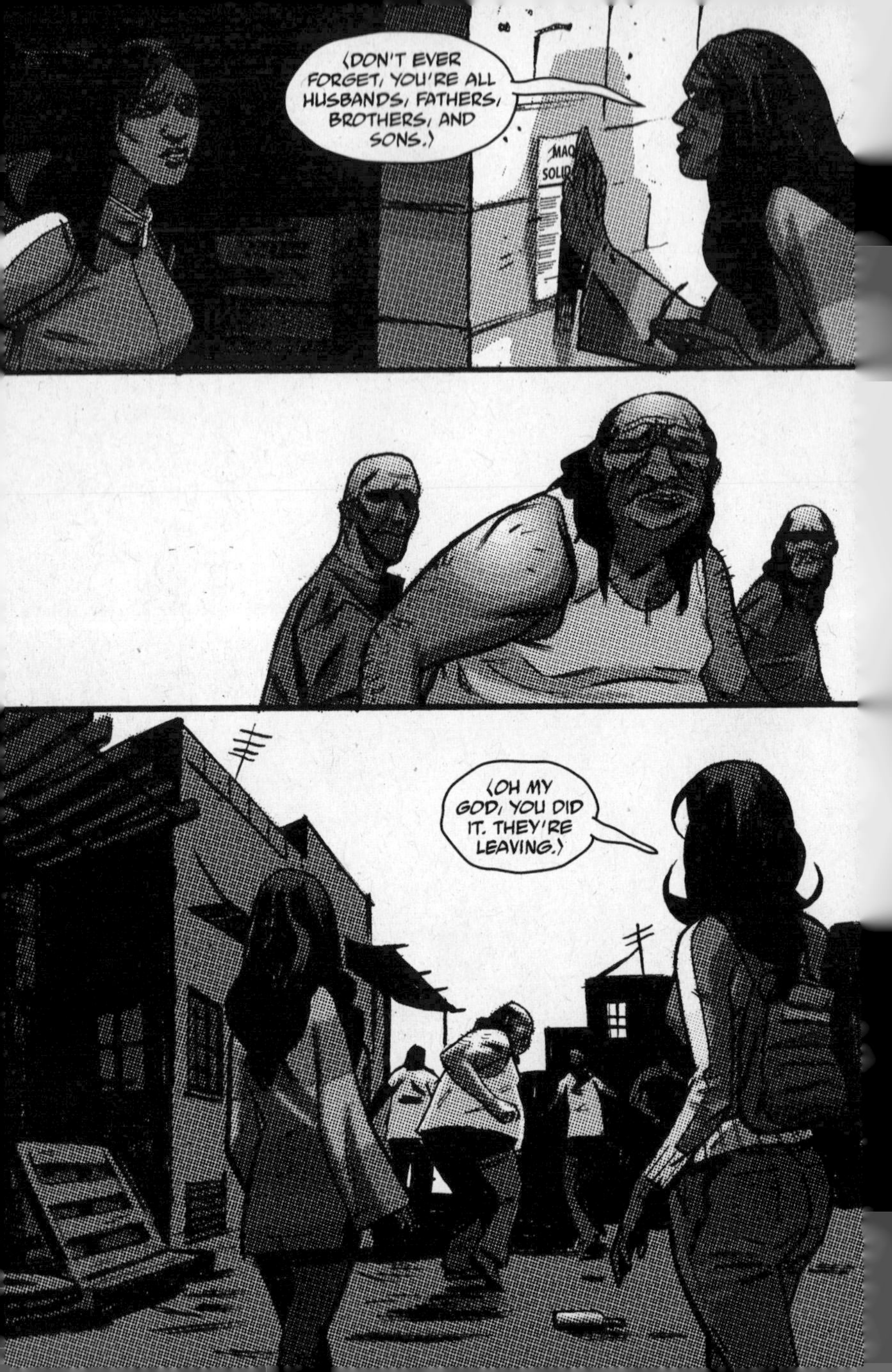
⟨DON'T EVER FORGET, YOU'RE ALL HUSBANDS, FATHERS, BROTHERS, AND SONS.⟩
⟨OH MY GOD, YOU DID IT. THEY'RE LEAVING.⟩

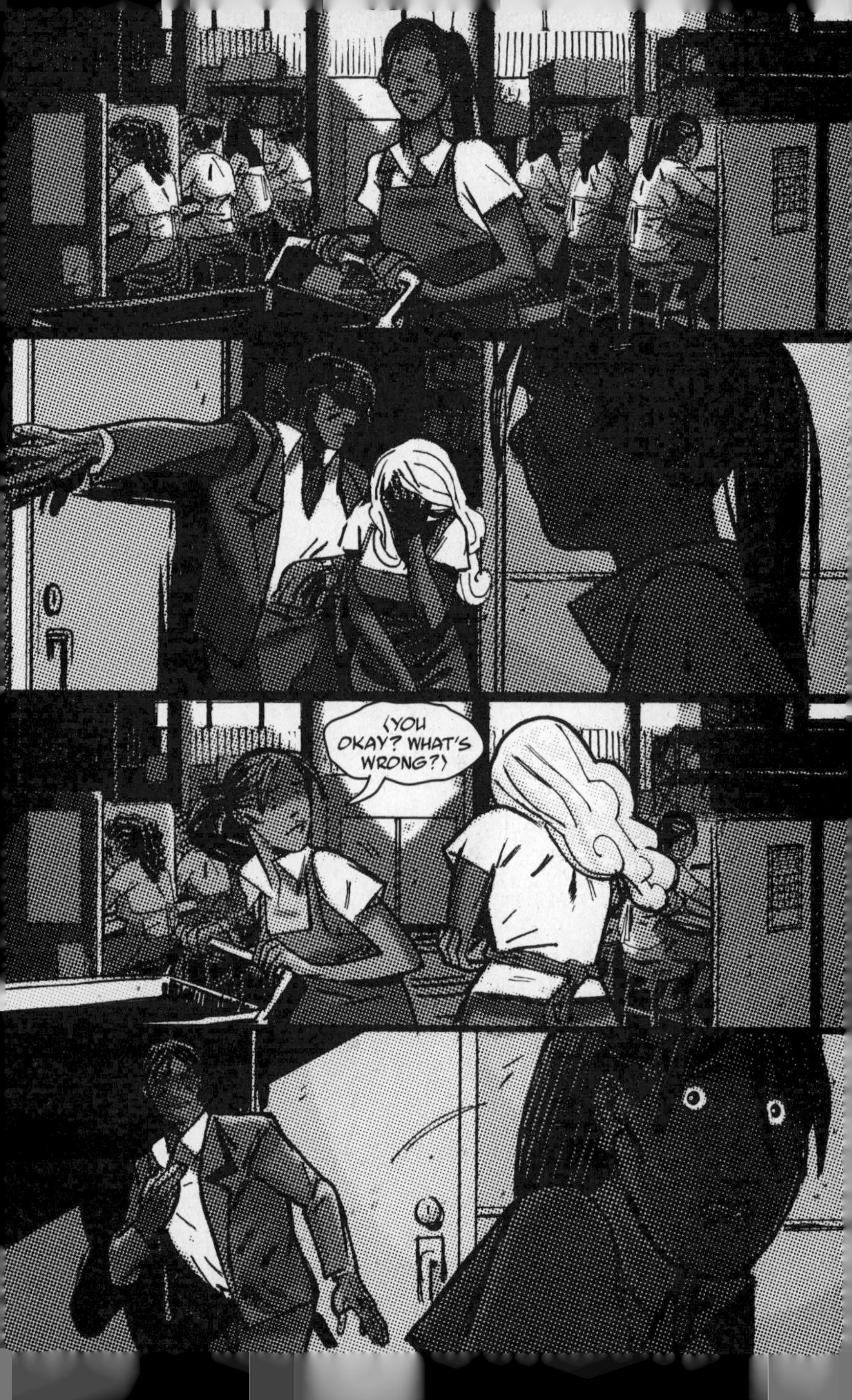
⟨YOU OKAY? WHAT'S WRONG?⟩

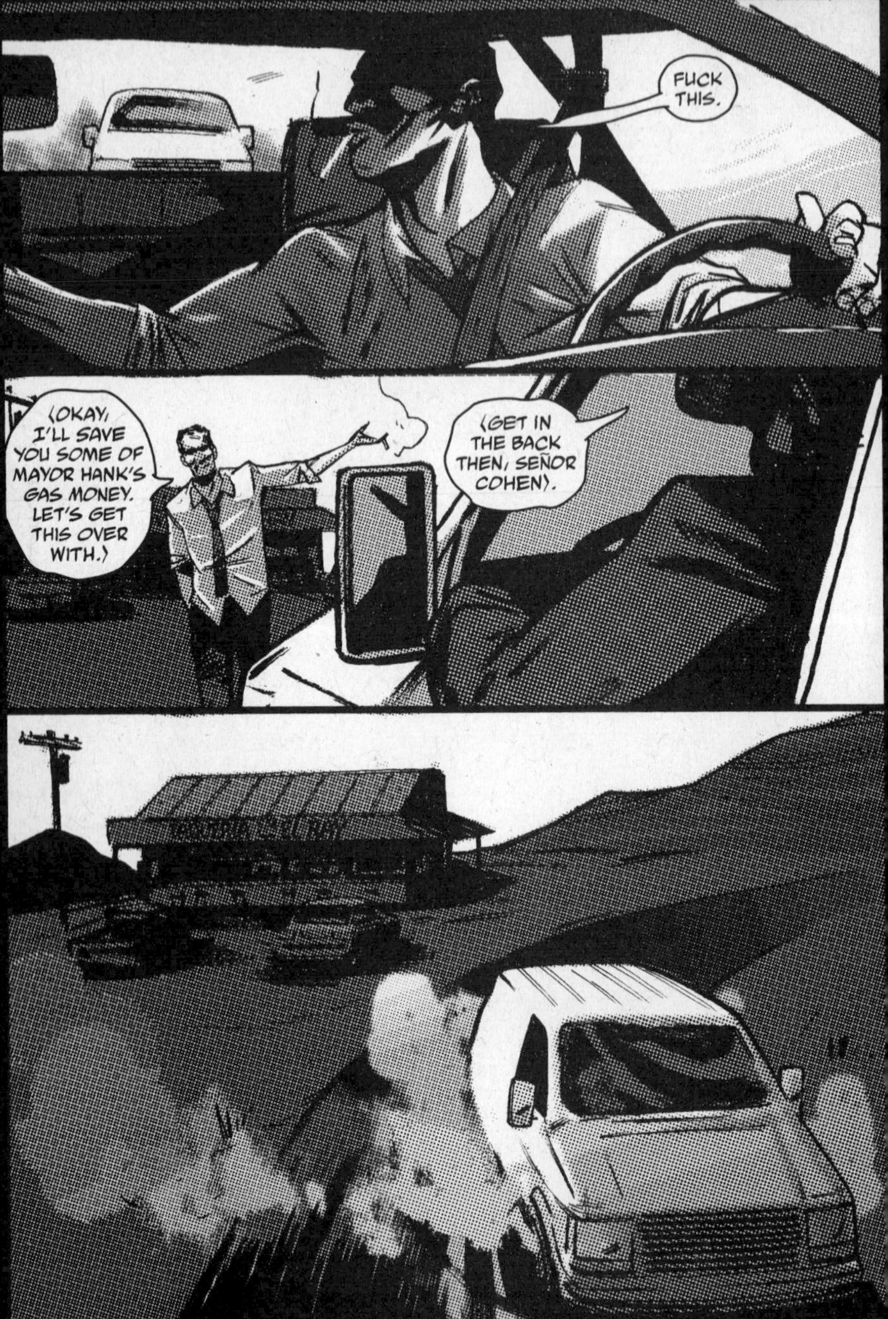
FUCK THIS.
⟨OKAY, I'LL SAVE YOU SOME OF MAYOR HANK'S GAS MONEY. LET'S GET THIS OVER WITH.⟩
⟨GET IN THE BACK THEN, SEÑOR COHEN⟩.

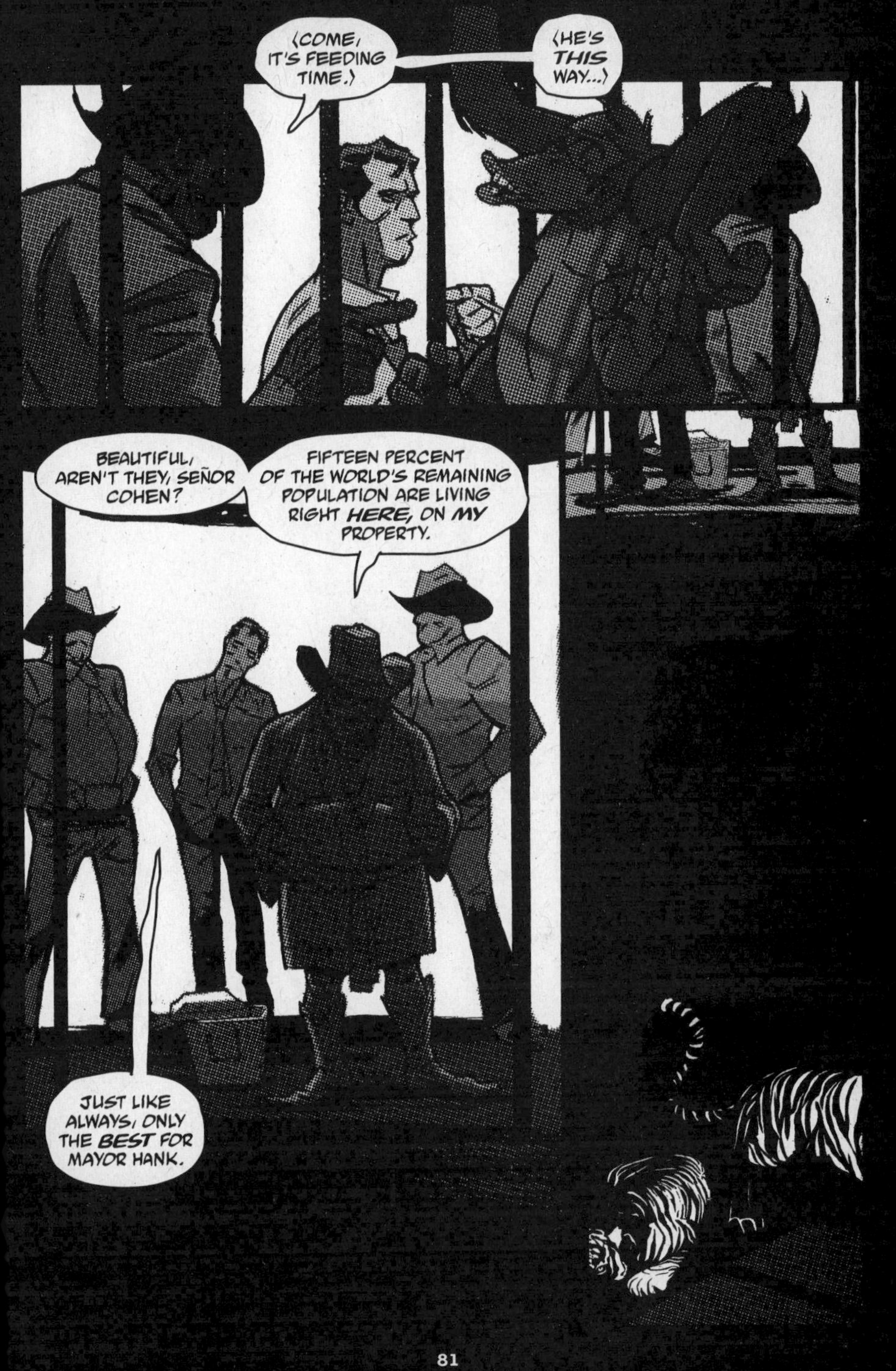

⟨COME, IT'S FEEDING TIME.⟩
⟨HE'S THIS WAY...⟩
BEAUTIFUL, AREN'T THEY, SEÑOR COHEN?
FIFTEEN PERCENT OF THE WORLD'S REMAINING POPULATION ARE LIVING RIGHT HERE, ON MY PROPERTY.
JUST LIKE ALWAYS, ONLY THE BEST FOR MAYOR HANK.

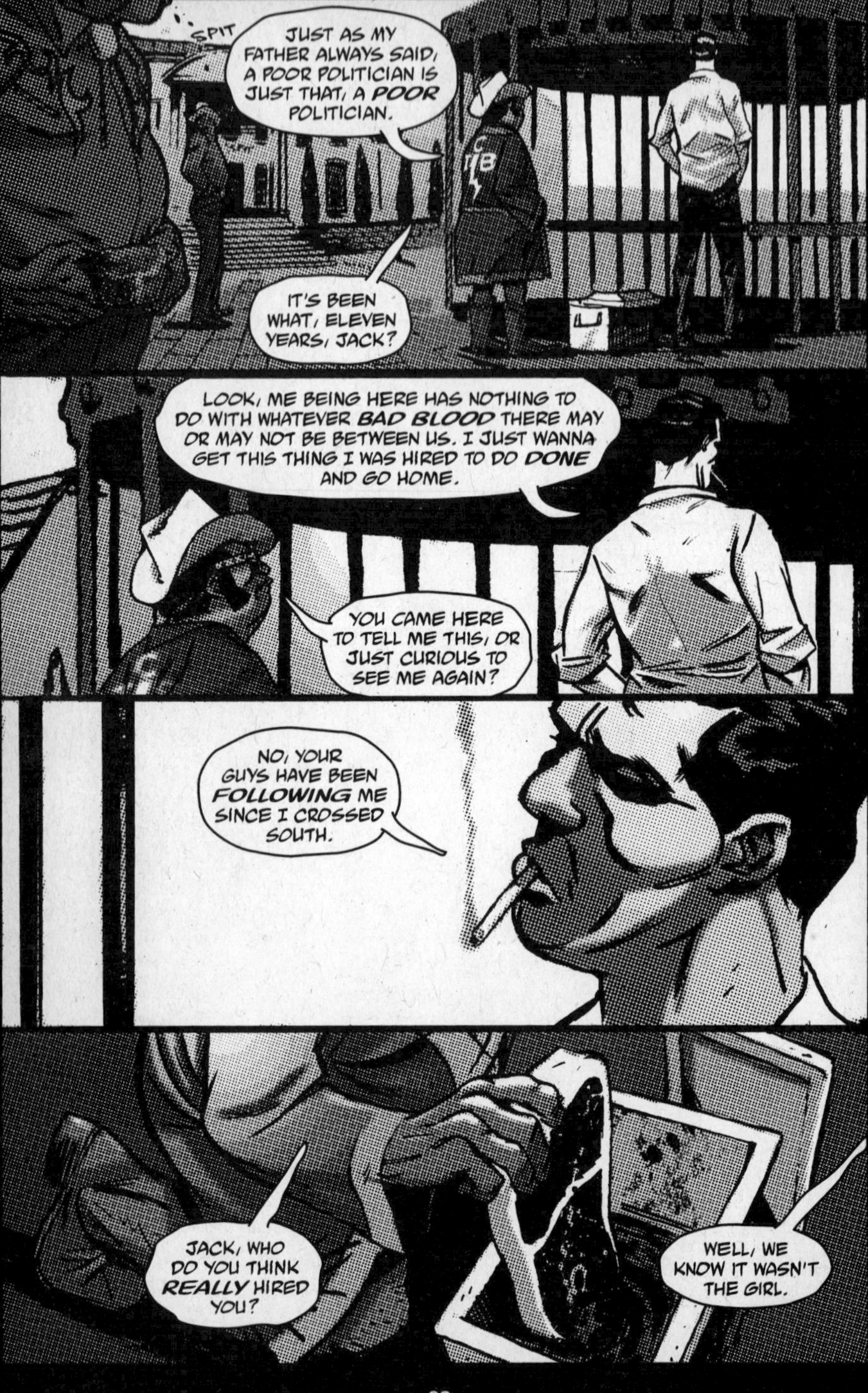
SPIT
JUST AS MY FATHER ALWAYS SAID, A POOR POLITICIAN IS JUST THAT, A POOR POLITICIAN.
IT'S BEEN WHAT, ELEVEN YEARS, JACK?
LOOK, ME BEING HERE HAS NOTHING TO DO WITH WHATEVER BAD BLOOD THERE MAY OR MAY NOT BE BETWEEN US. I JUST WANNA GET THIS THING I WAS HIRED TO DO DONE AND GO HOME.
YOU CAME HERE TO TELL ME THIS, OR JUST CURIOUS TO SEE ME AGAIN?
NO, YOUR GUYS HAVE BEEN FOLLOWING ME SINCE I CROSSED SOUTH.
JACK, WHO DO YOU THINK REALLY HIRED YOU?
WELL, WE KNOW IT WASN'T THE GIRL.

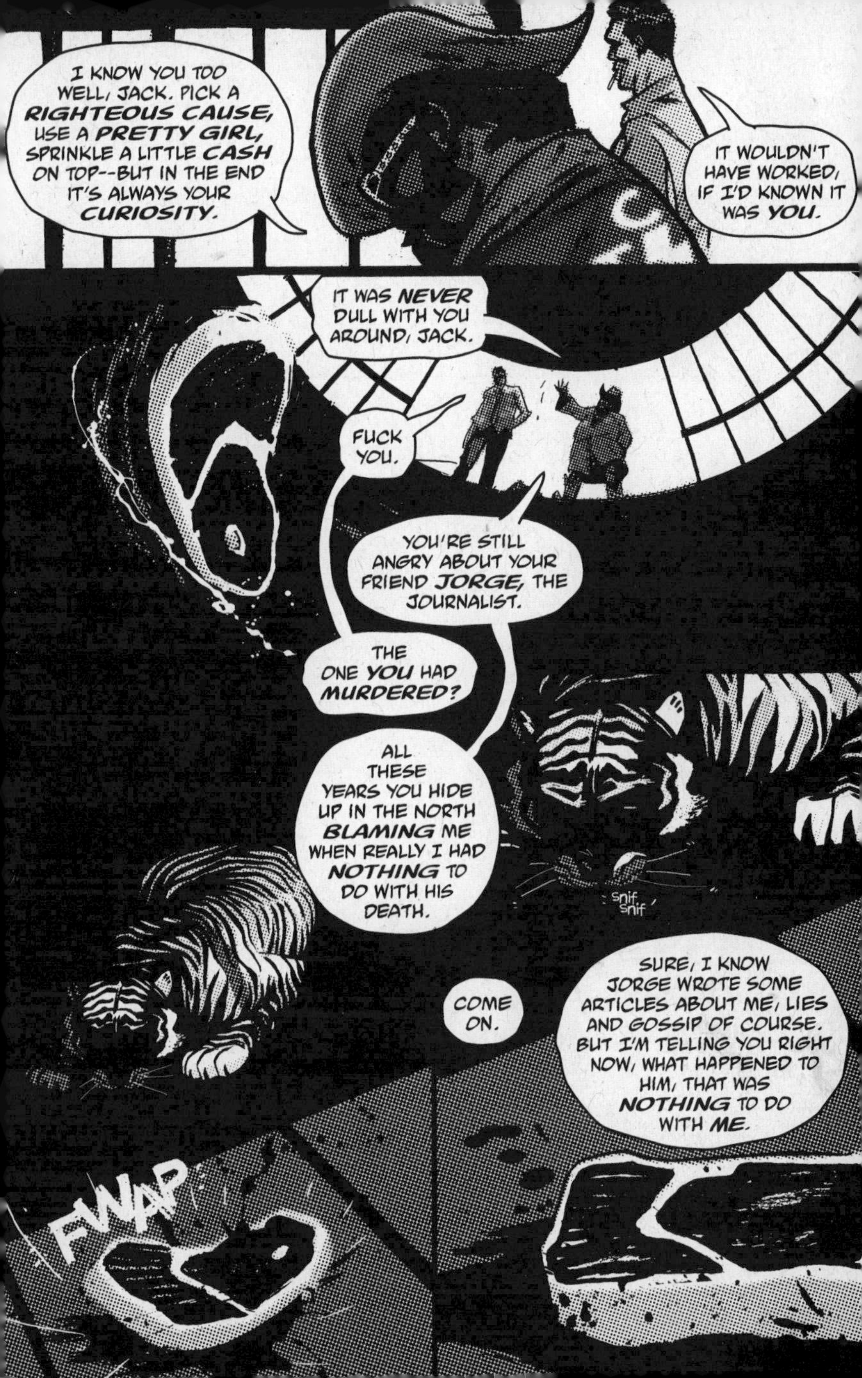
I KNOW YOU TOO WELL, JACK. PICK A RIGHTEOUS CAUSE, USE A PRETTY GIRL, SPRINKLE A LITTLE CASH ON TOP--BUT IN THE END IT'S ALWAYS YOUR CURIOSITY.
IT WOULDN'T HAVE WORKED, IF I'D KNOWN IT WAS YOU.
IT WAS NEVER DULL WITH YOU AROUND, JACK.
FUCK YOU.
YOU'RE STILL ANGRY ABOUT YOUR FRIEND JORGE, THE JOURNALIST.
THE ONE YOU HAD MURDERED?
ALL THESE YEARS YOU HIDE UP IN THE NORTH BLAMING ME WHEN REALLY I HAD NOTHING TO DO WITH HIS DEATH.
snif snif
COME ON.
SURE, I KNOW JORGE WROTE SOME ARTICLES ABOUT ME, LIES AND GOSSIP OF COURSE. BUT I'M TELLING YOU RIGHT NOW, WHAT HAPPENED TO HIM, THAT WAS NOTHING TO DO WITH ME.
FWAP

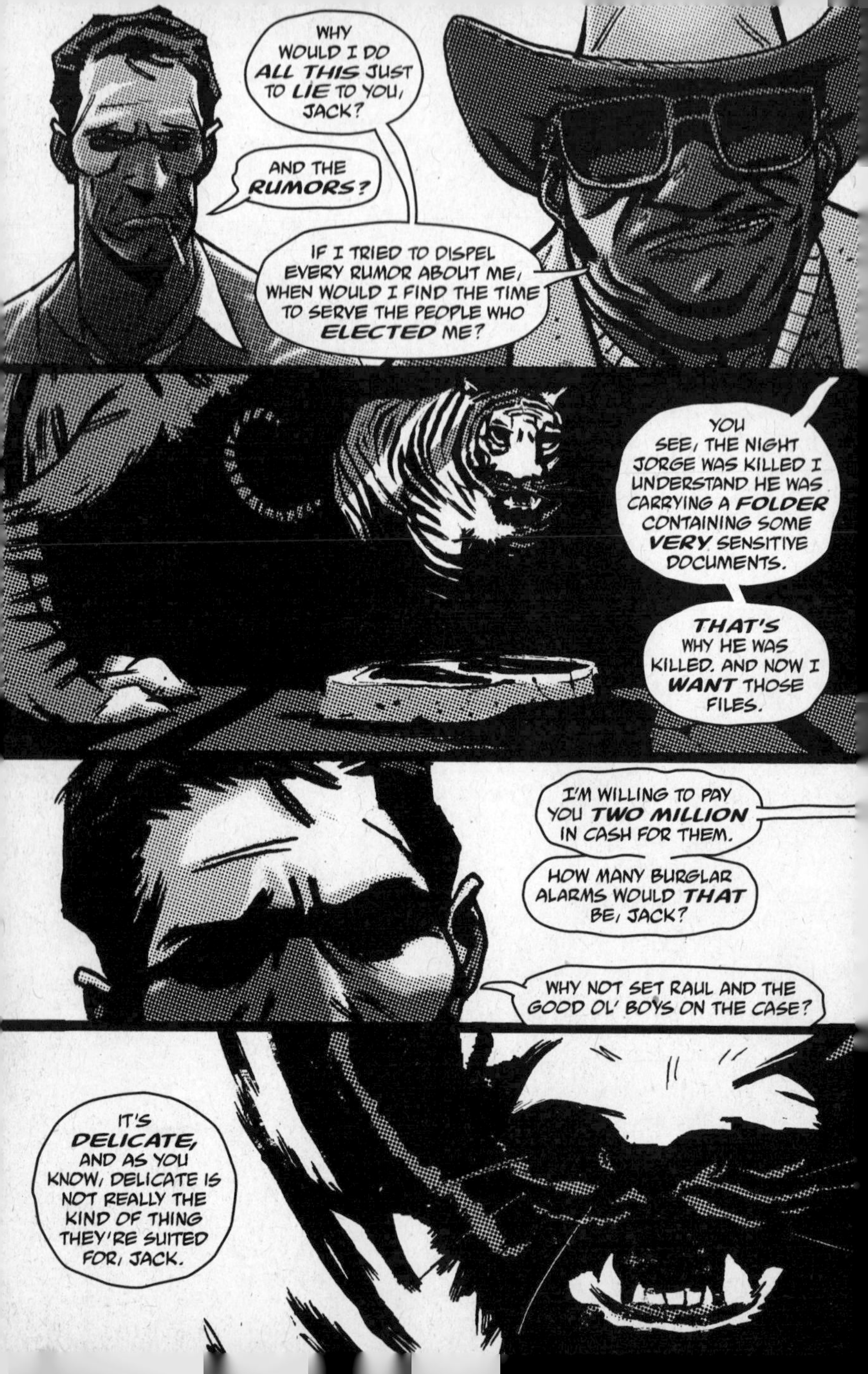
WHY WOULD I DO ALL THIS JUST TO LIE TO YOU, JACK?
AND THE RUMORS?
IF I TRIED TO DISPEL EVERY RUMOR ABOUT ME, WHEN WOULD I FIND THE TIME TO SERVE THE PEOPLE WHO ELECTED ME?
YOU SEE, THE NIGHT JORGE WAS KILLED I UNDERSTAND HE WAS CARRYING A FOLDER CONTAINING SOME VERY SENSITIVE DOCUMENTS.
THAT'S WHY HE WAS KILLED. AND NOW I WANT THOSE FILES.
I'M WILLING TO PAY YOU TWO MILLION IN CASH FOR THEM.
HOW MANY BURGLAR ALARMS WOULD THAT BE, JACK?
WHY NOT SET RAUL AND THE GOOD OL' BOYS ON THE CASE?
IT'S DELICATE, AND AS YOU KNOW, DELICATE IS NOT REALLY THE KIND OF THING THEY'RE SUITED FOR, JACK.

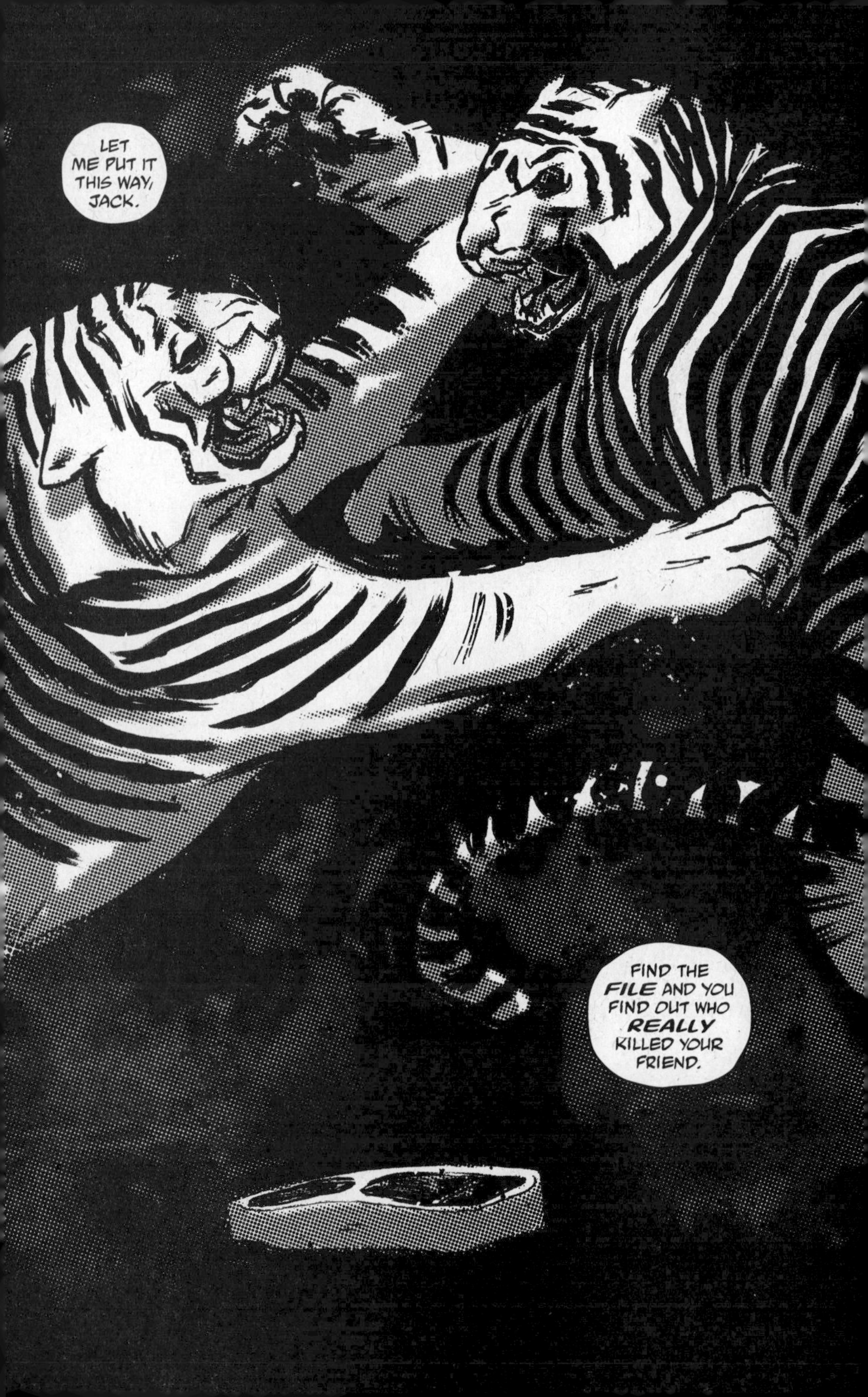
LET ME PUT IT THIS WAY, JACK.
FIND THE FILE AND YOU FIND OUT WHO REALLY KILLED YOUR FRIEND.

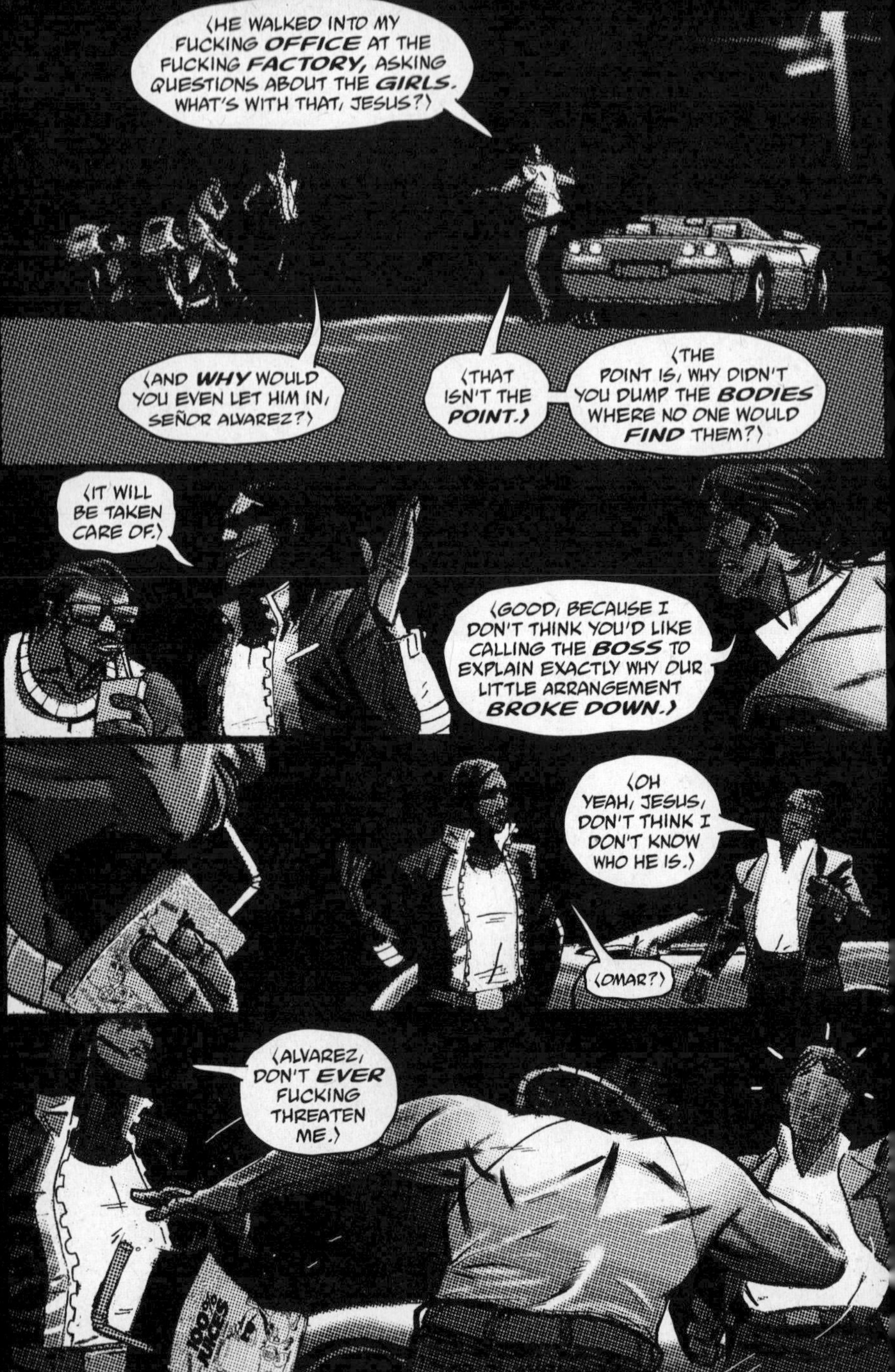
⟨HE WALKED INTO MY FUCKING OFFICE AT THE FUCKING FACTORY, ASKING QUESTIONS ABOUT THE GIRLS. WHAT'S WITH THAT, JESUS?⟩
⟨AND WHY WOULD YOU EVEN LET HIM IN, SEÑOR ALVAREZ?⟩
⟨THAT ISN'T THE POINT.⟩
⟨THE POINT IS, WHY DIDN'T YOU DUMP THE BODIES WHERE NO ONE WOULD FIND THEM?⟩
⟨IT WILL BE TAKEN CARE OF.⟩
⟨GOOD, BECAUSE I DON'T THINK YOU'D LIKE CALLING THE BOSS TO EXPLAIN EXACTLY WHY OUR LITTLE ARRANGEMENT BROKE DOWN.⟩
⟨OH YEAH, JESUS, DON'T THINK I DON'T KNOW WHO HE IS.⟩
⟨OMAR?⟩
⟨ALVAREZ, DON'T EVER FUCKING THREATEN ME.⟩

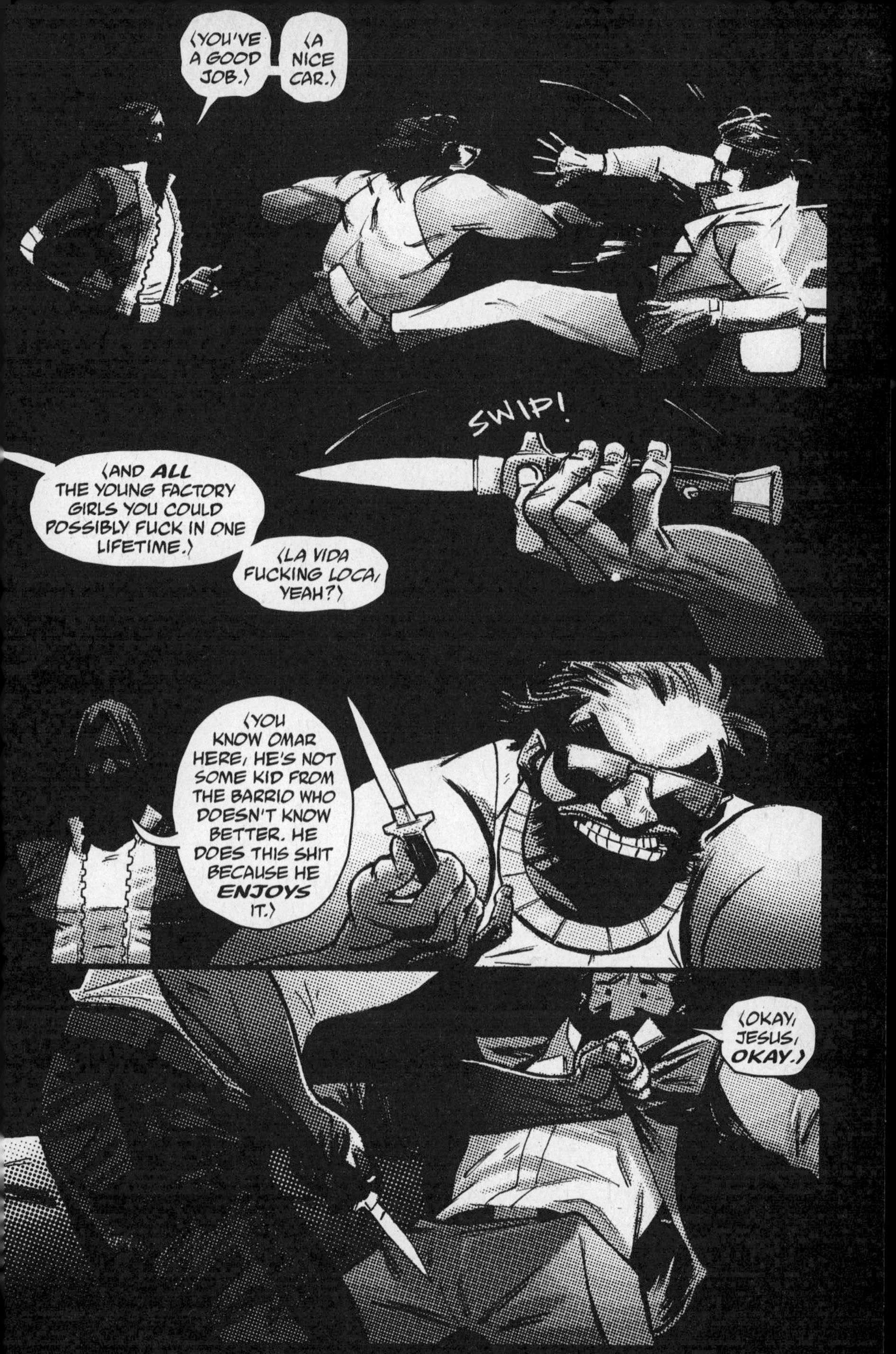

(YOU'VE A GOOD JOB.)
(A NICE CAR.)
SWIP!
(AND **ALL** THE YOUNG FACTORY GIRLS YOU COULD POSSIBLY FUCK IN ONE LIFETIME.)
(LA VIDA FUCKING LOCA, YEAH?)
(YOU KNOW OMAR HERE, HE'S NOT SOME KID FROM THE BARRIO WHO DOESN'T KNOW BETTER. HE DOES THIS SHIT BECAUSE HE **ENJOYS** IT.)
(OKAY, JESUS, **OKAY**.)

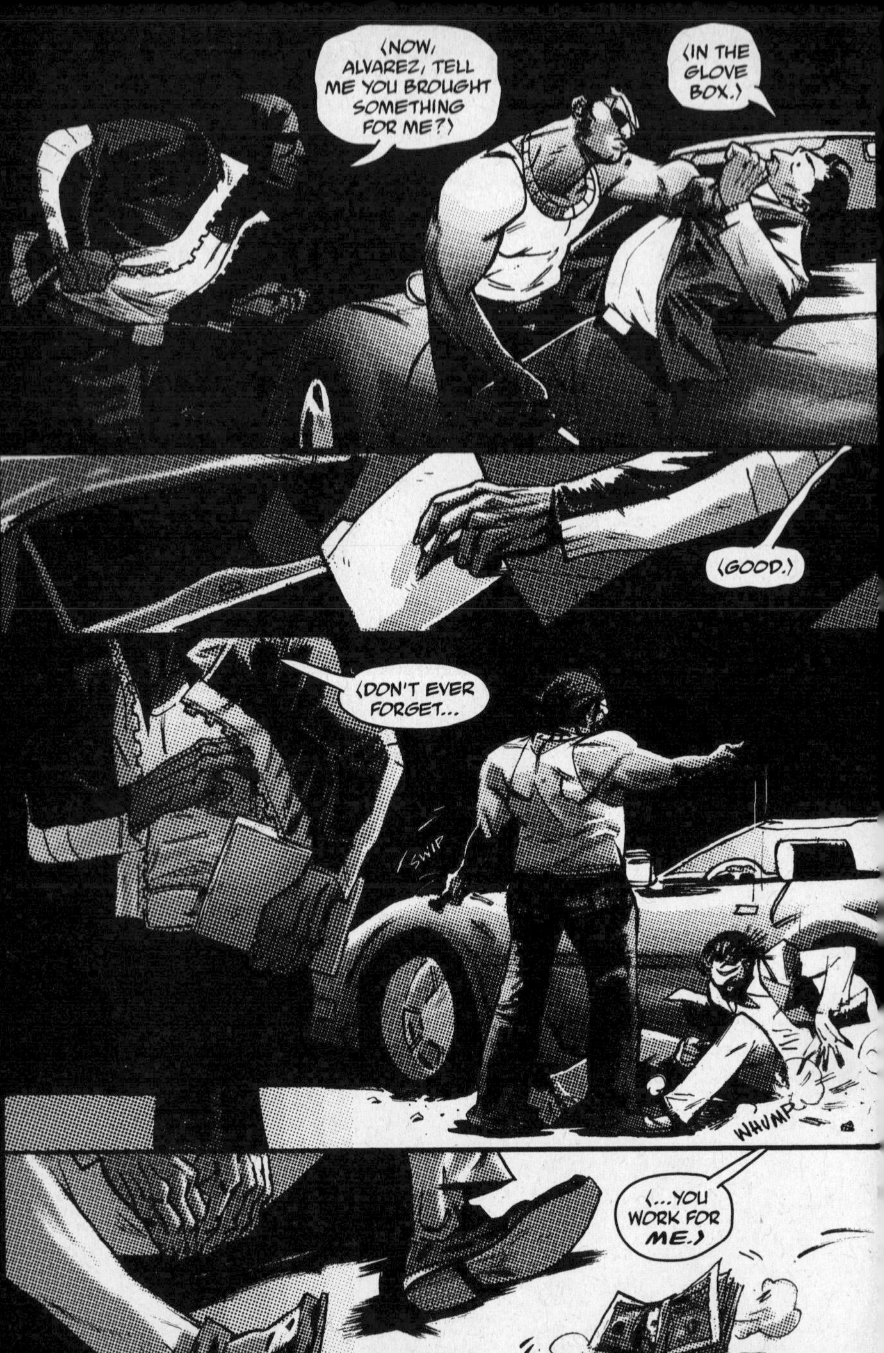
⟨NOW, ALVAREZ, TELL ME YOU BROUGHT SOMETHING FOR ME?⟩
⟨IN THE GLOVE BOX.⟩
⟨GOOD.⟩
⟨DON'T EVER FORGET...
SWIP
WHUMP
⟨...YOU WORK FOR ME.⟩

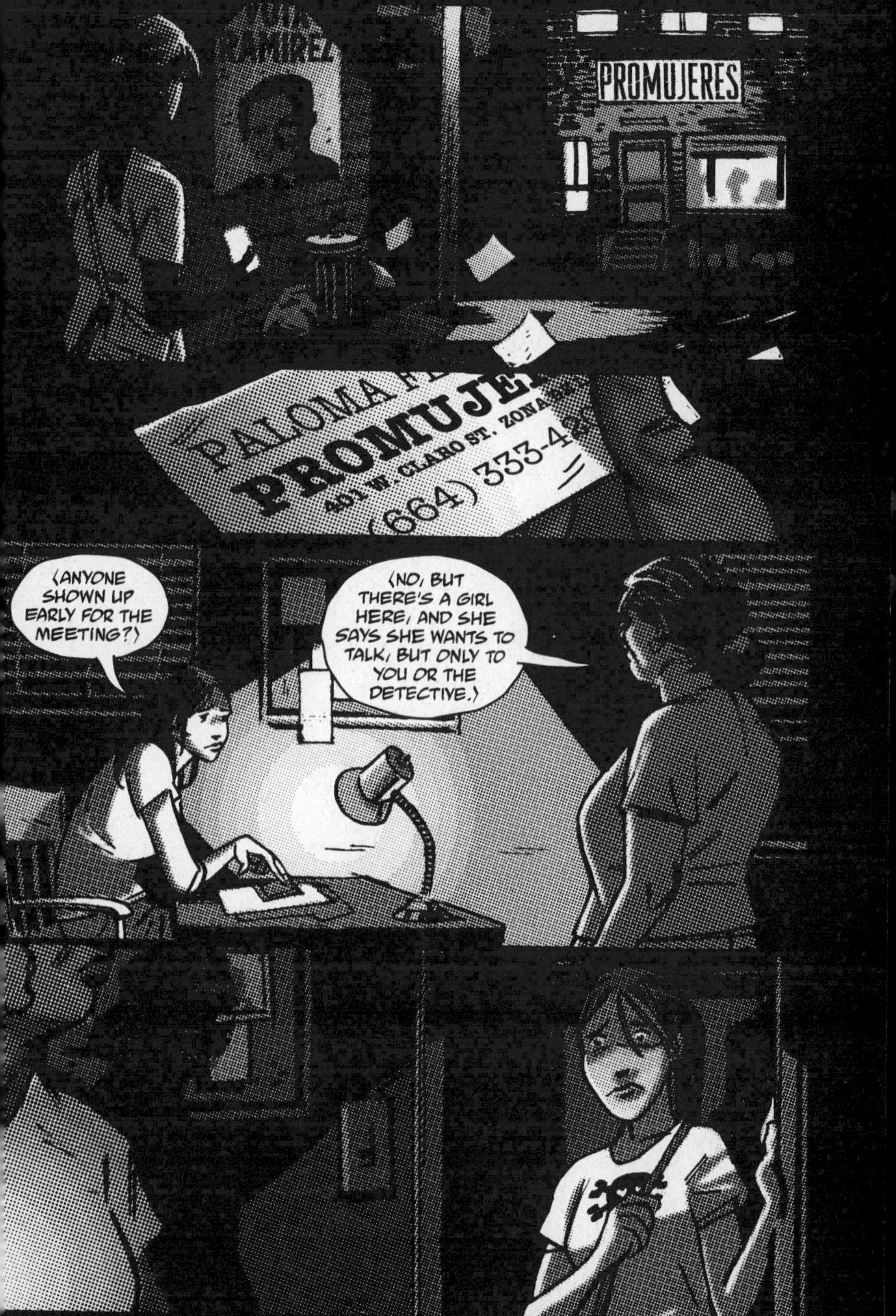
PROMUJERES
PALOMA
PROMUJE
401 W. CLARO ST. ZONA
(664) 333-42
⟨ANYONE SHOWN UP EARLY FOR THE MEETING?⟩
⟨NO, BUT THERE'S A GIRL HERE, AND SHE SAYS SHE WANTS TO TALK, BUT ONLY TO YOU OR THE DETECTIVE.⟩

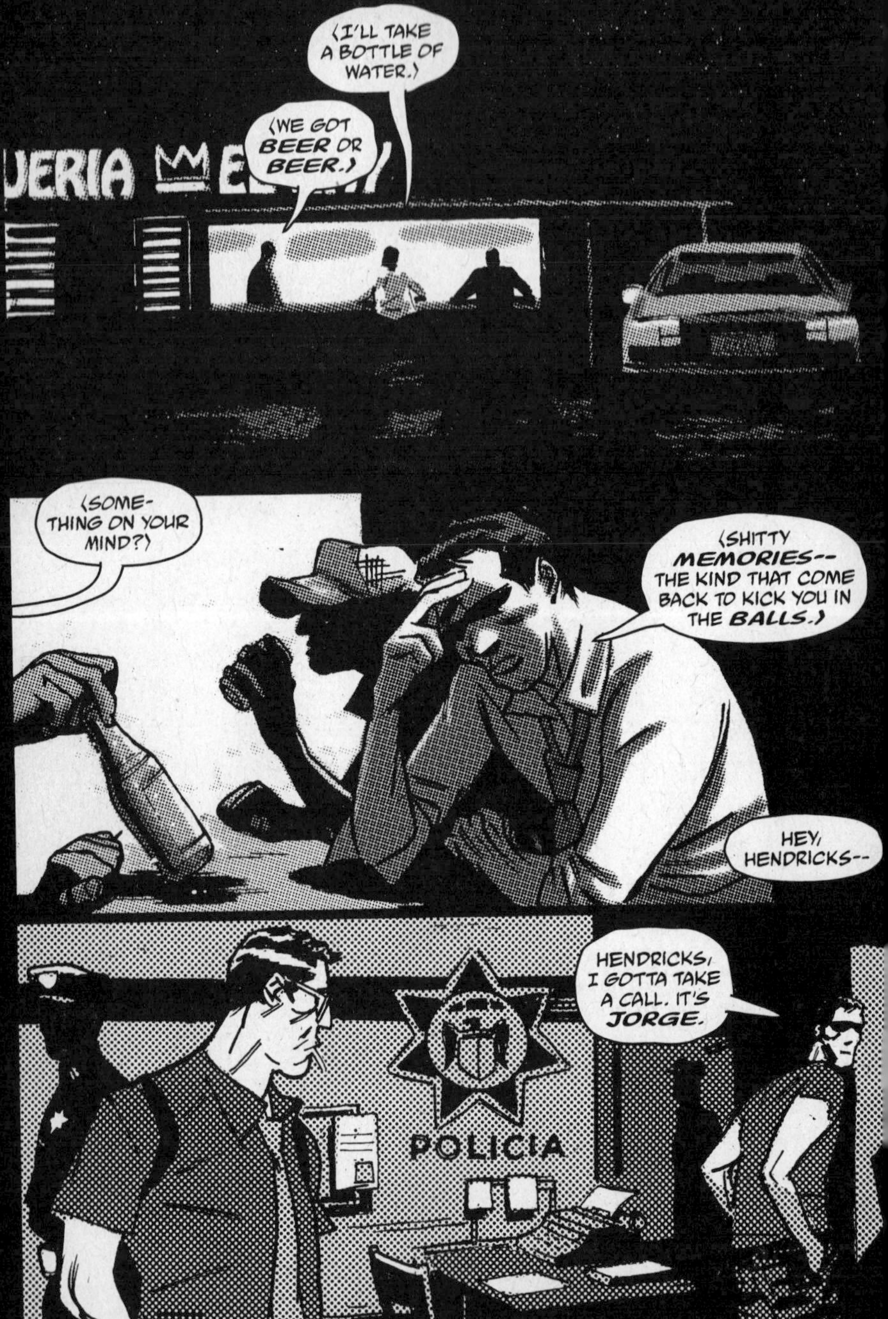
UERIA
⟨WE GOT BEER OR BEER.⟩
⟨I'LL TAKE A BOTTLE OF WATER.⟩
⟨SOME-THING ON YOUR MIND?⟩
⟨SHITTY MEMORIES-- THE KIND THAT COME BACK TO KICK YOU IN THE BALLS.⟩
HEY, HENDRICKS--
HENDRICKS, I GOTTA TAKE A CALL. IT'S JORGE.
POLICIA

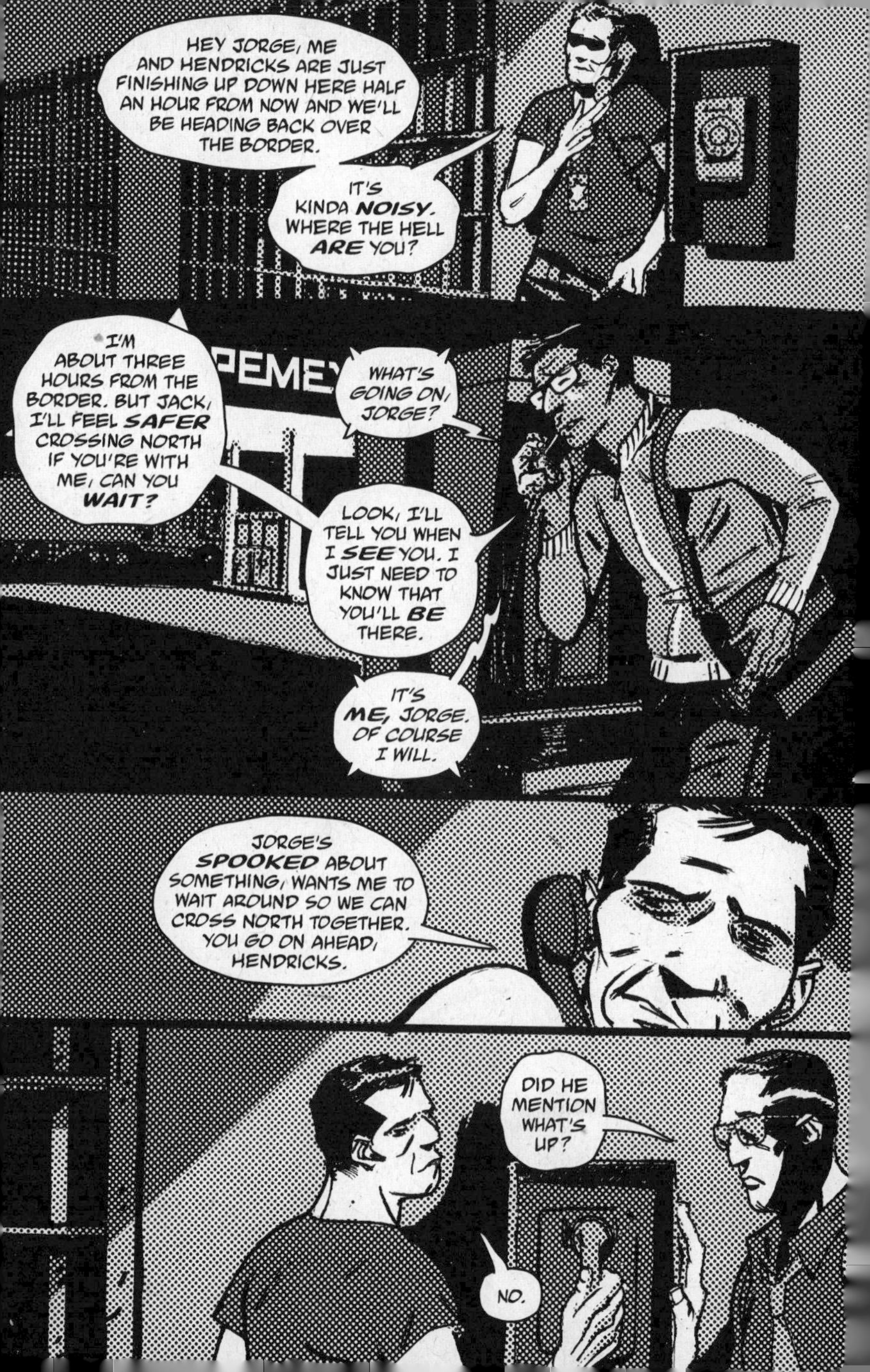
HEY JORGE, ME AND HENDRICKS ARE JUST FINISHING UP DOWN HERE HALF AN HOUR FROM NOW AND WE'LL BE HEADING BACK OVER THE BORDER.
IT'S KINDA NOISY. WHERE THE HELL ARE YOU?
I'M ABOUT THREE HOURS FROM THE BORDER. BUT JACK, I'LL FEEL SAFER CROSSING NORTH IF YOU'RE WITH ME, CAN YOU WAIT?
PEMEX
WHAT'S GOING ON, JORGE?
LOOK, I'LL TELL YOU WHEN I SEE YOU. I JUST NEED TO KNOW THAT YOU'LL BE THERE.
IT'S ME, JORGE. OF COURSE I WILL.
JORGE'S SPOOKED ABOUT SOMETHING, WANTS ME TO WAIT AROUND SO WE CAN CROSS NORTH TOGETHER. YOU GO ON AHEAD, HENDRICKS.
DID HE MENTION WHAT'S UP?
NO.

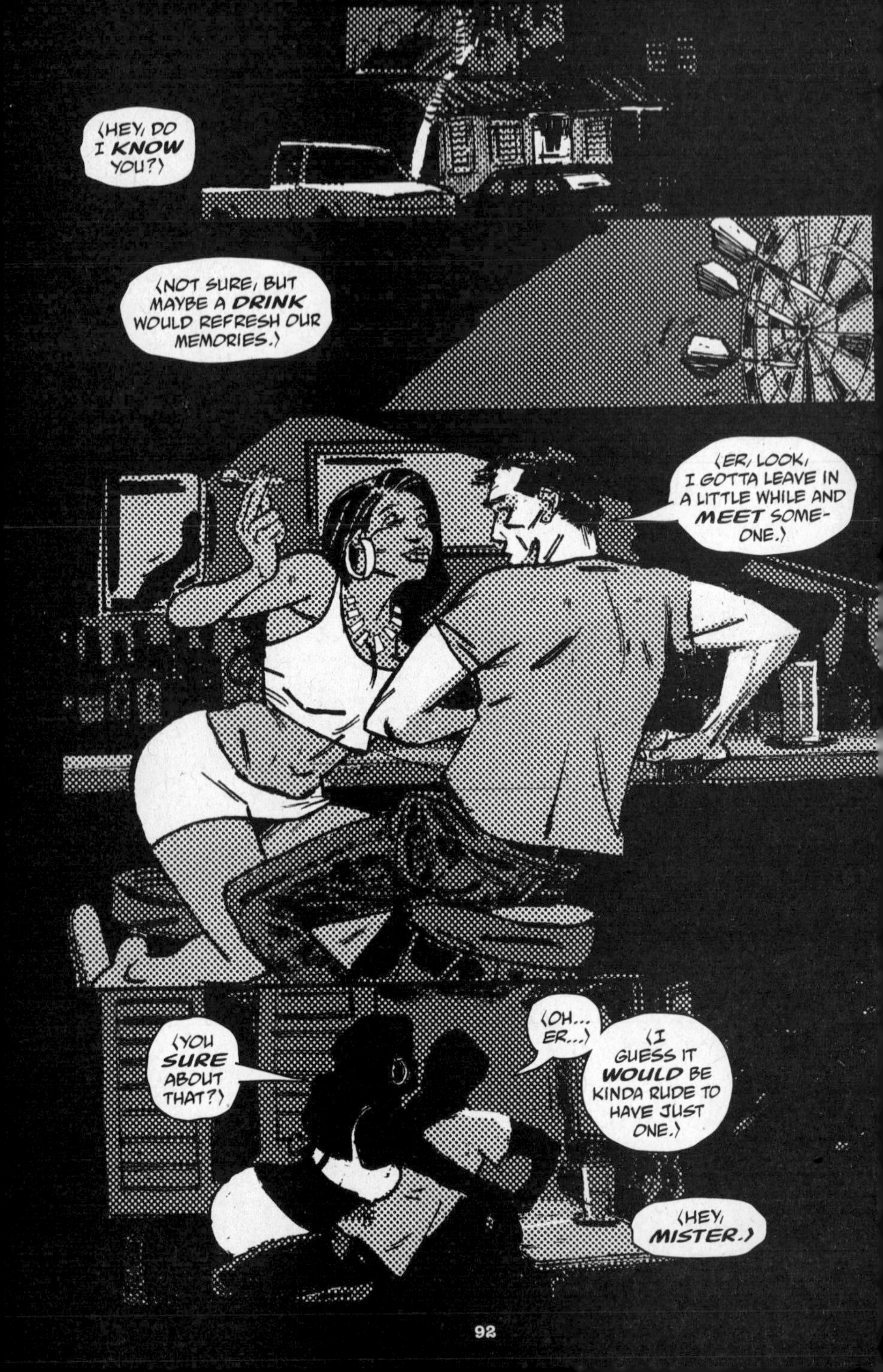

‹HEY, DO I KNOW YOU?›
‹NOT SURE, BUT MAYBE A DRINK WOULD REFRESH OUR MEMORIES.›
‹ER, LOOK, I GOTTA LEAVE IN A LITTLE WHILE AND MEET SOME-ONE.›
‹YOU SURE ABOUT THAT?›
‹OH... ER...›
‹I GUESS IT WOULD BE KINDA RUDE TO HAVE JUST ONE.›
‹HEY, MISTER.›

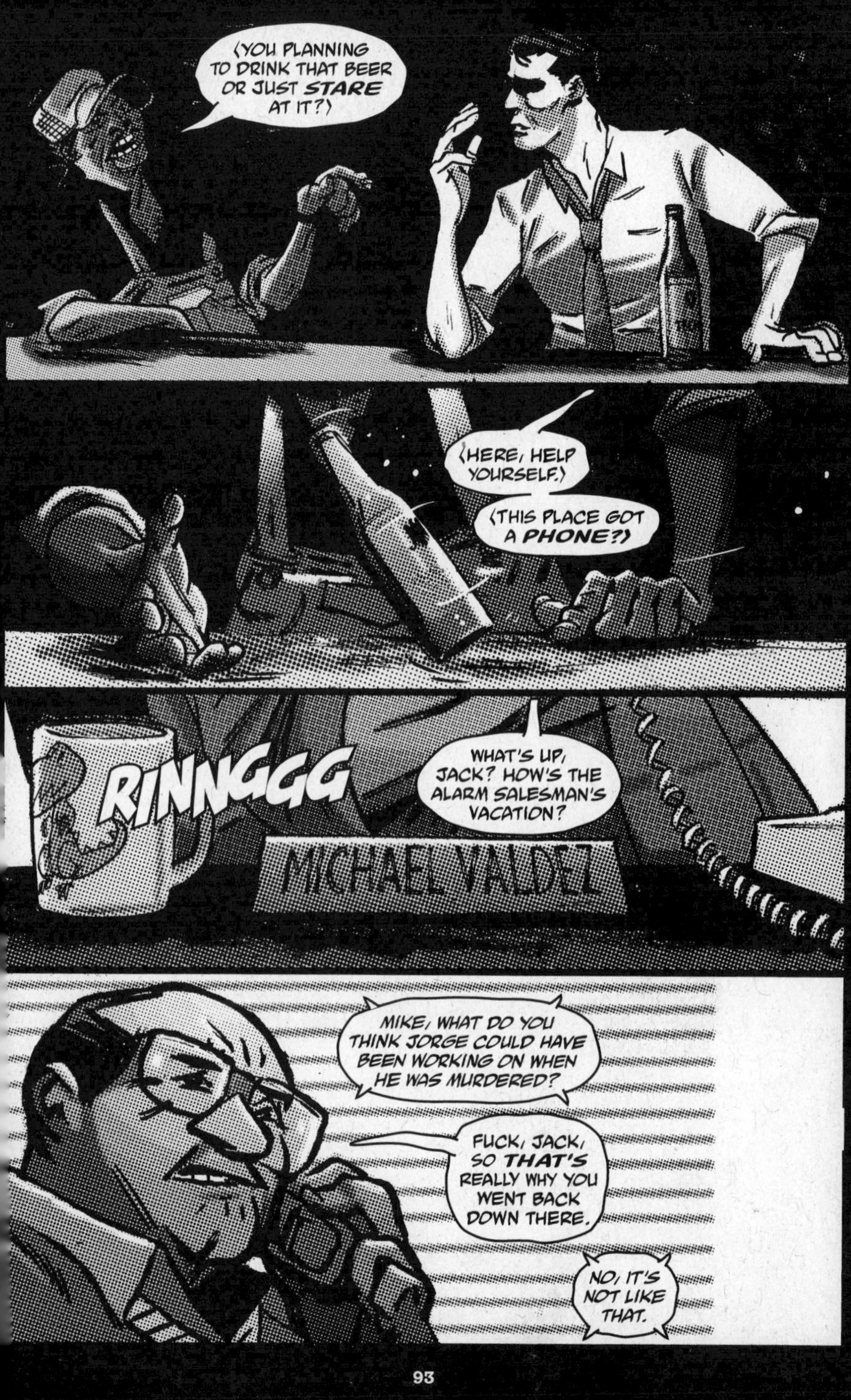
‹YOU PLANNING TO DRINK THAT BEER OR JUST STARE AT IT?›
‹HERE, HELP YOURSELF.›
‹THIS PLACE GOT A PHONE?›
RINNGGG
WHAT'S UP, JACK? HOW'S THE ALARM SALESMAN'S VACATION?
MICHAEL VALDEZ
MIKE, WHAT DO YOU THINK JORGE COULD HAVE BEEN WORKING ON WHEN HE WAS MURDERED?
FUCK, JACK, SO THAT'S REALLY WHY YOU WENT BACK DOWN THERE.
NO, IT'S NOT LIKE THAT.

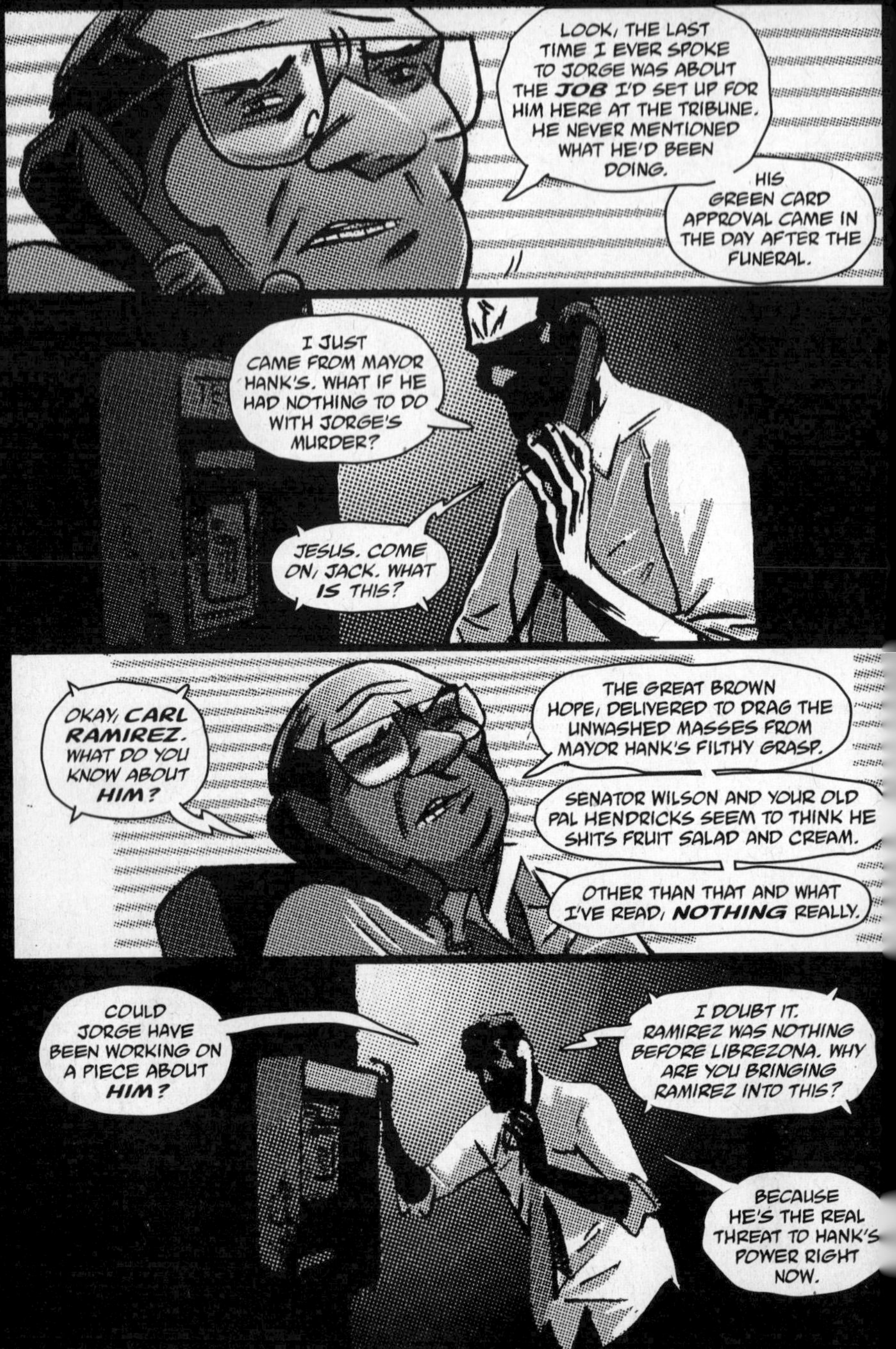
LOOK, THE LAST TIME I EVER SPOKE TO JORGE WAS ABOUT THE JOB I'D SET UP FOR HIM HERE AT THE TRIBUNE. HE NEVER MENTIONED WHAT HE'D BEEN DOING.
HIS GREEN CARD APPROVAL CAME IN THE DAY AFTER THE FUNERAL.
I JUST CAME FROM MAYOR HANK'S. WHAT IF HE HAD NOTHING TO DO WITH JORGE'S MURDER?
JESUS. COME ON, JACK. WHAT IS THIS?
OKAY, CARL RAMIREZ. WHAT DO YOU KNOW ABOUT HIM?
THE GREAT BROWN HOPE, DELIVERED TO DRAG THE UNWASHED MASSES FROM MAYOR HANK'S FILTHY GRASP.
SENATOR WILSON AND YOUR OLD PAL HENDRICKS SEEM TO THINK HE SHITS FRUIT SALAD AND CREAM.
OTHER THAN THAT AND WHAT I'VE READ, NOTHING REALLY.
COULD JORGE HAVE BEEN WORKING ON A PIECE ABOUT HIM?
I DOUBT IT. RAMIREZ WAS NOTHING BEFORE LIBREZONA. WHY ARE YOU BRINGING RAMIREZ INTO THIS?
BECAUSE HE'S THE REAL THREAT TO HANK'S POWER RIGHT NOW.

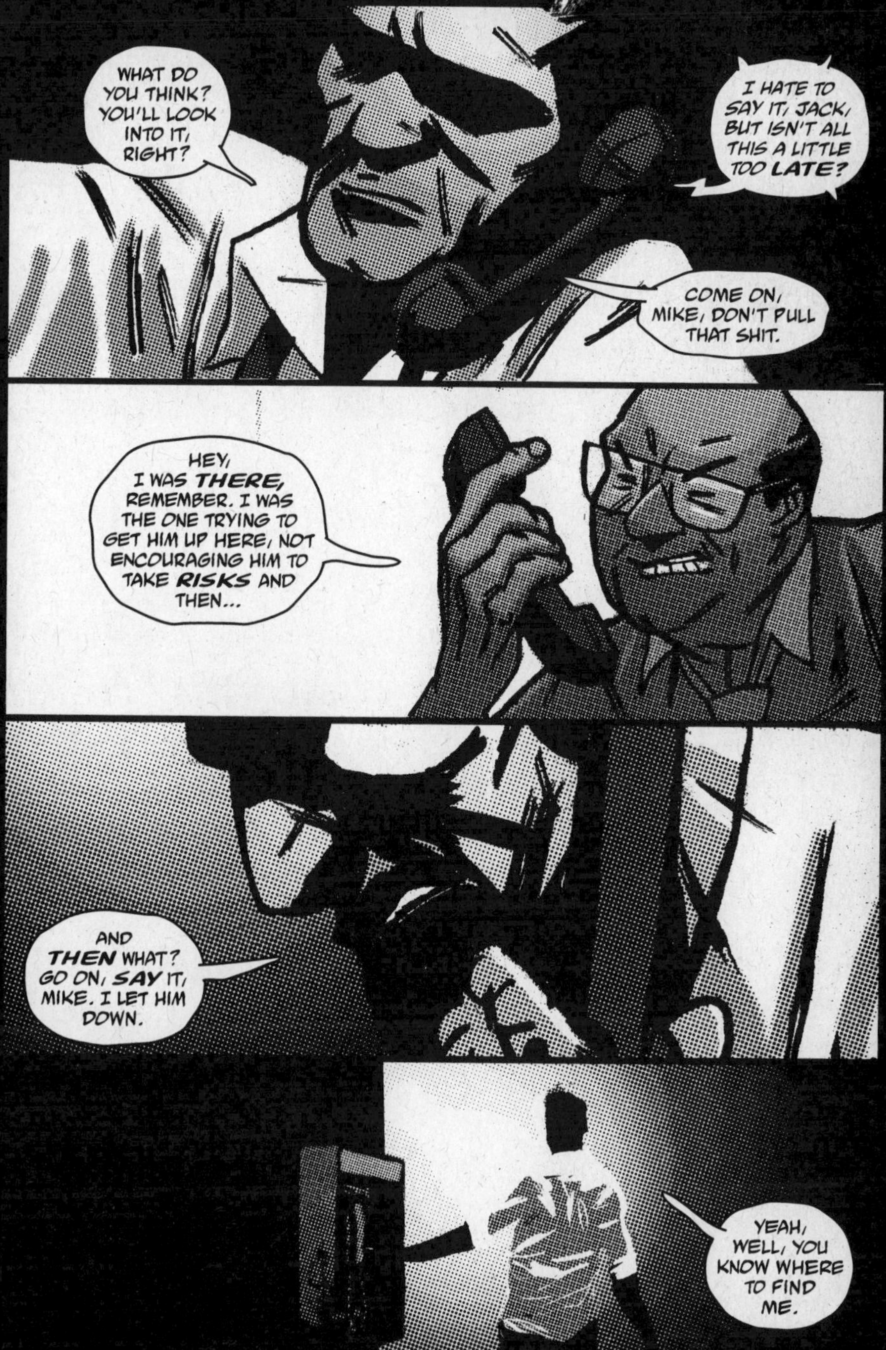
WHAT DO YOU THINK? YOU'LL LOOK INTO IT, RIGHT?
I HATE TO SAY IT, JACK, BUT ISN'T ALL THIS A LITTLE TOO LATE?
COME ON, MIKE, DON'T PULL THAT SHIT.
HEY, I WAS THERE, REMEMBER. I WAS THE ONE TRYING TO GET HIM UP HERE, NOT ENCOURAGING HIM TO TAKE RISKS AND THEN...
AND THEN WHAT? GO ON, SAY IT, MIKE. I LET HIM DOWN.
YEAH, WELL, YOU KNOW WHERE TO FIND ME.

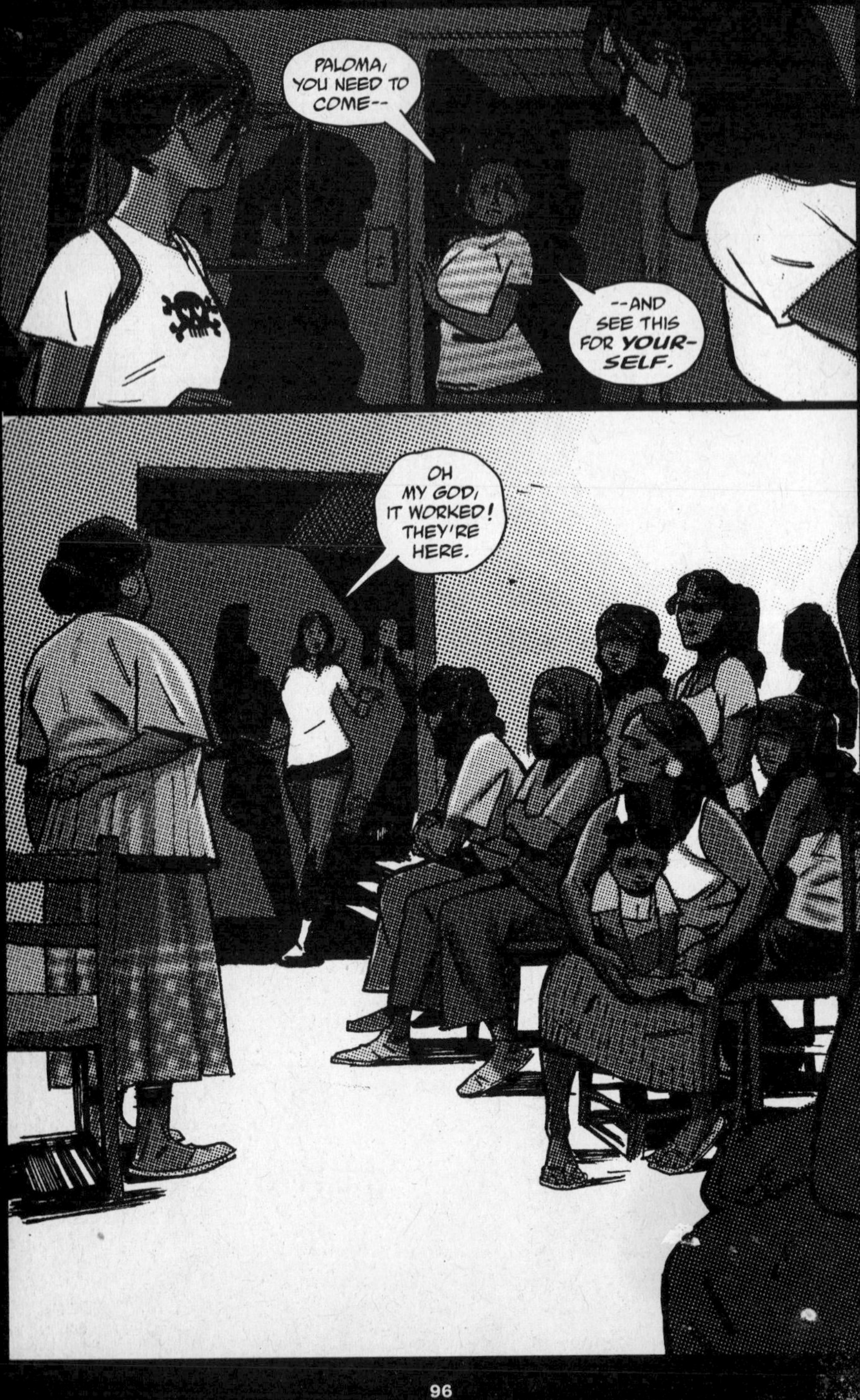
PALOMA, YOU NEED TO COME--
--AND SEE THIS FOR YOURSELF.
OH MY GOD, IT WORKED! THEY'RE HERE.

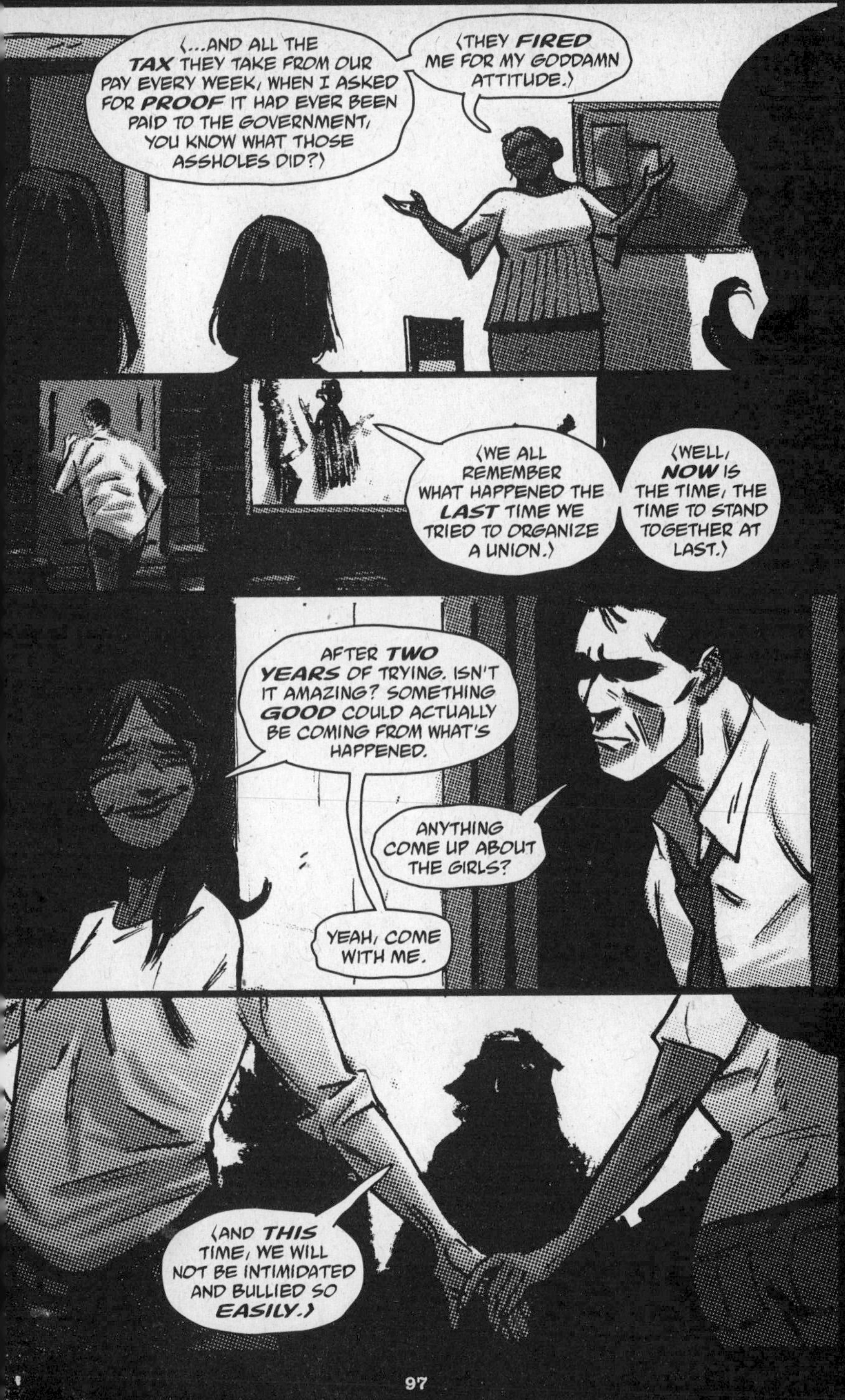
⟨...AND ALL THE TAX THEY TAKE FROM OUR PAY EVERY WEEK, WHEN I ASKED FOR PROOF IT HAD EVER BEEN PAID TO THE GOVERNMENT, YOU KNOW WHAT THOSE ASSHOLES DID?⟩
⟨THEY FIRED ME FOR MY GODDAMN ATTITUDE.⟩
⟨WE ALL REMEMBER WHAT HAPPENED THE LAST TIME WE TRIED TO ORGANIZE A UNION.⟩
⟨WELL, NOW IS THE TIME, THE TIME TO STAND TOGETHER AT LAST.⟩
AFTER TWO YEARS OF TRYING. ISN'T IT AMAZING? SOMETHING GOOD COULD ACTUALLY BE COMING FROM WHAT'S HAPPENED.
ANYTHING COME UP ABOUT THE GIRLS?
YEAH, COME WITH ME.
⟨AND THIS TIME, WE WILL NOT BE INTIMIDATED AND BULLIED SO EASILY.⟩

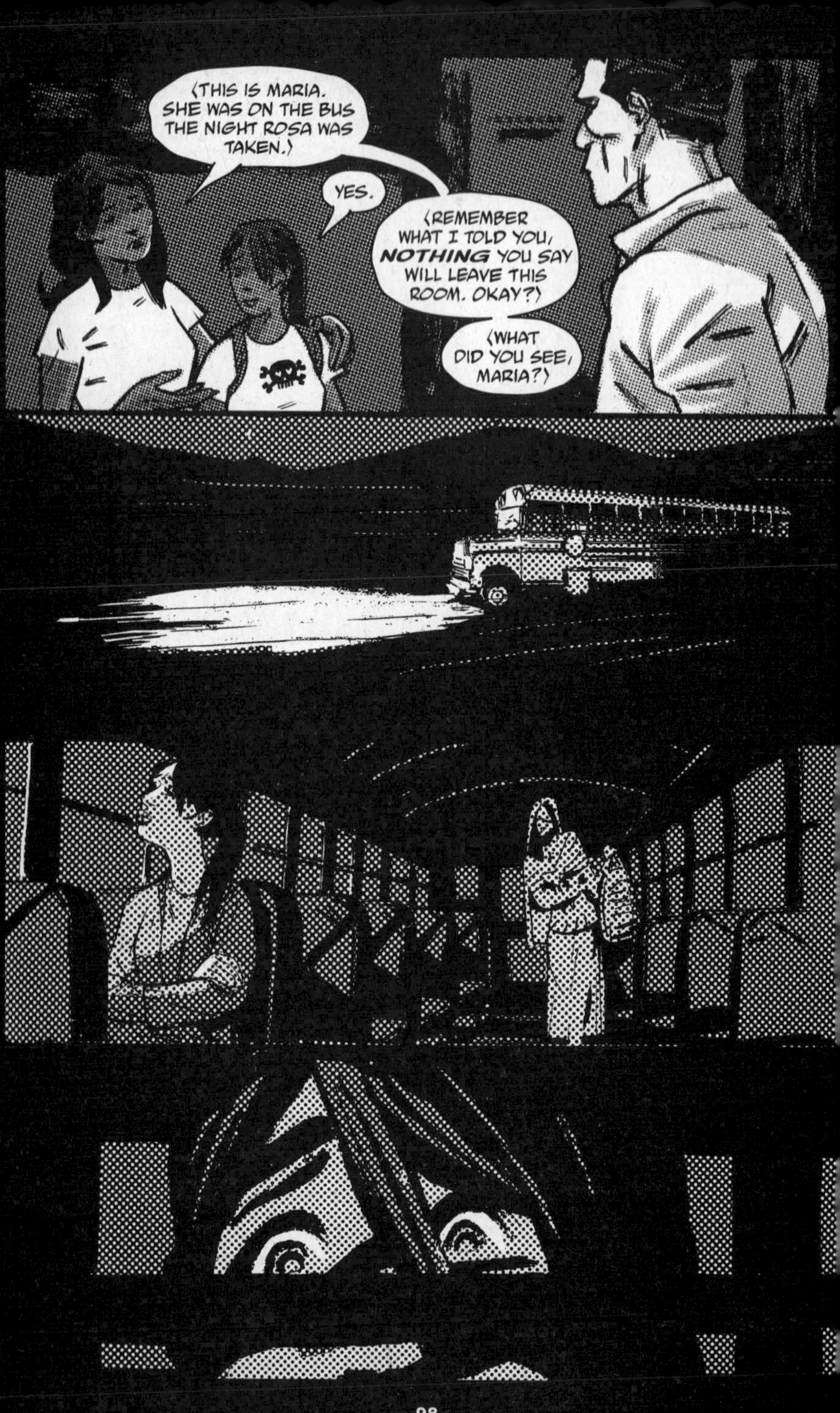

⟨THIS IS MARIA. SHE WAS ON THE BUS THE NIGHT ROSA WAS TAKEN.⟩
YES.
⟨REMEMBER WHAT I TOLD YOU, **NOTHING** YOU SAY WILL LEAVE THIS ROOM. OKAY?⟩
⟨WHAT DID YOU SEE, MARIA?⟩

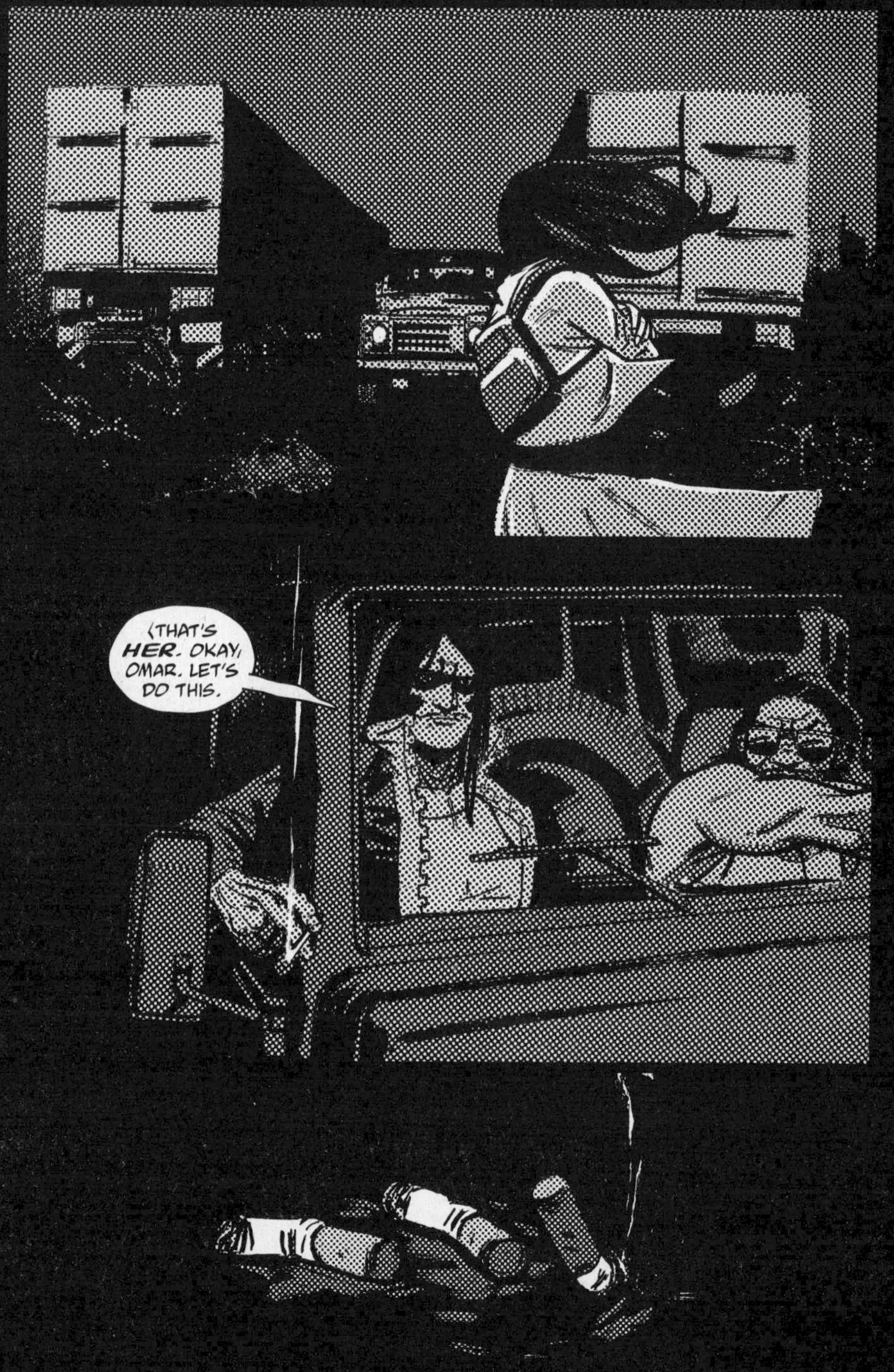
‹THAT'S *HER*. OKAY, OMAR. LET'S DO THIS.

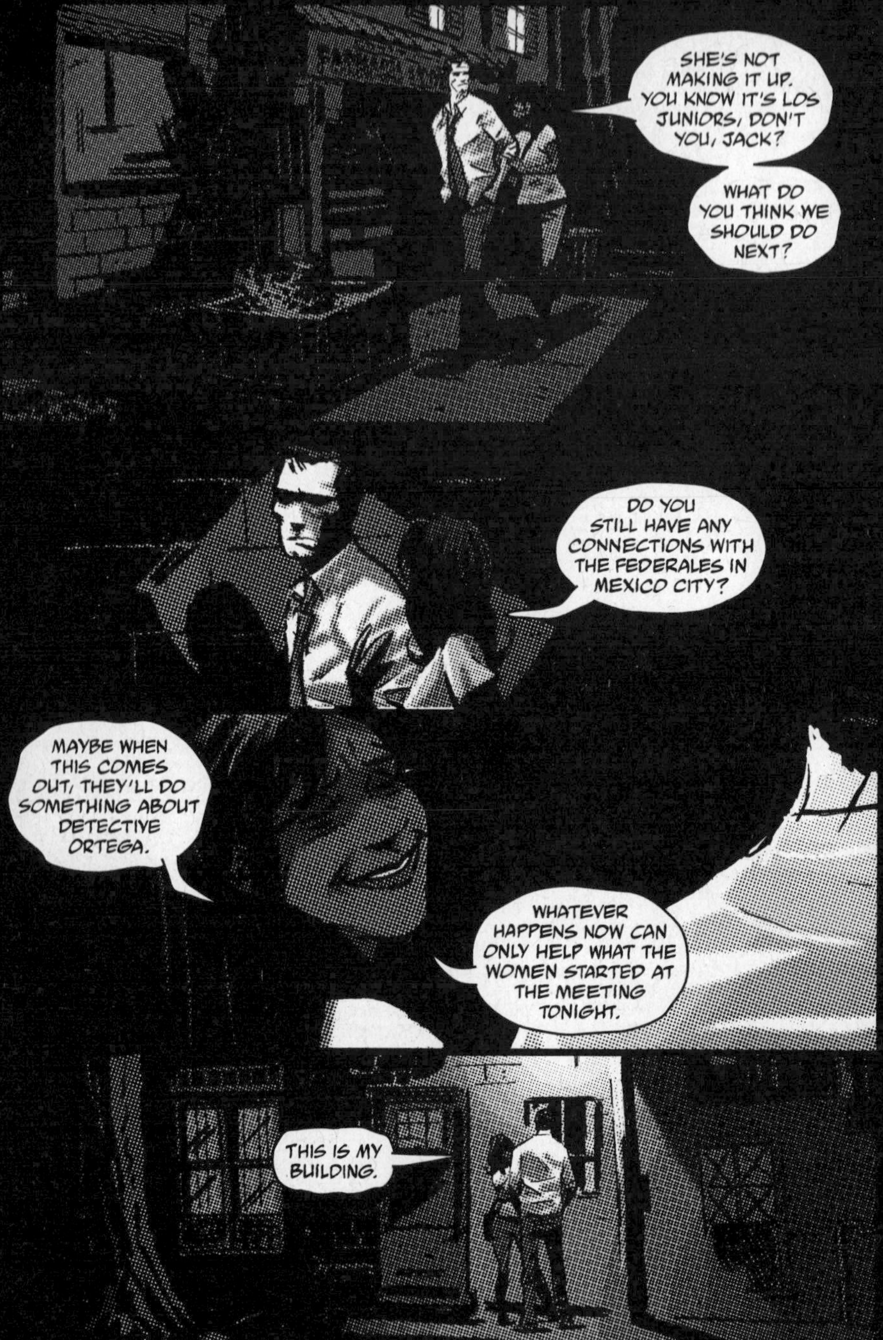
SHE'S NOT MAKING IT UP. YOU KNOW IT'S LOS JUNIORS, DON'T YOU, JACK?
WHAT DO YOU THINK WE SHOULD DO NEXT?
DO YOU STILL HAVE ANY CONNECTIONS WITH THE FEDERALES IN MEXICO CITY?
MAYBE WHEN THIS COMES OUT, THEY'LL DO SOMETHING ABOUT DETECTIVE ORTEGA.
WHATEVER HAPPENS NOW CAN ONLY HELP WHAT THE WOMEN STARTED AT THE MEETING TONIGHT.
THIS IS MY BUILDING.

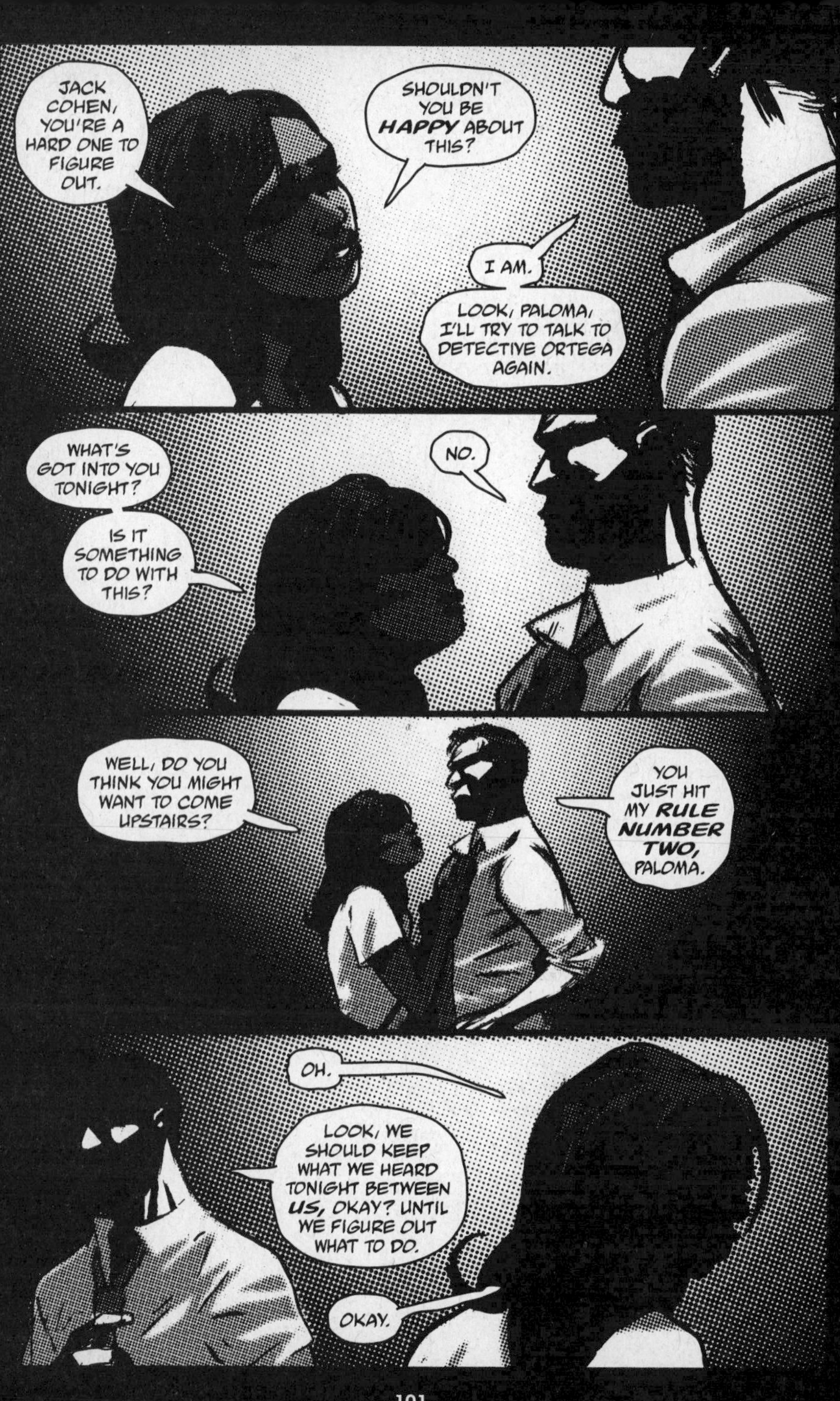
JACK COHEN, YOU'RE A HARD ONE TO FIGURE OUT.
SHOULDN'T YOU BE **HAPPY** ABOUT THIS?
I AM.
LOOK, PALOMA, I'LL TRY TO TALK TO DETECTIVE ORTEGA AGAIN.
WHAT'S GOT INTO YOU TONIGHT?
IS IT SOMETHING TO DO WITH THIS?
NO.
WELL, DO YOU THINK YOU MIGHT WANT TO COME UPSTAIRS?
YOU JUST HIT MY **RULE NUMBER TWO,** PALOMA.
OH.
LOOK, WE SHOULD KEEP WHAT WE HEARD TONIGHT BETWEEN **US,** OKAY? UNTIL WE FIGURE OUT WHAT TO DO.
OKAY.

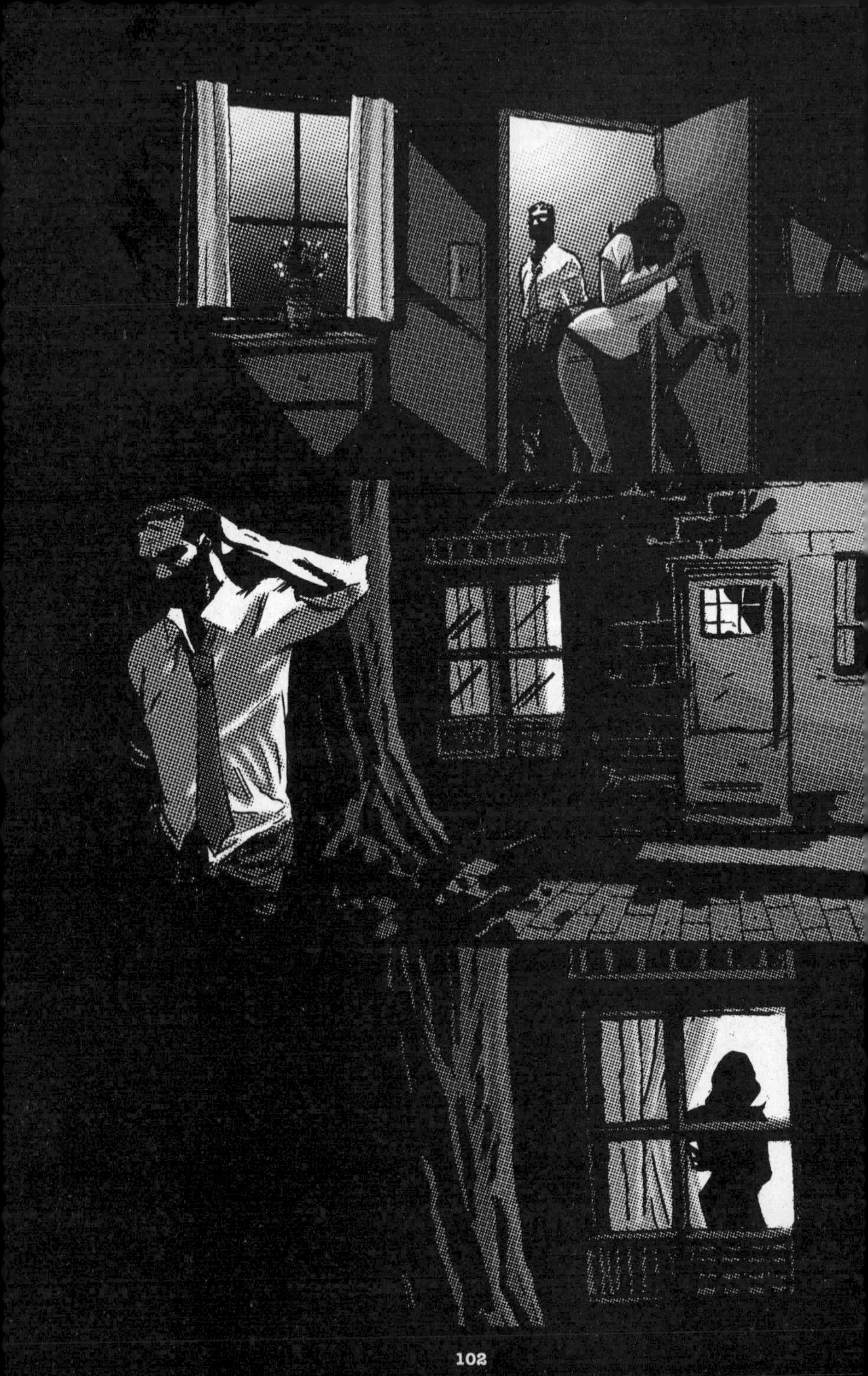

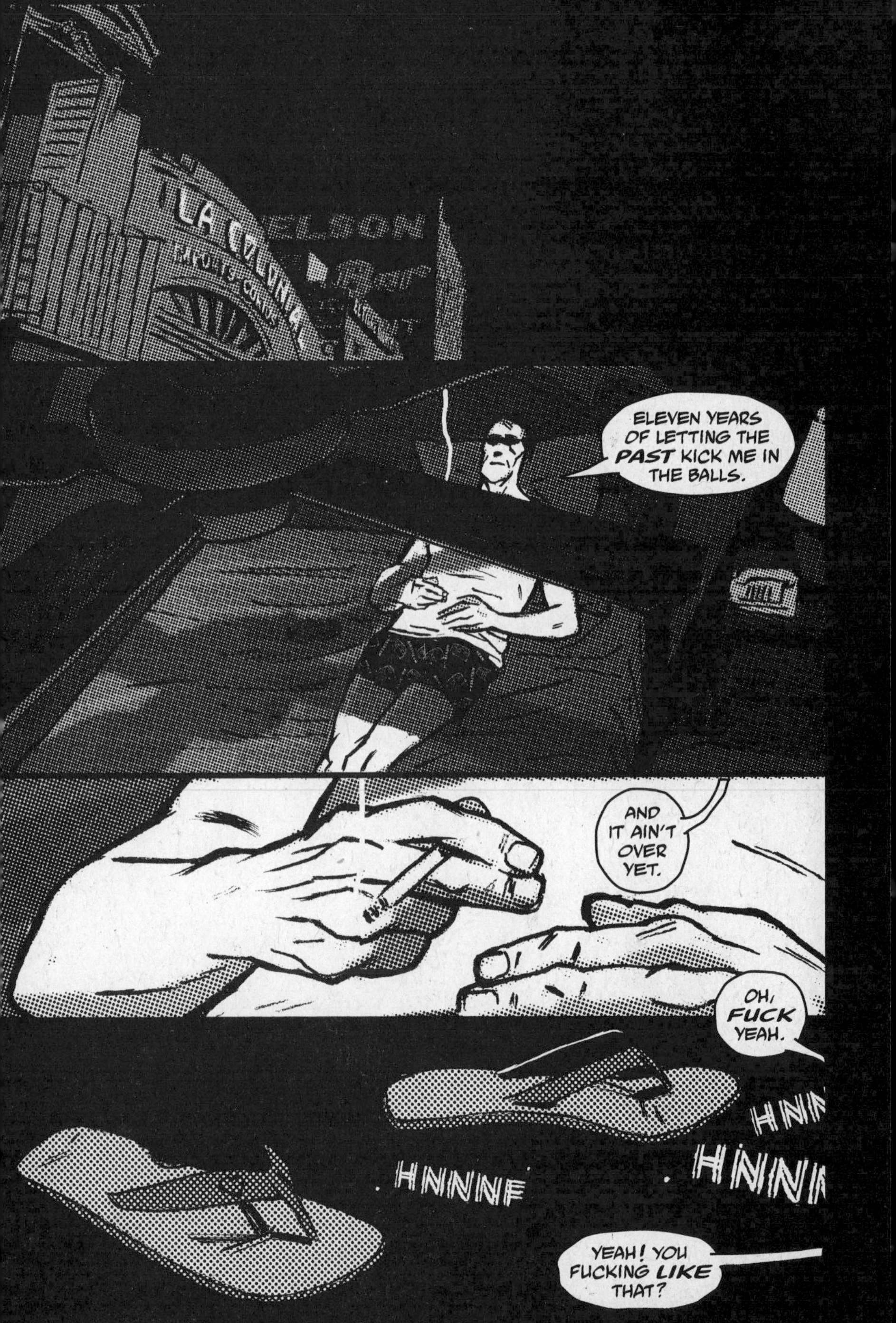
ELEVEN YEARS OF LETTING THE PAST KICK ME IN THE BALLS.
AND IT AIN'T OVER YET.
OH, FUCK YEAH.
HNNF
HNNNF
HNNNF
YEAH! YOU FUCKING LIKE THAT?

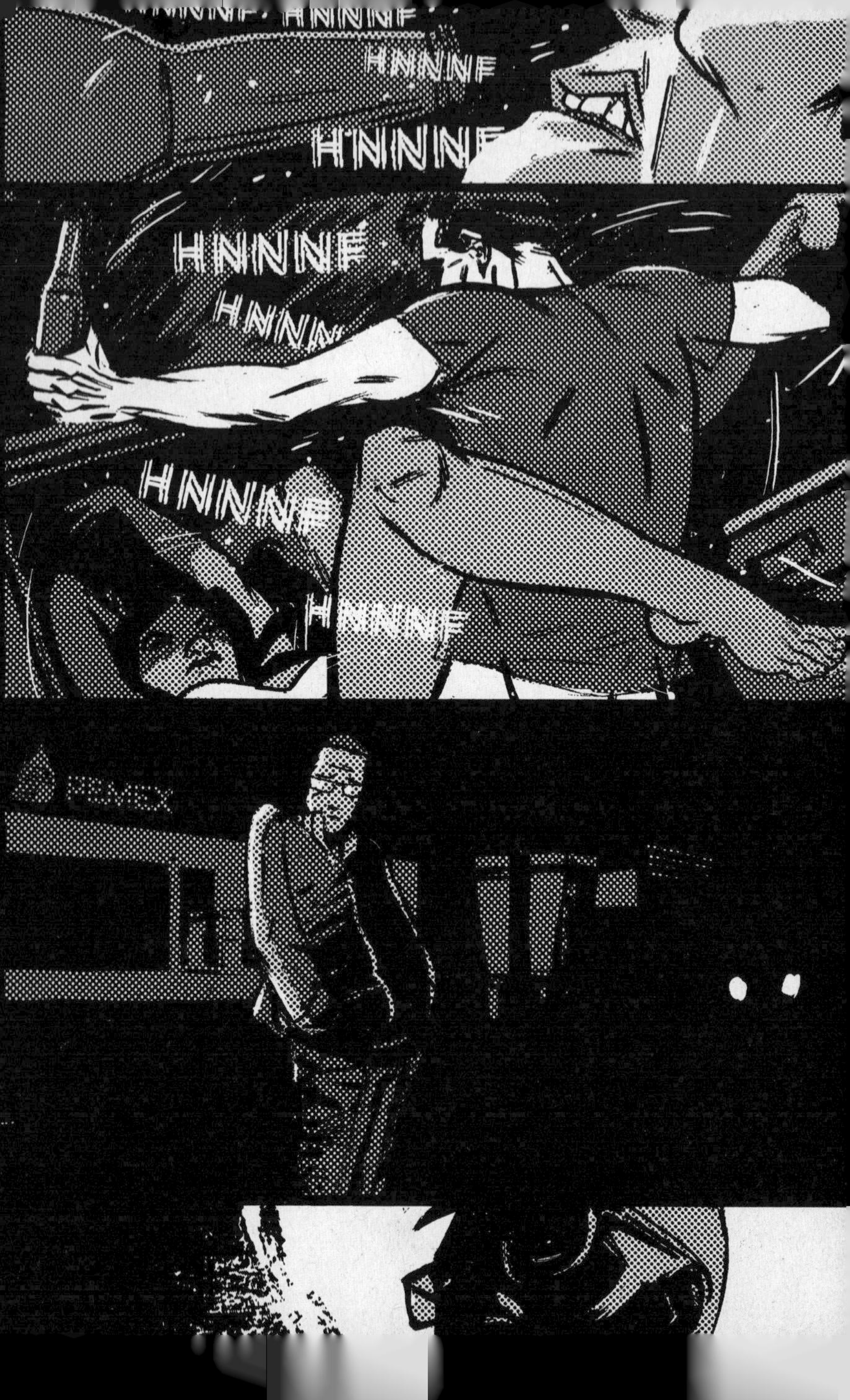

HNNNF
HNNNF
HNNNF
HNNNF
HNNNF
..

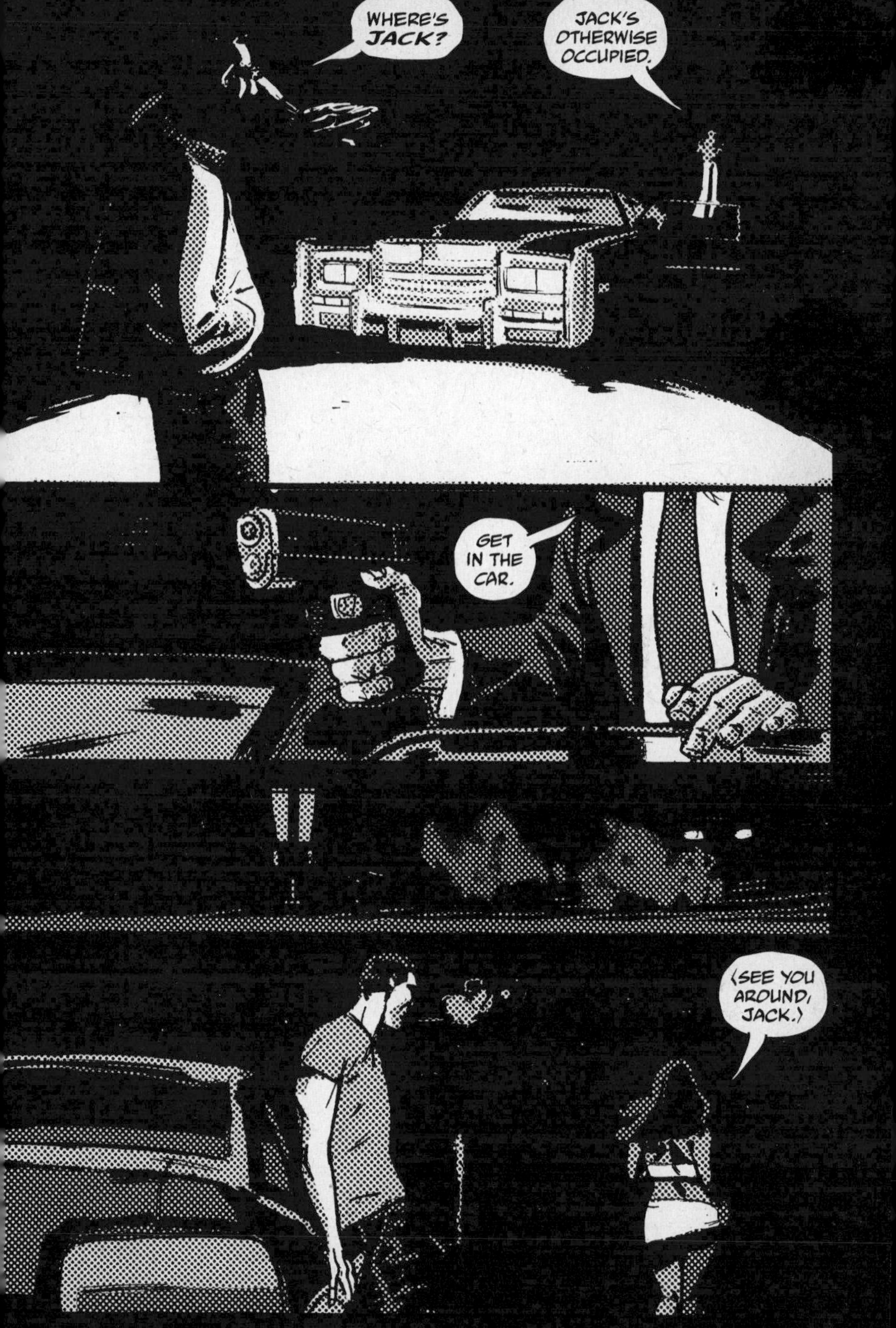
WHERE'S JACK?
JACK'S OTHERWISE OCCUPIED.
GET IN THE CAR.
‹SEE YOU AROUND, JACK.›

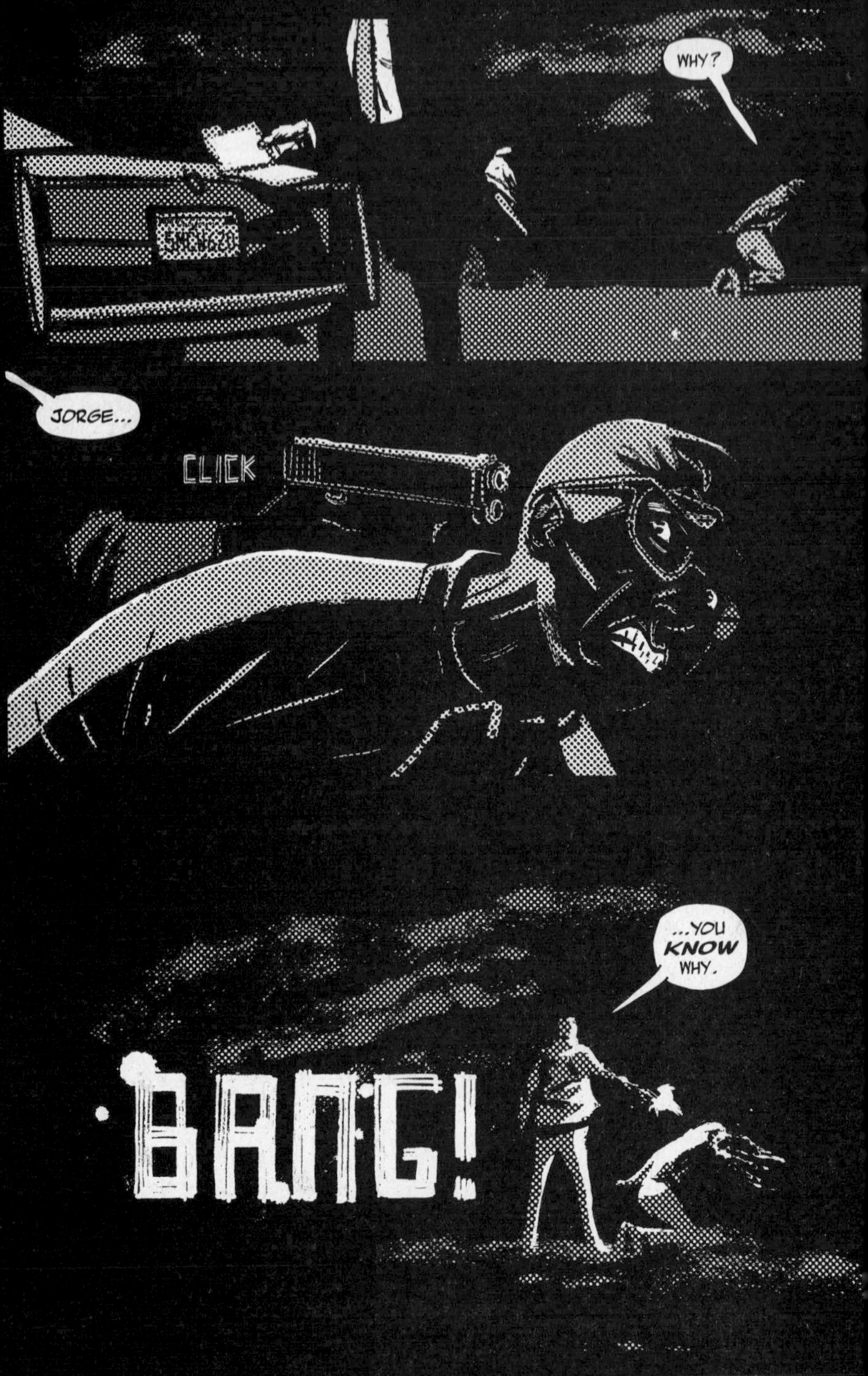
WHY?
JORGE...
CLICK
...YOU KNOW WHY.
BANG!

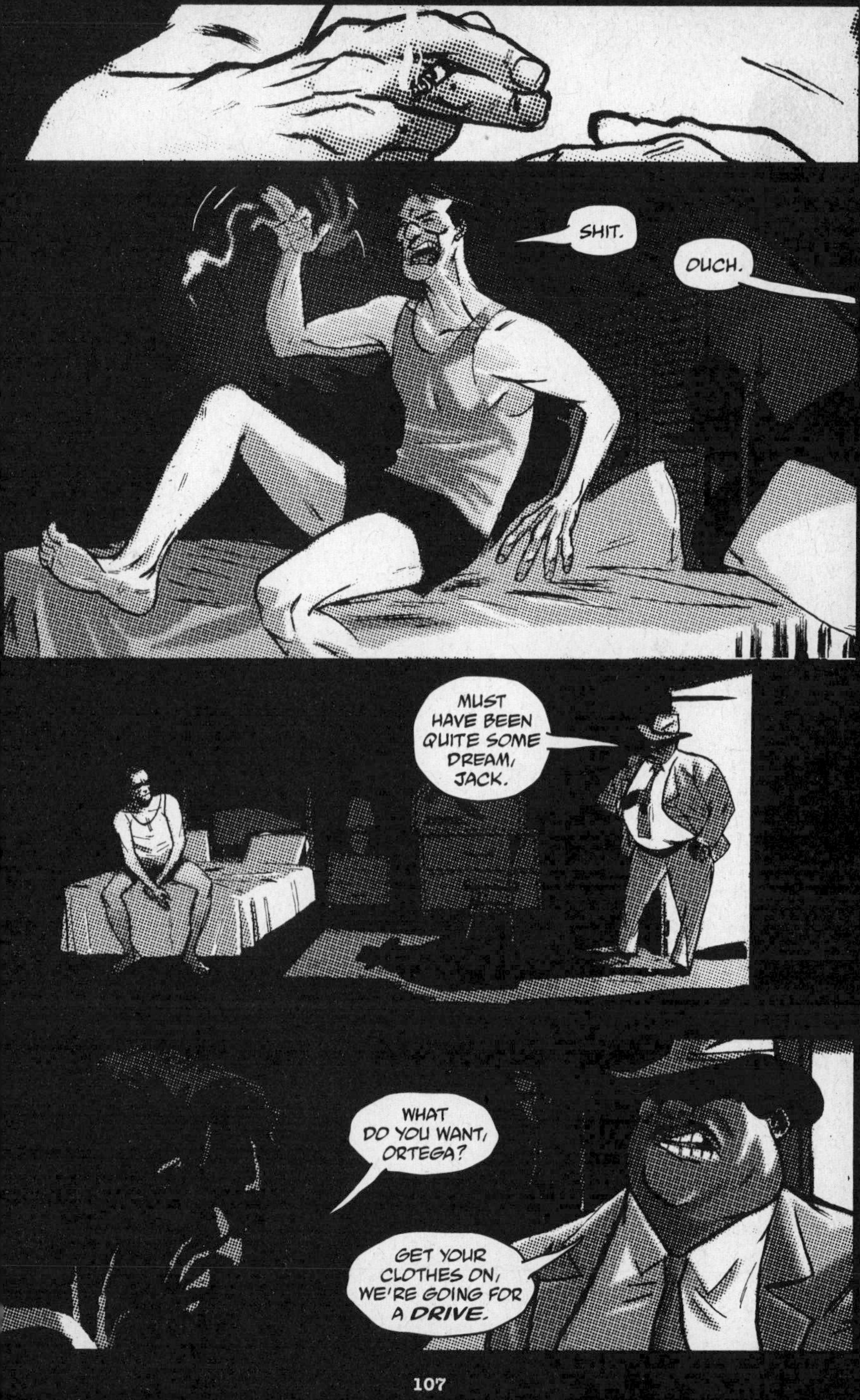
SHIT.
OUCH.
MUST HAVE BEEN QUITE SOME DREAM, JACK.
WHAT DO YOU WANT, ORTEGA?
GET YOUR CLOTHES ON, WE'RE GOING FOR A **DRIVE.**

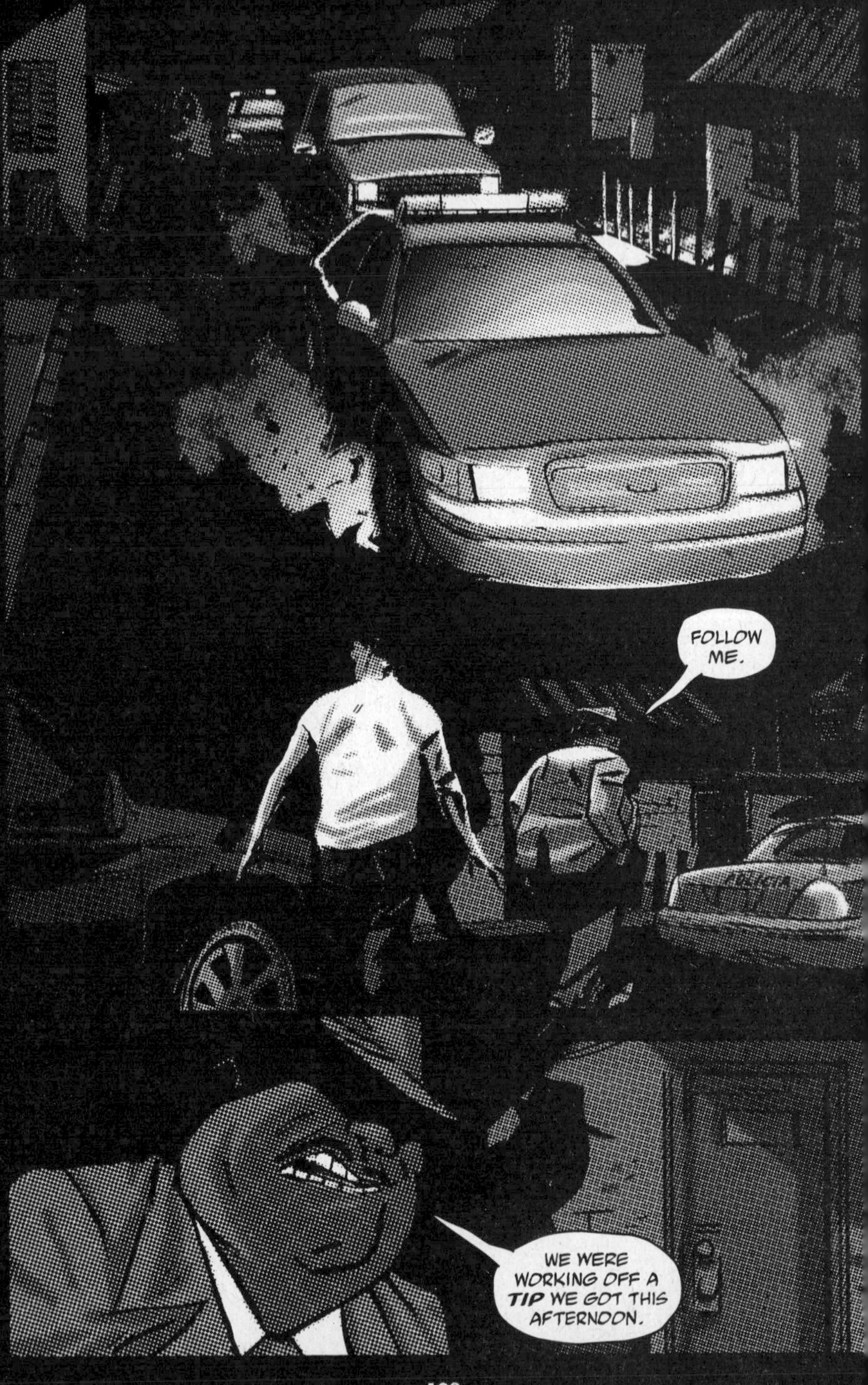
FOLLOW ME.
WE WERE WORKING OFF A TIP WE GOT THIS AFTERNOON.

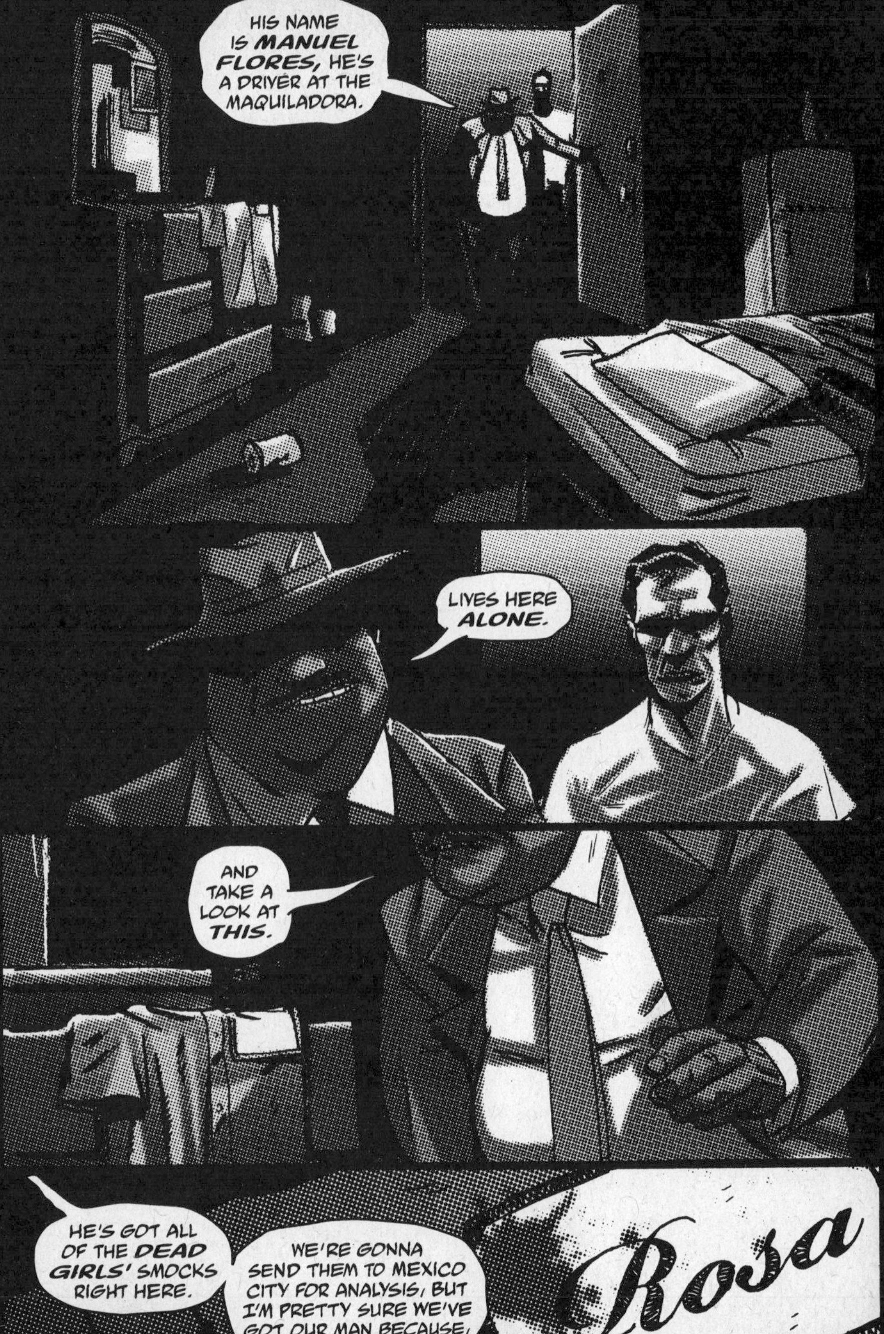

HIS NAME IS MANUEL FLORES, HE'S A DRIVER AT THE MAQUILADORA.
LIVES HERE ALONE.
AND TAKE A LOOK AT THIS.
HE'S GOT ALL OF THE DEAD GIRLS' SMOCKS RIGHT HERE.
WE'RE GONNA SEND THEM TO MEXICO CITY FOR ANALYSIS, BUT I'M PRETTY SURE WE'VE GOT OUR MAN BECAUSE, GET THIS...
Rosa

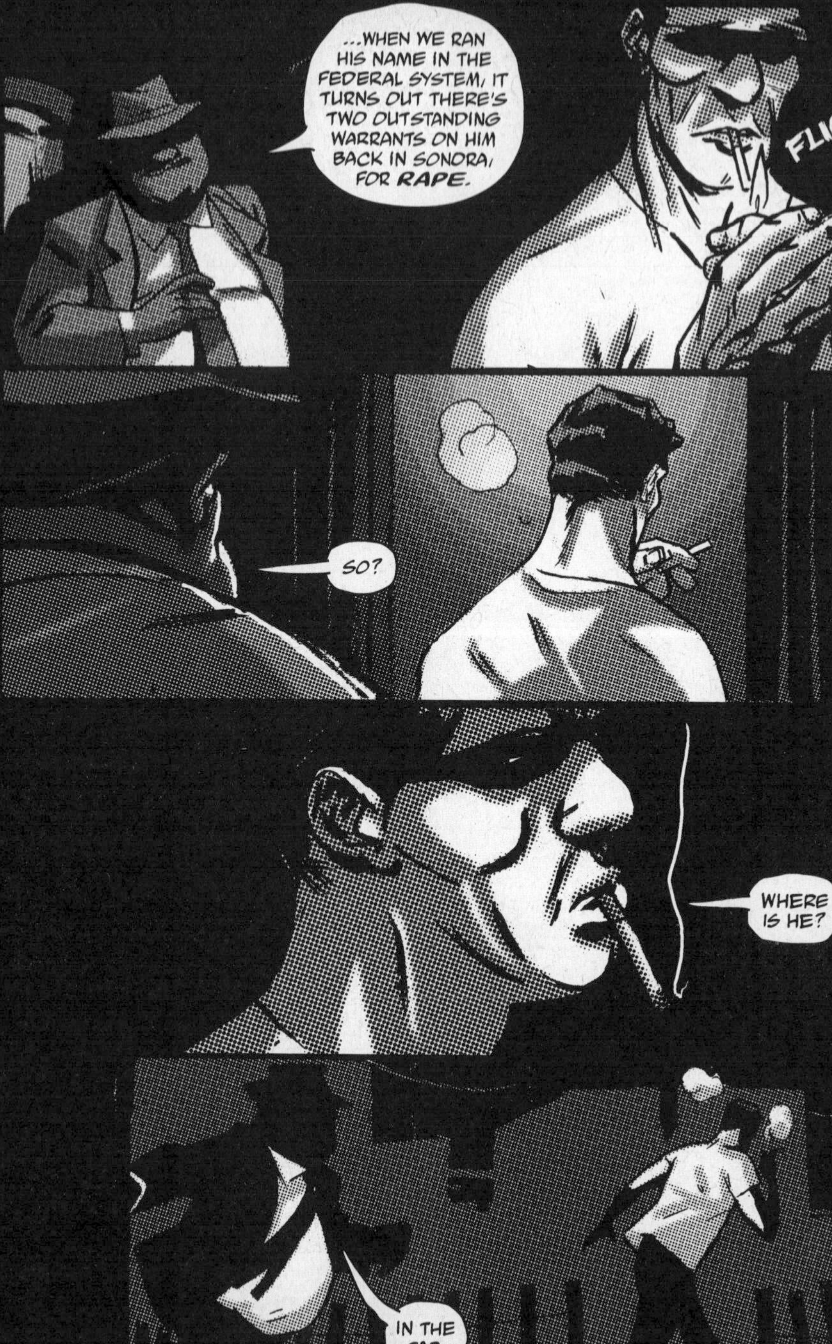
...WHEN WE RAN HIS NAME IN THE FEDERAL SYSTEM, IT TURNS OUT THERE'S TWO OUTSTANDING WARRANTS ON HIM BACK IN SONORA, FOR RAPE.
FLICK
SO?
WHERE IS HE?
IN THE CAR.

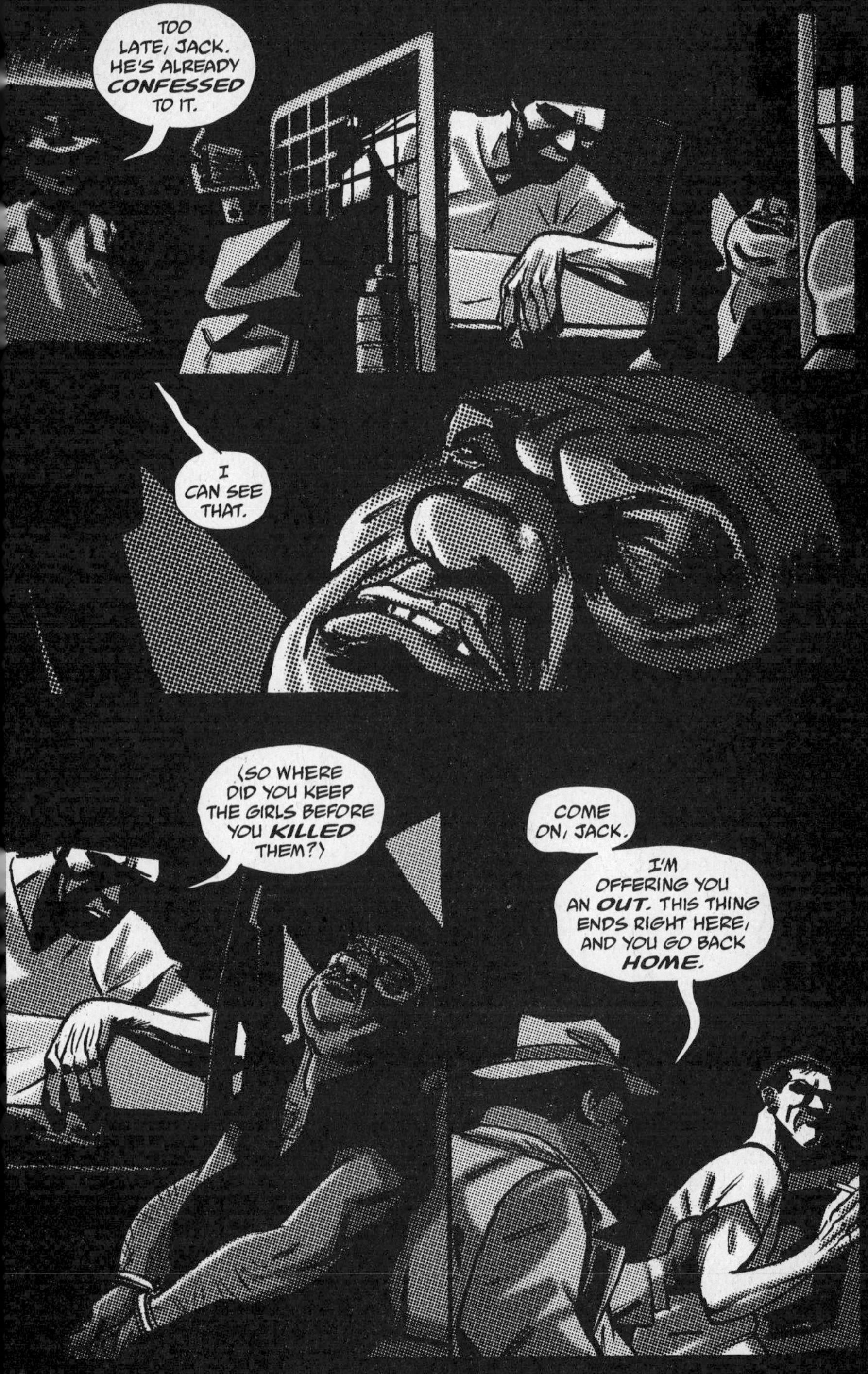
TOO LATE, JACK. HE'S ALREADY CONFESSED TO IT.
I CAN SEE THAT.
<SO WHERE DID YOU KEEP THE GIRLS BEFORE YOU KILLED THEM?>
COME ON, JACK.
I'M OFFERING YOU AN OUT. THIS THING ENDS RIGHT HERE, AND YOU GO BACK HOME.

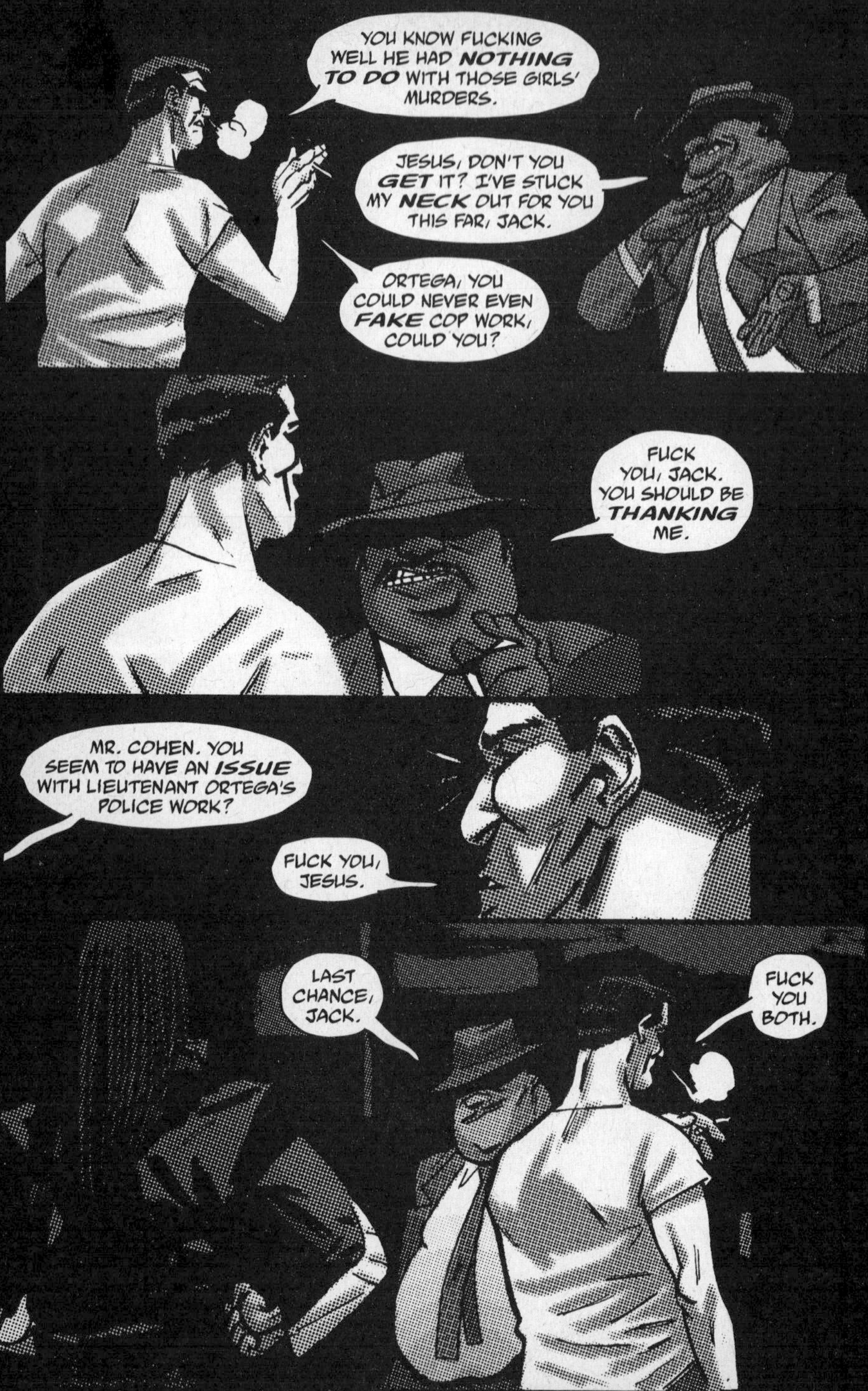
YOU KNOW FUCKING WELL HE HAD NOTHING TO DO WITH THOSE GIRLS' MURDERS.
JESUS, DON'T YOU GET IT? I'VE STUCK MY NECK OUT FOR YOU THIS FAR, JACK.
ORTEGA, YOU COULD NEVER EVEN FAKE COP WORK, COULD YOU?
FUCK YOU, JACK. YOU SHOULD BE THANKING ME.
MR. COHEN. YOU SEEM TO HAVE AN ISSUE WITH LIEUTENANT ORTEGA'S POLICE WORK?
FUCK YOU, JESUS.
LAST CHANCE, JACK.
FUCK YOU BOTH.

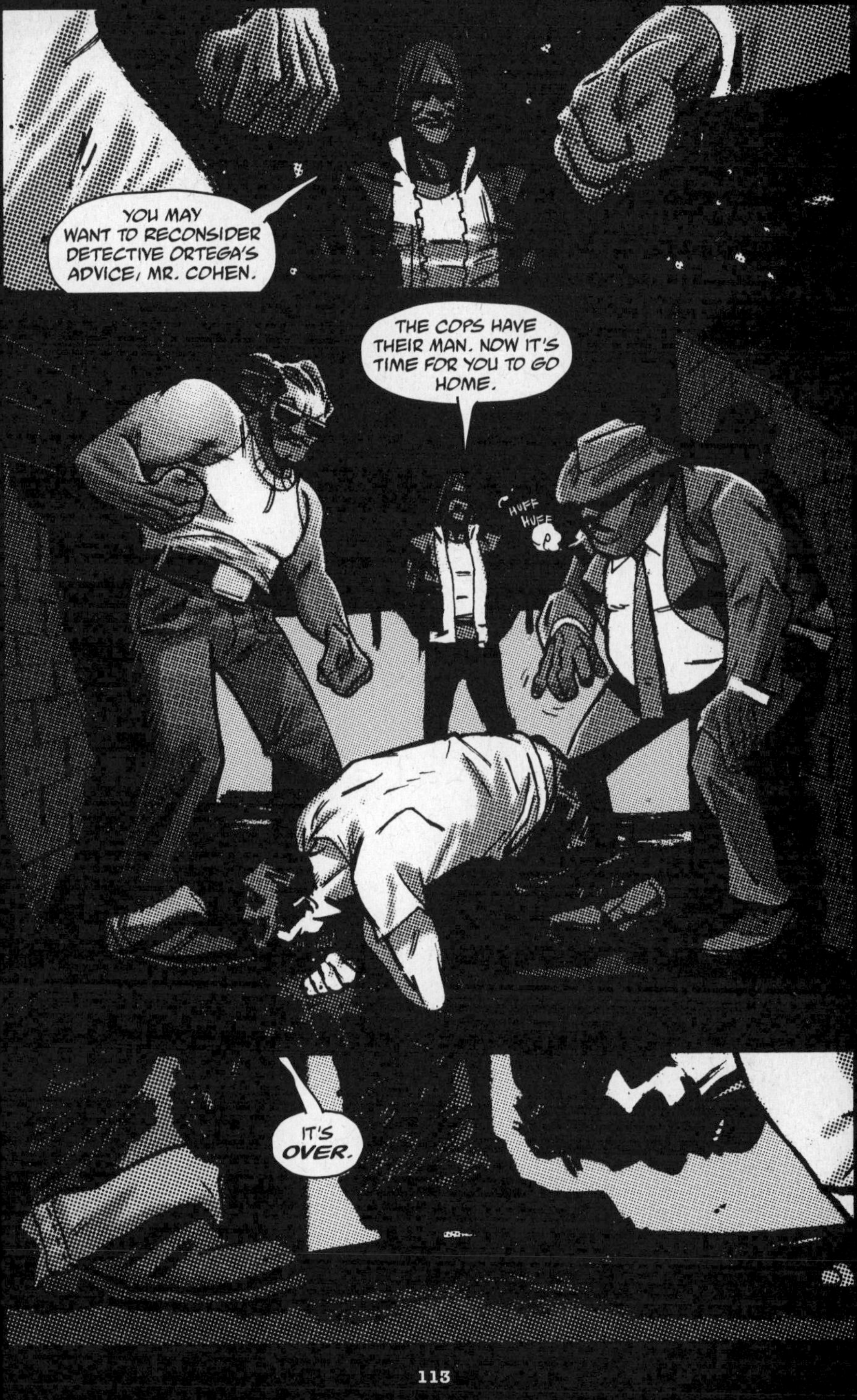
YOU MAY WANT TO RECONSIDER DETECTIVE ORTEGA'S ADVICE, MR. COHEN.
THE COPS HAVE THEIR MAN. NOW IT'S TIME FOR YOU TO GO HOME.
HUFF HUFF
IT'S OVER.

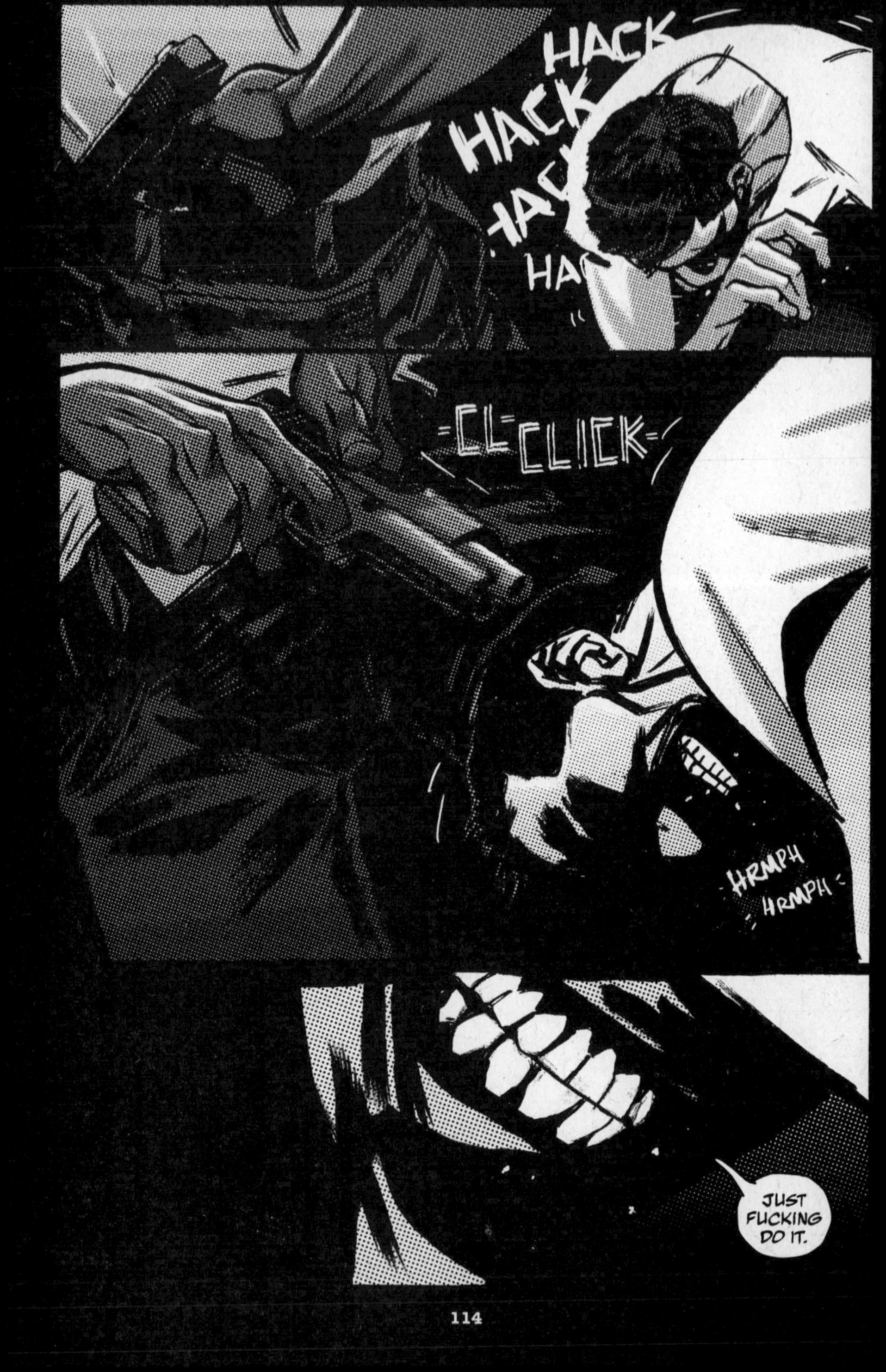
HACK
HACK
HAC
CL CLICK
HRMPH
HRMPH
JUST FUCKING DO IT.

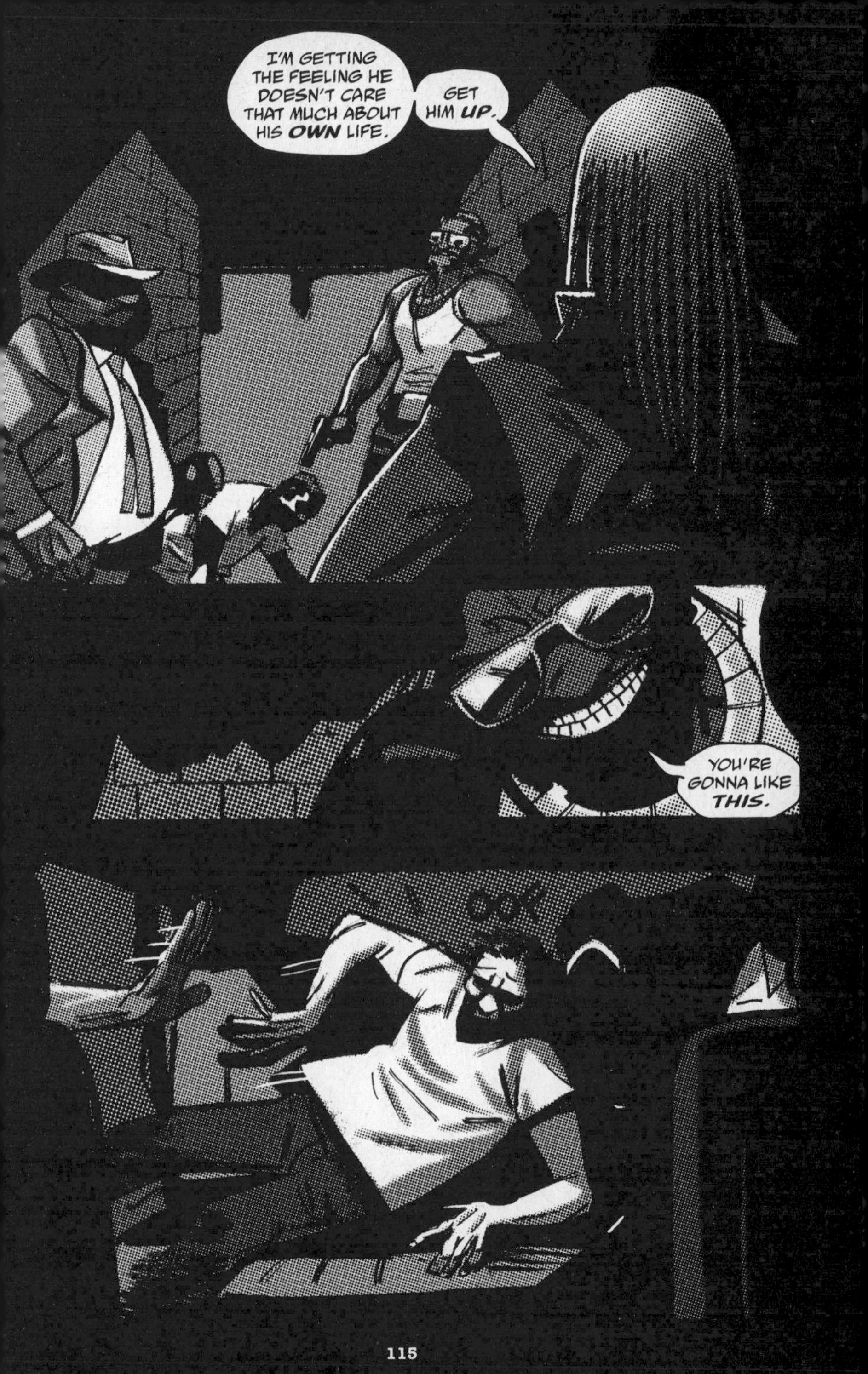
I'M GETTING THE FEELING HE DOESN'T CARE THAT MUCH ABOUT HIS OWN LIFE.
GET HIM UP.
YOU'RE GONNA LIKE THIS.

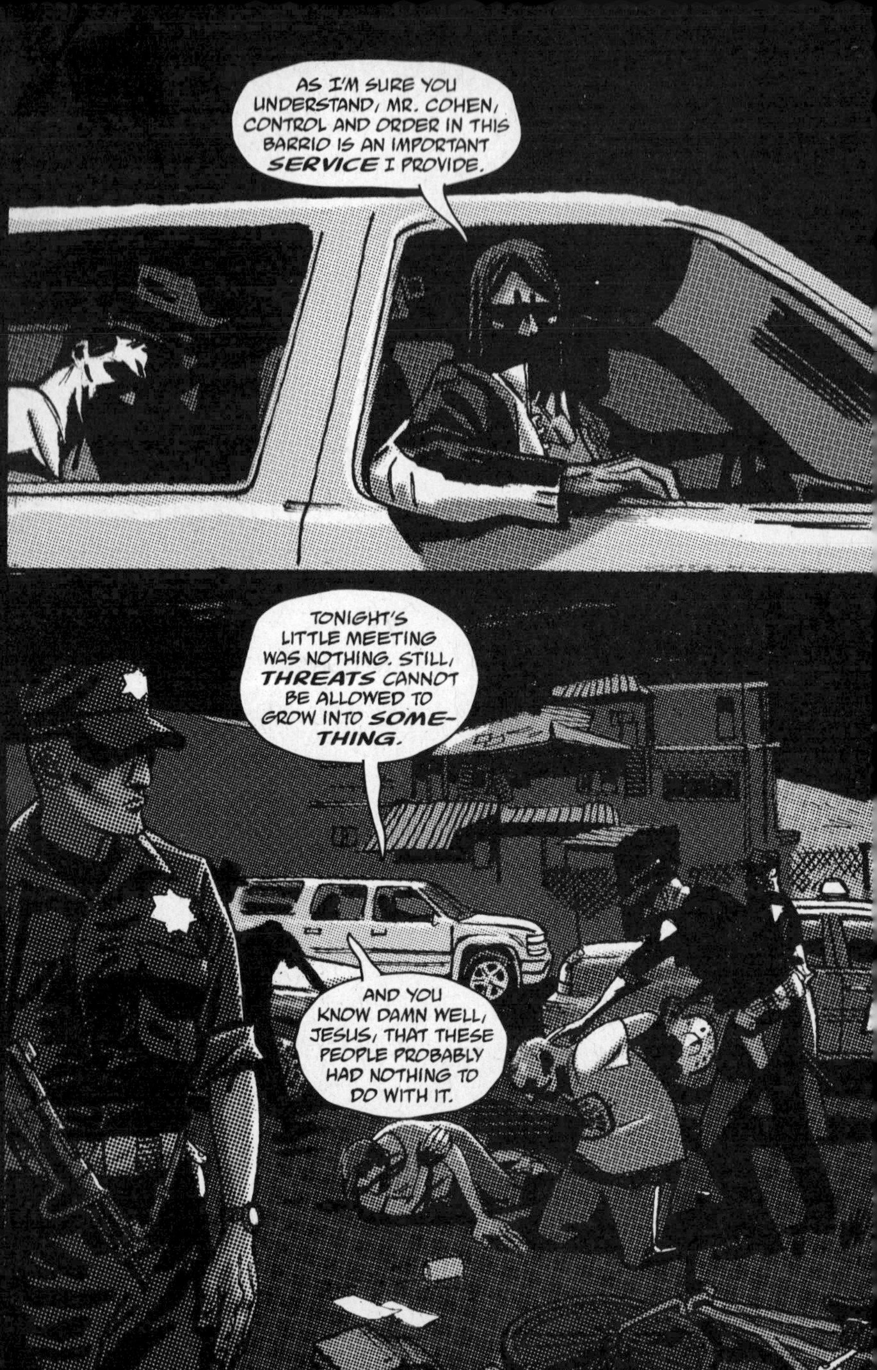
AS I'M SURE YOU UNDERSTAND, MR. COHEN, CONTROL AND ORDER IN THIS BARRIO IS AN IMPORTANT SERVICE I PROVIDE.
TONIGHT'S LITTLE MEETING WAS NOTHING. STILL, THREATS CANNOT BE ALLOWED TO GROW INTO SOME-THING.
AND YOU KNOW DAMN WELL, JESUS, THAT THESE PEOPLE PROBABLY HAD NOTHING TO DO WITH IT.

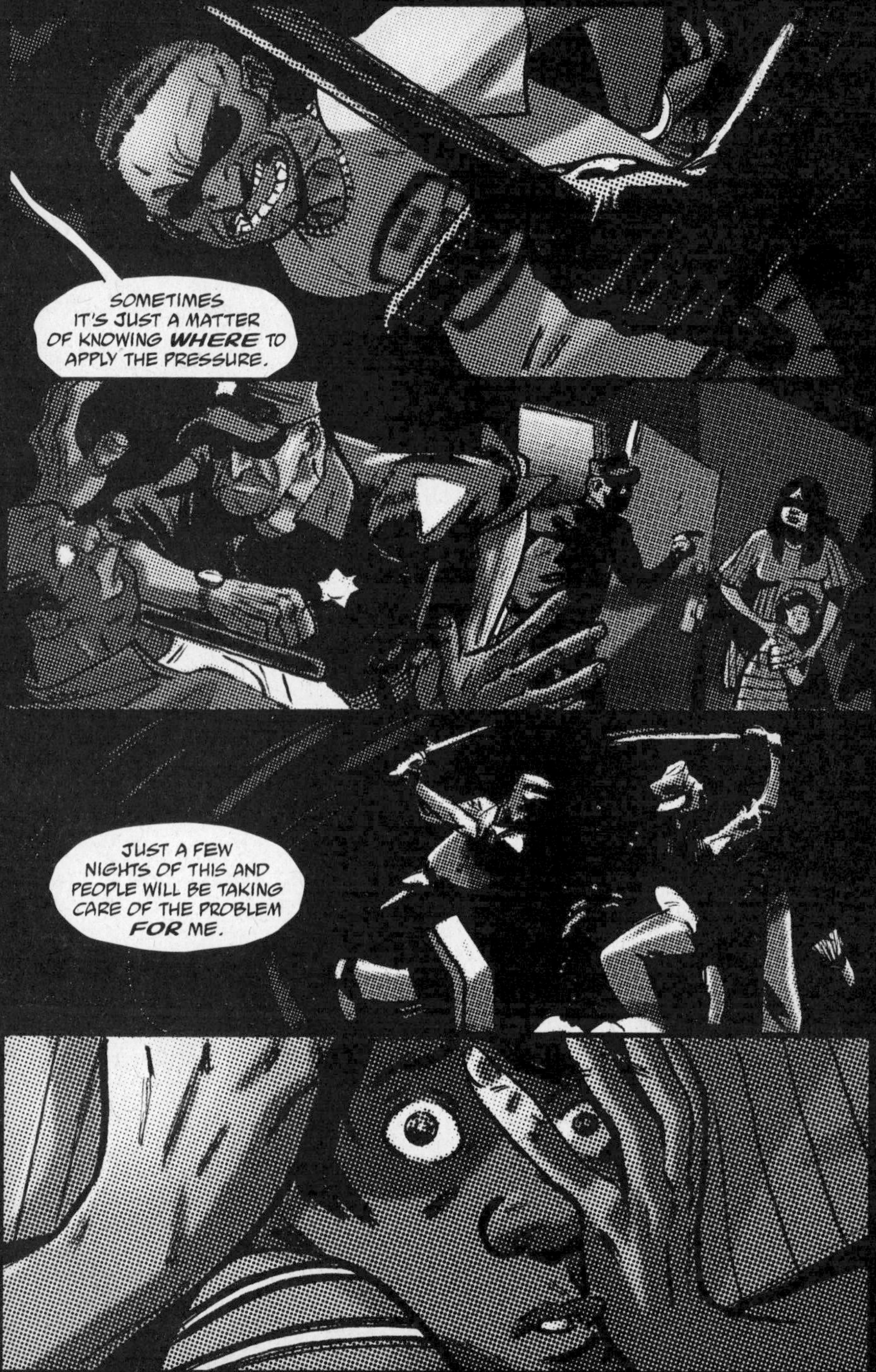
SOMETIMES IT'S JUST A MATTER OF KNOWING **WHERE** TO APPLY THE PRESSURE.
JUST A FEW NIGHTS OF THIS AND PEOPLE WILL BE TAKING CARE OF THE PROBLEM **FOR** ME.

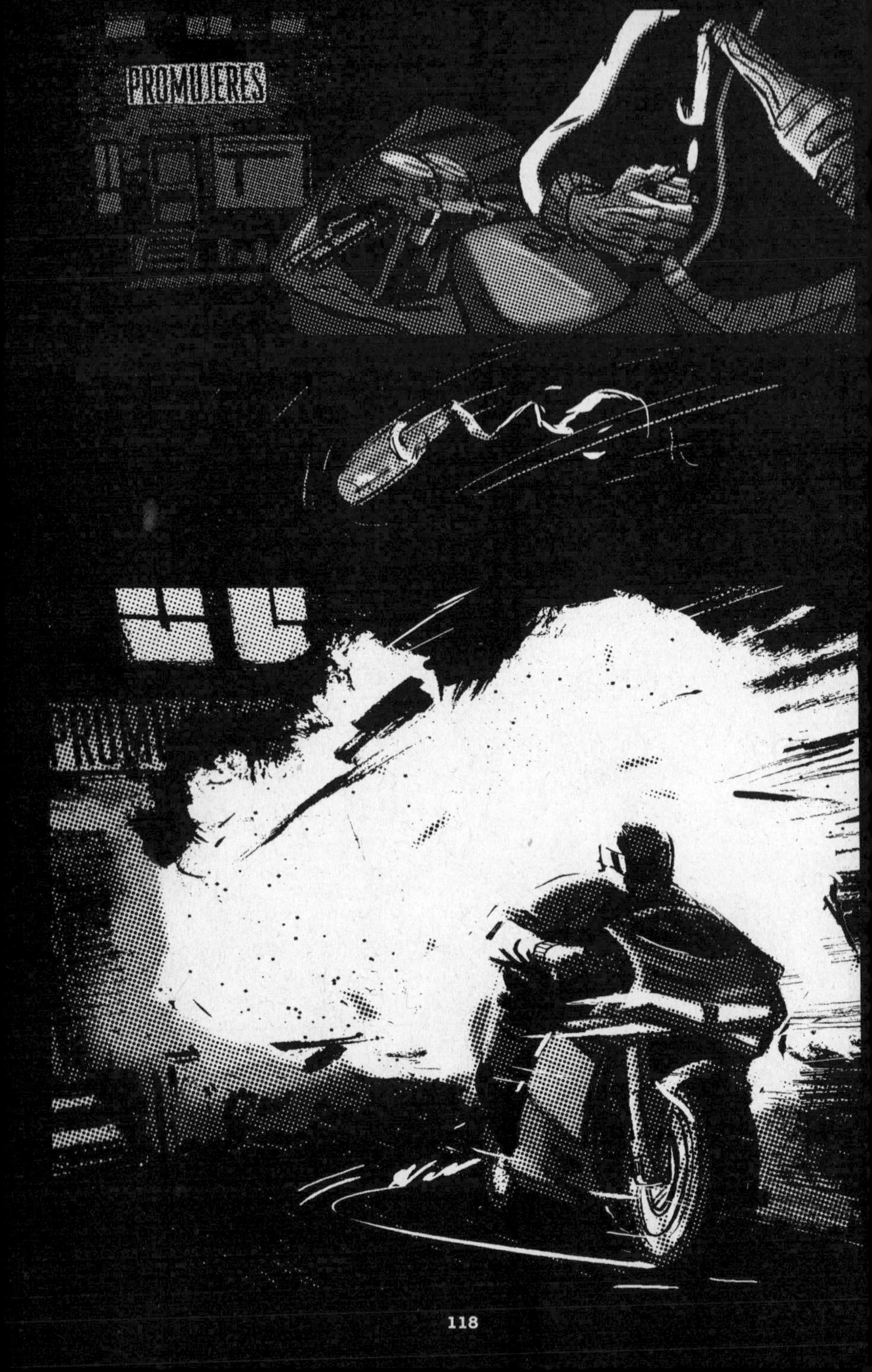
PROMUJERES

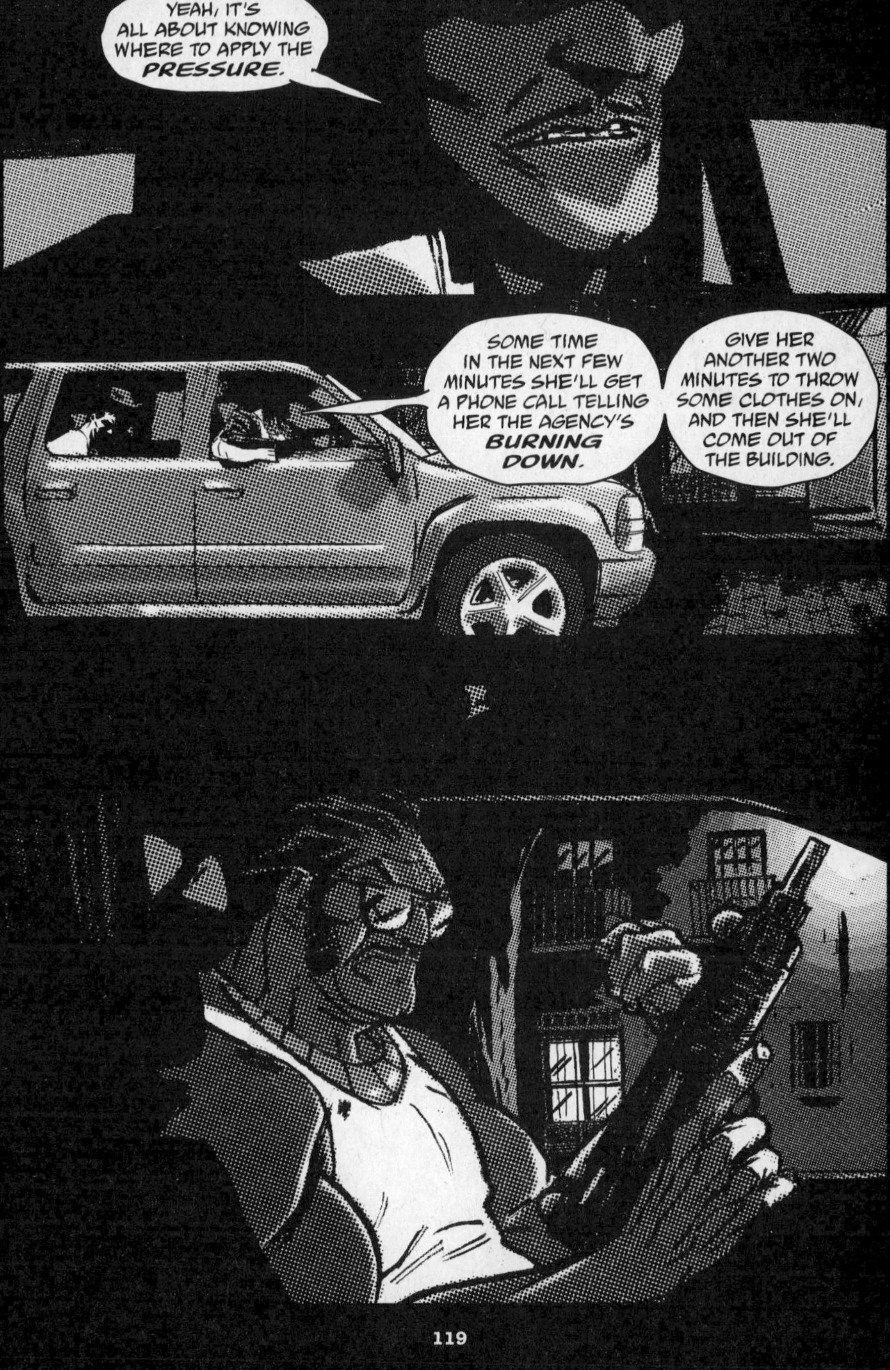
YEAH, IT'S ALL ABOUT KNOWING WHERE TO APPLY THE PRESSURE.
SOME TIME IN THE NEXT FEW MINUTES SHE'LL GET A PHONE CALL TELLING HER THE AGENCY'S BURNING DOWN.
GIVE HER ANOTHER TWO MINUTES TO THROW SOME CLOTHES ON, AND THEN SHE'LL COME OUT OF THE BUILDING.

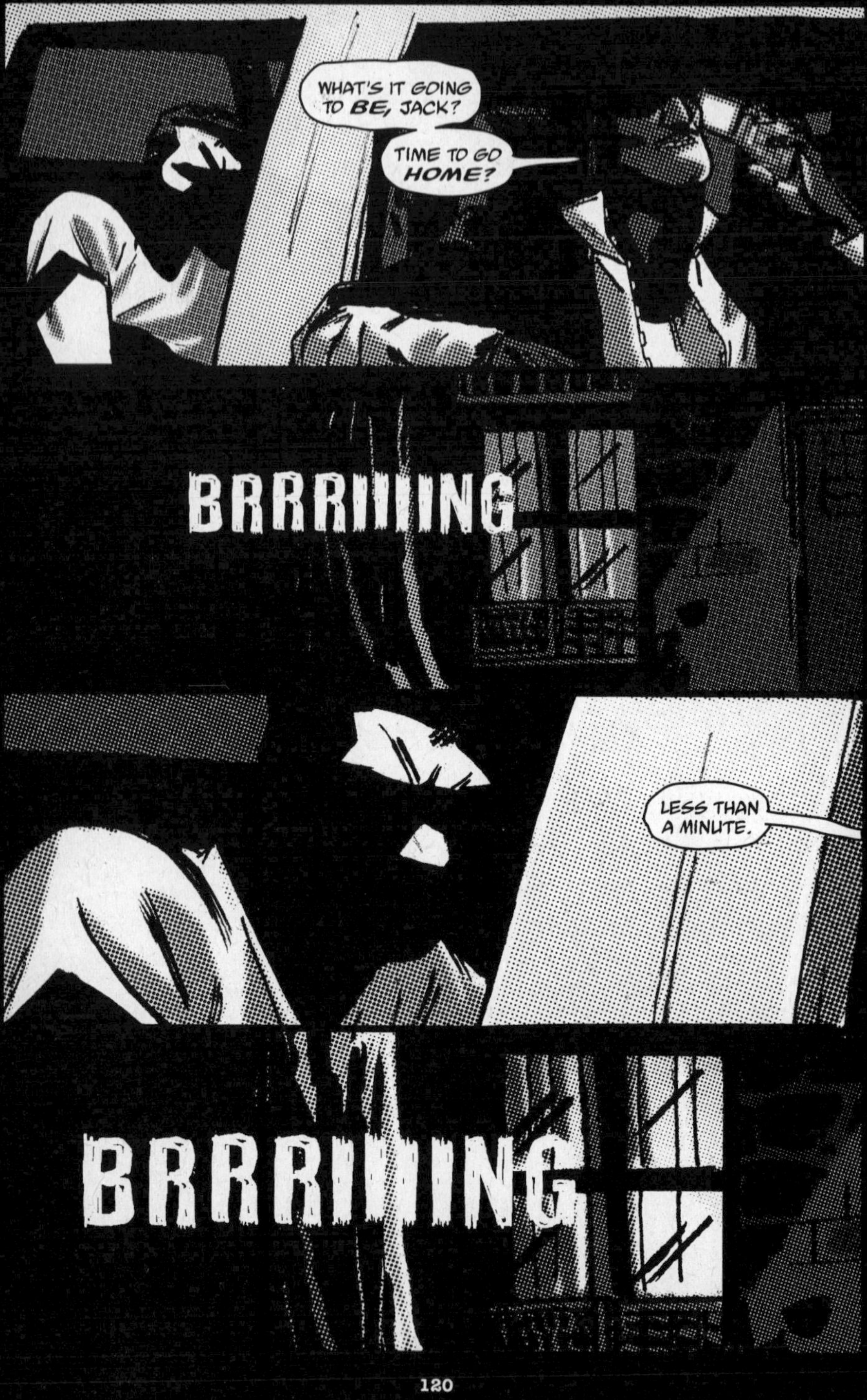
WHAT'S IT GOING TO BE, JACK?
TIME TO GO HOME?
BRRRIIIING
LESS THAN A MINUTE.
BRRRIIIING

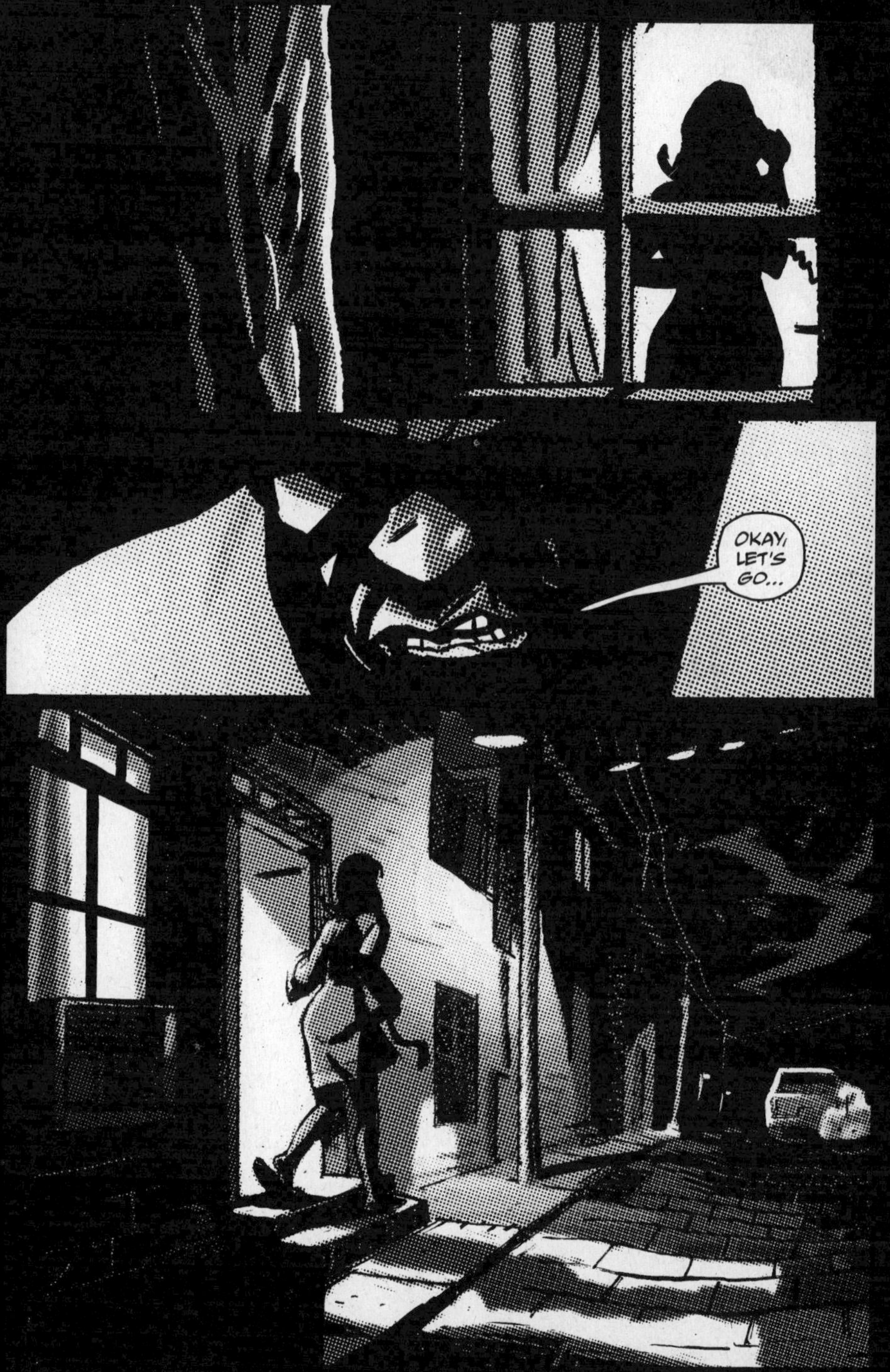
OKAY, LET'S GO...

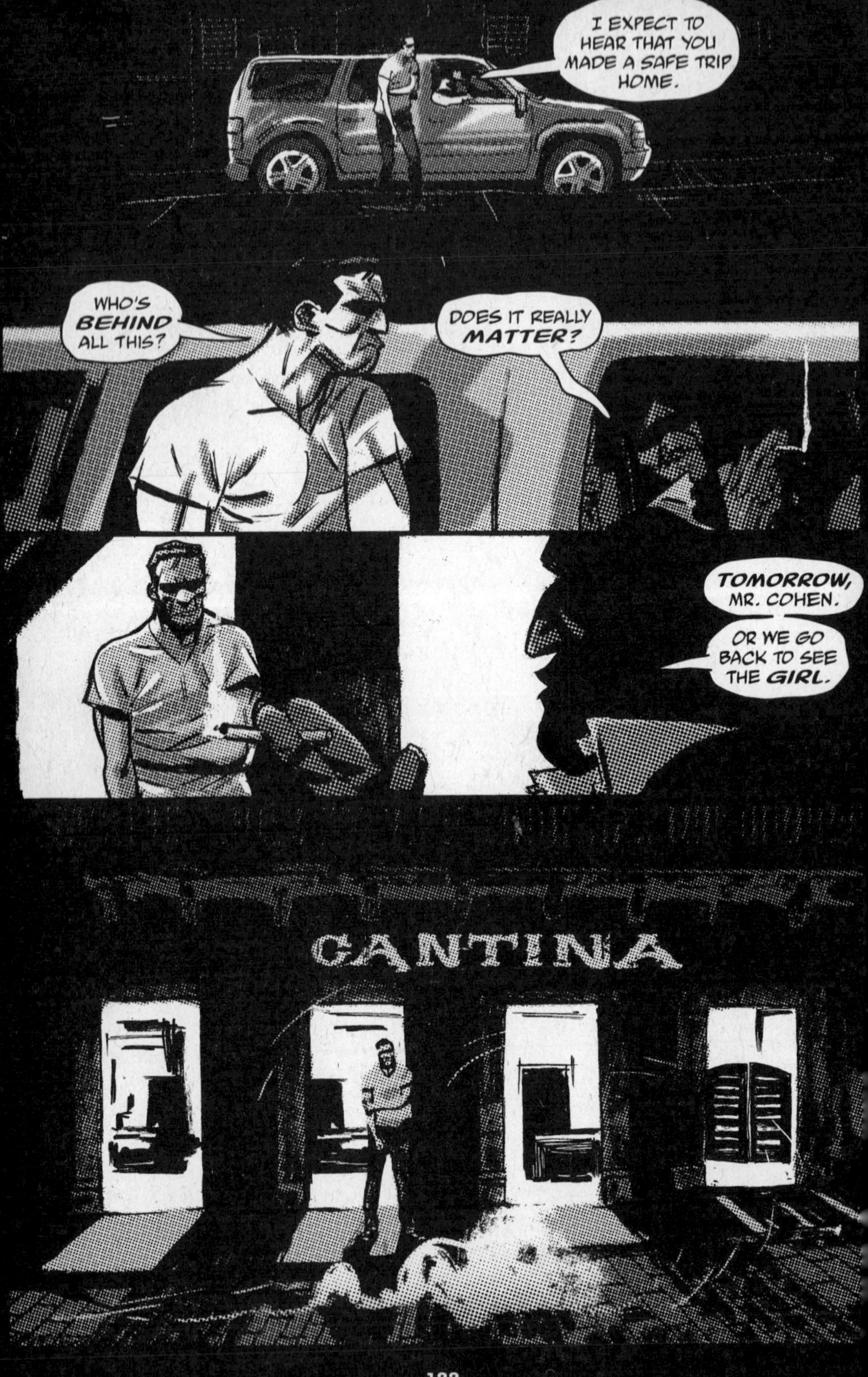
I EXPECT TO HEAR THAT YOU MADE A SAFE TRIP HOME.
WHO'S BEHIND ALL THIS?
DOES IT REALLY MATTER?
TOMORROW, MR. COHEN.
OR WE GO BACK TO SEE THE GIRL.
CANTINA

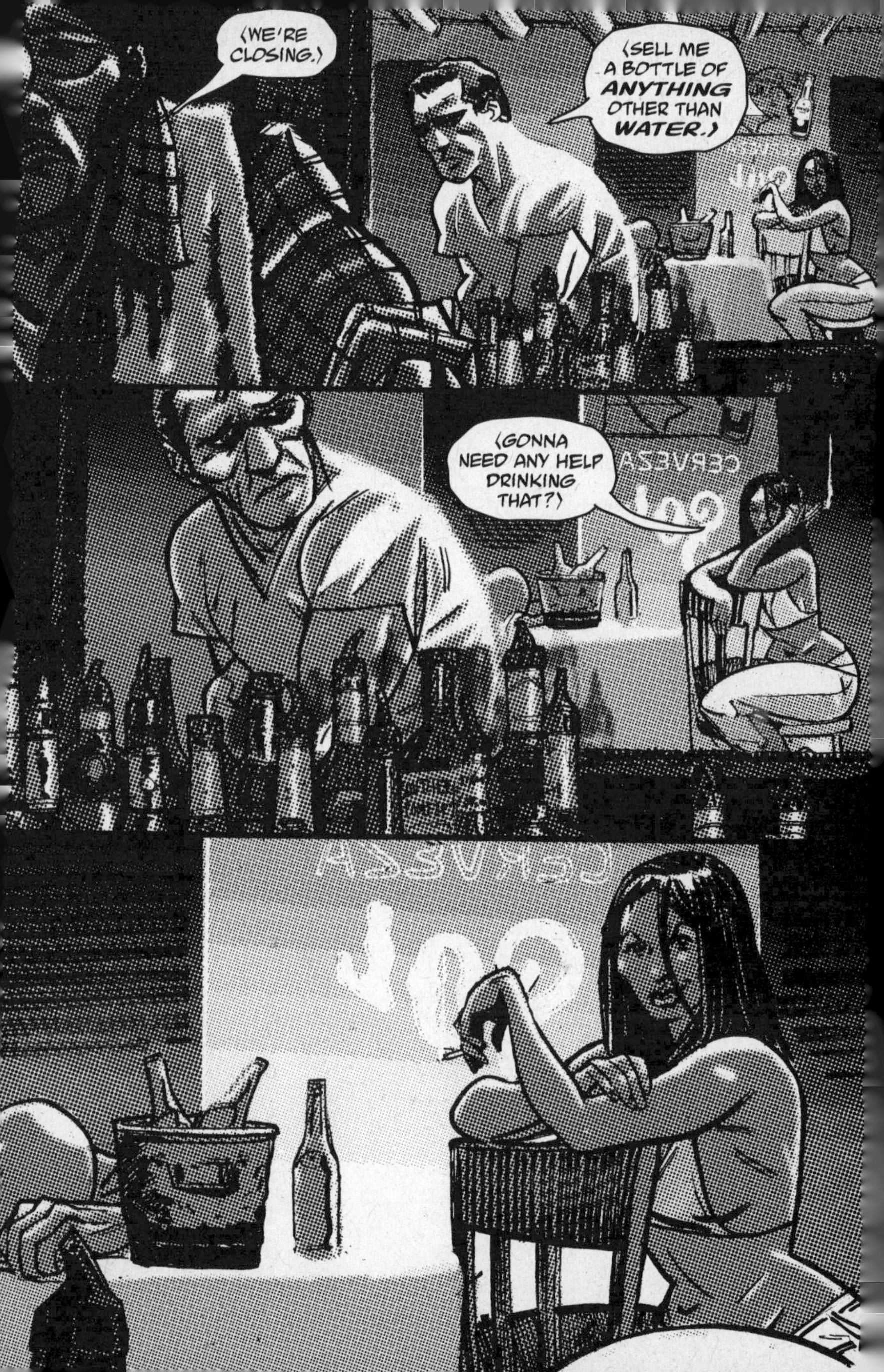
‹WE'RE CLOSING.›
‹SELL ME A BOTTLE OF ANYTHING OTHER THAN WATER.›
‹GONNA NEED ANY HELP DRINKING THAT?›

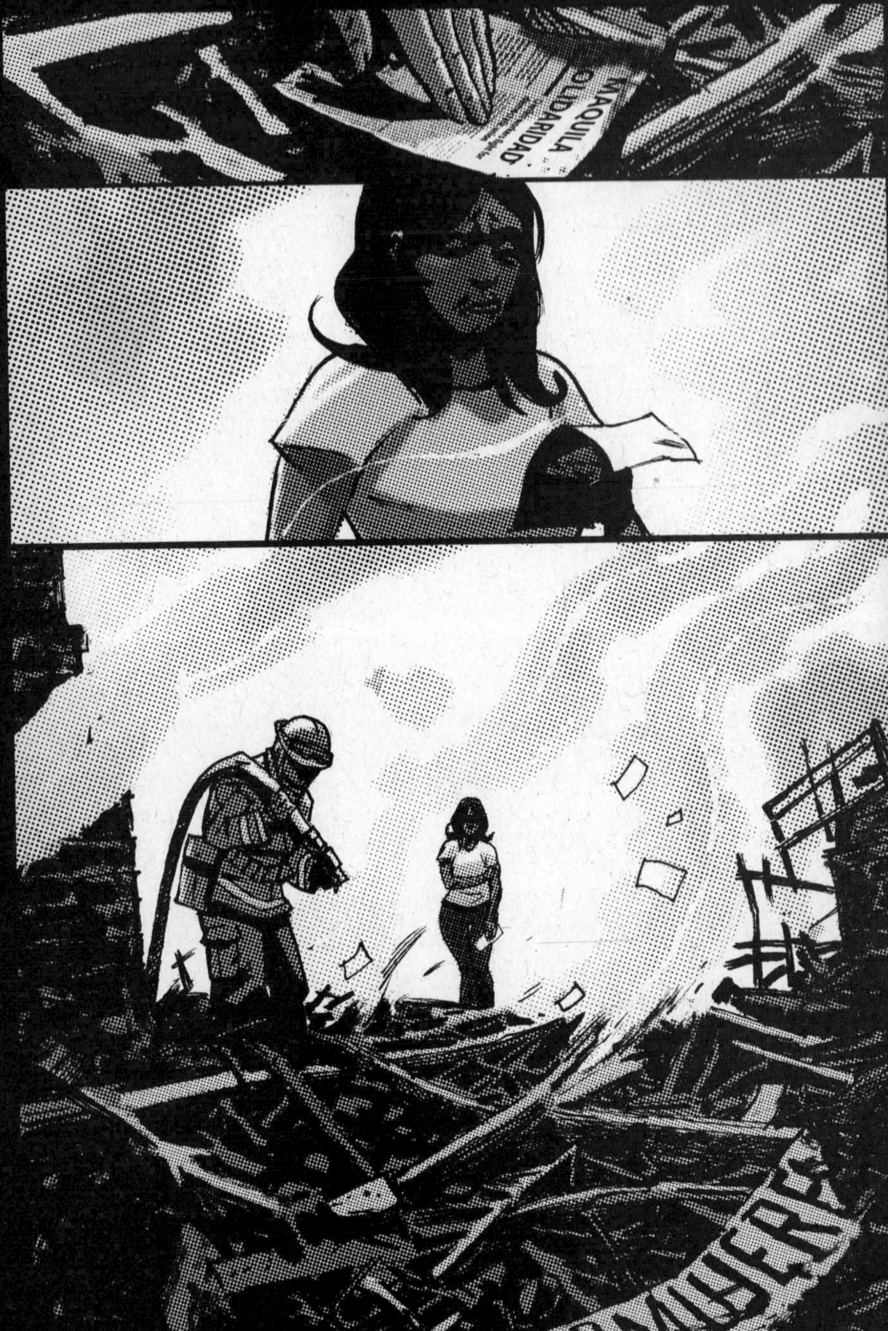
MAQUILA
OLIDARIDAD
ORO MUJERE

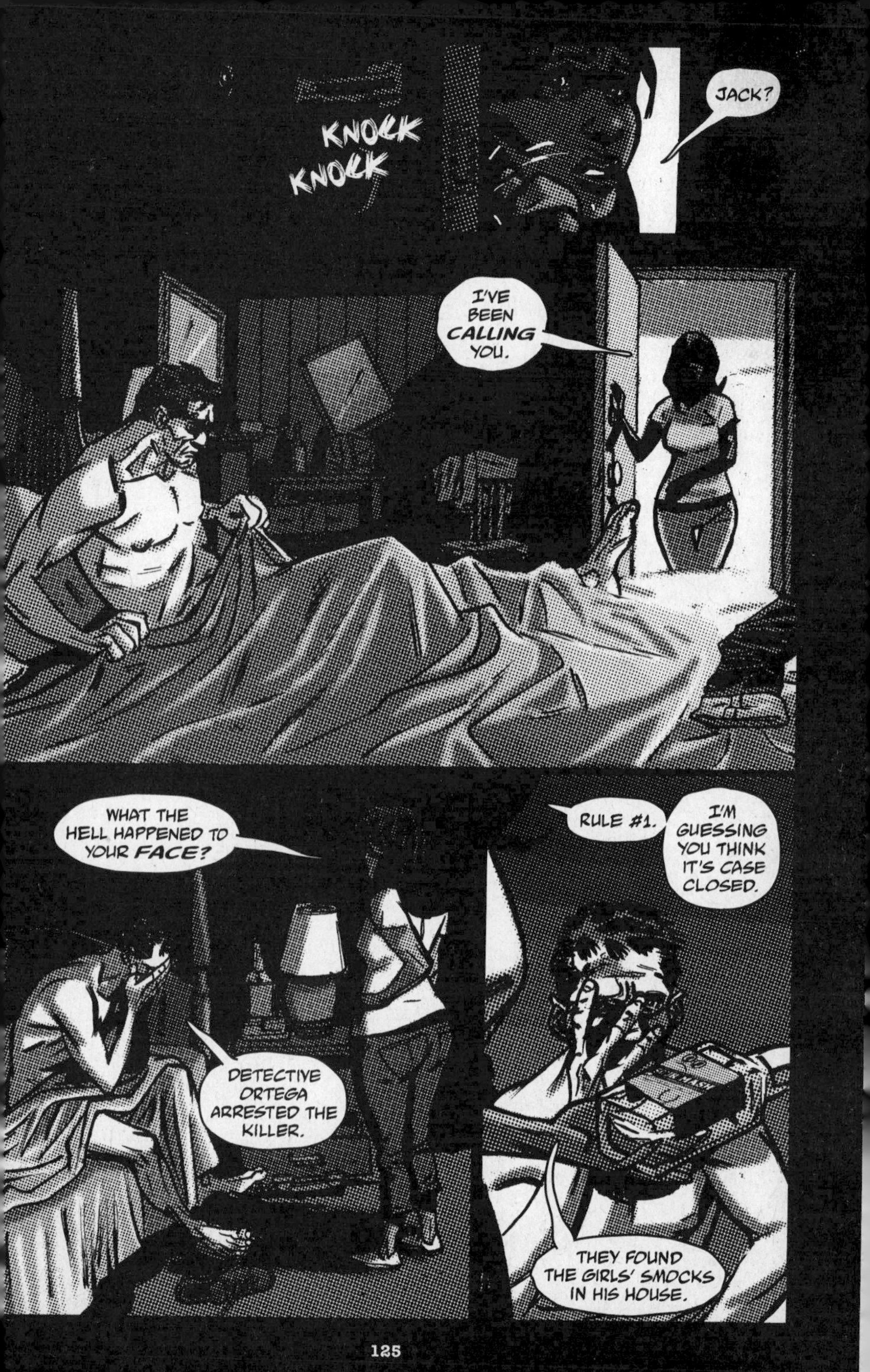
KNOCK
KNOCK
JACK?
I'VE BEEN CALLING YOU.
WHAT THE HELL HAPPENED TO YOUR FACE?
DETECTIVE ORTEGA ARRESTED THE KILLER.
RULE #1.
I'M GUESSING YOU THINK IT'S CASE CLOSED.
THEY FOUND THE GIRLS' SMOCKS IN HIS HOUSE.

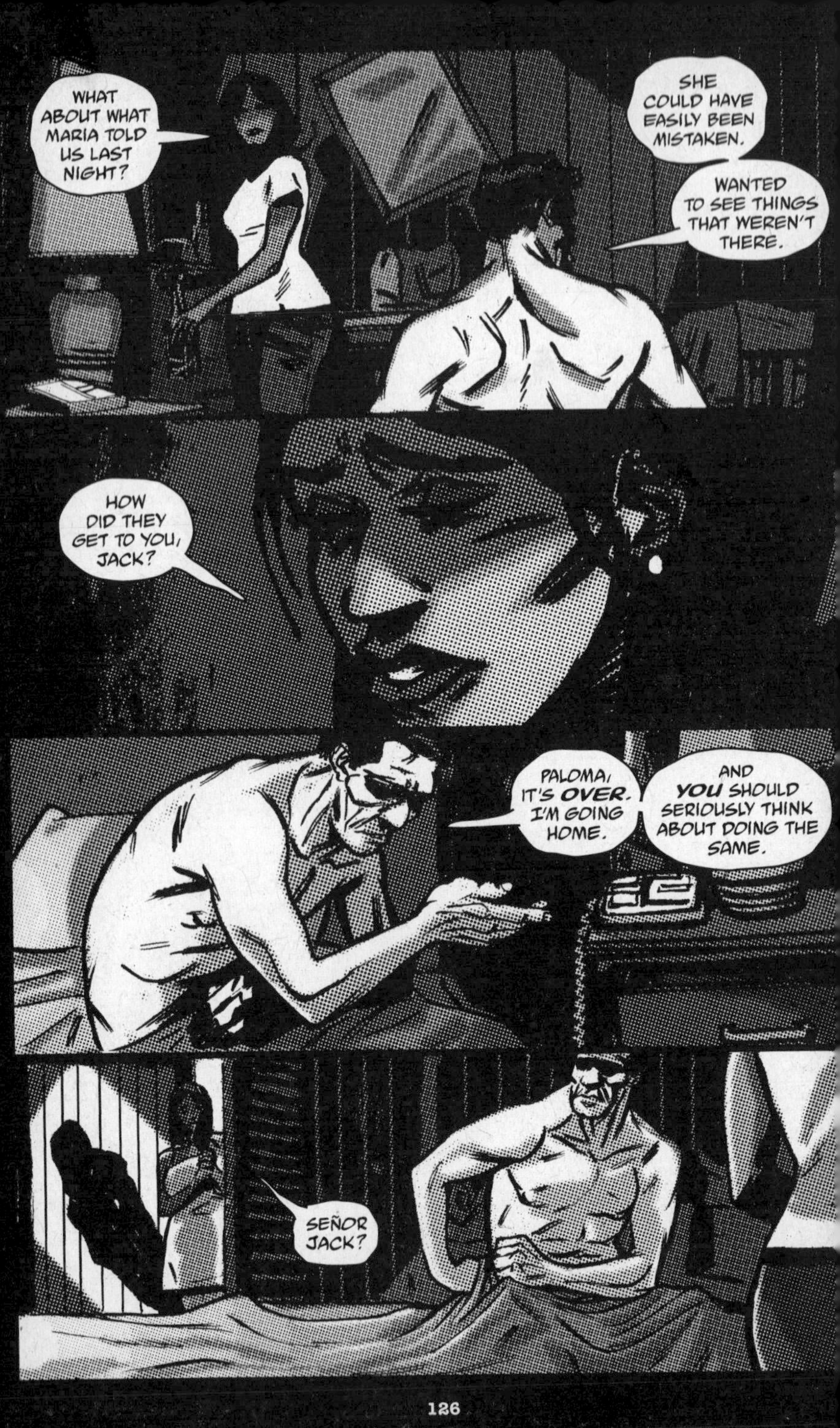
WHAT ABOUT WHAT MARIA TOLD US LAST NIGHT?
SHE COULD HAVE EASILY BEEN MISTAKEN.
WANTED TO SEE THINGS THAT WEREN'T THERE.
HOW DID THEY GET TO YOU, JACK?
PALOMA, IT'S **OVER**. I'M GOING HOME.
AND **YOU** SHOULD SERIOUSLY THINK ABOUT DOING THE SAME.
SEÑOR JACK?

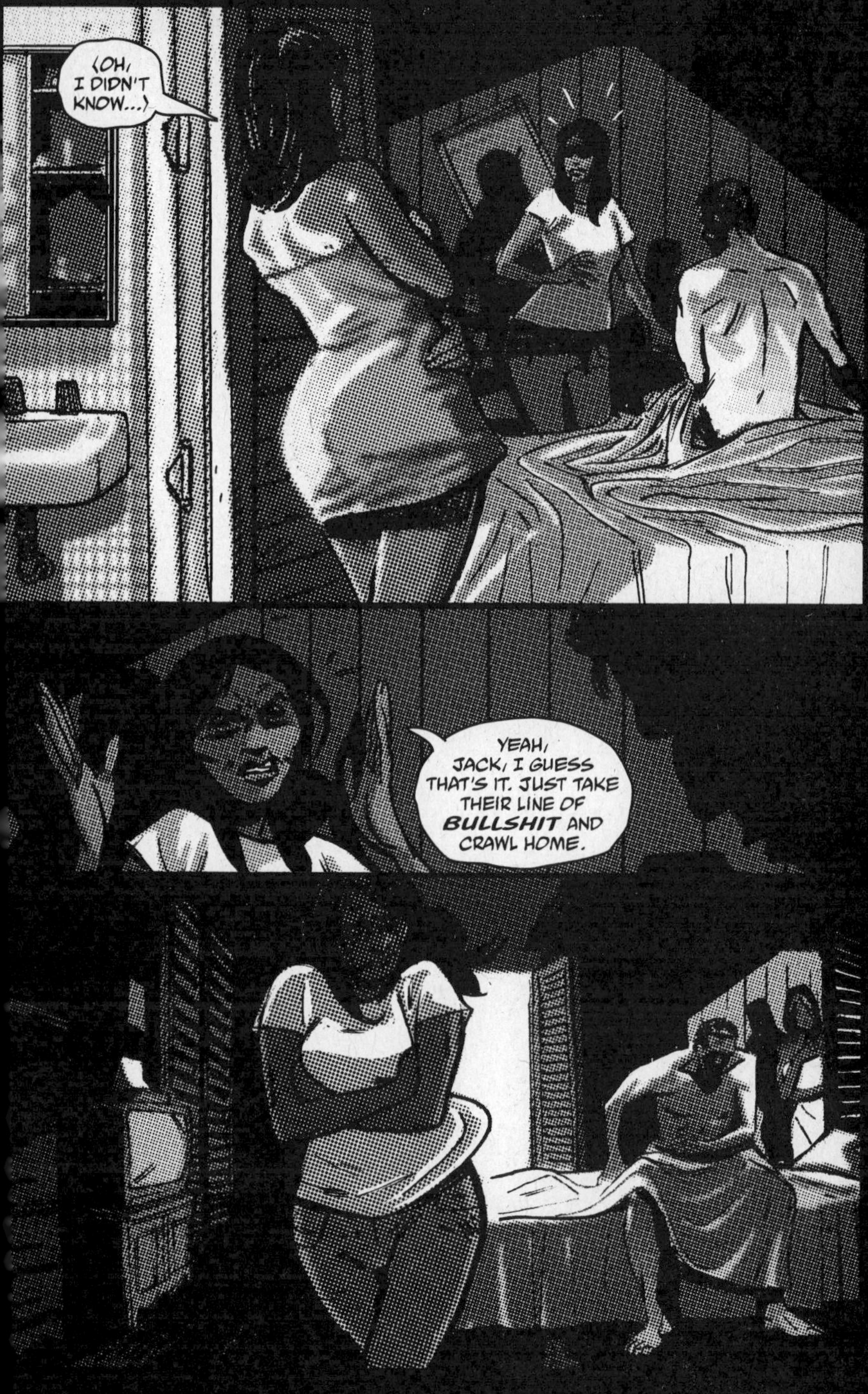

‹OH, I DIDN'T KNOW...›
YEAH, JACK, I GUESS THAT'S IT. JUST TAKE THEIR LINE OF BULLSHIT AND CRAWL HOME.

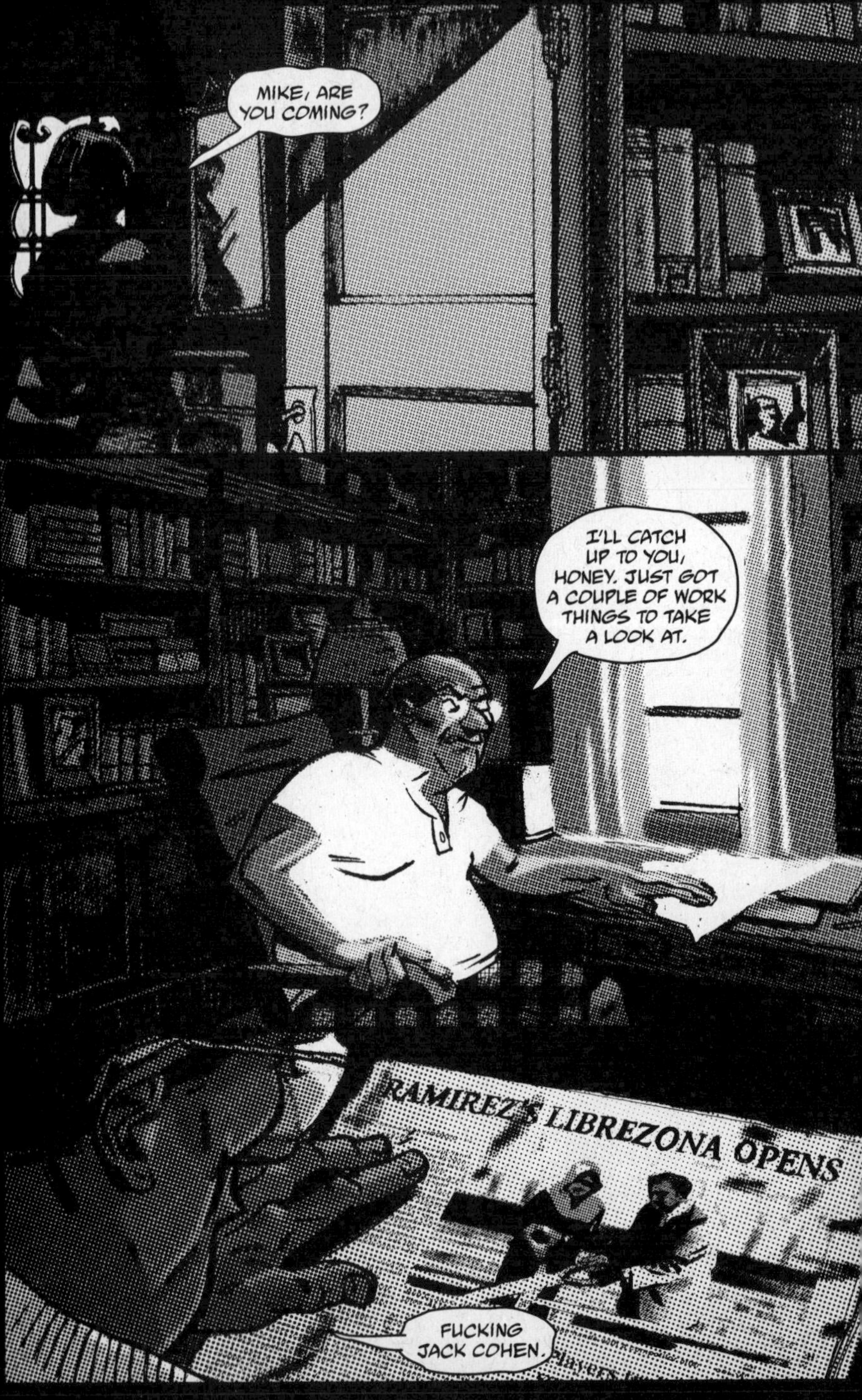
MIKE, ARE YOU COMING?
I'LL CATCH UP TO YOU, HONEY. JUST GOT A COUPLE OF WORK THINGS TO TAKE A LOOK AT.
RAMIREZ'S LIBREZONA OPENS
FUCKING JACK COHEN.

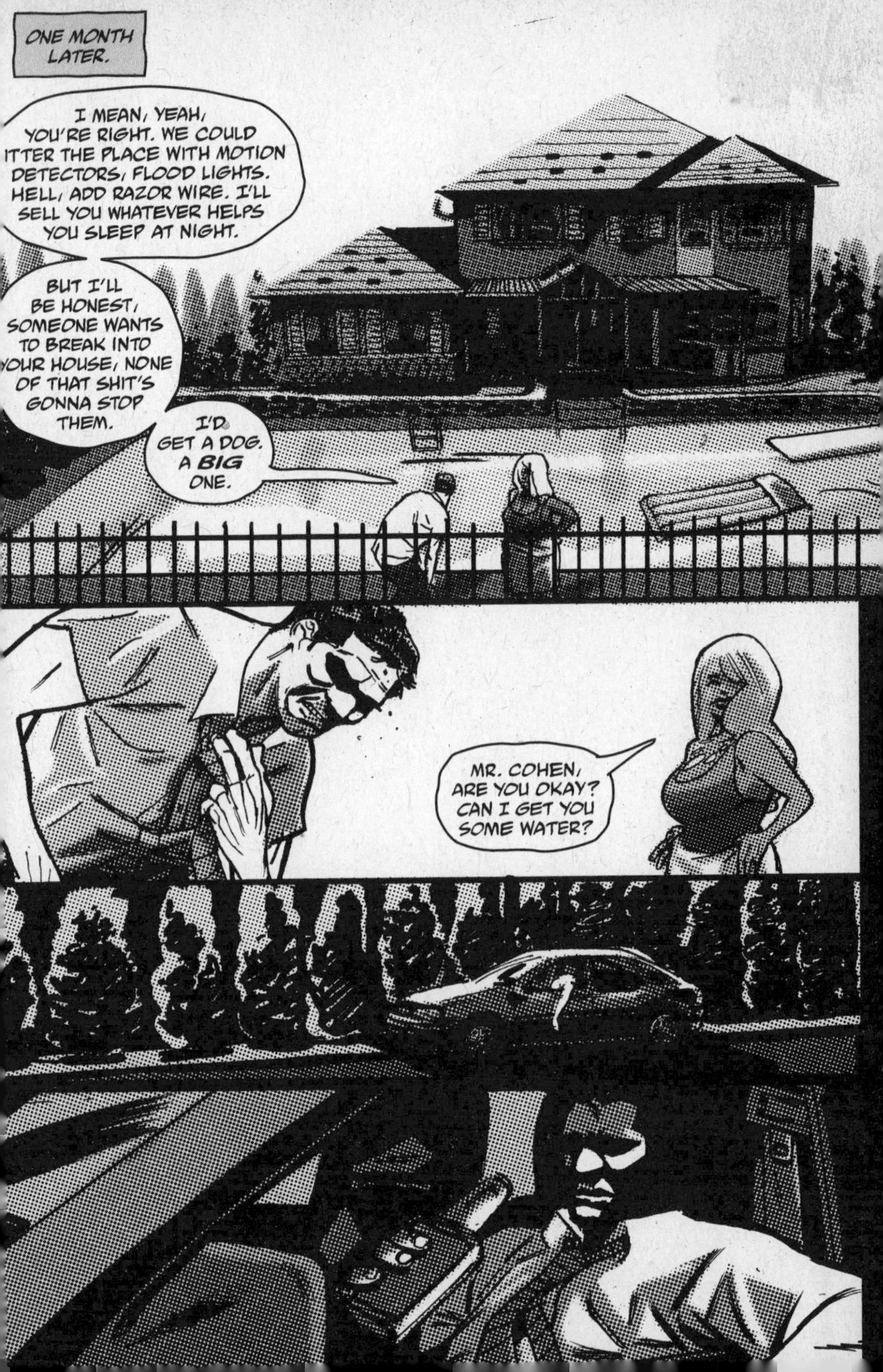
ONE MONTH LATER.
I MEAN, YEAH, YOU'RE RIGHT. WE COULD ITTER THE PLACE WITH MOTION DETECTORS, FLOOD LIGHTS. HELL, ADD RAZOR WIRE. I'LL SELL YOU WHATEVER HELPS YOU SLEEP AT NIGHT.
BUT I'LL BE HONEST, SOMEONE WANTS TO BREAK INTO YOUR HOUSE, NONE OF THAT SHIT'S GONNA STOP THEM.
I'D GET A DOG. A BIG ONE.
MR. COHEN, ARE YOU OKAY? CAN I GET YOU SOME WATER?

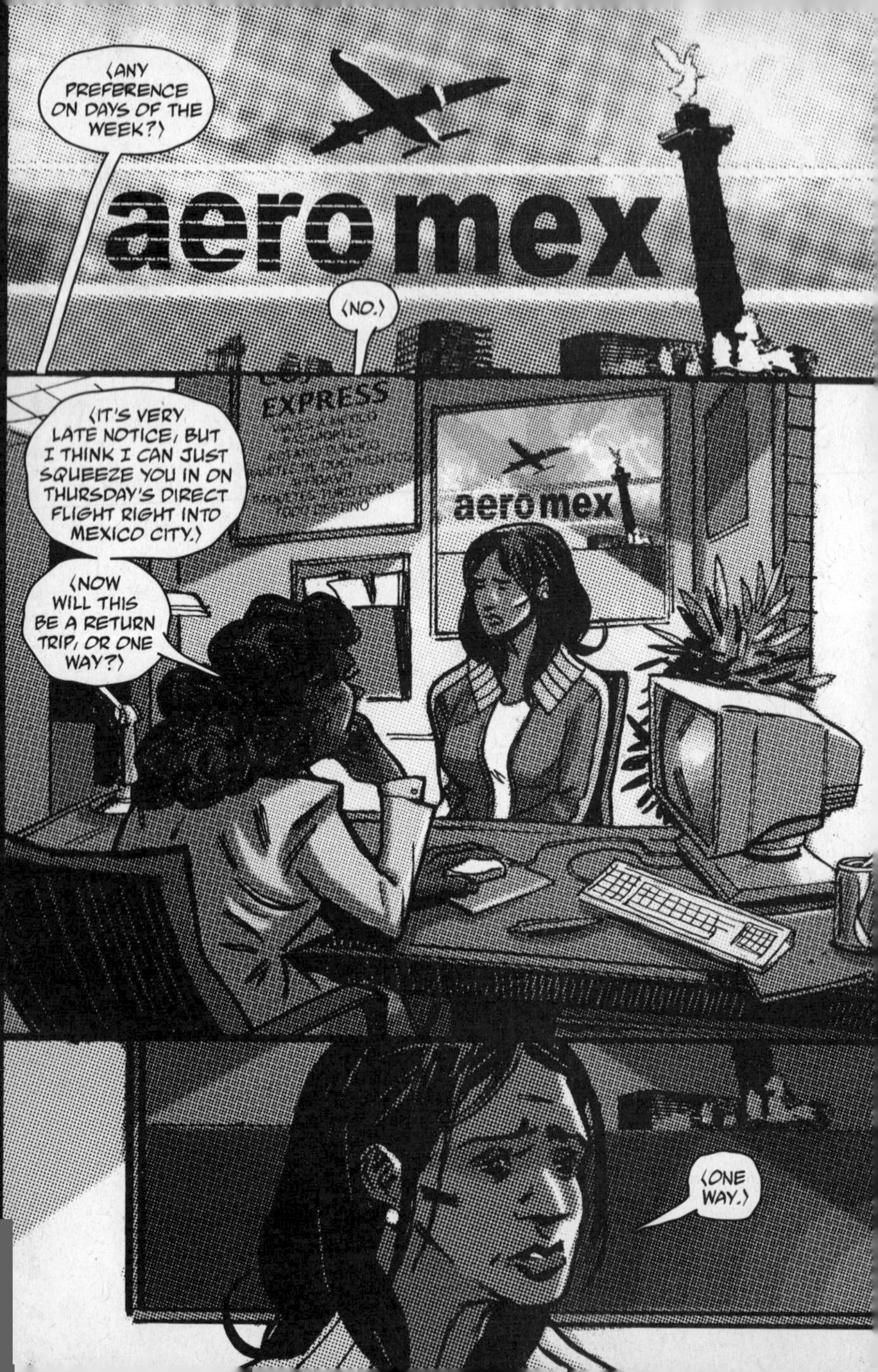
aeromex
⟨ANY PREFERENCE ON DAYS OF THE WEEK?⟩
⟨NO.⟩
EXPRESS
aeromex
⟨IT'S VERY LATE NOTICE, BUT I THINK I CAN JUST SQUEEZE YOU IN ON THURSDAY'S DIRECT FLIGHT RIGHT INTO MEXICO CITY.⟩
⟨NOW WILL THIS BE A RETURN TRIP, OR ONE WAY?⟩
⟨ONE WAY.⟩

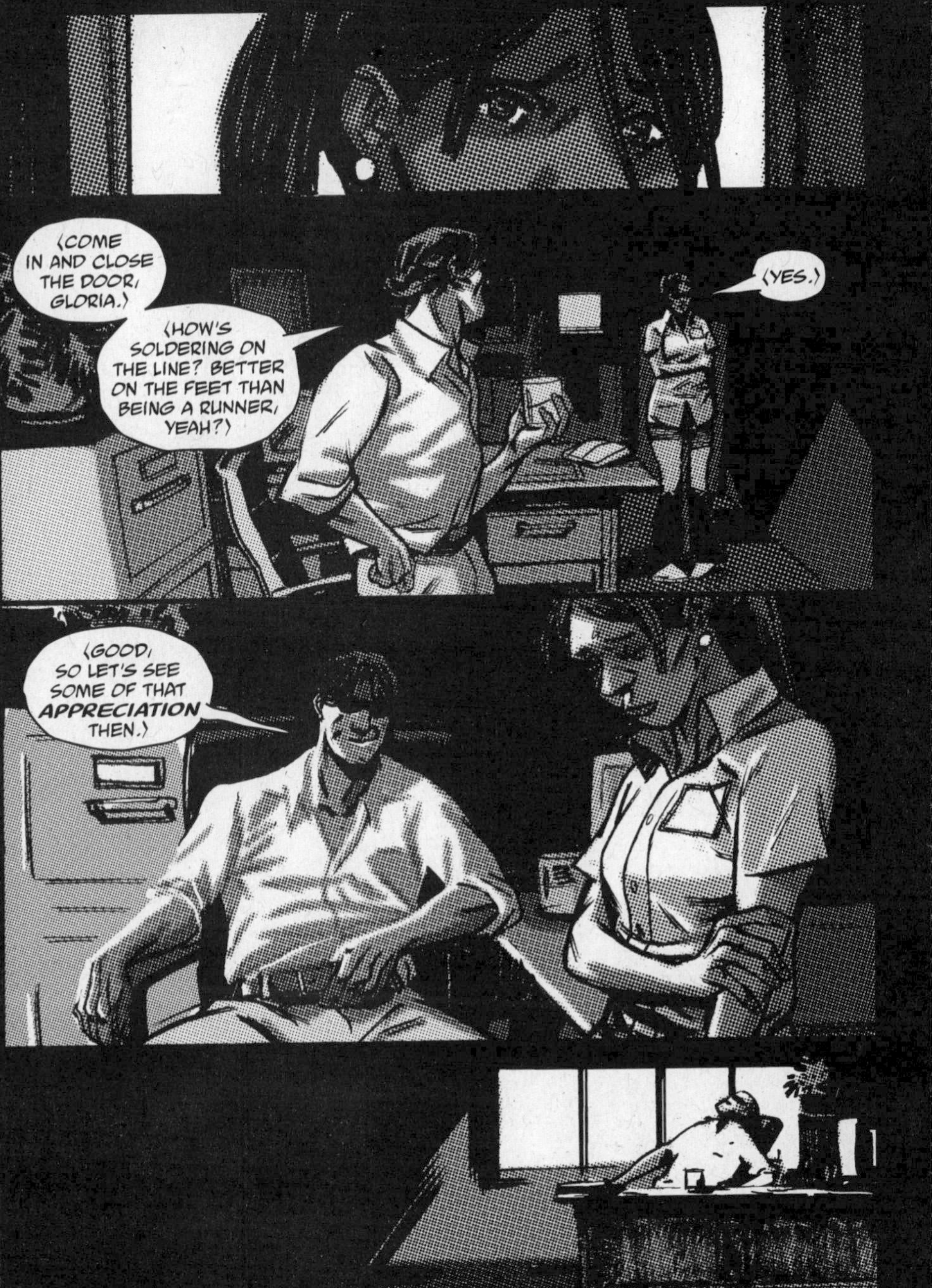

⟨COME IN AND CLOSE THE DOOR, GLORIA.⟩
⟨YES.⟩
⟨HOW'S SOLDERING ON THE LINE? BETTER ON THE FEET THAN BEING A RUNNER, YEAH?⟩
⟨GOOD, SO LET'S SEE SOME OF THAT **APPRECIATION** THEN.⟩

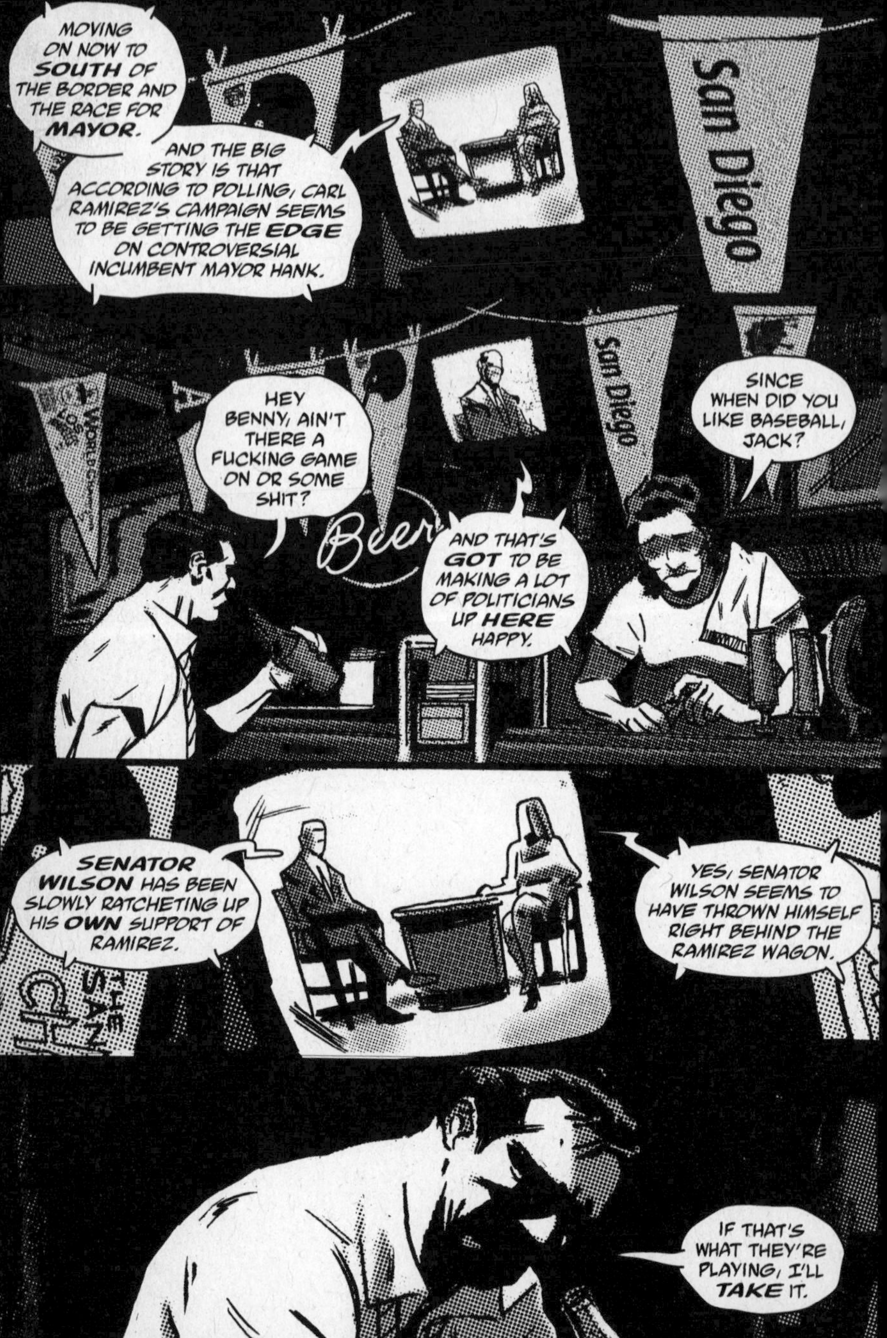
MOVING ON NOW TO SOUTH OF THE BORDER AND THE RACE FOR MAYOR.
AND THE BIG STORY IS THAT ACCORDING TO POLLING, CARL RAMIREZ'S CAMPAIGN SEEMS TO BE GETTING THE EDGE ON CONTROVERSIAL INCUMBENT MAYOR HANK.
San Diego
HEY BENNY, AIN'T THERE A FUCKING GAME ON OR SOME SHIT?
AND THAT'S GOT TO BE MAKING A LOT OF POLITICIANS UP HERE HAPPY.
SINCE WHEN DID YOU LIKE BASEBALL, JACK?
San Diego
Beer
SENATOR WILSON HAS BEEN SLOWLY RATCHETING UP HIS OWN SUPPORT OF RAMIREZ.
YES, SENATOR WILSON SEEMS TO HAVE THROWN HIMSELF RIGHT BEHIND THE RAMIREZ WAGON.
IF THAT'S WHAT THEY'RE PLAYING, I'LL TAKE IT.

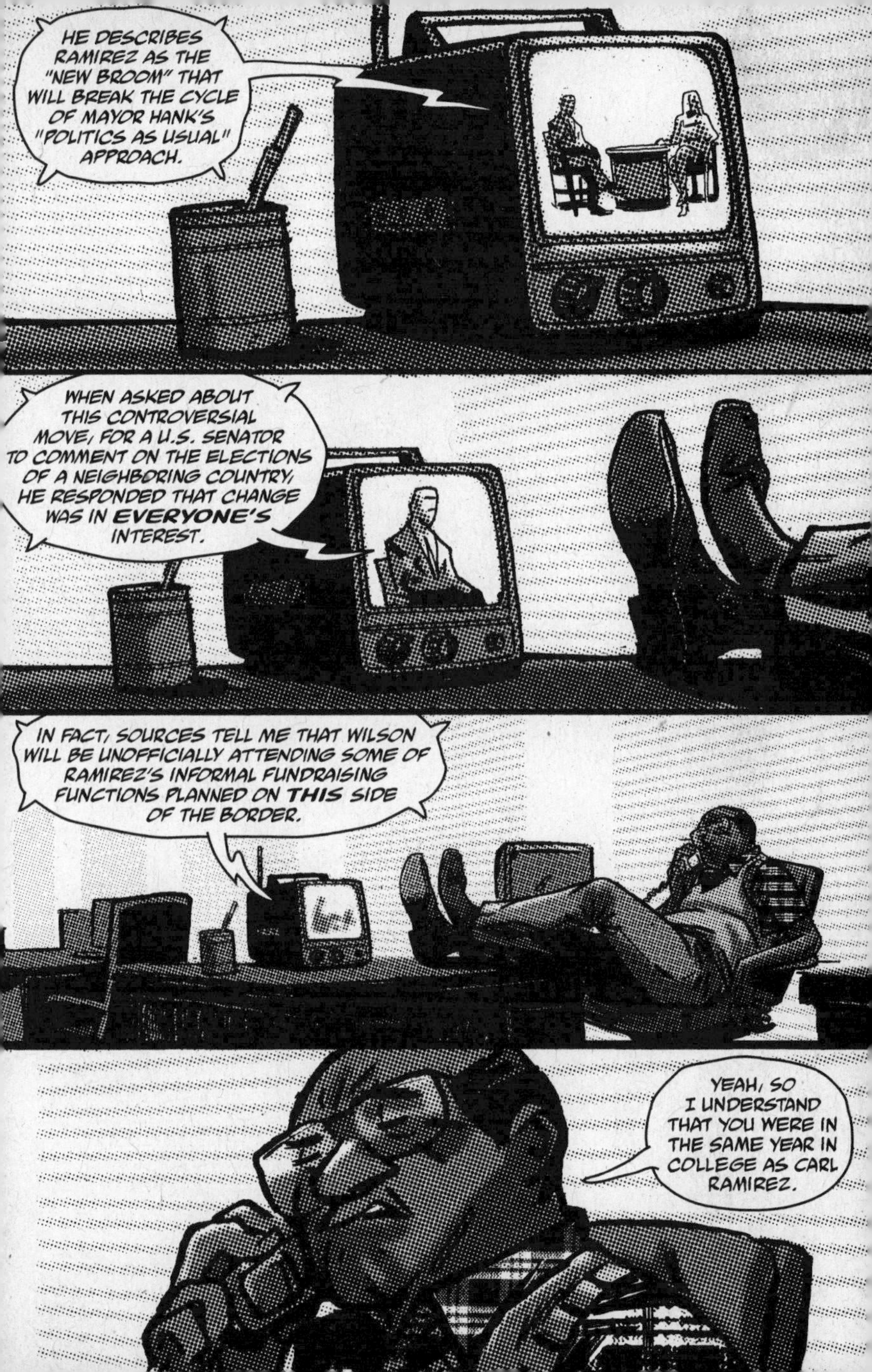
HE DESCRIBES RAMIREZ AS THE "NEW BROOM" THAT WILL BREAK THE CYCLE OF MAYOR HANK'S "POLITICS AS USUAL" APPROACH.
WHEN ASKED ABOUT THIS CONTROVERSIAL MOVE, FOR A U.S. SENATOR TO COMMENT ON THE ELECTIONS OF A NEIGHBORING COUNTRY, HE RESPONDED THAT CHANGE WAS IN EVERYONE'S INTEREST.
IN FACT, SOURCES TELL ME THAT WILSON WILL BE UNOFFICIALLY ATTENDING SOME OF RAMIREZ'S INFORMAL FUNDRAISING FUNCTIONS PLANNED ON THIS SIDE OF THE BORDER.
YEAH, SO I UNDERSTAND THAT YOU WERE IN THE SAME YEAR IN COLLEGE AS CARL RAMIREZ.

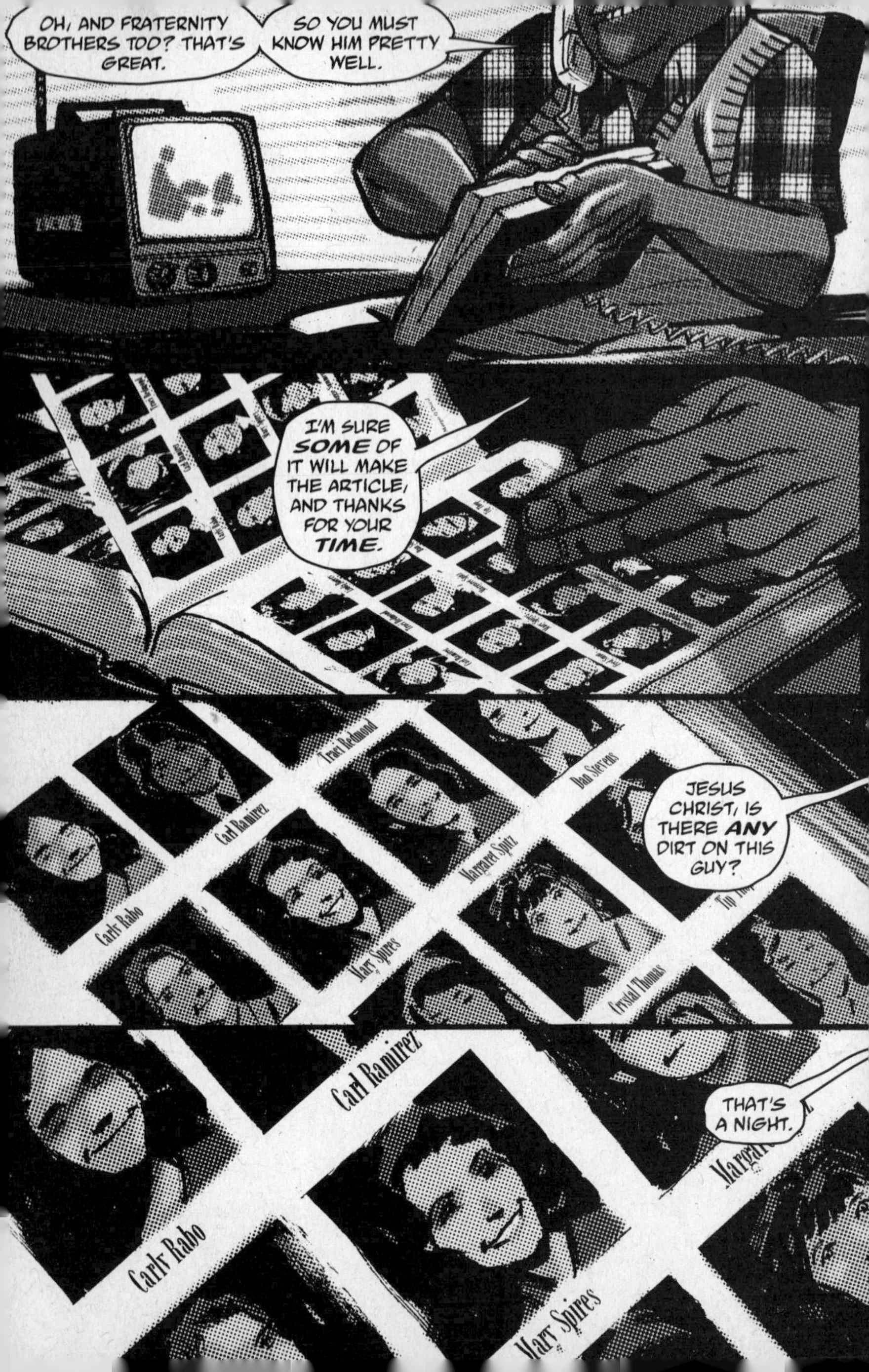
OH, AND FRATERNITY BROTHERS TOO? THAT'S GREAT.
SO YOU MUST KNOW HIM PRETTY WELL.
I'M SURE SOME OF IT WILL MAKE THE ARTICLE, AND THANKS FOR YOUR TIME.
Traci Redmond
Carl Ramirez
Dan Stevens
Margaret Spitz
Carly Rabo
Mary Spires
Crystal Thomas
JESUS CHRIST, IS THERE ANY DIRT ON THIS GUY?
Carl Ramirez
Carly Rabo
Mary Spires
THAT'S A NIGHT.

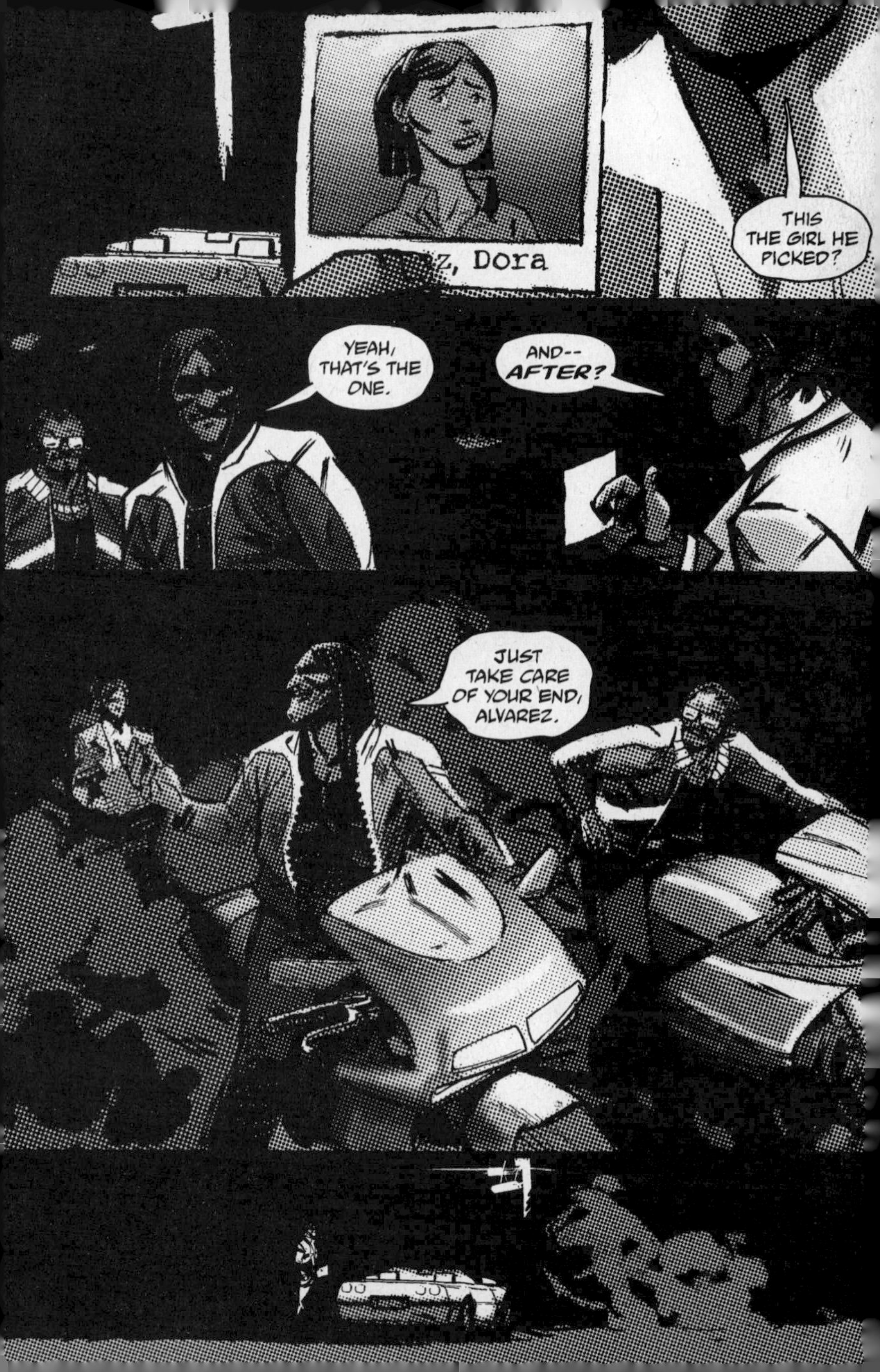
z, Dora
THIS THE GIRL HE PICKED?
YEAH, THAT'S THE ONE.
AND-- AFTER?
JUST TAKE CARE OF YOUR END, ALVAREZ.

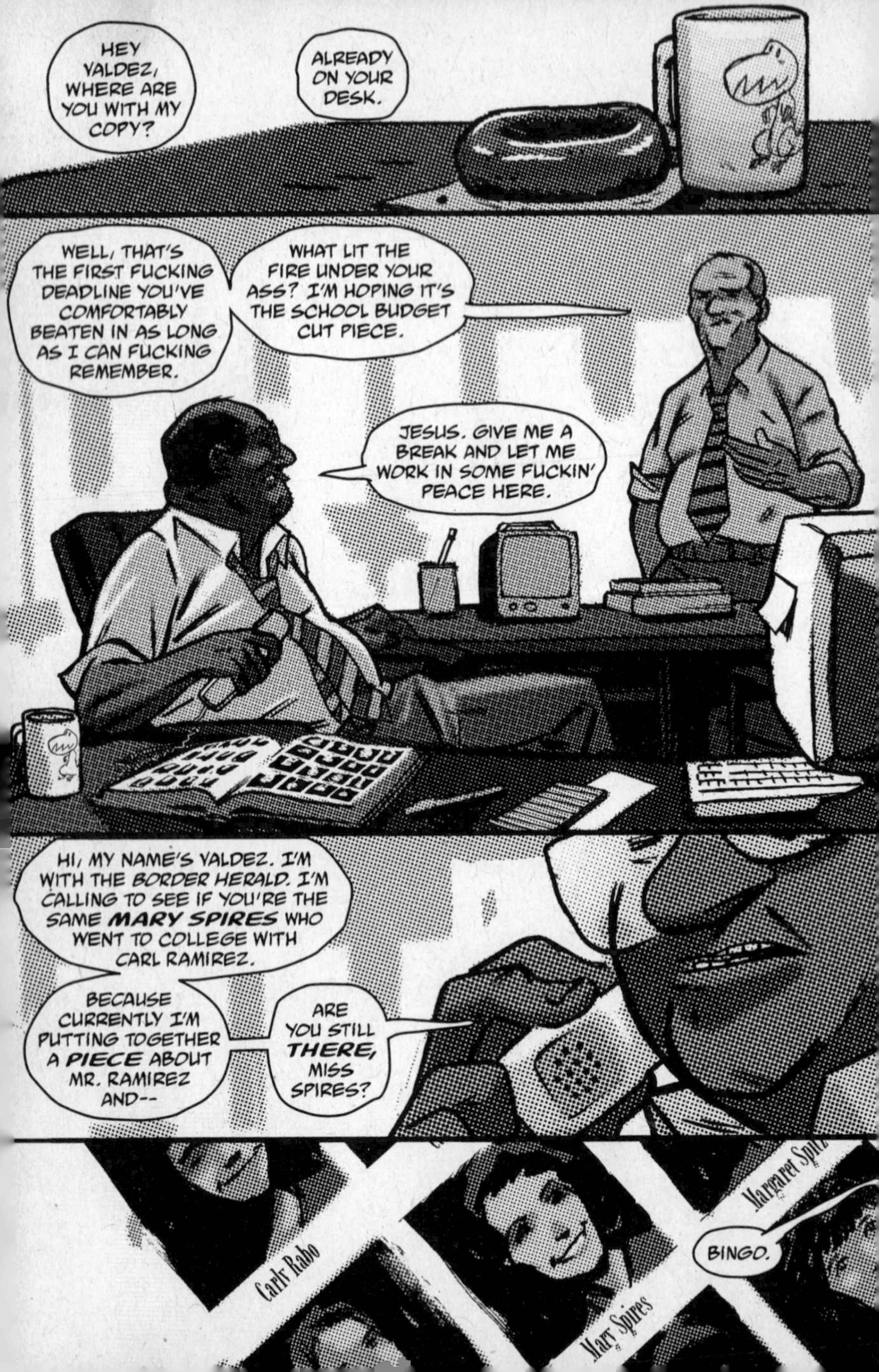
HEY YALDEZ, WHERE ARE YOU WITH MY COPY?
ALREADY ON YOUR DESK.
WELL, THAT'S THE FIRST FUCKING DEADLINE YOU'VE COMFORTABLY BEATEN IN AS LONG AS I CAN FUCKING REMEMBER.
WHAT LIT THE FIRE UNDER YOUR ASS? I'M HOPING IT'S THE SCHOOL BUDGET CUT PIECE.
JESUS. GIVE ME A BREAK AND LET ME WORK IN SOME FUCKIN' PEACE HERE.
HI, MY NAME'S YALDEZ. I'M WITH THE BORDER HERALD. I'M CALLING TO SEE IF YOU'RE THE SAME MARY SPIRES WHO WENT TO COLLEGE WITH CARL RAMIREZ.
BECAUSE CURRENTLY I'M PUTTING TOGETHER A PIECE ABOUT MR. RAMIREZ AND--
ARE YOU STILL THERE, MISS SPIRES?
Carla Rabo
Mary Spires
BINGO.

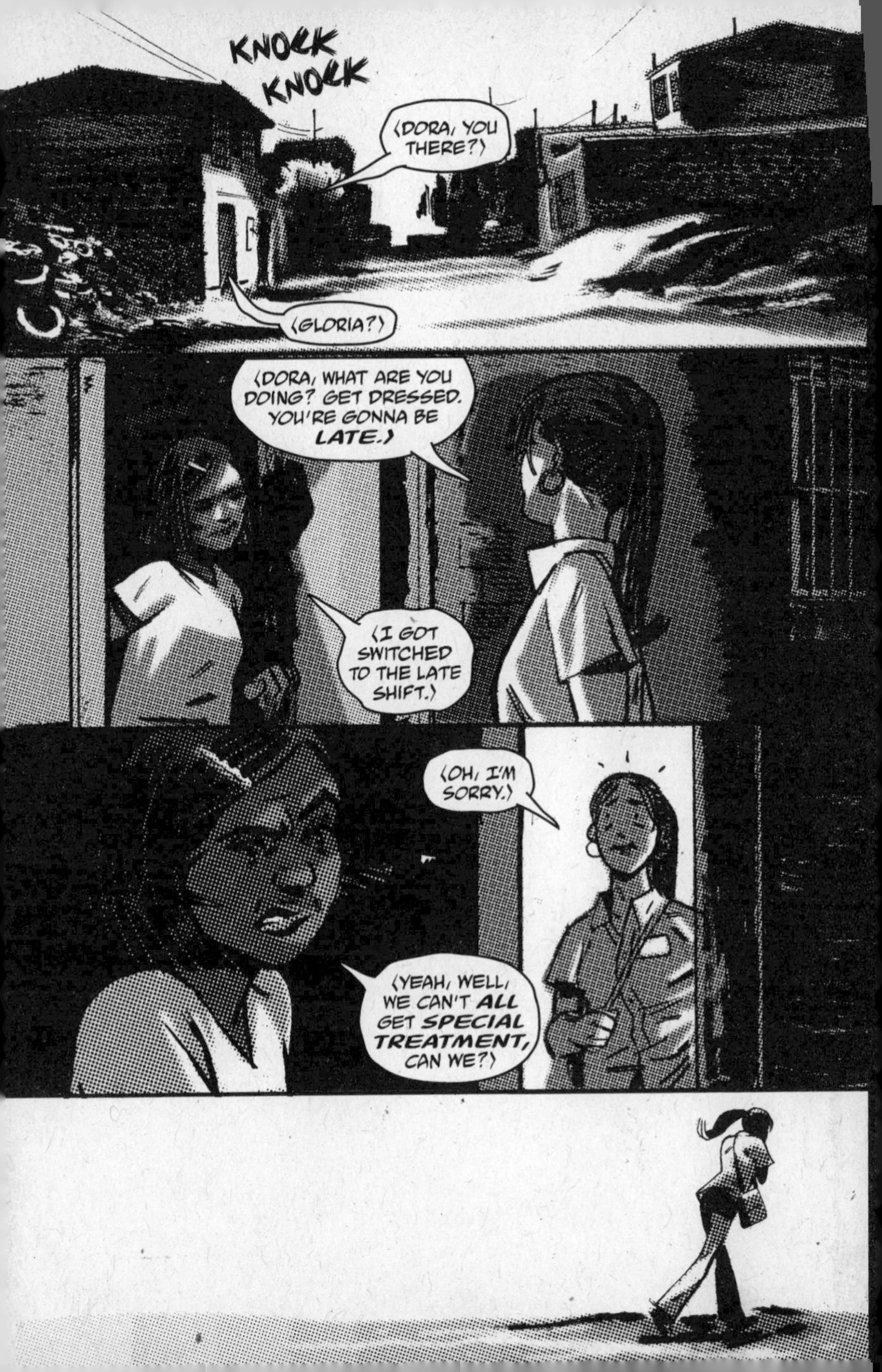
KNOCK KNOCK
⟨DORA, YOU THERE?⟩
⟨GLORIA?⟩
⟨DORA, WHAT ARE YOU DOING? GET DRESSED. YOU'RE GONNA BE LATE.⟩
⟨I GOT SWITCHED TO THE LATE SHIFT.⟩
⟨OH, I'M SORRY.⟩
⟨YEAH, WELL, WE CAN'T ALL GET SPECIAL TREATMENT, CAN WE?⟩

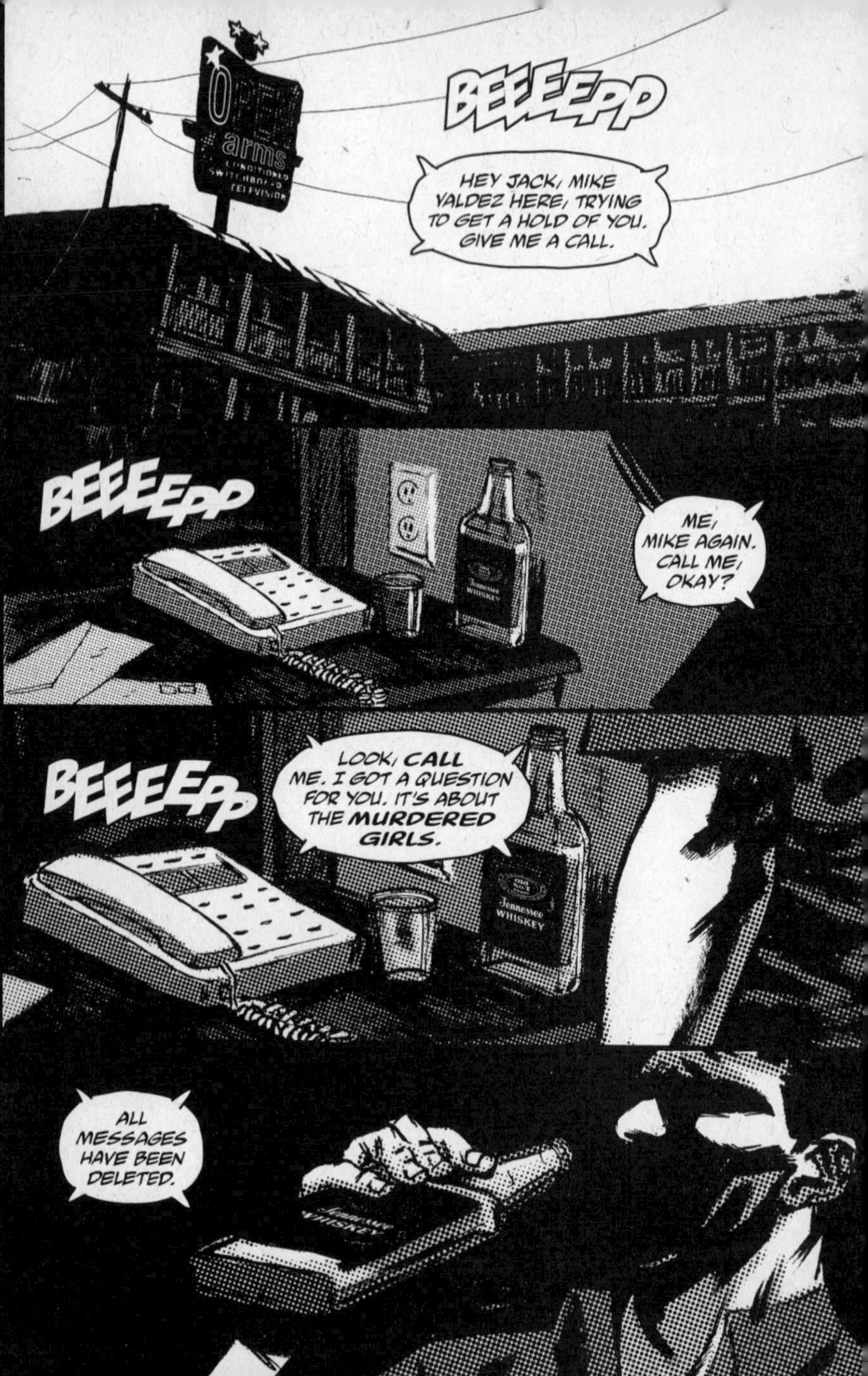
BEEEEPP
HEY JACK, MIKE VALDEZ HERE, TRYING TO GET A HOLD OF YOU. GIVE ME A CALL.
BEEEEPP
ME, MIKE AGAIN. CALL ME, OKAY?
BEEEEPP
LOOK, CALL ME. I GOT A QUESTION FOR YOU. IT'S ABOUT THE MURDERED GIRLS.
ALL MESSAGES HAVE BEEN DELETED.

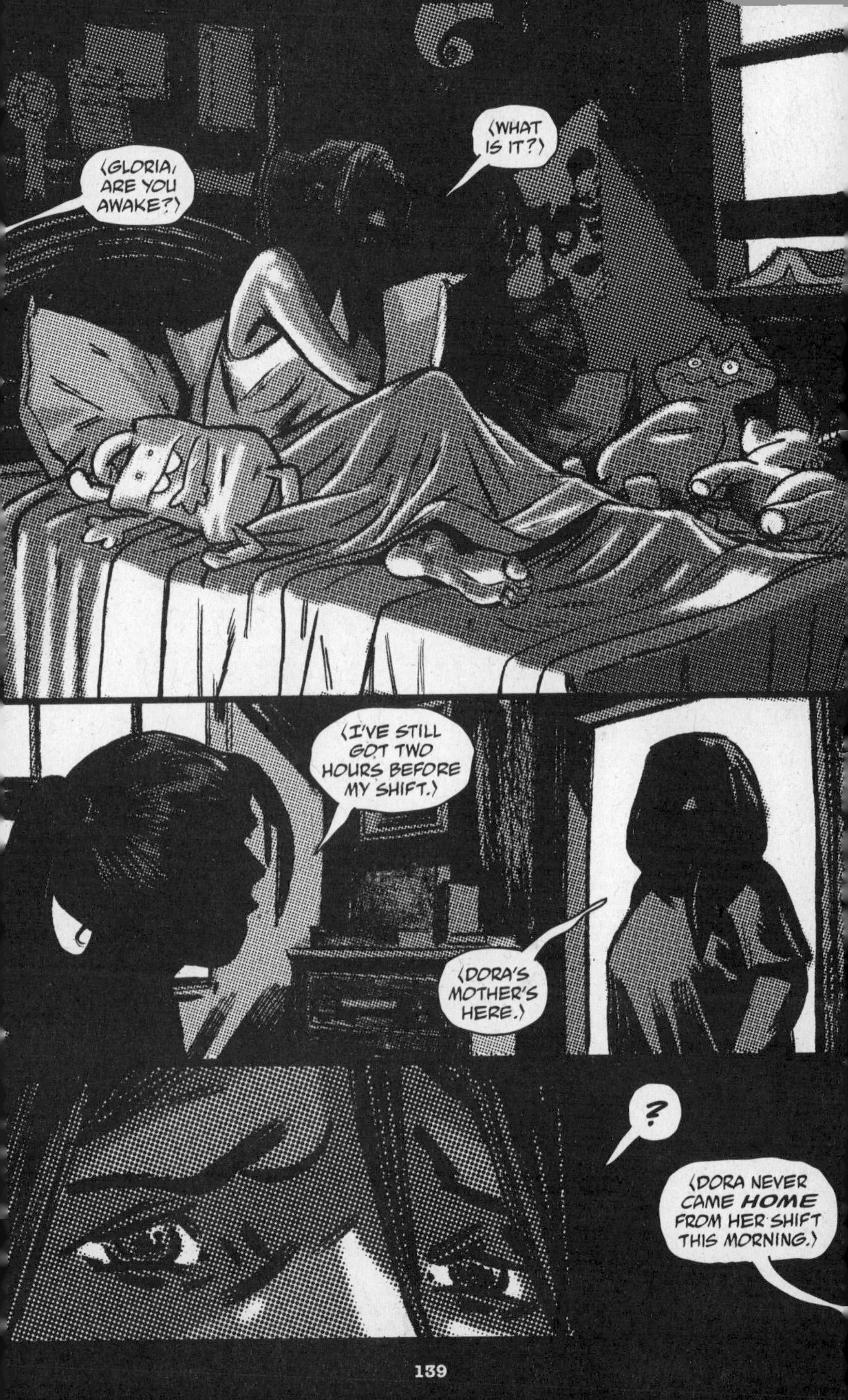
⟨GLORIA, ARE YOU AWAKE?⟩
⟨WHAT IS IT?⟩
⟨I'VE STILL GOT TWO HOURS BEFORE MY SHIFT.⟩
⟨DORA'S MOTHER'S HERE.⟩
?
⟨DORA NEVER CAME **HOME** FROM HER SHIFT THIS MORNING.⟩

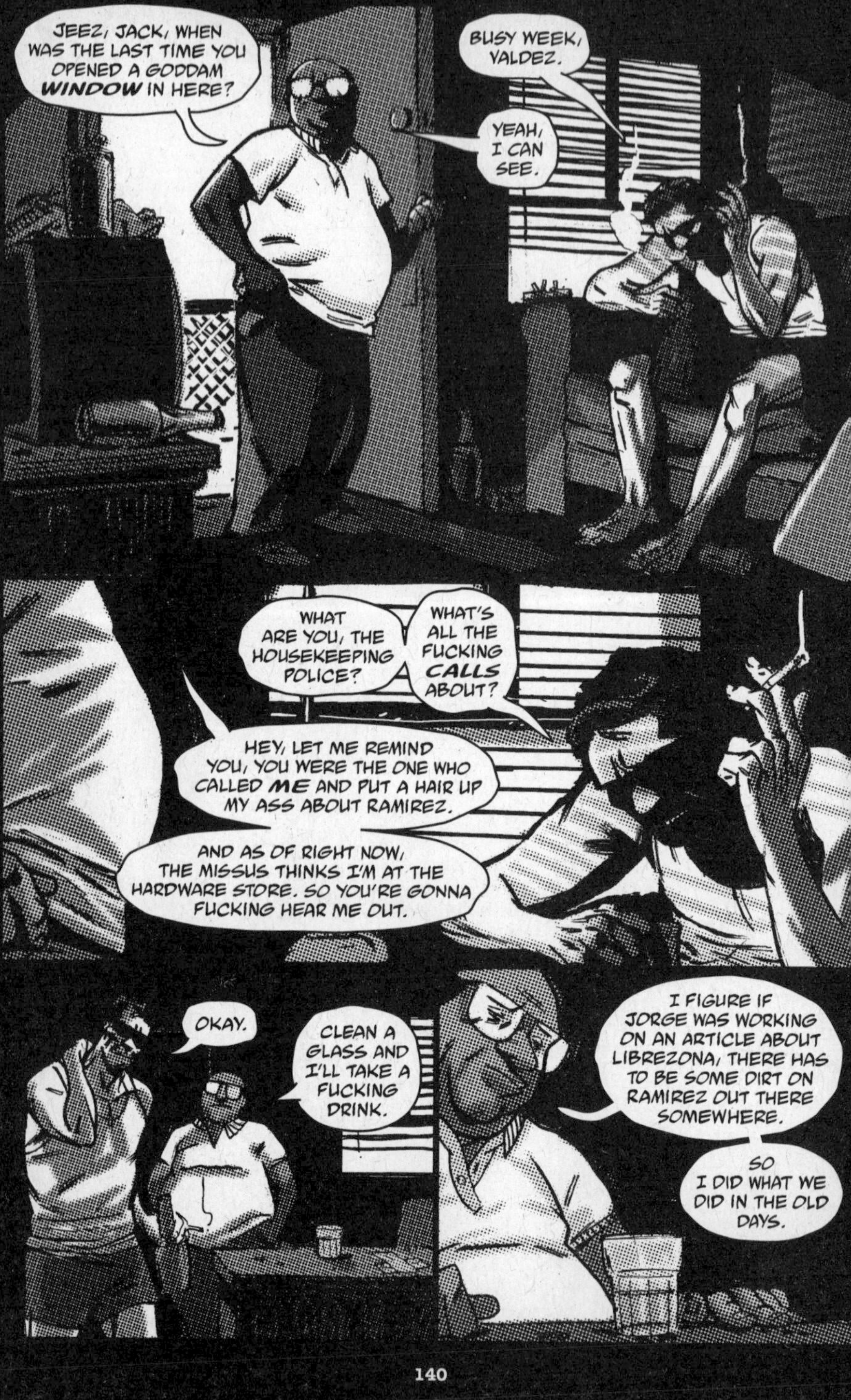
JEEZ, JACK, WHEN WAS THE LAST TIME YOU OPENED A GODDAM WINDOW IN HERE?
BUSY WEEK, VALDEZ.
YEAH, I CAN SEE.
WHAT ARE YOU, THE HOUSEKEEPING POLICE?
WHAT'S ALL THE FUCKING CALLS ABOUT?
HEY, LET ME REMIND YOU, YOU WERE THE ONE WHO CALLED ME AND PUT A HAIR UP MY ASS ABOUT RAMIREZ.
AND AS OF RIGHT NOW, THE MISSUS THINKS I'M AT THE HARDWARE STORE. SO YOU'RE GONNA FUCKING HEAR ME OUT.
OKAY.
CLEAN A GLASS AND I'LL TAKE A FUCKING DRINK.
I FIGURE IF JORGE WAS WORKING ON AN ARTICLE ABOUT LIBREZONA, THERE HAS TO BE SOME DIRT ON RAMIREZ OUT THERE SOMEWHERE.
SO I DID WHAT WE DID IN THE OLD DAYS.

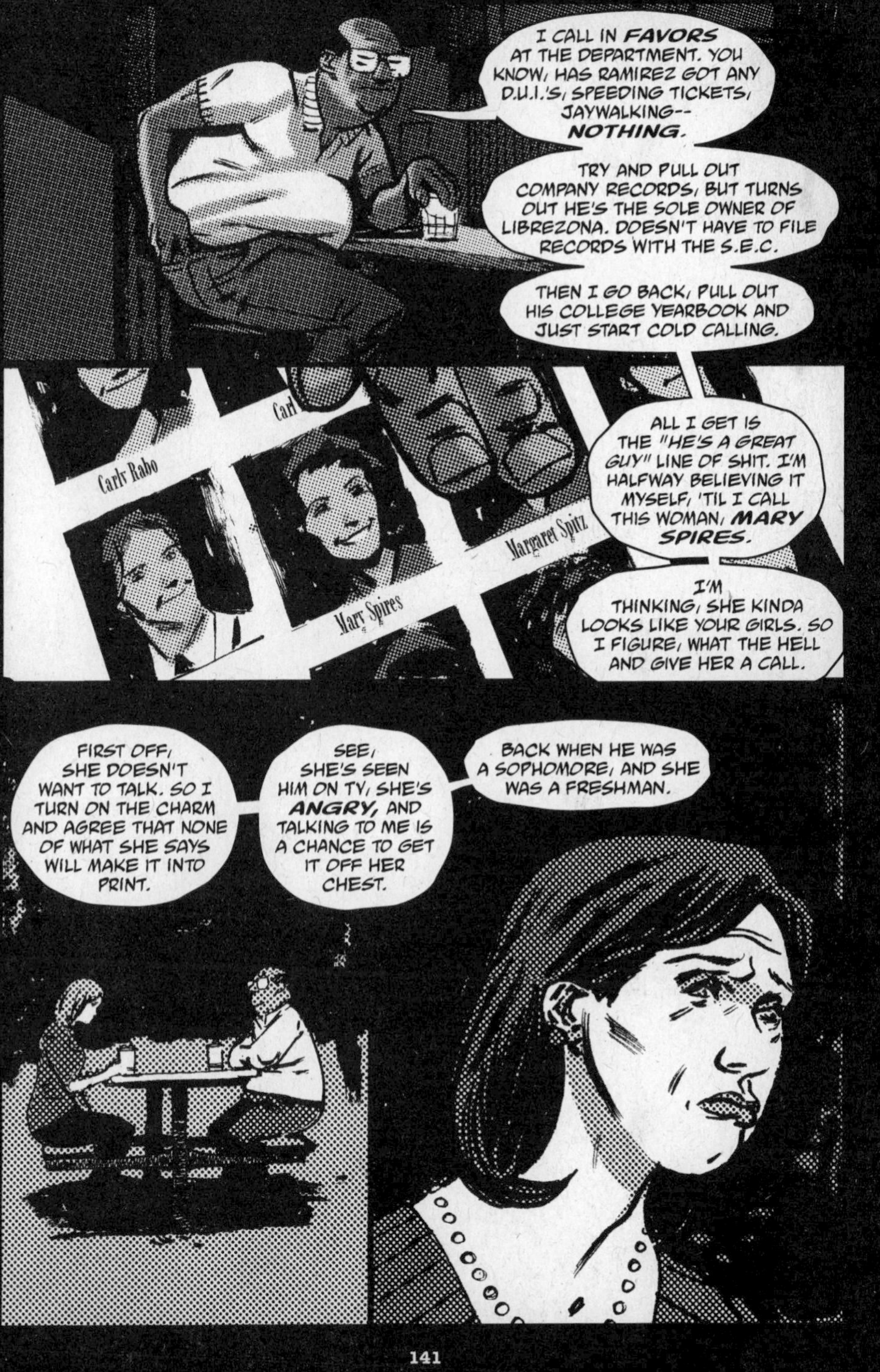
I CALL IN FAVORS AT THE DEPARTMENT. YOU KNOW, HAS RAMIREZ GOT ANY D.U.I.'S, SPEEDING TICKETS, JAYWALKING-- NOTHING.
TRY AND PULL OUT COMPANY RECORDS, BUT TURNS OUT HE'S THE SOLE OWNER OF LIBREZONA. DOESN'T HAVE TO FILE RECORDS WITH THE S.E.C.
THEN I GO BACK, PULL OUT HIS COLLEGE YEARBOOK AND JUST START COLD CALLING.
Carly Rabo
Carl
Margaret Spitz
Mary Spires
ALL I GET IS THE "HE'S A GREAT GUY" LINE OF SHIT. I'M HALFWAY BELIEVING IT MYSELF, 'TIL I CALL THIS WOMAN, MARY SPIRES.
I'M THINKING, SHE KINDA LOOKS LIKE YOUR GIRLS. SO I FIGURE, WHAT THE HELL AND GIVE HER A CALL.
FIRST OFF, SHE DOESN'T WANT TO TALK. SO I TURN ON THE CHARM AND AGREE THAT NONE OF WHAT SHE SAYS WILL MAKE IT INTO PRINT.
SEE, SHE'S SEEN HIM ON TV, SHE'S ANGRY, AND TALKING TO ME IS A CHANCE TO GET IT OFF HER CHEST.
BACK WHEN HE WAS A SOPHOMORE, AND SHE WAS A FRESHMAN.

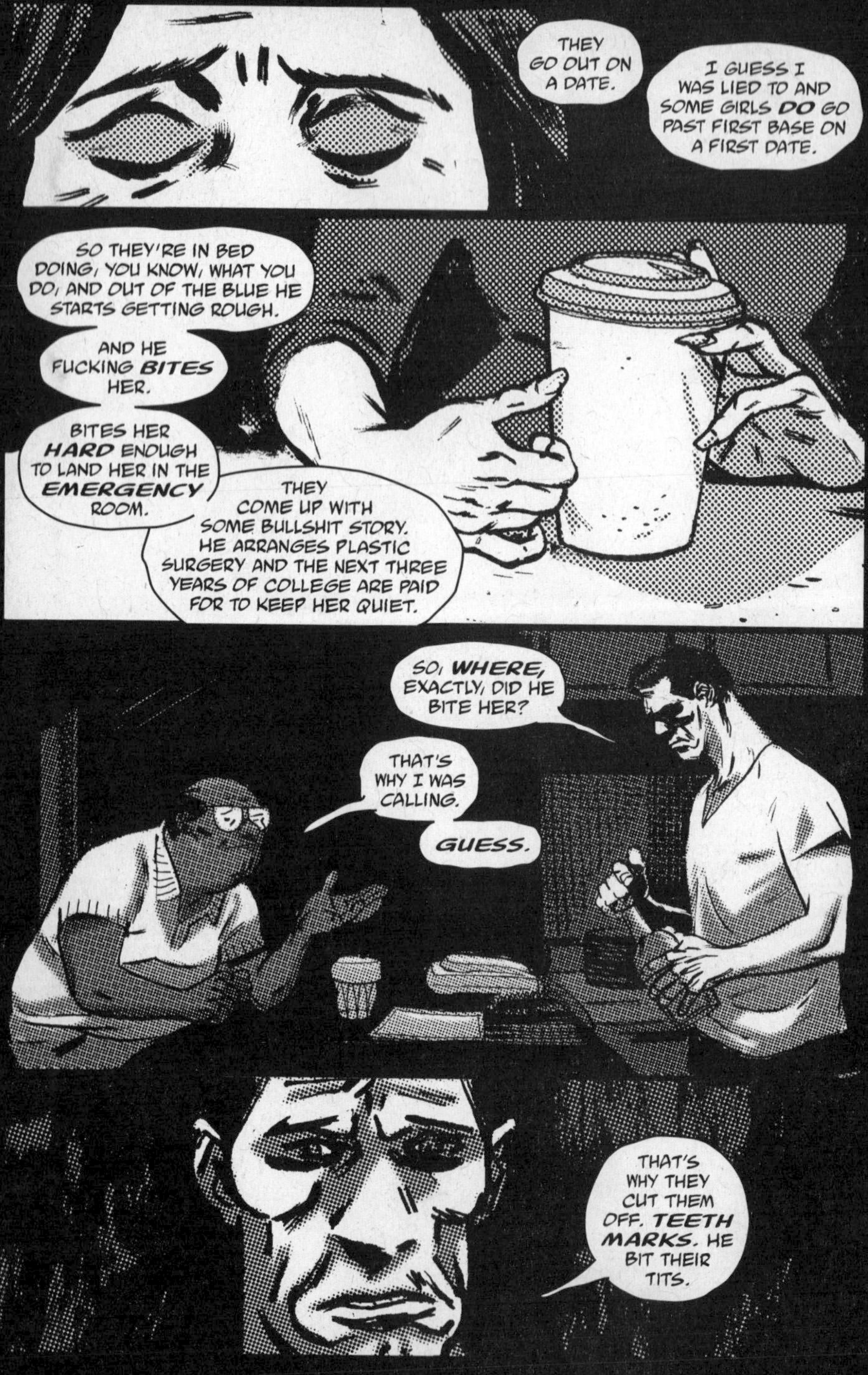
THEY GO OUT ON A DATE.
I GUESS I WAS LIED TO AND SOME GIRLS DO GO PAST FIRST BASE ON A FIRST DATE.
SO THEY'RE IN BED DOING, YOU KNOW, WHAT YOU DO, AND OUT OF THE BLUE HE STARTS GETTING ROUGH.
AND HE FUCKING BITES HER.
BITES HER HARD ENOUGH TO LAND HER IN THE EMERGENCY ROOM.
THEY COME UP WITH SOME BULLSHIT STORY. HE ARRANGES PLASTIC SURGERY AND THE NEXT THREE YEARS OF COLLEGE ARE PAID FOR TO KEEP HER QUIET.
SO, WHERE, EXACTLY, DID HE BITE HER?
THAT'S WHY I WAS CALLING.
GUESS.
THAT'S WHY THEY CUT THEM OFF. TEETH MARKS. HE BIT THEIR TITS.

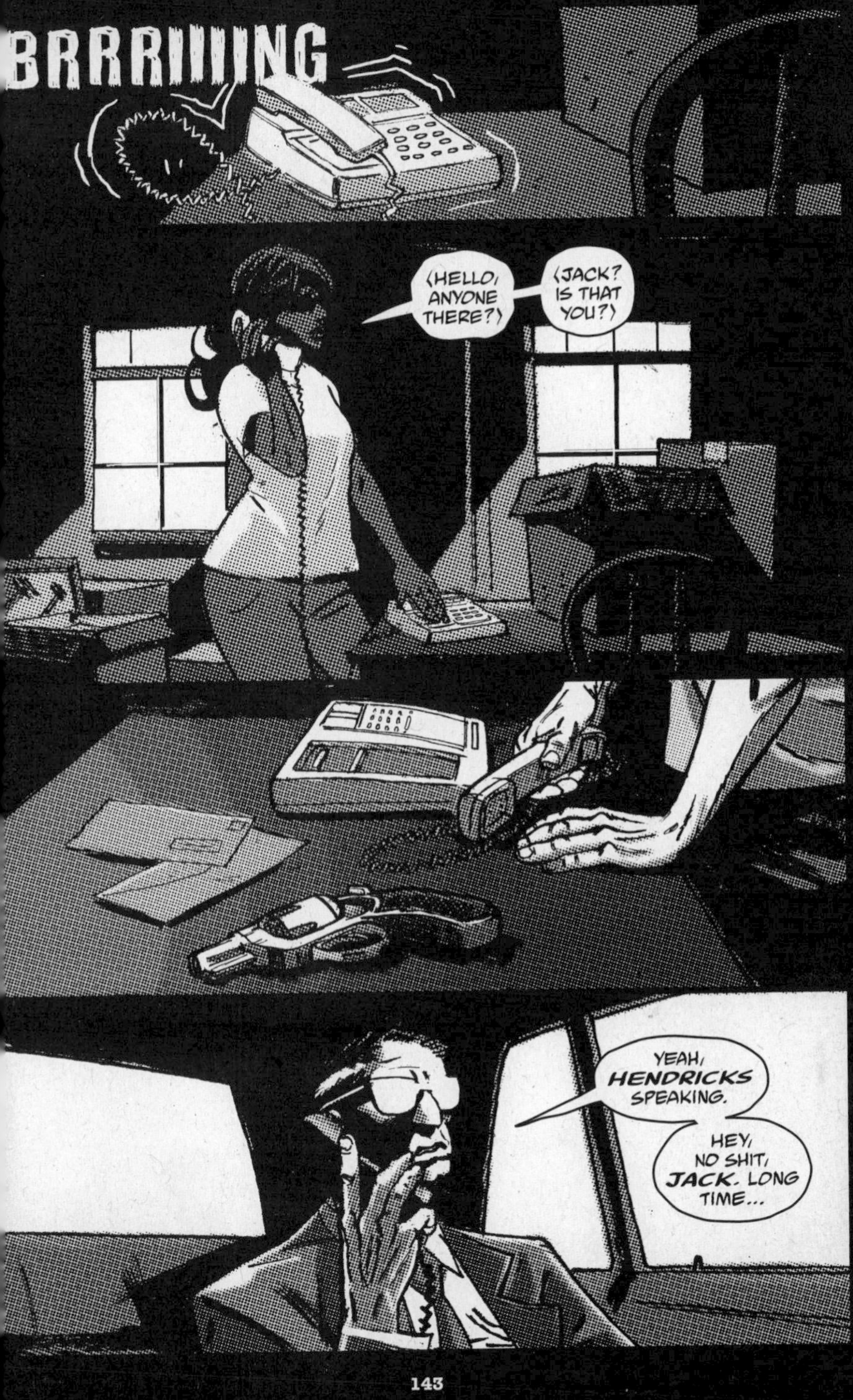
BRRRIIIING
(HELLO, ANYONE THERE?)
(JACK? IS THAT YOU?)
YEAH, HENDRICKS SPEAKING.
HEY, NO SHIT, JACK. LONG TIME...

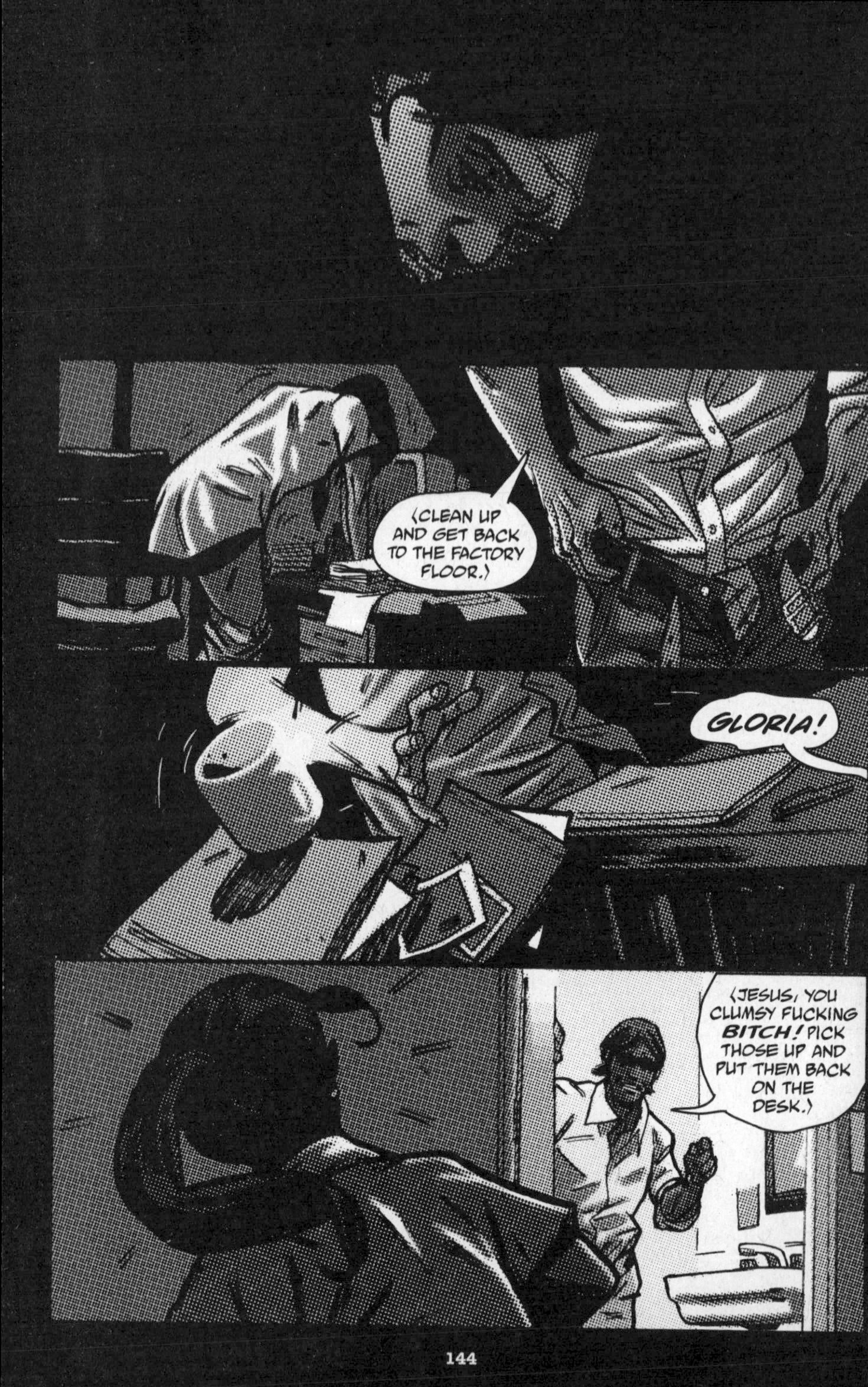
⟨CLEAN UP AND GET BACK TO THE FACTORY FLOOR.⟩
GLORIA!
⟨JESUS, YOU CLUMSY FUCKING **BITCH!** PICK THOSE UP AND PUT THEM BACK ON THE DESK.⟩

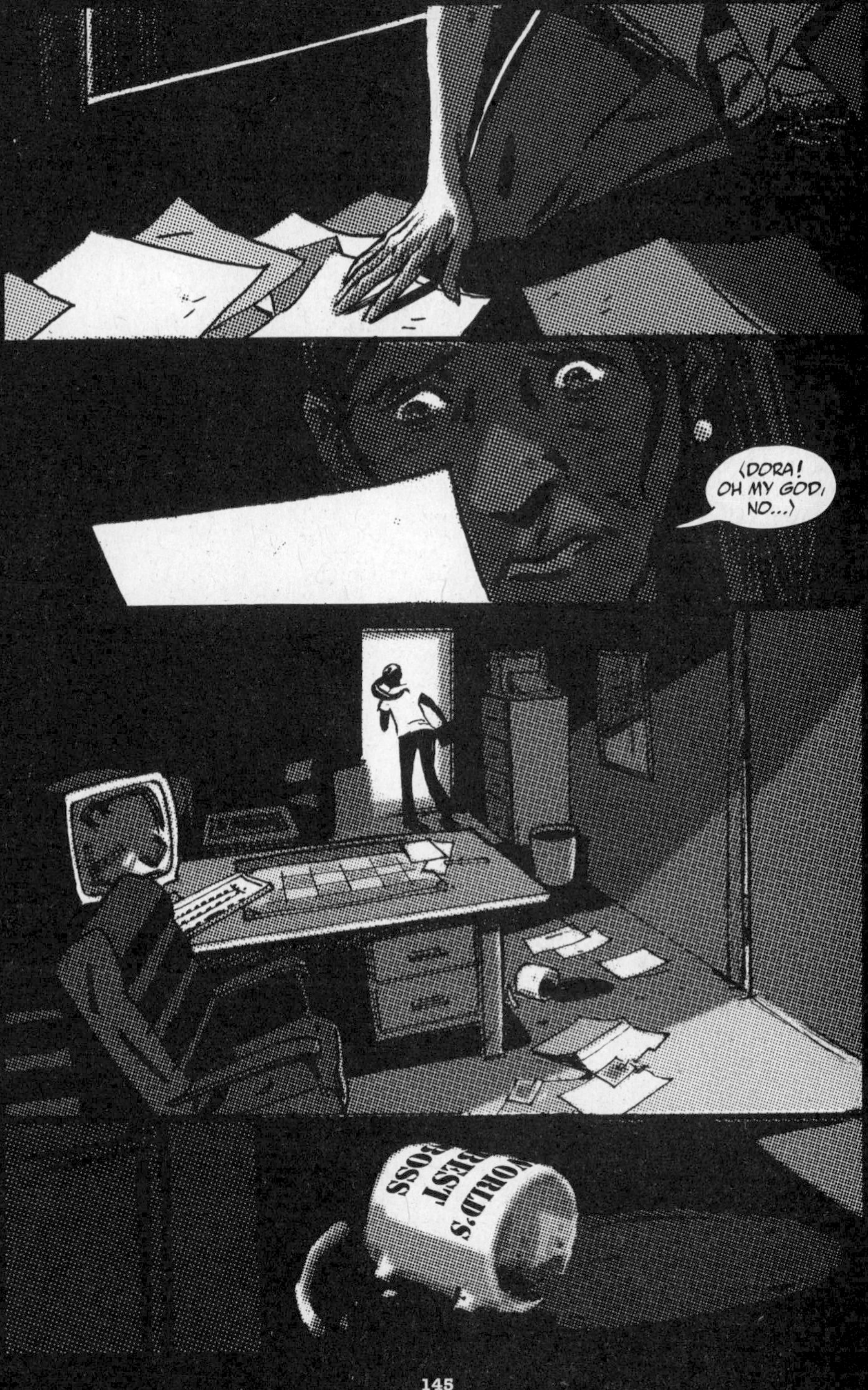
⟨DORA! OH MY GOD, NO...⟩
WORLD'S BEST BOSS

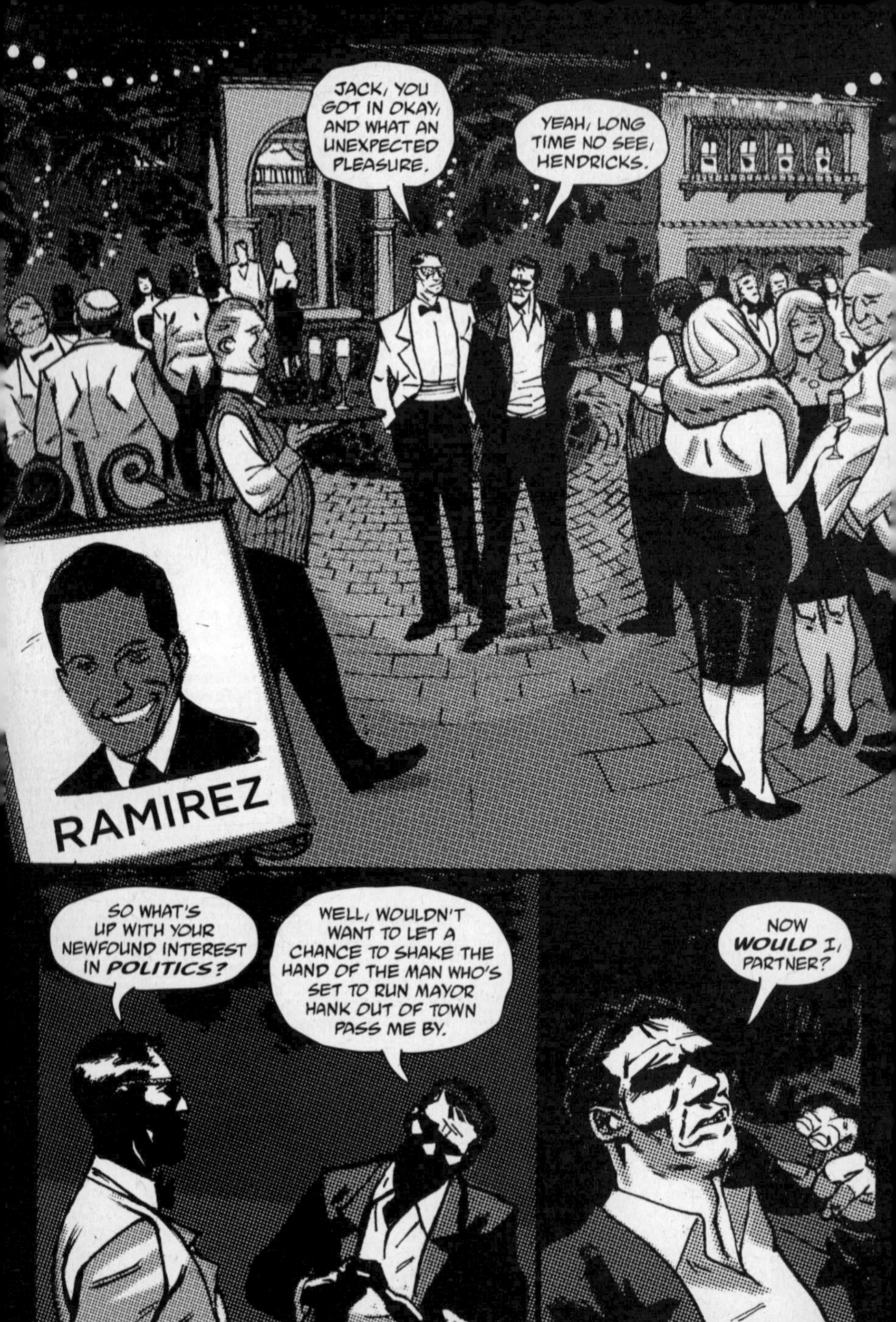
JACK, YOU GOT IN OKAY, AND WHAT AN UNEXPECTED PLEASURE.
YEAH, LONG TIME NO SEE, HENDRICKS.
RAMIREZ
SO WHAT'S UP WITH YOUR NEWFOUND INTEREST IN *POLITICS?*
WELL, WOULDN'T WANT TO LET A CHANCE TO SHAKE THE HAND OF THE MAN WHO'S SET TO RUN MAYOR HANK OUT OF TOWN PASS ME BY.
NOW *WOULD* I, PARTNER?

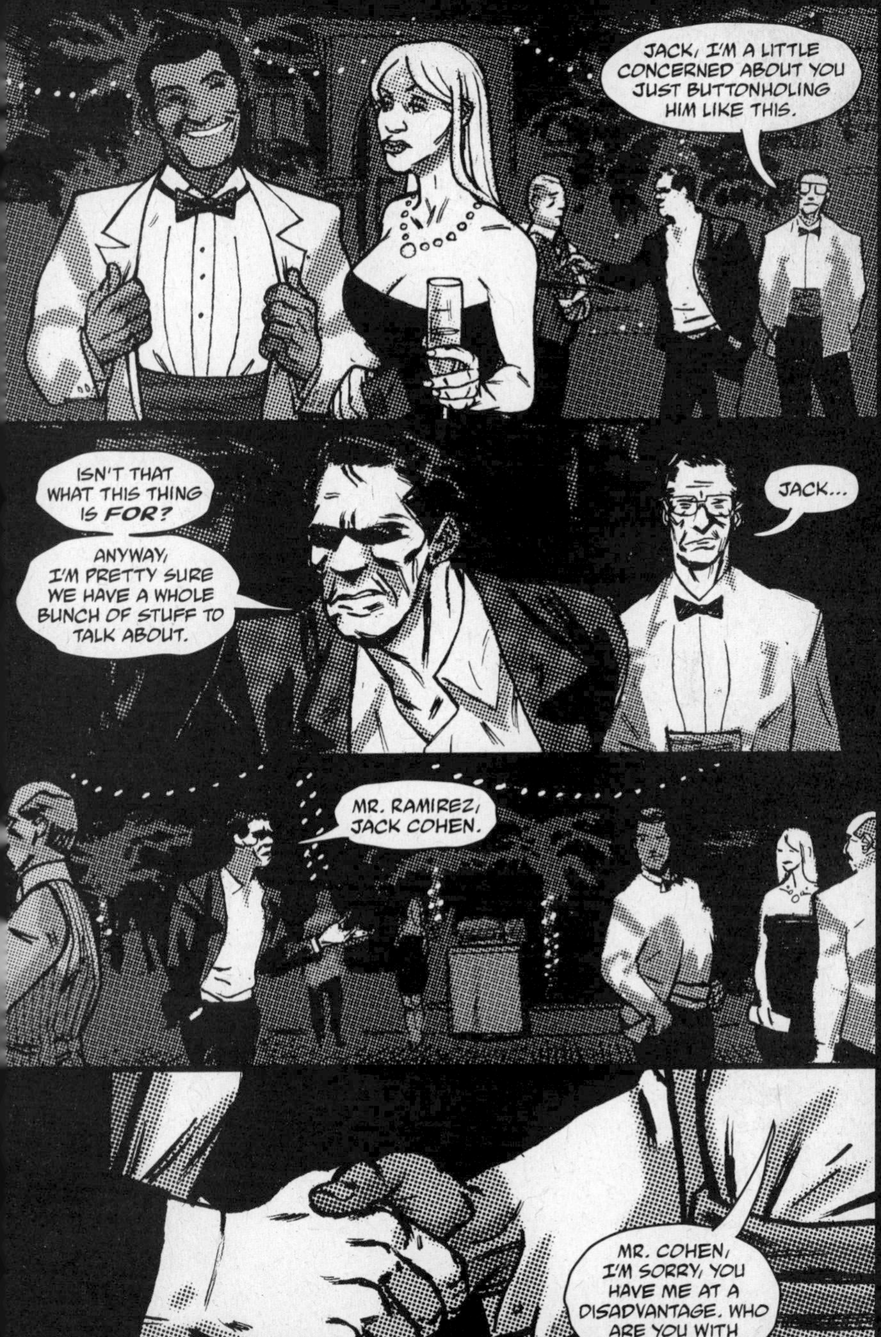
JACK, I'M A LITTLE CONCERNED ABOUT YOU JUST BUTTONHOLING HIM LIKE THIS.
ISN'T THAT WHAT THIS THING IS FOR?
ANYWAY, I'M PRETTY SURE WE HAVE A WHOLE BUNCH OF STUFF TO TALK ABOUT.
JACK...
MR. RAMIREZ, JACK COHEN.
MR. COHEN, I'M SORRY, YOU HAVE ME AT A DISADVANTAGE. WHO ARE YOU WITH AGAIN?

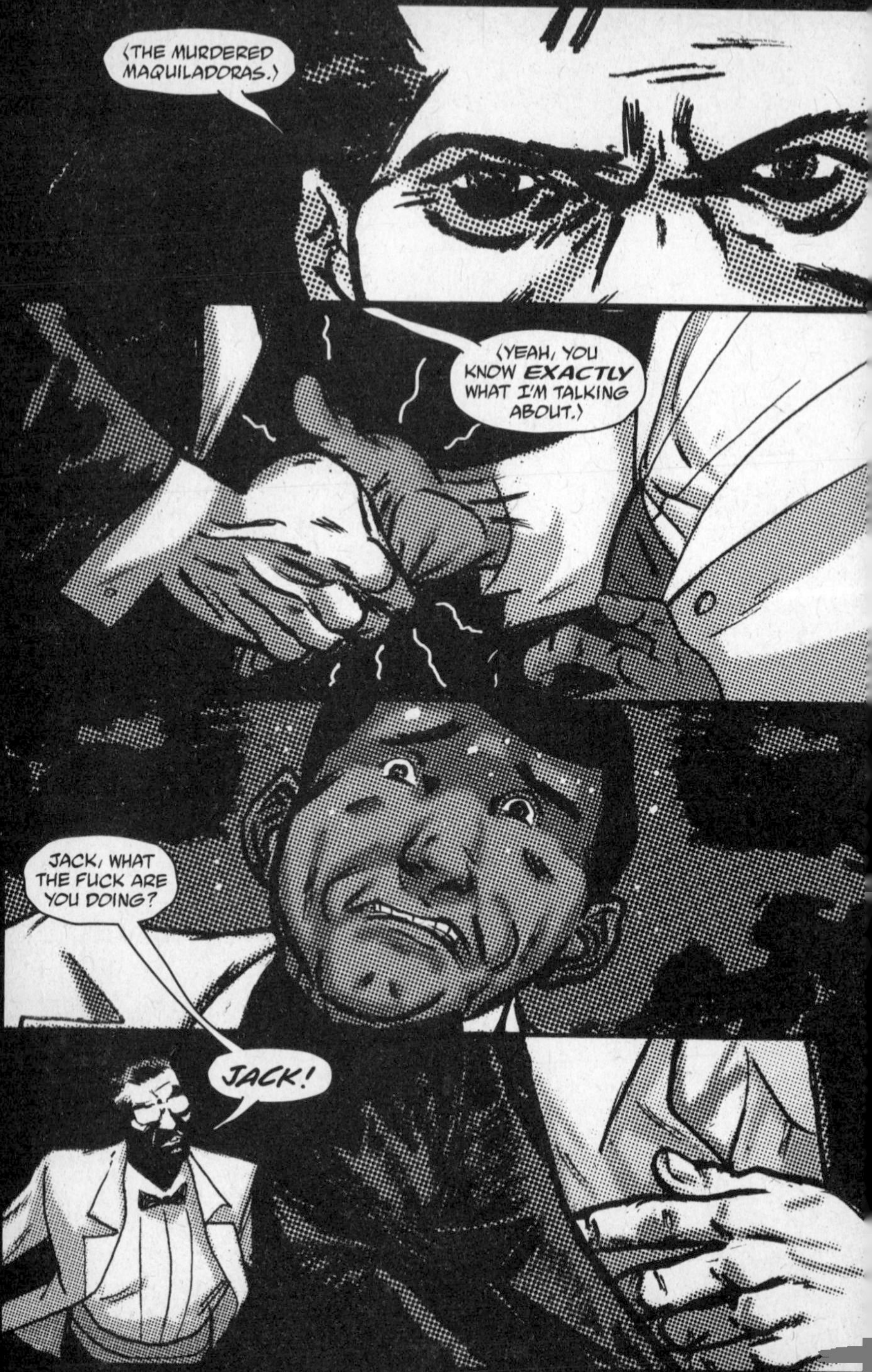
⟨THE MURDERED MAQUILADORAS.⟩
⟨YEAH, YOU KNOW **EXACTLY** WHAT I'M TALKING ABOUT.⟩
JACK, WHAT THE FUCK ARE YOU DOING?
JACK!

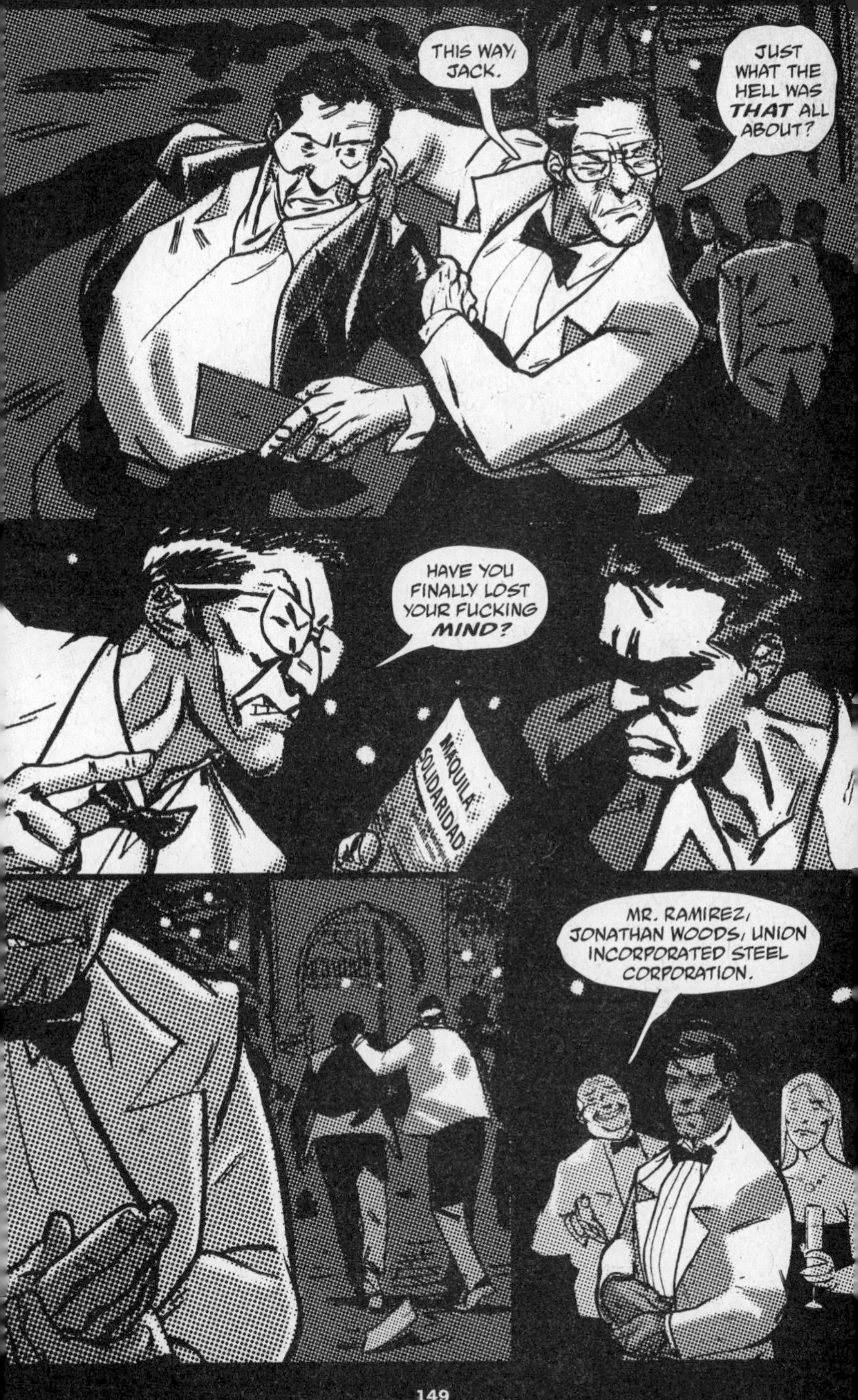
THIS WAY, JACK.
JUST WHAT THE HELL WAS THAT ALL ABOUT?
HAVE YOU FINALLY LOST YOUR FUCKING MIND?
MAQUILA SOLIDARIDAD
MR. RAMIREZ, JONATHAN WOODS, UNION INCORPORATED STEEL CORPORATION.

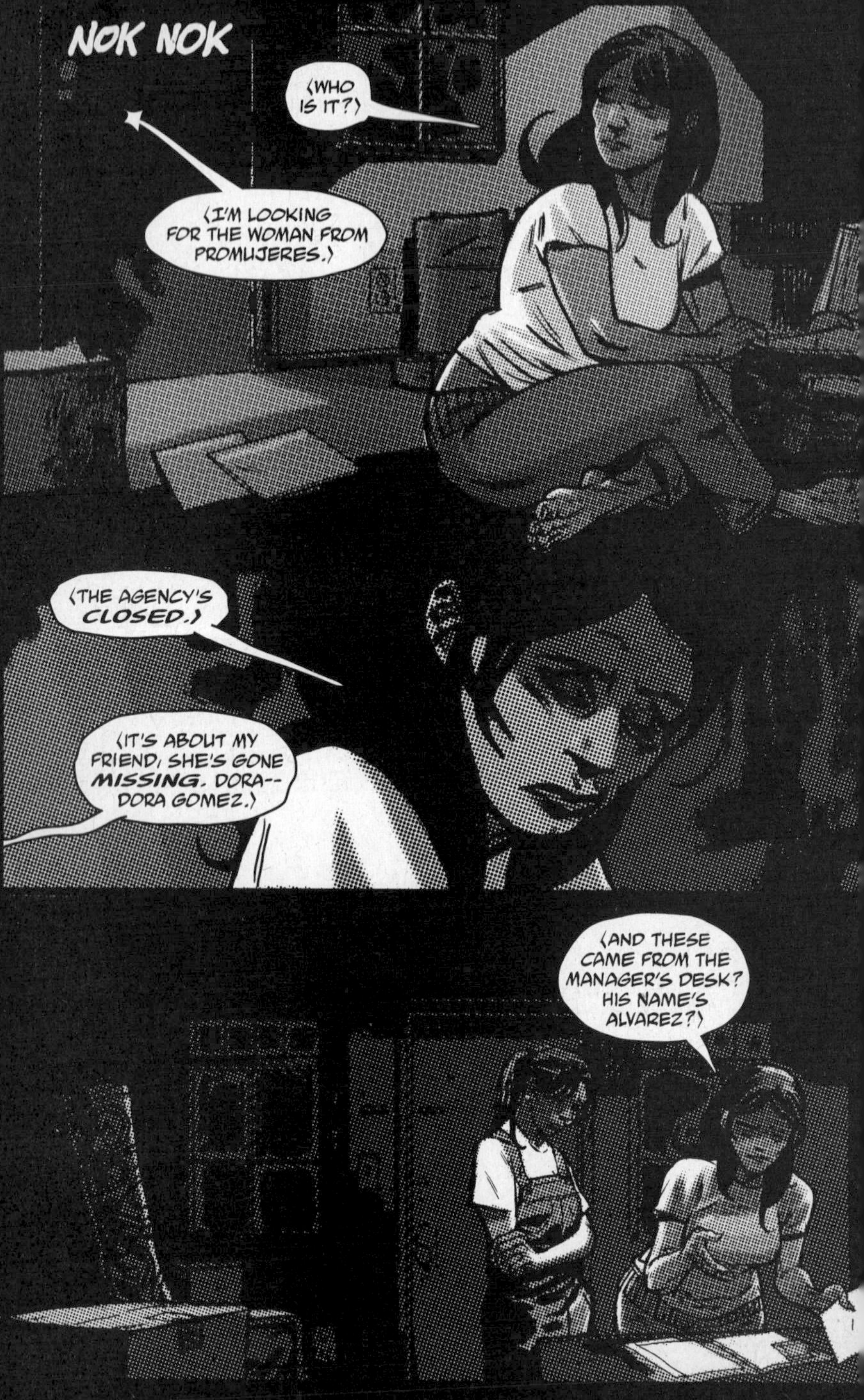
NOK NOK
⟨WHO IS IT?⟩
⟨I'M LOOKING FOR THE WOMAN FROM PROMUJERES.⟩
⟨THE AGENCY'S CLOSED.⟩
⟨IT'S ABOUT MY FRIEND, SHE'S GONE MISSING. DORA-- DORA GOMEZ.⟩
⟨AND THESE CAME FROM THE MANAGER'S DESK? HIS NAME'S ALVAREZ?⟩

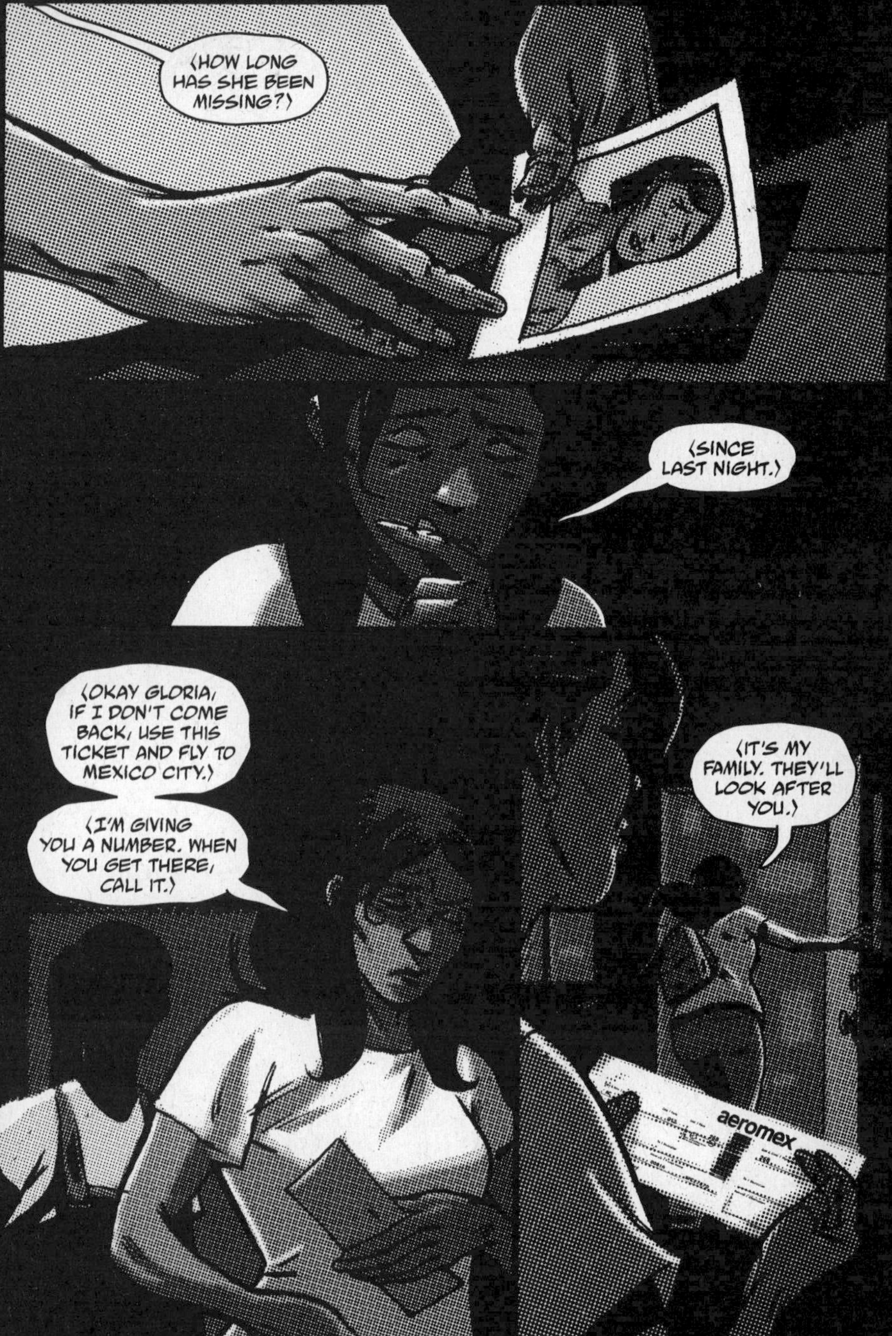
⟨HOW LONG HAS SHE BEEN MISSING?⟩
⟨SINCE LAST NIGHT.⟩
⟨OKAY GLORIA, IF I DON'T COME BACK, USE THIS TICKET AND FLY TO MEXICO CITY.⟩
⟨I'M GIVING YOU A NUMBER. WHEN YOU GET THERE, CALL IT.⟩
⟨IT'S MY FAMILY. THEY'LL LOOK AFTER YOU.⟩
aeromex

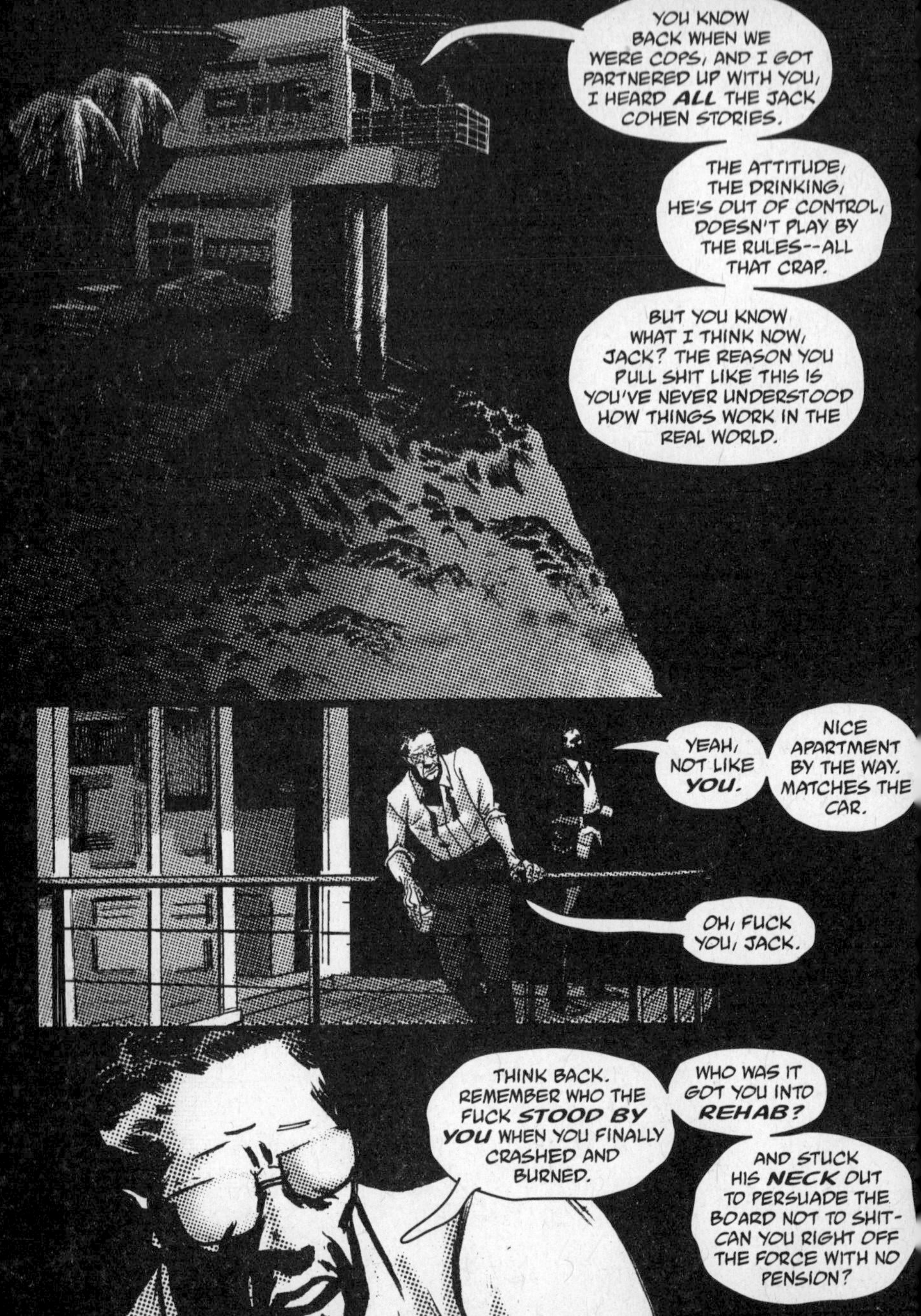
YOU KNOW BACK WHEN WE WERE COPS, AND I GOT PARTNERED UP WITH YOU, I HEARD ALL THE JACK COHEN STORIES.
THE ATTITUDE, THE DRINKING, HE'S OUT OF CONTROL, DOESN'T PLAY BY THE RULES--ALL THAT CRAP.
BUT YOU KNOW WHAT I THINK NOW, JACK? THE REASON YOU PULL SHIT LIKE THIS IS YOU'VE NEVER UNDERSTOOD HOW THINGS WORK IN THE REAL WORLD.
YEAH, NOT LIKE YOU.
NICE APARTMENT BY THE WAY. MATCHES THE CAR.
OH, FUCK YOU, JACK.
THINK BACK. REMEMBER WHO THE FUCK STOOD BY YOU WHEN YOU FINALLY CRASHED AND BURNED.
WHO WAS IT GOT YOU INTO REHAB?
AND STUCK HIS NECK OUT TO PERSUADE THE BOARD NOT TO SHIT-CAN YOU RIGHT OFF THE FORCE WITH NO PENSION?

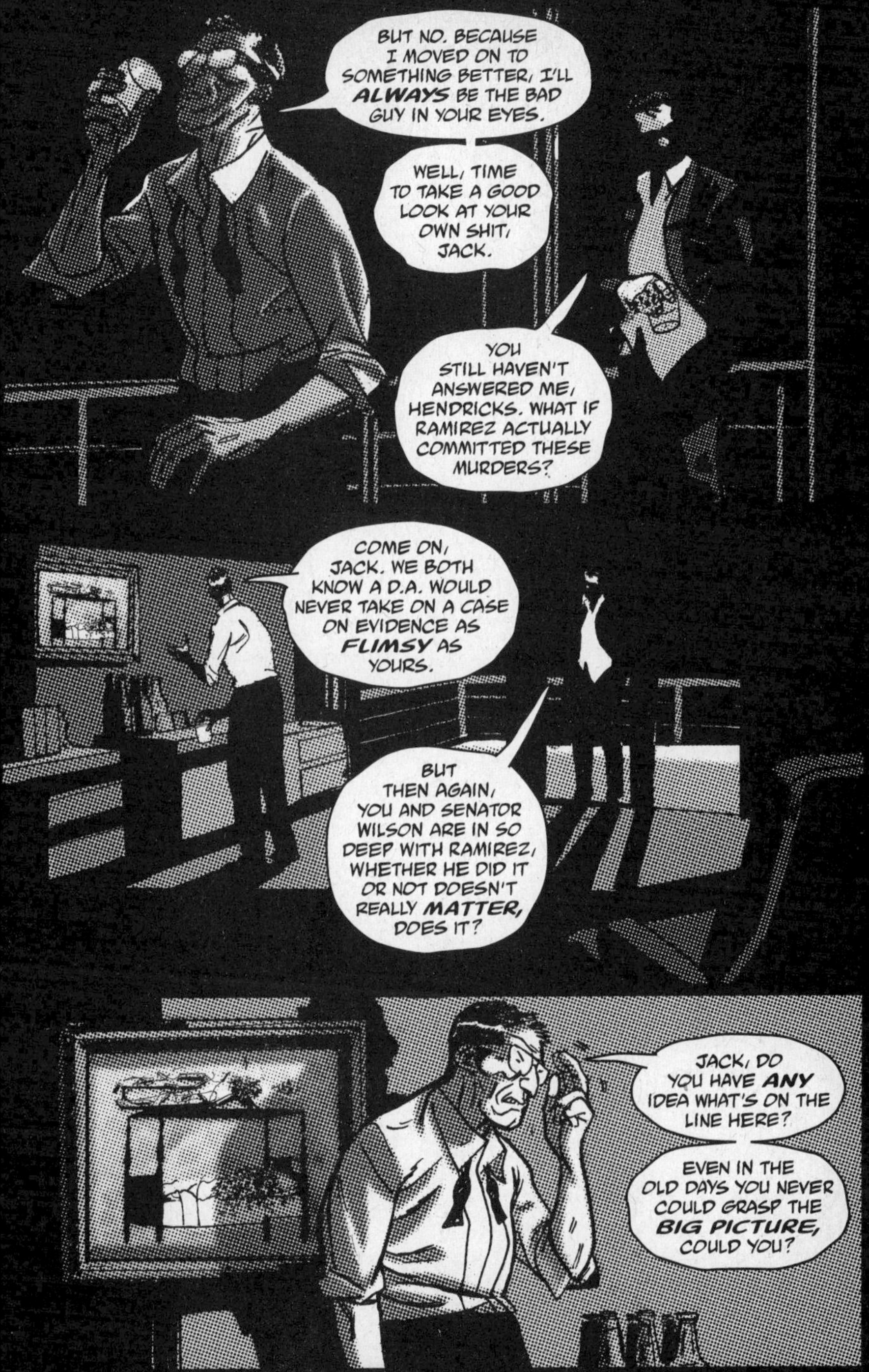
BUT NO. BECAUSE I MOVED ON TO SOMETHING BETTER, I'LL ALWAYS BE THE BAD GUY IN YOUR EYES.
WELL, TIME TO TAKE A GOOD LOOK AT YOUR OWN SHIT, JACK.
YOU STILL HAVEN'T ANSWERED ME, HENDRICKS. WHAT IF RAMIREZ ACTUALLY COMMITTED THESE MURDERS?
COME ON, JACK. WE BOTH KNOW A D.A. WOULD NEVER TAKE ON A CASE ON EVIDENCE AS FLIMSY AS YOURS.
BUT THEN AGAIN, YOU AND SENATOR WILSON ARE IN SO DEEP WITH RAMIREZ, WHETHER HE DID IT OR NOT DOESN'T REALLY MATTER, DOES IT?
JACK, DO YOU HAVE ANY IDEA WHAT'S ON THE LINE HERE?
EVEN IN THE OLD DAYS YOU NEVER COULD GRASP THE BIG PICTURE, COULD YOU?

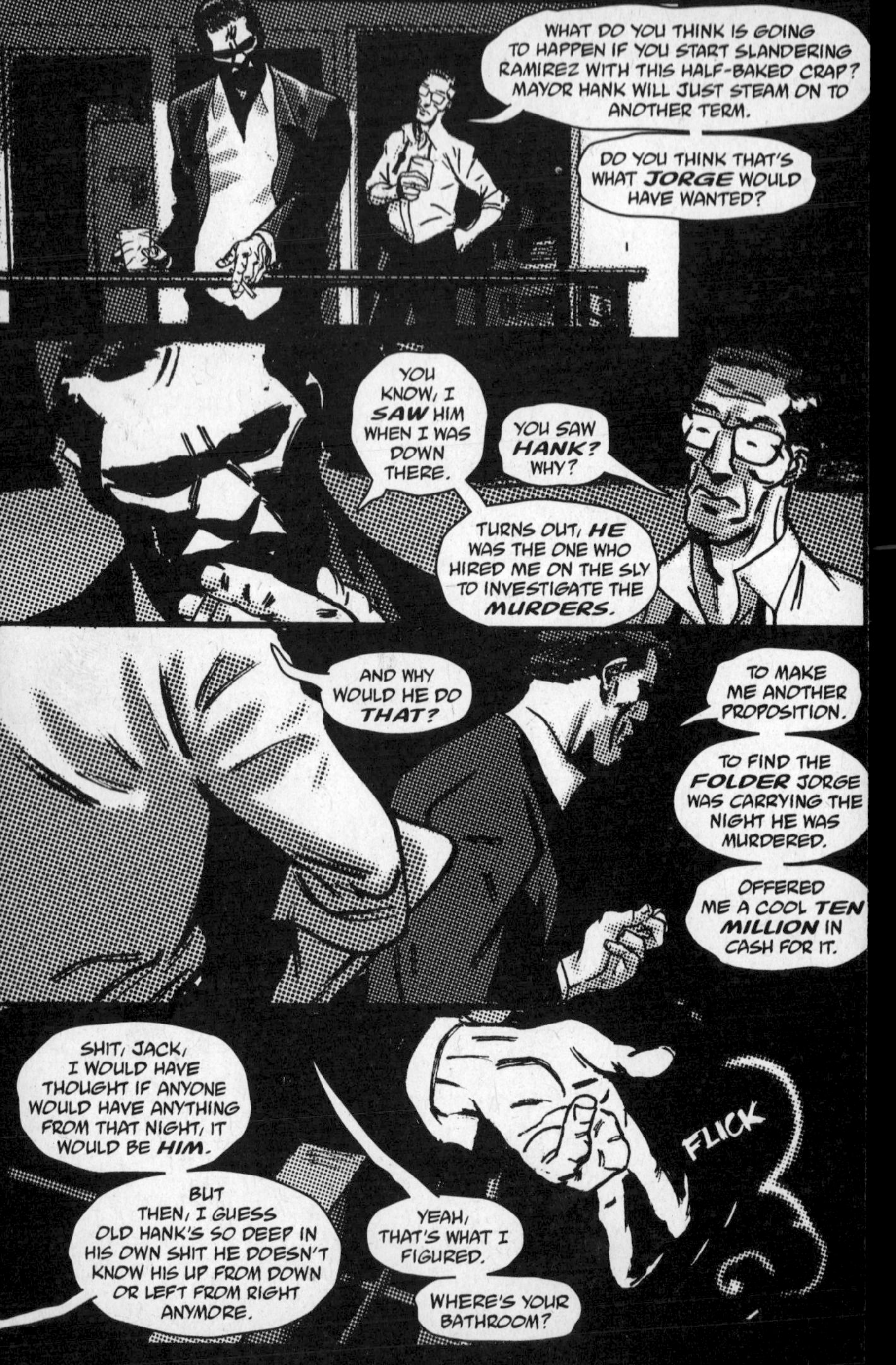
WHAT DO YOU THINK IS GOING TO HAPPEN IF YOU START SLANDERING RAMIREZ WITH THIS HALF-BAKED CRAP? MAYOR HANK WILL JUST STEAM ON TO ANOTHER TERM.
DO YOU THINK THAT'S WHAT JORGE WOULD HAVE WANTED?
YOU KNOW, I SAW HIM WHEN I WAS DOWN THERE.
YOU SAW HANK? WHY?
TURNS OUT, HE WAS THE ONE WHO HIRED ME ON THE SLY TO INVESTIGATE THE MURDERS.
AND WHY WOULD HE DO THAT?
TO MAKE ME ANOTHER PROPOSITION.
TO FIND THE FOLDER JORGE WAS CARRYING THE NIGHT HE WAS MURDERED.
OFFERED ME A COOL TEN MILLION IN CASH FOR IT.
SHIT, JACK, I WOULD HAVE THOUGHT IF ANYONE WOULD HAVE ANYTHING FROM THAT NIGHT, IT WOULD BE HIM.
FLICK
BUT THEN, I GUESS OLD HANK'S SO DEEP IN HIS OWN SHIT HE DOESN'T KNOW HIS UP FROM DOWN OR LEFT FROM RIGHT ANYMORE.
YEAH, THAT'S WHAT I FIGURED.
WHERE'S YOUR BATHROOM?

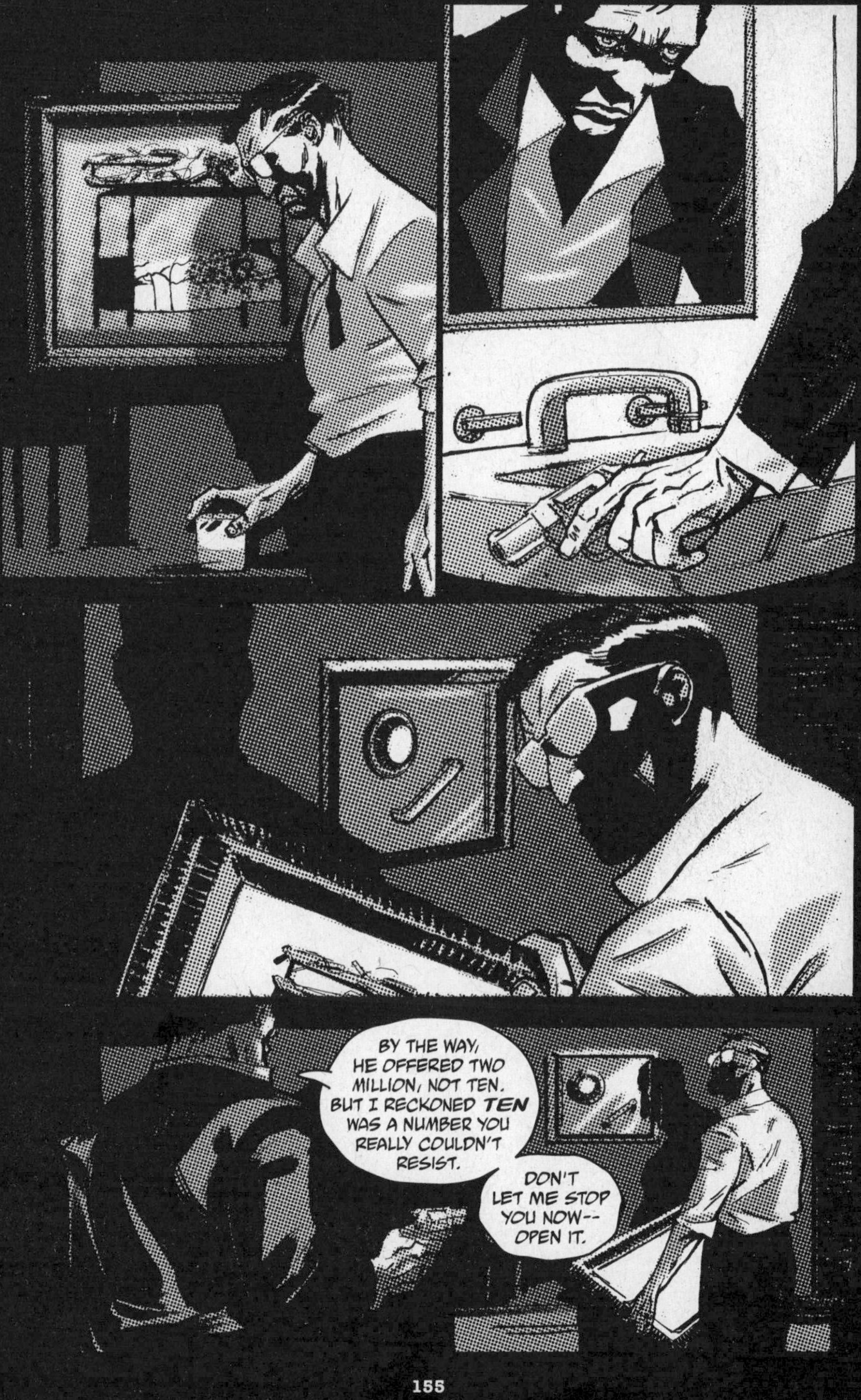
BY THE WAY, HE OFFERED TWO MILLION, NOT TEN. BUT I RECKONED TEN WAS A NUMBER YOU REALLY COULDN'T RESIST.
DON'T LET ME STOP YOU NOW-- OPEN IT.

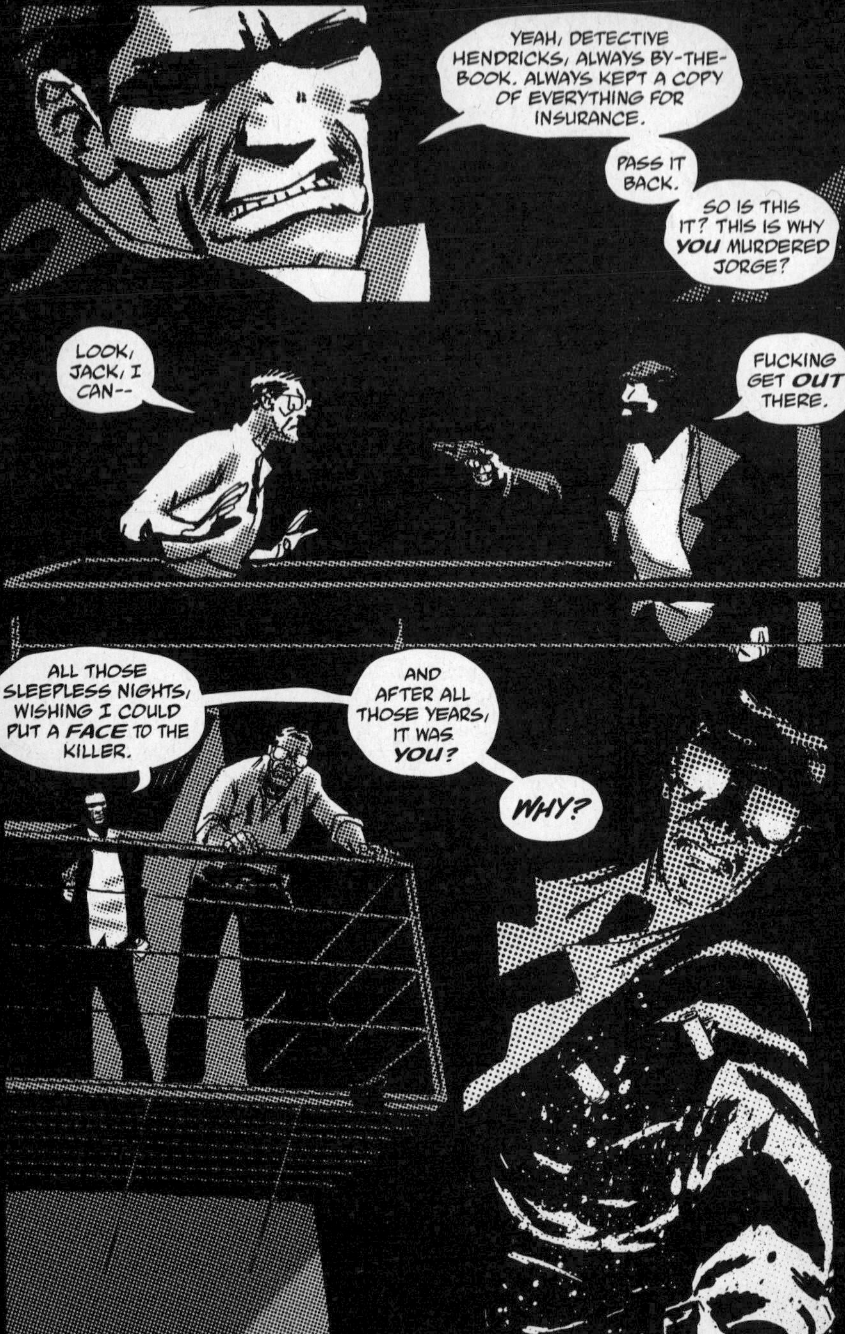
YEAH, DETECTIVE HENDRICKS, ALWAYS BY-THE-BOOK. ALWAYS KEPT A COPY OF EVERYTHING FOR INSURANCE.
PASS IT BACK.
SO IS THIS IT? THIS IS WHY *YOU* MURDERED JORGE?
LOOK, JACK, I CAN--
FUCKING GET *OUT* THERE.
ALL THOSE SLEEPLESS NIGHTS, WISHING I COULD PUT A *FACE* TO THE KILLER.
AND AFTER ALL THOSE YEARS, IT WAS *YOU*?
WHY?

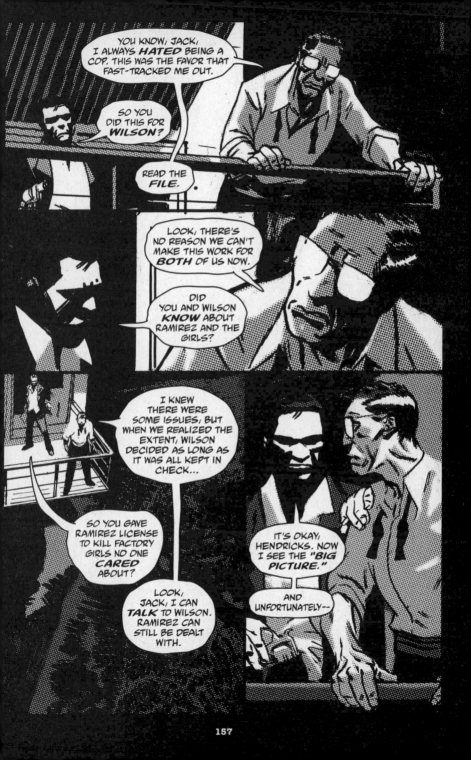

YOU KNOW, JACK, I ALWAYS *HATED* BEING A COP. THIS WAS THE FAVOR THAT FAST-TRACKED ME OUT.

SO YOU DID THIS FOR *WILSON?*

READ THE *FILE.*

LOOK, THERE'S NO REASON WE CAN'T MAKE THIS WORK FOR *BOTH* OF US NOW.

DID YOU AND WILSON *KNOW* ABOUT RAMIREZ AND THE GIRLS?

I KNEW THERE WERE SOME ISSUES, BUT WHEN WE REALIZED THE EXTENT, WILSON DECIDED AS LONG AS IT WAS ALL KEPT IN CHECK...

SO YOU GAVE RAMIREZ LICENSE TO KILL FACTORY GIRLS NO ONE *CARED* ABOUT?

LOOK, JACK, I CAN *TALK* TO WILSON. RAMIREZ CAN STILL BE DEALT WITH.

IT'S OKAY, HENDRICKS. NOW I SEE THE *"BIG PICTURE."*

AND UNFORTUNATELY--

157

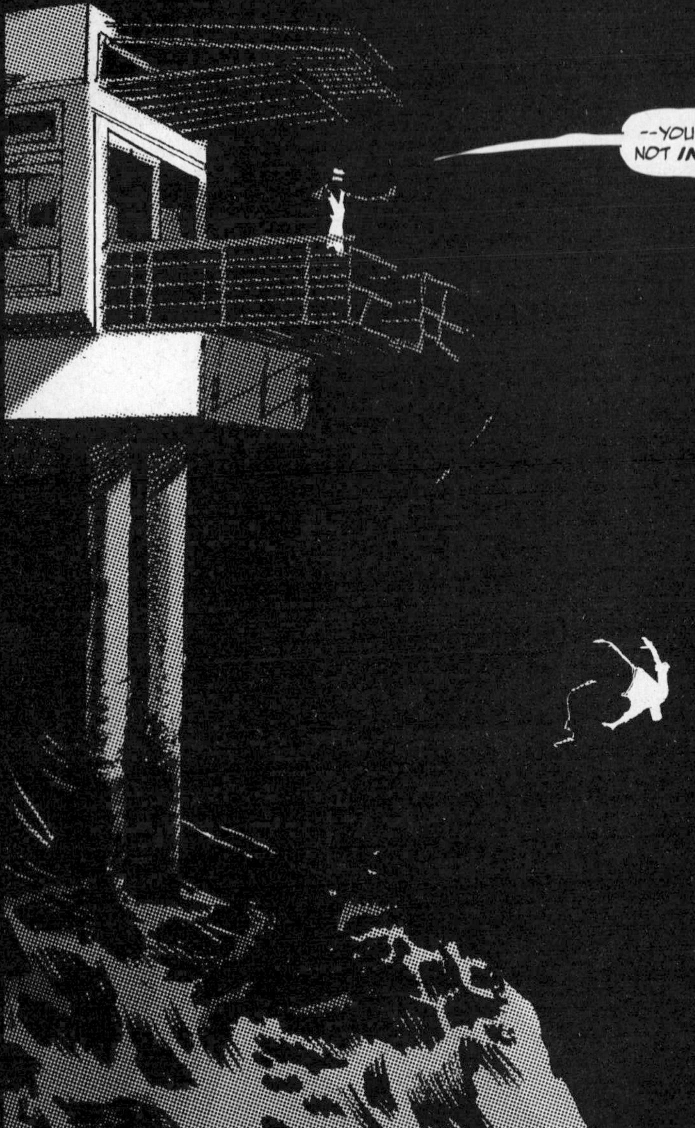
--YOU'RE NOT IN IT.

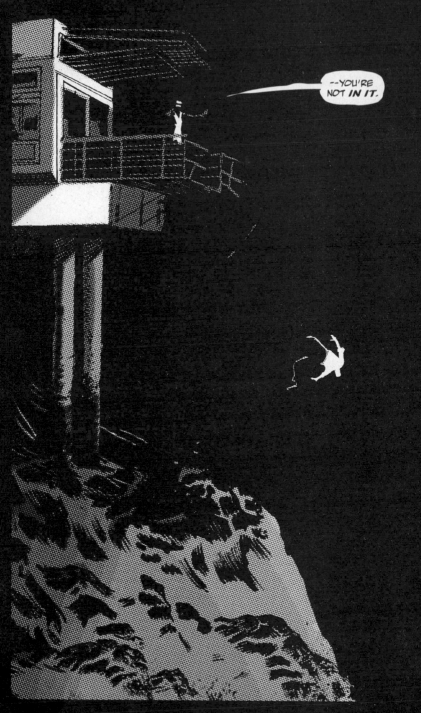

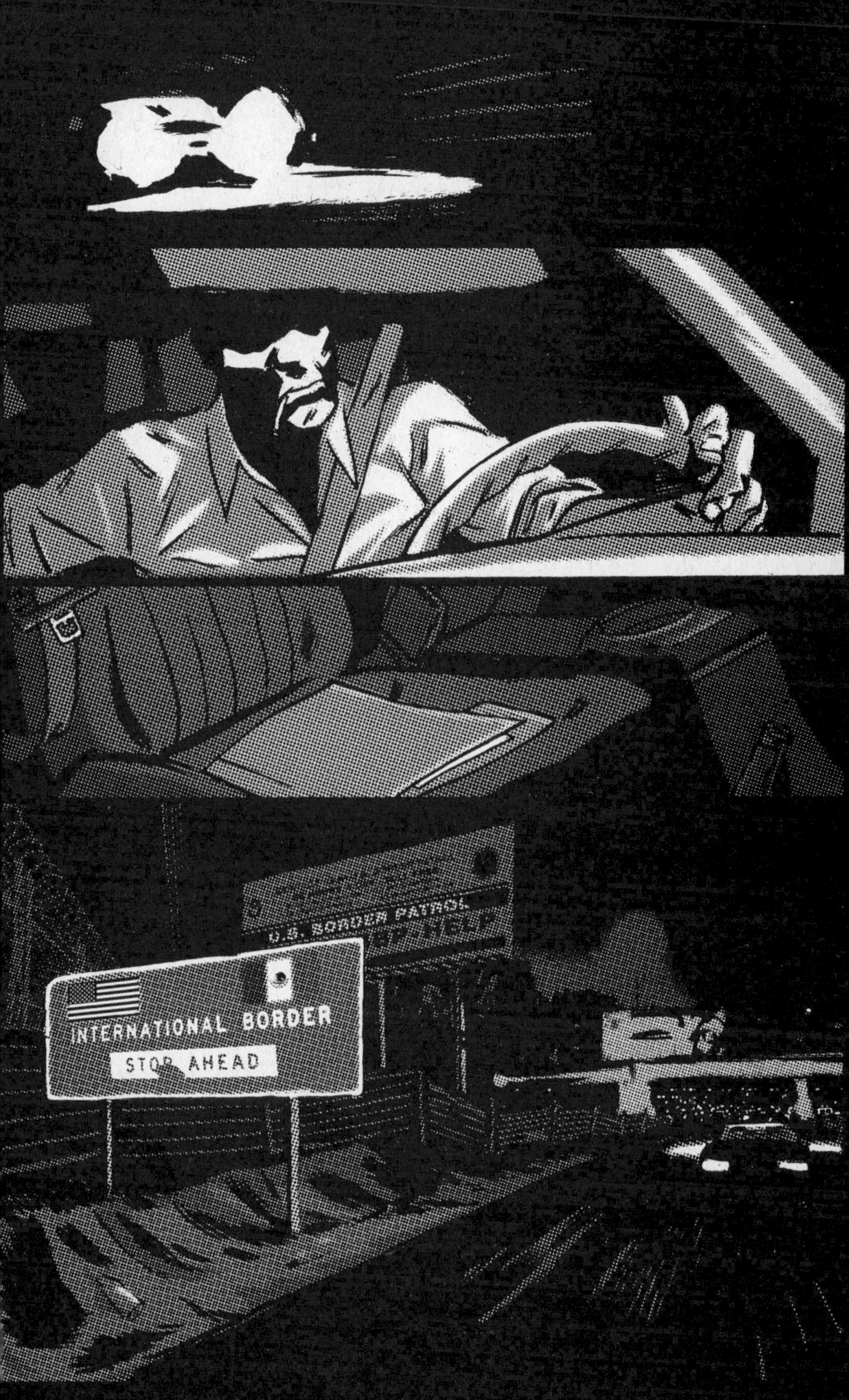
U.S. BORDER PATROL
INTERNATIONAL BORDER
STOP AHEAD

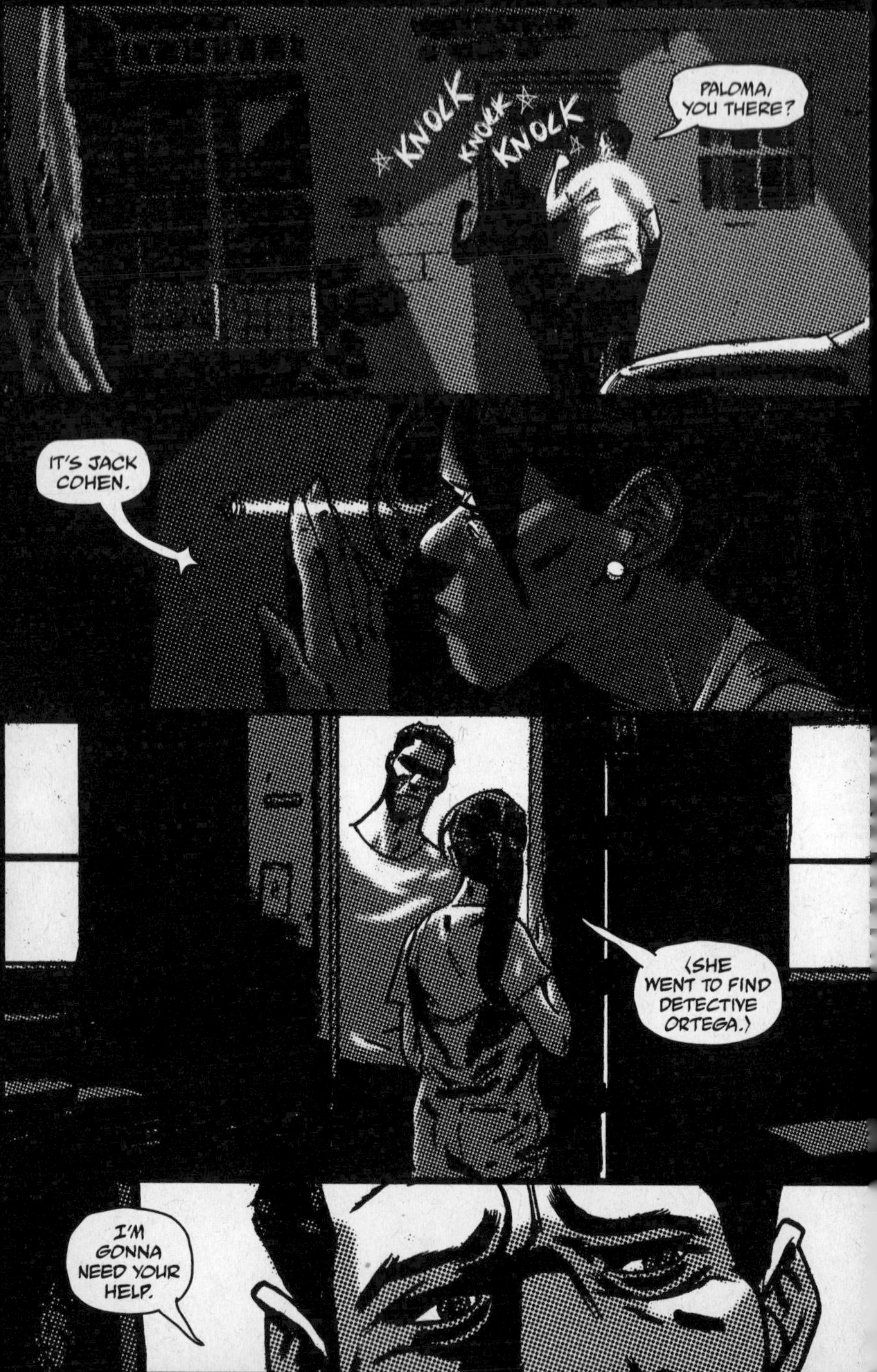
KNOCK KNOCK KNOCK
PALOMA, YOU THERE?
IT'S JACK COHEN.
(SHE WENT TO FIND DETECTIVE ORTEGA.)
I'M GONNA NEED YOUR HELP.

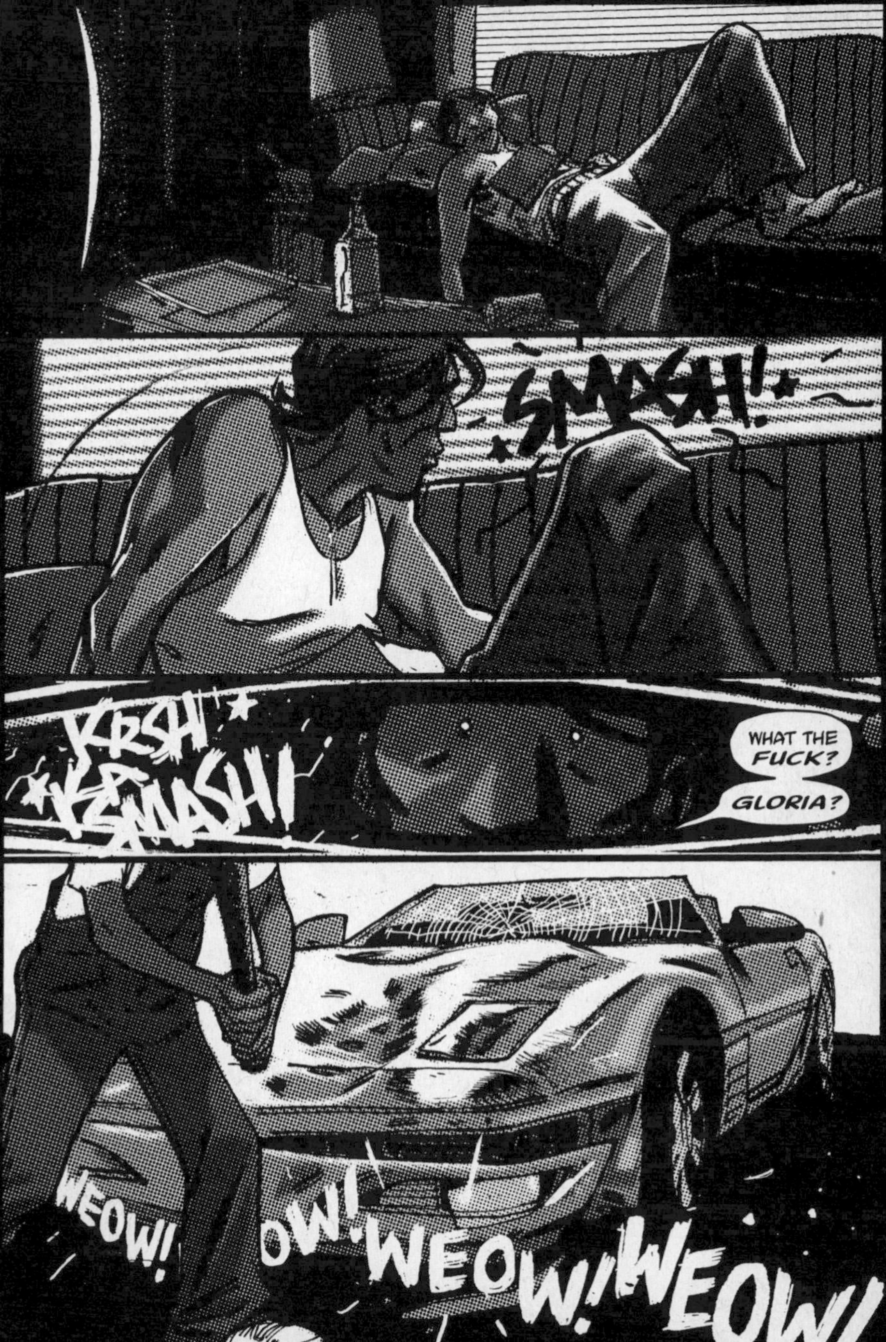
SMASH!
KRSH
KRSMASH!
WHAT THE FUCK?
GLORIA?
WEOW!
OW!
WEOW!
WEOW!

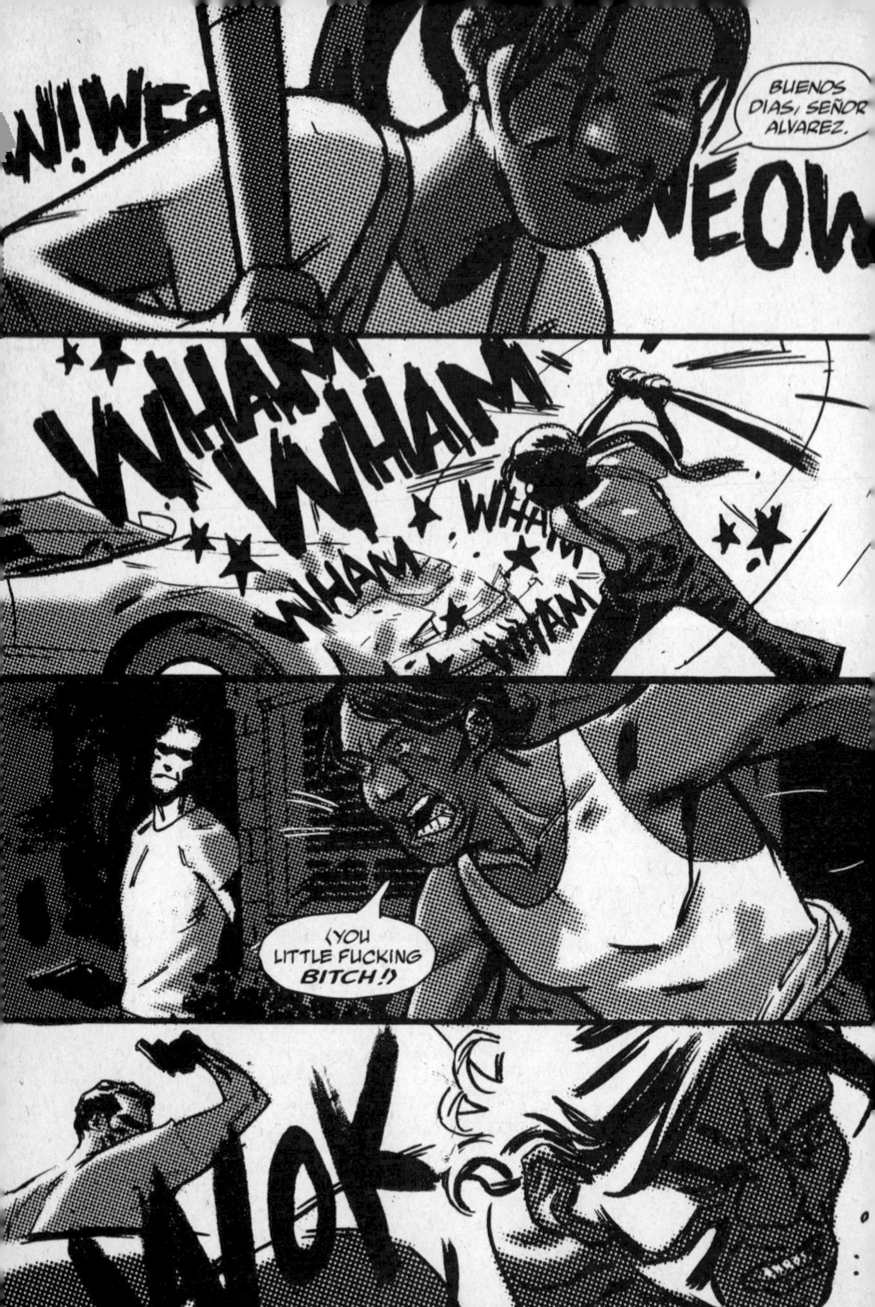
BUENOS DIAS, SEÑOR ALVAREZ.
WEOW
WHAM
WHAM
WHAM
WHAM
WHAM
‹YOU LITTLE FUCKING BITCH!›

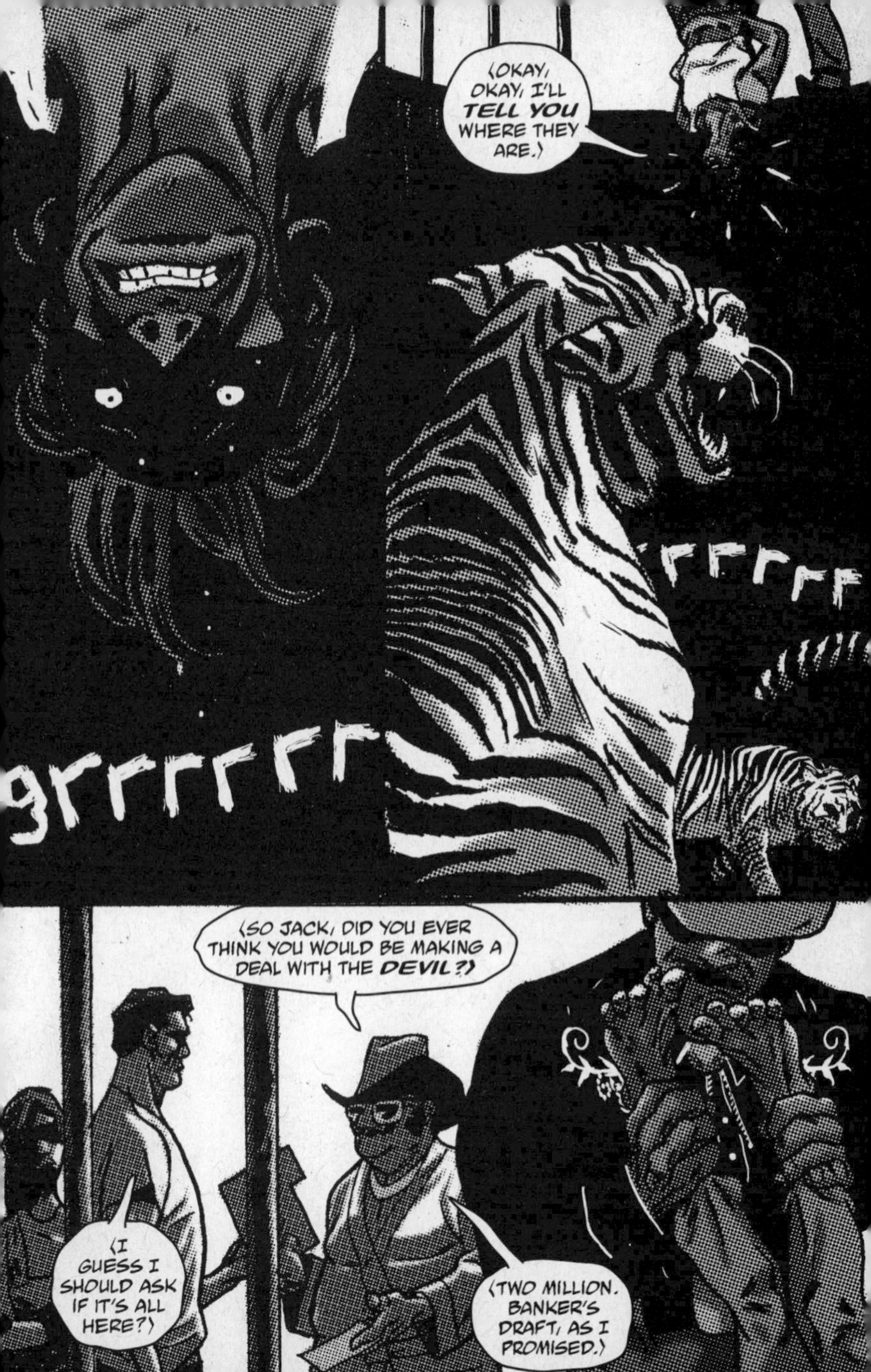

⟨OKAY, OKAY, I'LL TELL YOU WHERE THEY ARE.⟩
grrrrrr
rrrrrr
⟨SO JACK, DID YOU EVER THINK YOU WOULD BE MAKING A DEAL WITH THE DEVIL?⟩
⟨I GUESS I SHOULD ASK IF IT'S ALL HERE?⟩
⟨TWO MILLION. BANKER'S DRAFT, AS I PROMISED.⟩

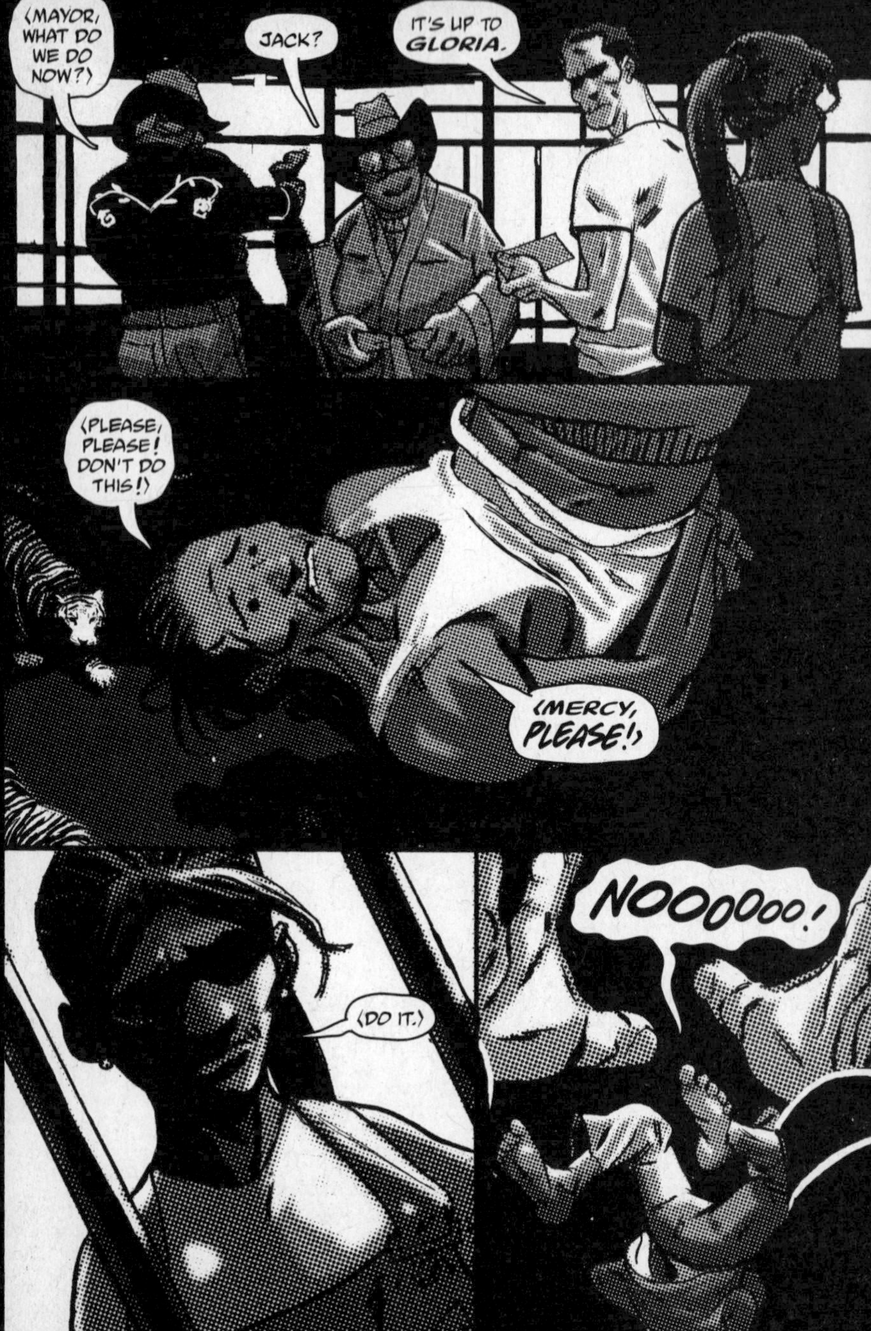
‹MAYOR, WHAT DO WE DO NOW?›
JACK?
IT'S UP TO GLORIA.
‹PLEASE, PLEASE! DON'T DO THIS!›
‹MERCY, PLEASE!›
‹DO IT.›
NOOOOOO!

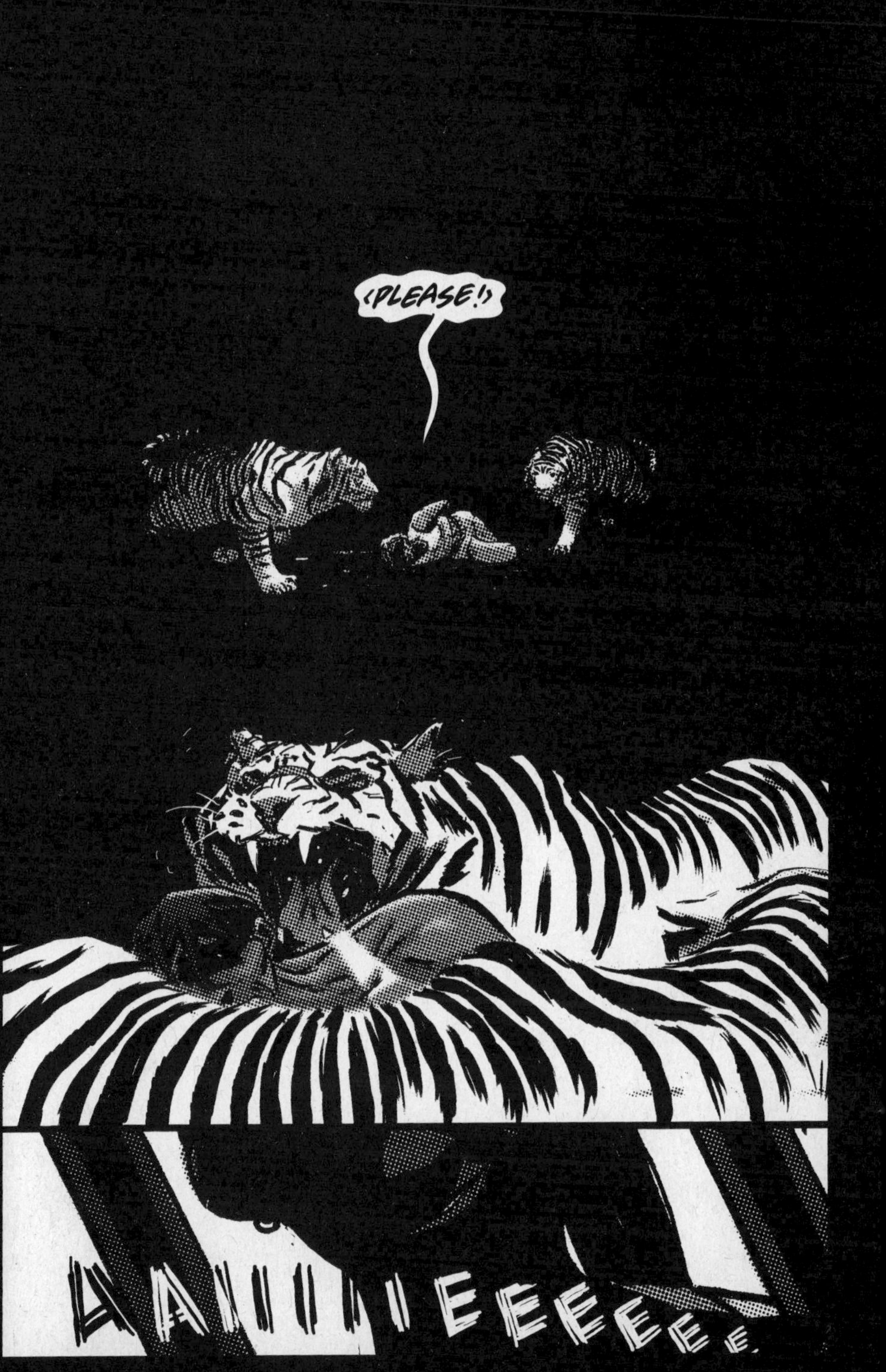
‹PLEASE!›
AAIIIIEEEEEEE

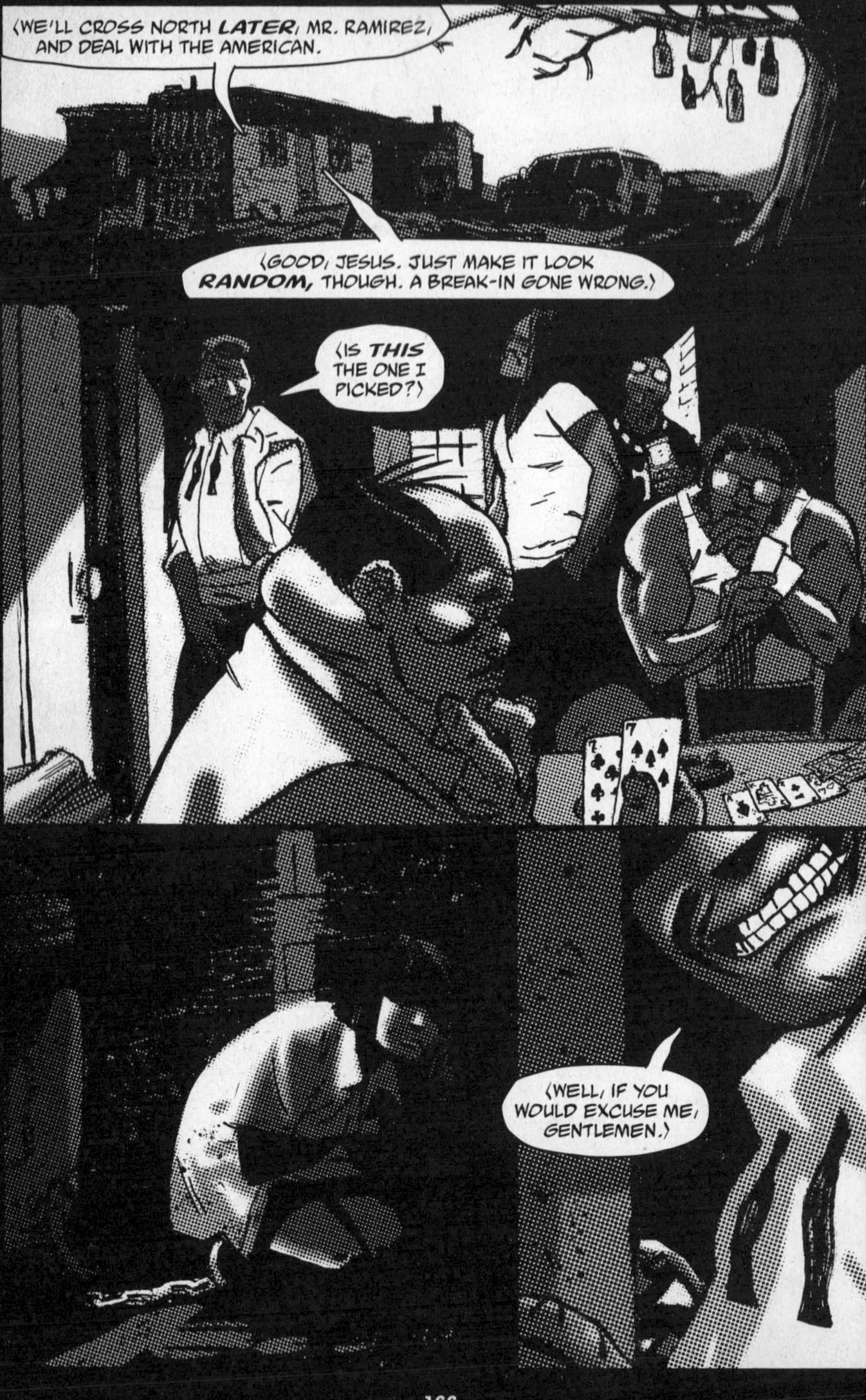
⟨WE'LL CROSS NORTH LATER, MR. RAMIREZ, AND DEAL WITH THE AMERICAN.
⟨GOOD, JESUS. JUST MAKE IT LOOK RANDOM, THOUGH. A BREAK-IN GONE WRONG.⟩
⟨IS THIS THE ONE I PICKED?⟩
⟨WELL, IF YOU WOULD EXCUSE ME, GENTLEMEN.⟩

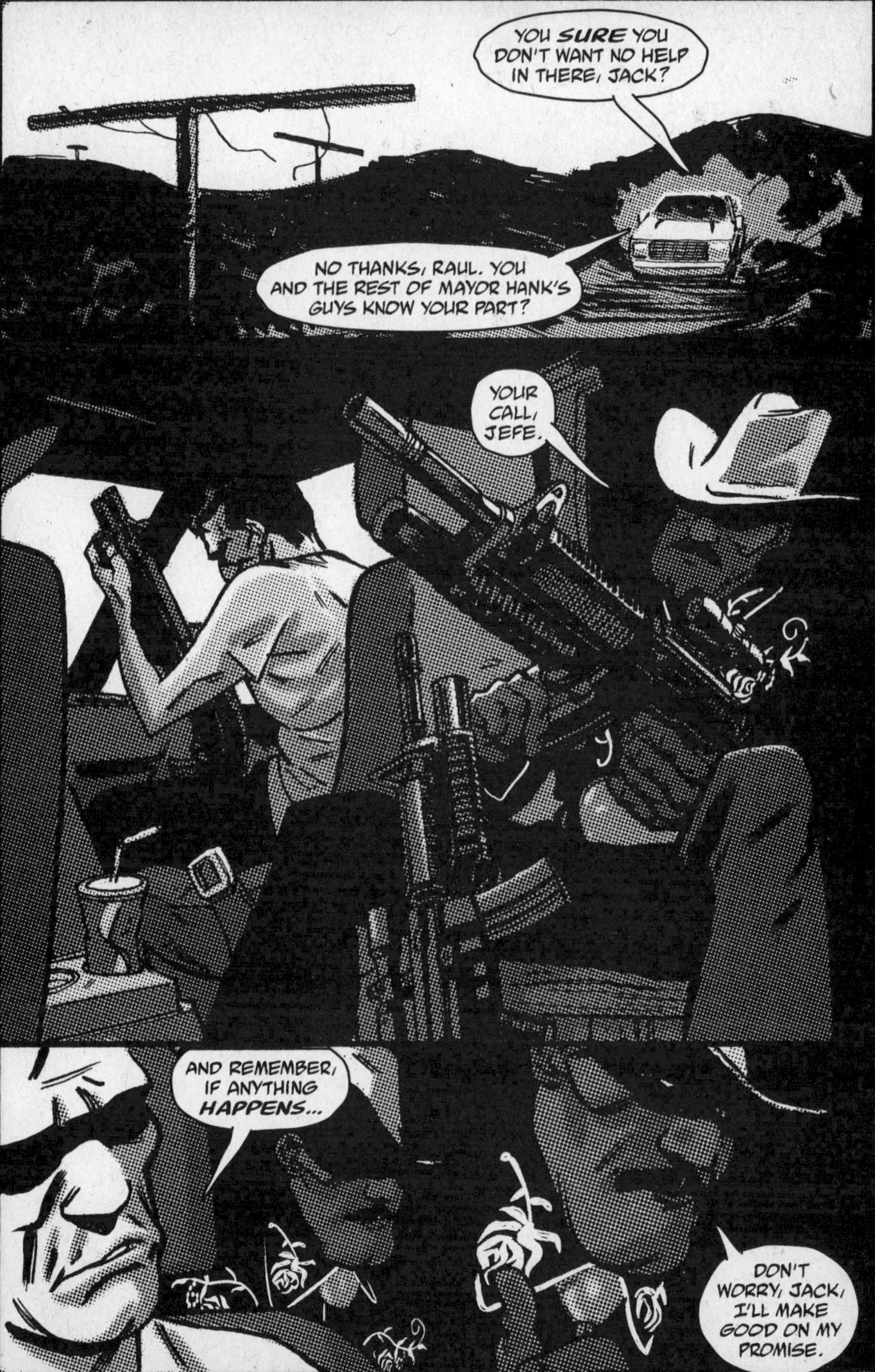
YOU *SURE* YOU DON'T WANT NO HELP IN THERE, JACK?
NO THANKS, RAUL. YOU AND THE REST OF MAYOR HANK'S GUYS KNOW YOUR PART?
YOUR CALL, JEFE.
AND REMEMBER, IF ANYTHING *HAPPENS*...
DON'T WORRY, JACK, I'LL MAKE GOOD ON MY PROMISE.

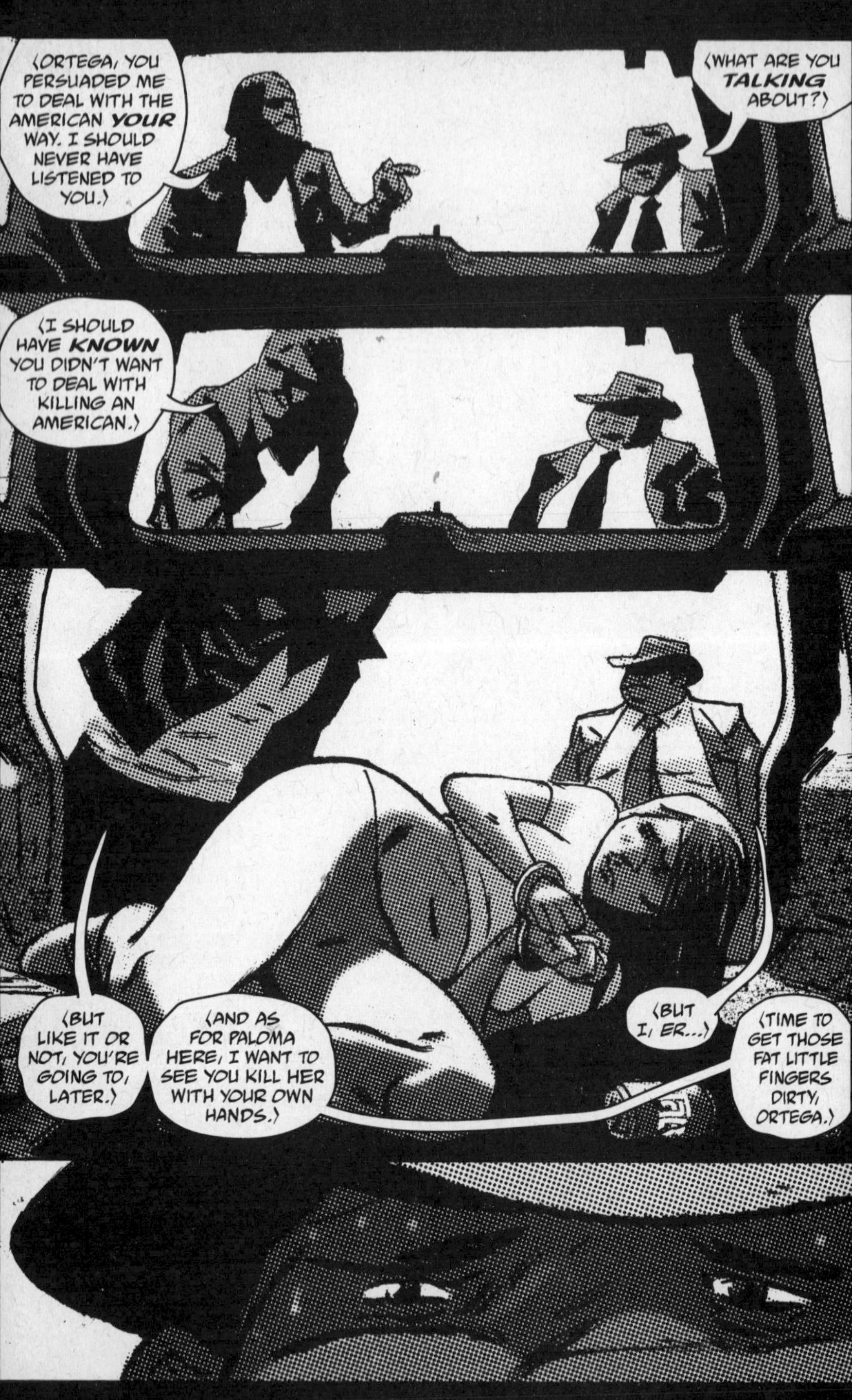
⟨ORTEGA, YOU PERSUADED ME TO DEAL WITH THE AMERICAN YOUR WAY. I SHOULD NEVER HAVE LISTENED TO YOU.⟩
⟨WHAT ARE YOU TALKING ABOUT?⟩
⟨I SHOULD HAVE KNOWN YOU DIDN'T WANT TO DEAL WITH KILLING AN AMERICAN.⟩
⟨BUT LIKE IT OR NOT, YOU'RE GOING TO, LATER.⟩
⟨AND AS FOR PALOMA HERE, I WANT TO SEE YOU KILL HER WITH YOUR OWN HANDS.⟩
⟨BUT I, ER...⟩
⟨TIME TO GET THOSE FAT LITTLE FINGERS DIRTY, ORTEGA.⟩

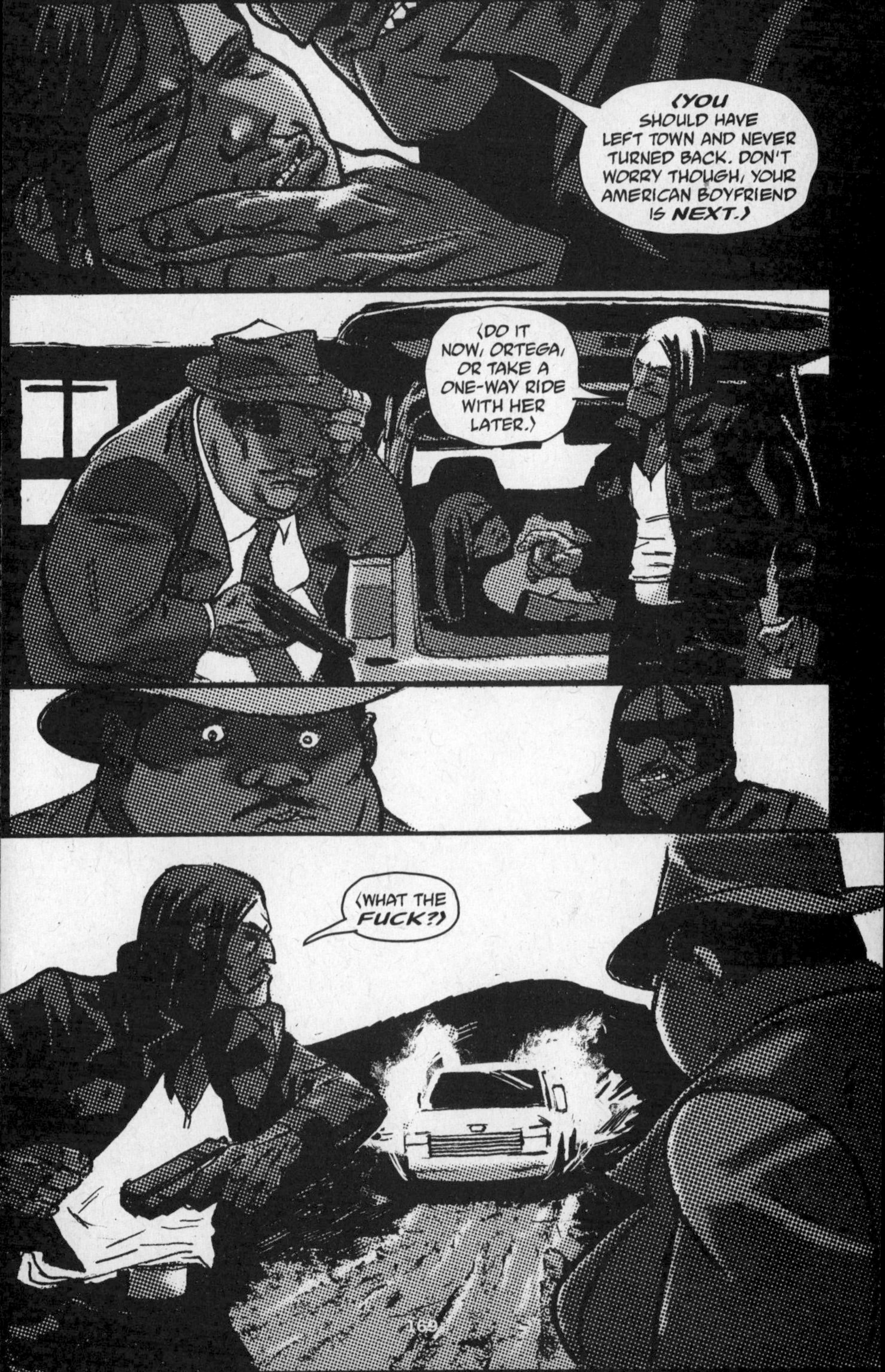
‹YOU SHOULD HAVE LEFT TOWN AND NEVER TURNED BACK. DON'T WORRY THOUGH, YOUR AMERICAN BOYFRIEND IS NEXT.›
‹DO IT NOW, ORTEGA, OR TAKE A ONE-WAY RIDE WITH HER LATER.›
‹WHAT THE FUCK?›

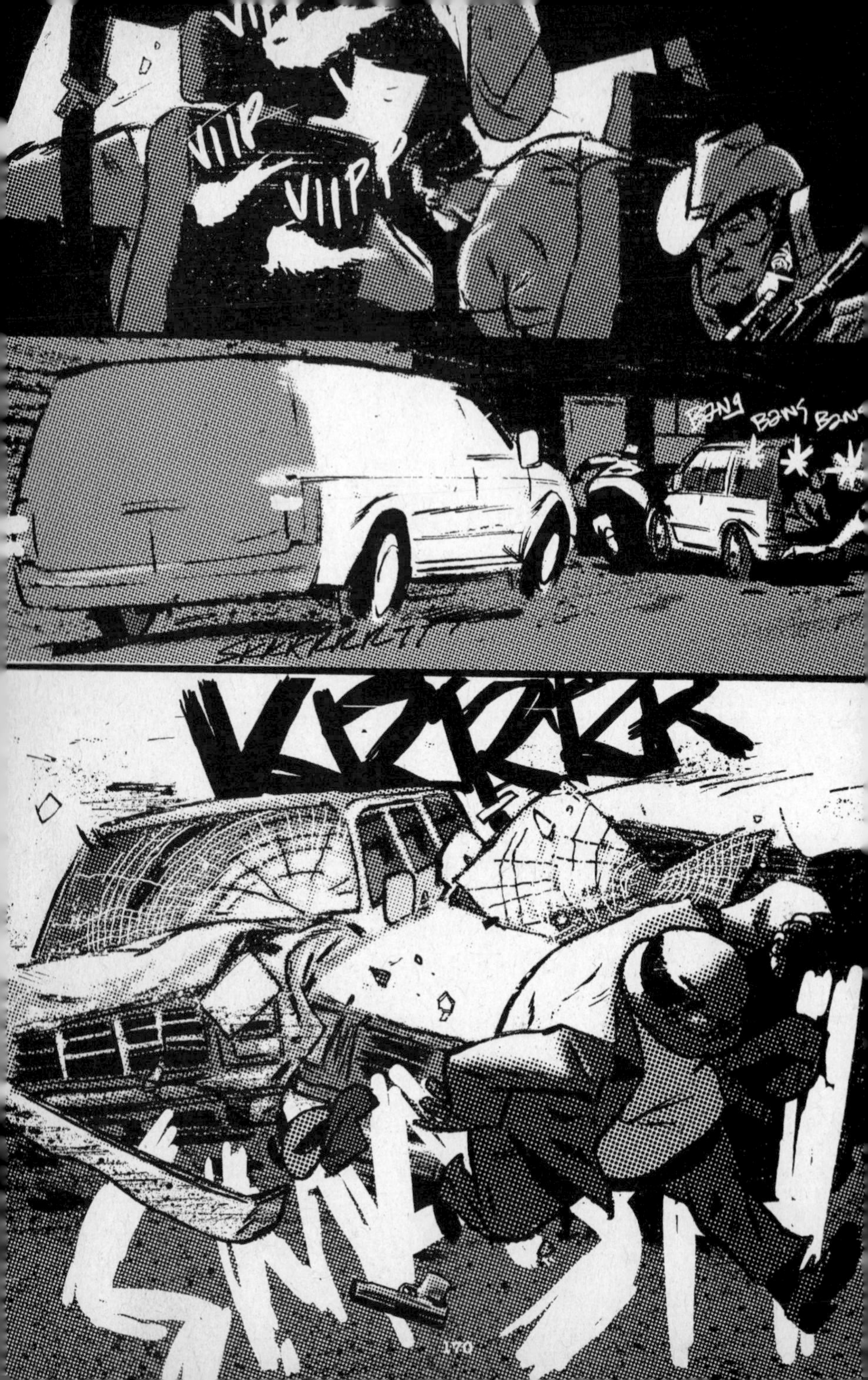
VIIP
VIIP
BANG
BANG

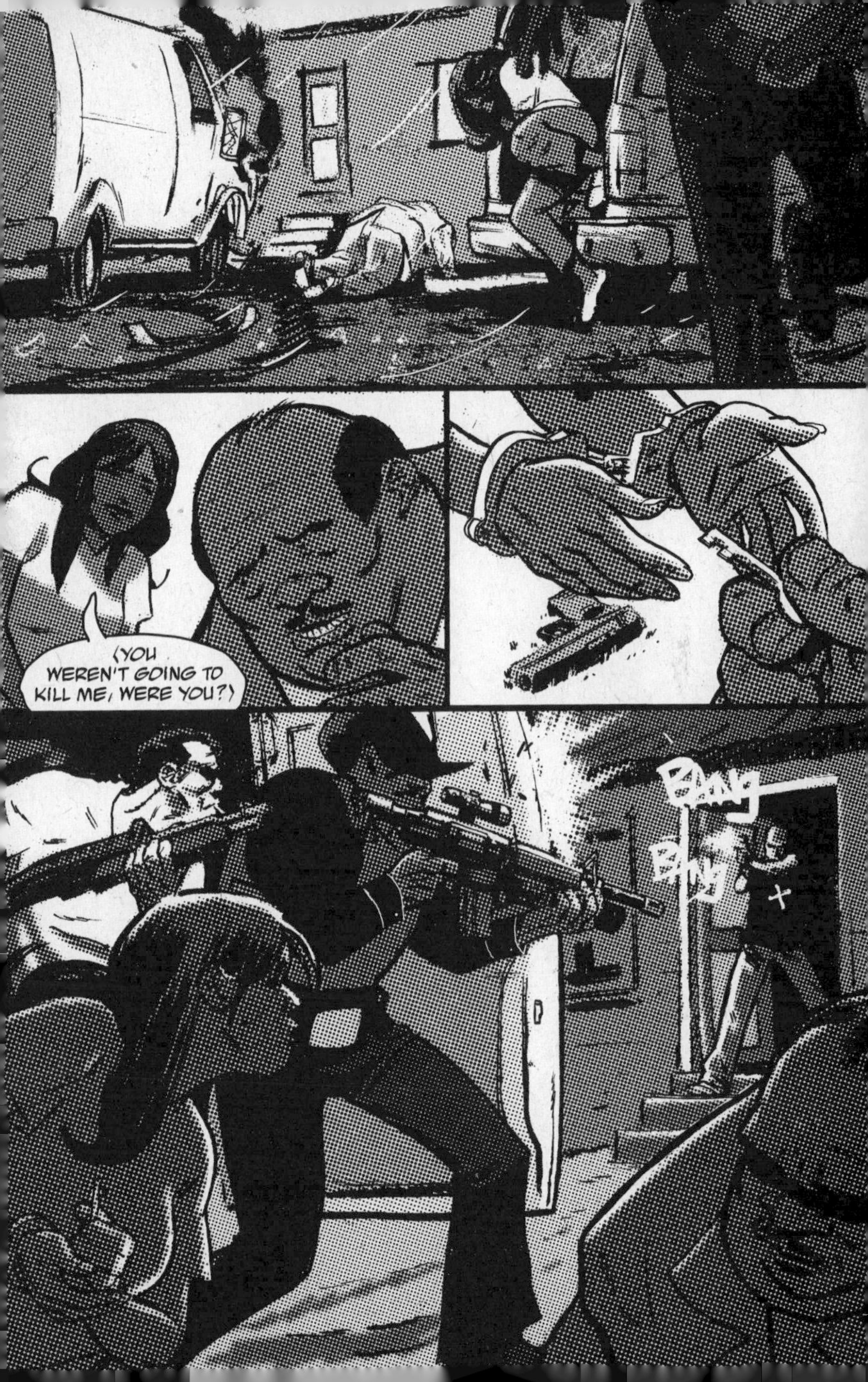
(YOU WEREN'T GOING TO KILL ME, WERE YOU?)
BLANG
BLANG

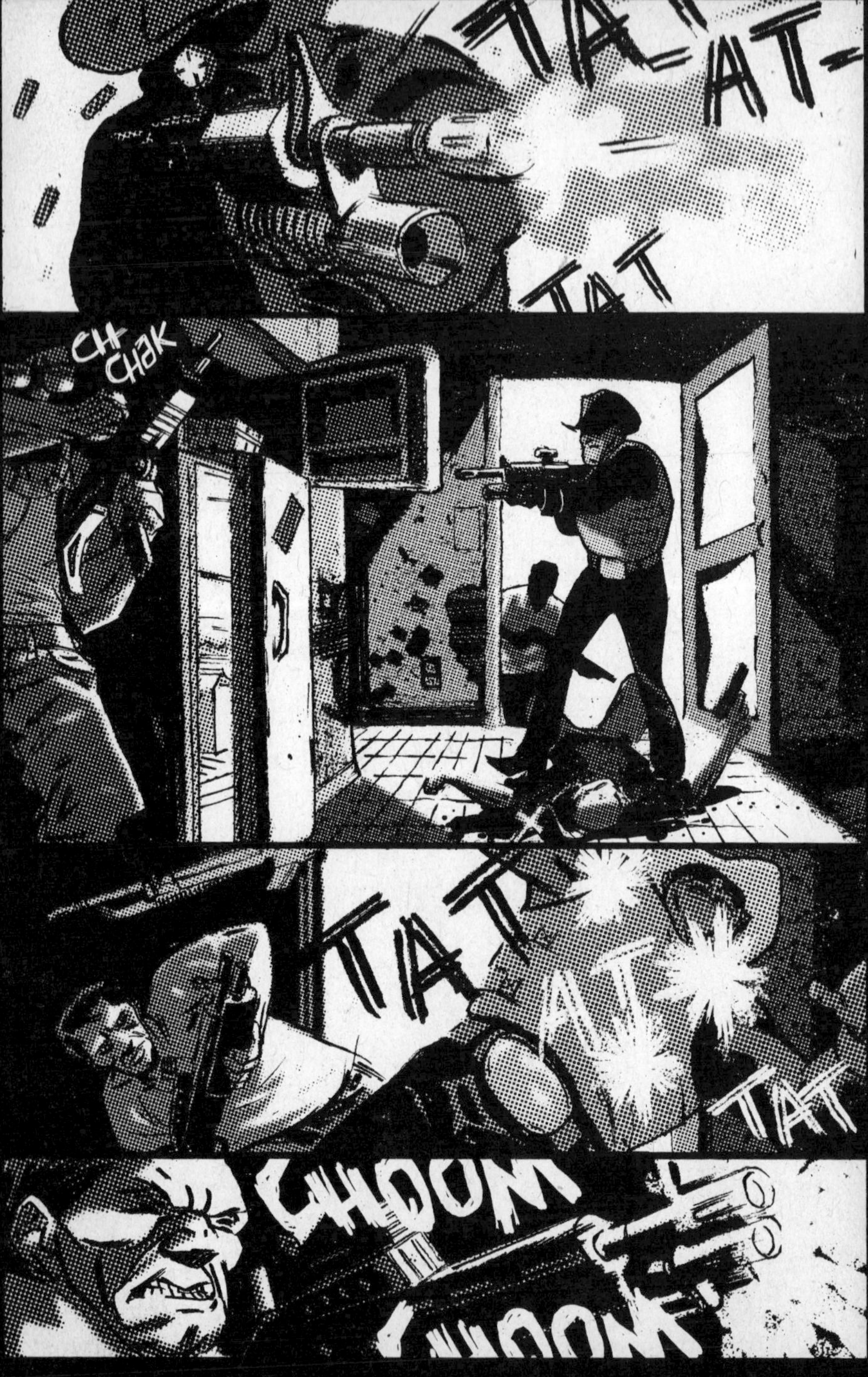
TAT-TAT-TAT
CH CHAK
TAT TAT TAT
CHOOM
CHOOM

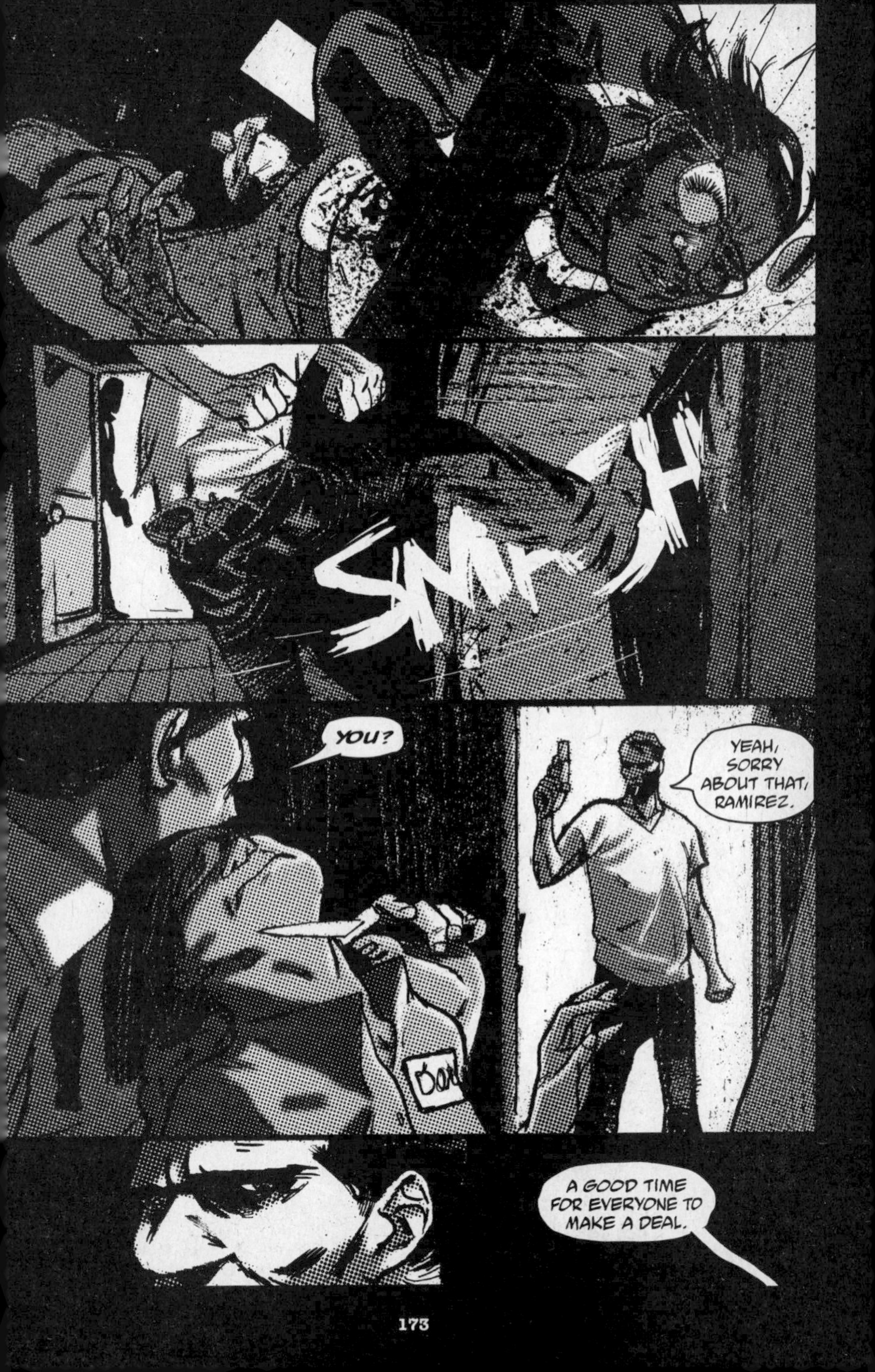
SMASH
YOU?
YEAH, SORRY ABOUT THAT, RAMIREZ.
A GOOD TIME FOR EVERYONE TO MAKE A DEAL.

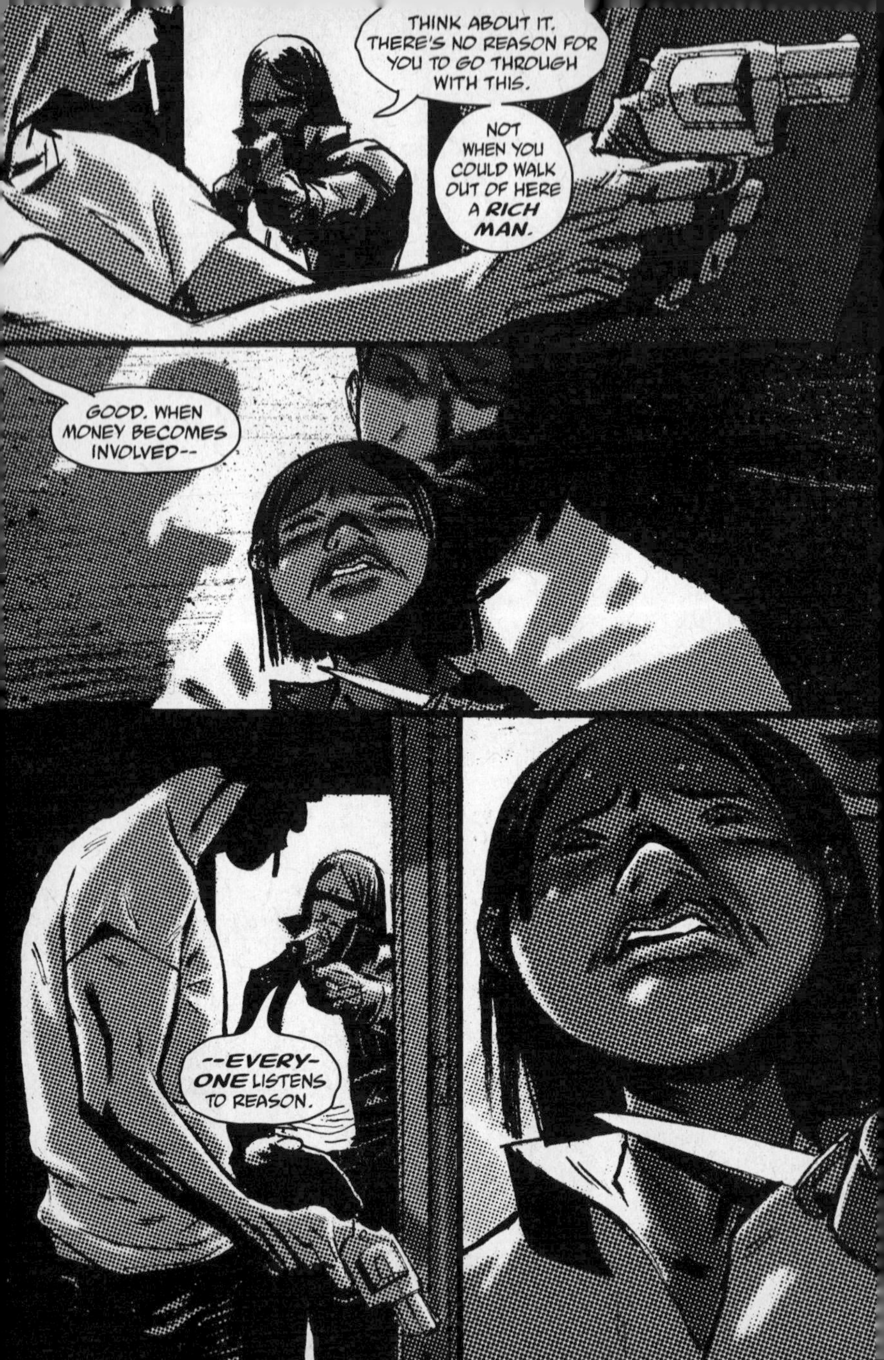
THINK ABOUT IT. THERE'S NO REASON FOR YOU TO GO THROUGH WITH THIS.
NOT WHEN YOU COULD WALK OUT OF HERE A RICH MAN.
GOOD. WHEN MONEY BECOMES INVOLVED--
--EVERY-ONE LISTENS TO REASON.

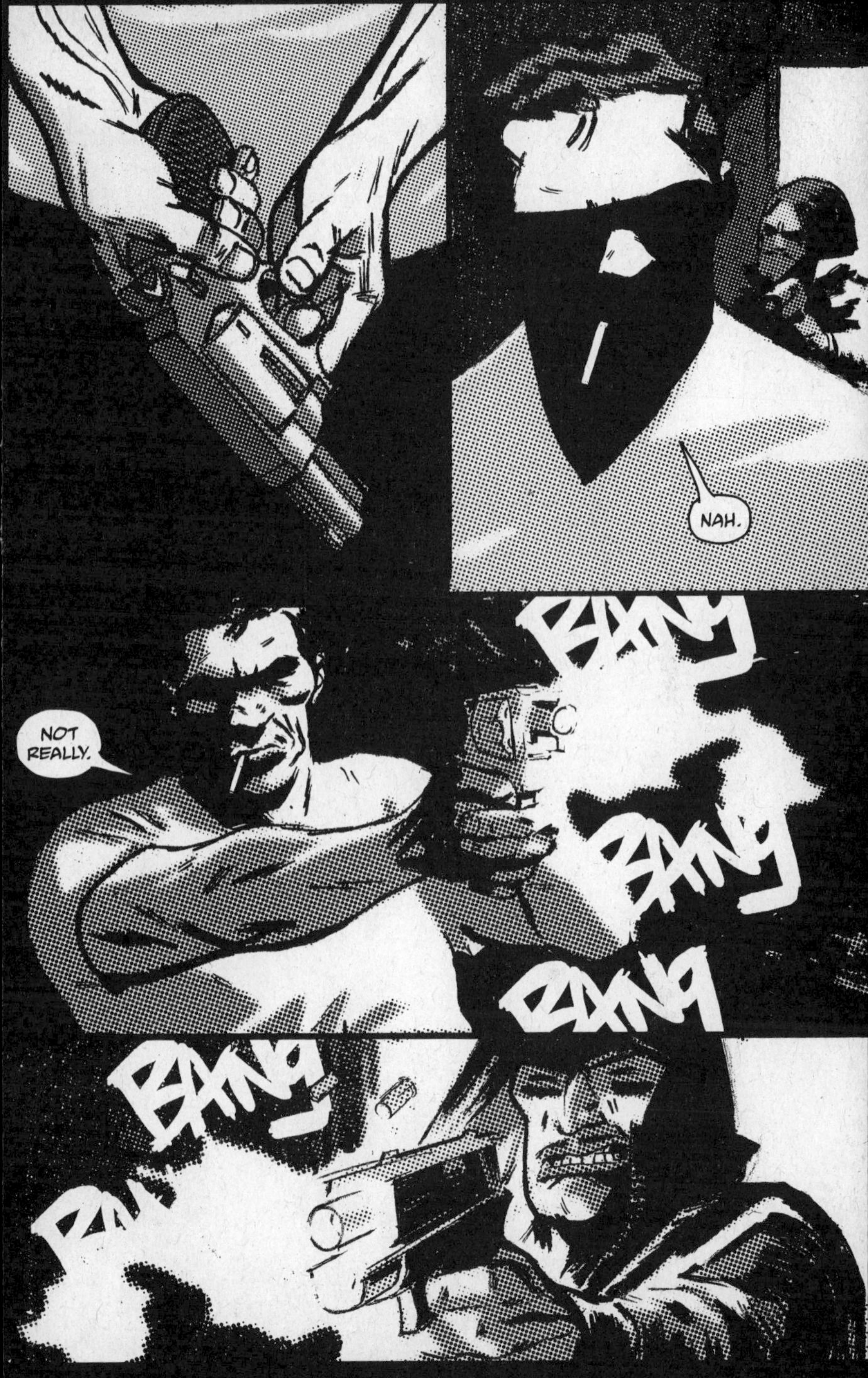

NAH.
NOT REALLY.
BANG
BANG
BANG
BANG

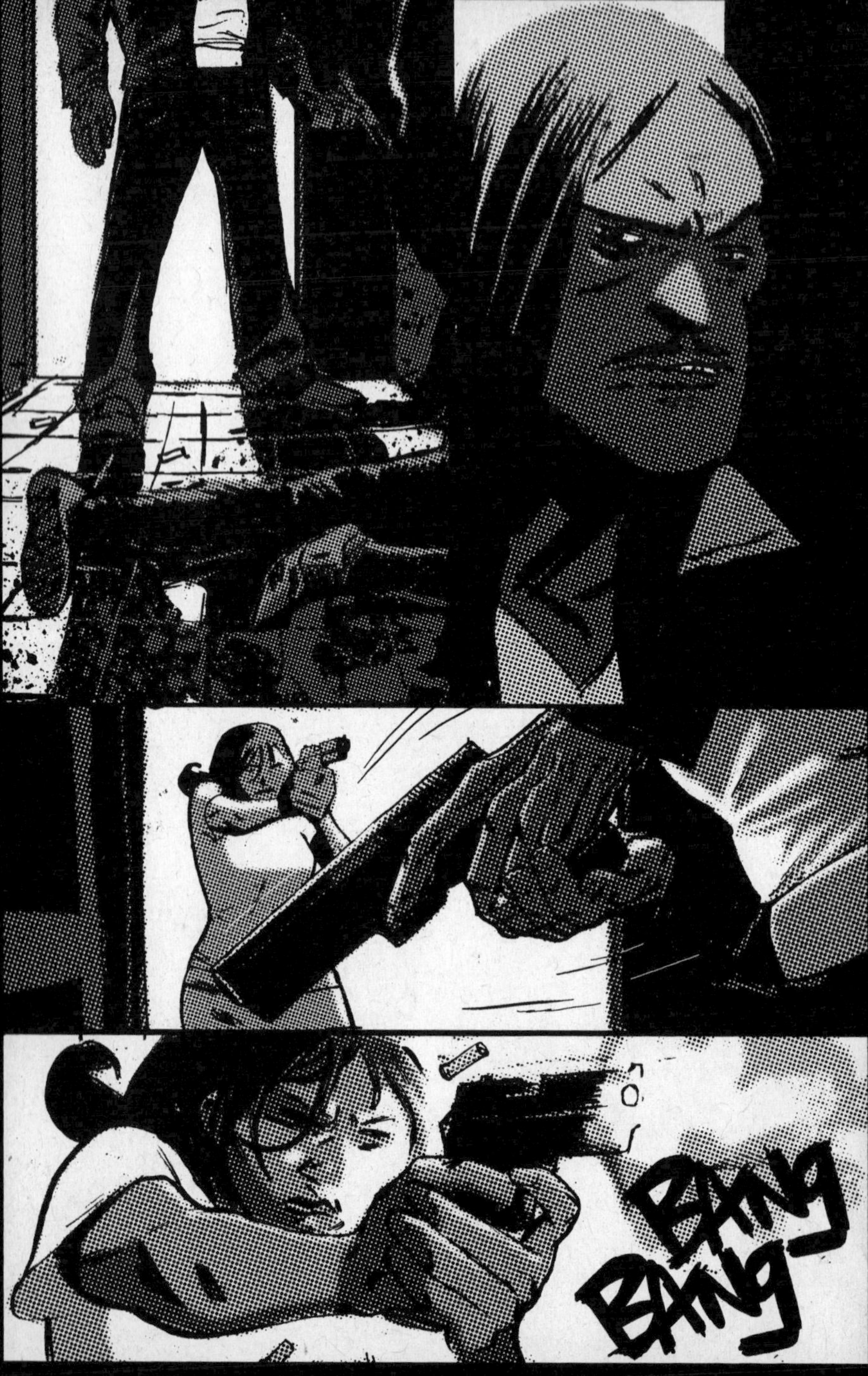
BANG
BANG

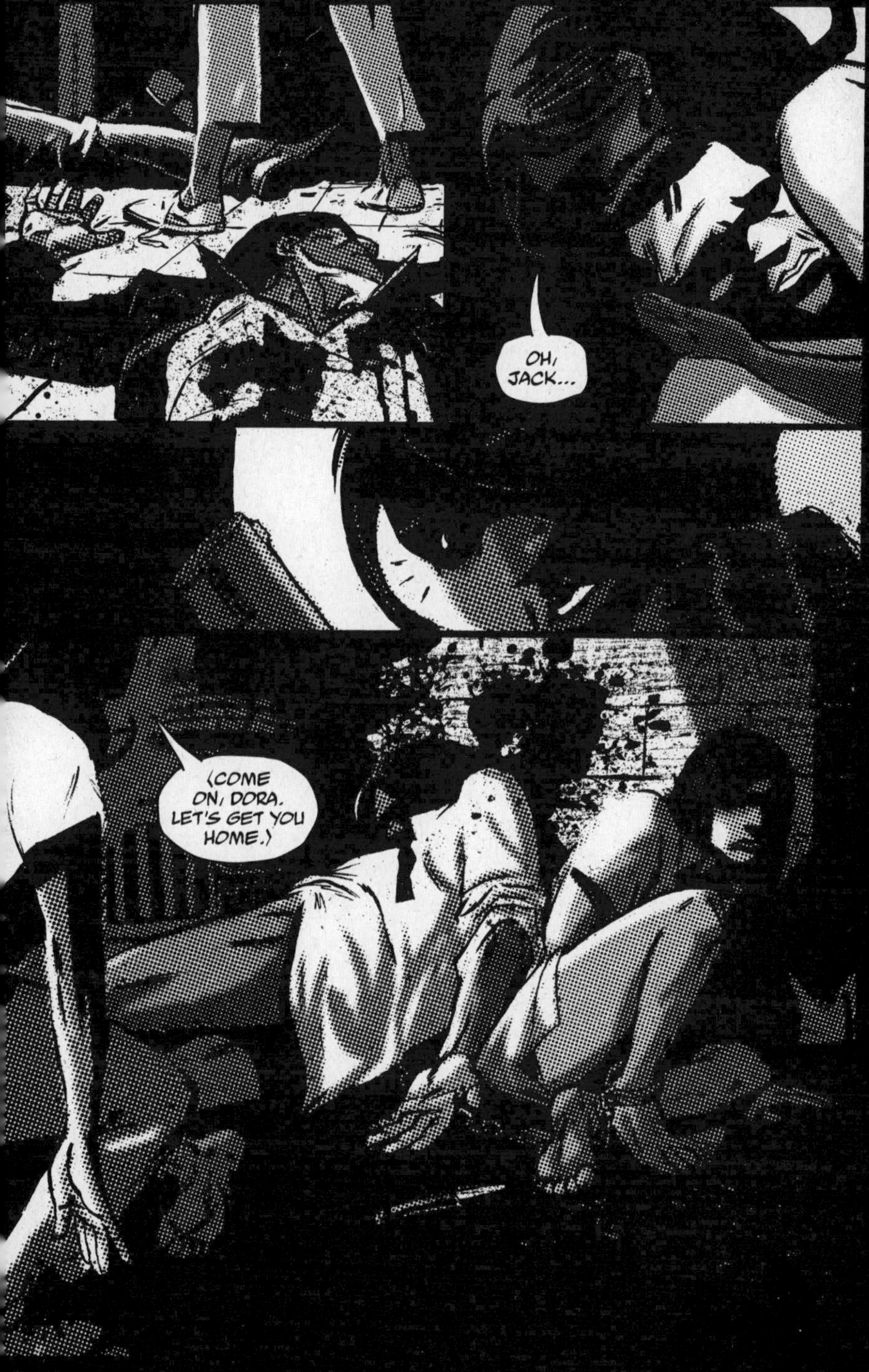
OH, JACK...
(COME ON, DORA. LET'S GET YOU HOME.)

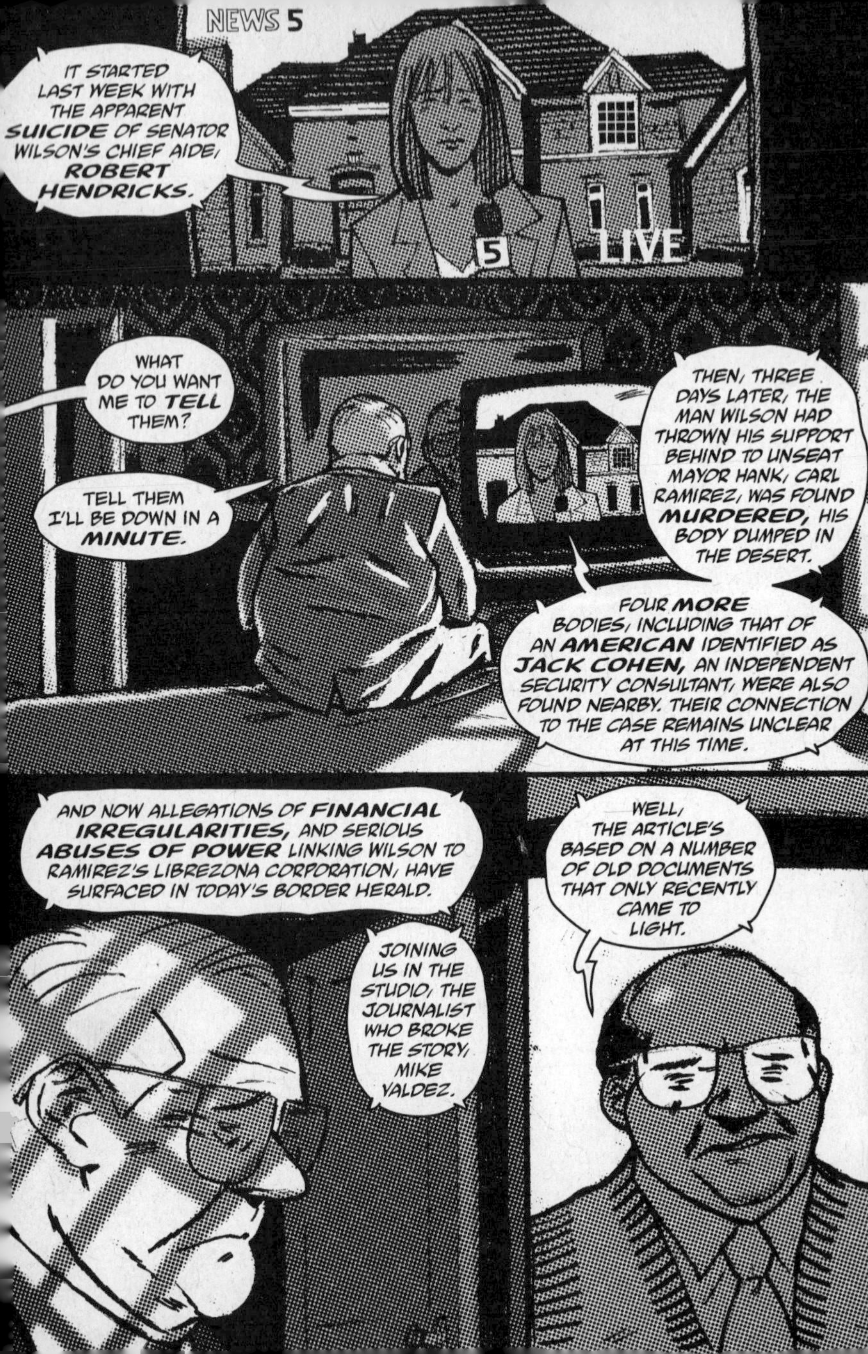
NEWS 5
IT STARTED LAST WEEK WITH THE APPARENT SUICIDE OF SENATOR WILSON'S CHIEF AIDE, ROBERT HENDRICKS.
5
LIVE
WHAT DO YOU WANT ME TO TELL THEM?
TELL THEM I'LL BE DOWN IN A MINUTE.
THEN, THREE DAYS LATER, THE MAN WILSON HAD THROWN HIS SUPPORT BEHIND TO UNSEAT MAYOR HANK, CARL RAMIREZ, WAS FOUND MURDERED, HIS BODY DUMPED IN THE DESERT.
FOUR MORE BODIES, INCLUDING THAT OF AN AMERICAN IDENTIFIED AS JACK COHEN, AN INDEPENDENT SECURITY CONSULTANT, WERE ALSO FOUND NEARBY. THEIR CONNECTION TO THE CASE REMAINS UNCLEAR AT THIS TIME.
AND NOW ALLEGATIONS OF FINANCIAL IRREGULARITIES, AND SERIOUS ABUSES OF POWER LINKING WILSON TO RAMIREZ'S LIBREZONA CORPORATION, HAVE SURFACED IN TODAY'S BORDER HERALD.
JOINING US IN THE STUDIO, THE JOURNALIST WHO BROKE THE STORY, MIKE VALDEZ.
WELL, THE ARTICLE'S BASED ON A NUMBER OF OLD DOCUMENTS THAT ONLY RECENTLY CAME TO LIGHT.

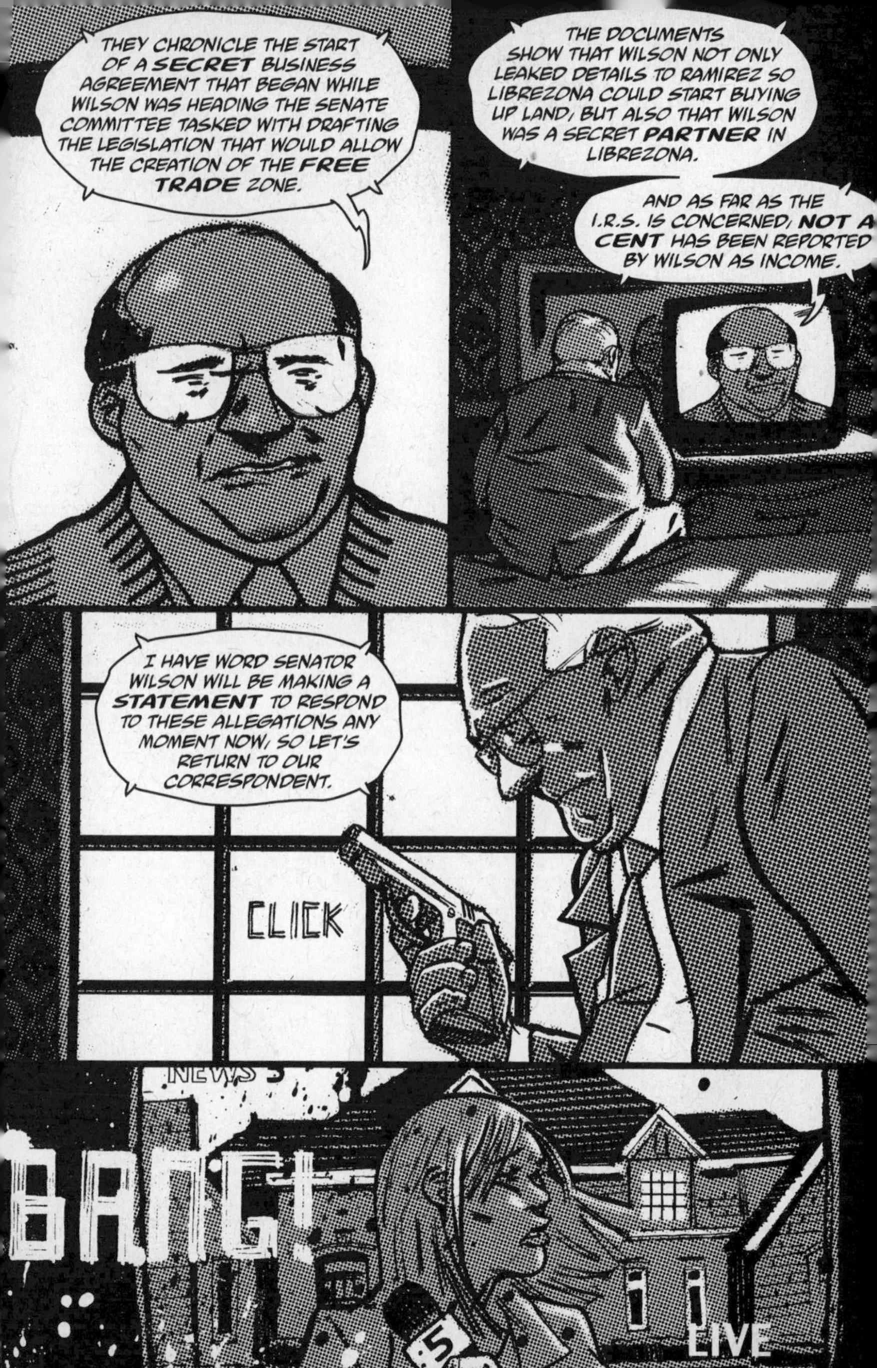
THEY CHRONICLE THE START OF A **SECRET** BUSINESS AGREEMENT THAT BEGAN WHILE WILSON WAS HEADING THE SENATE COMMITTEE TASKED WITH DRAFTING THE LEGISLATION THAT WOULD ALLOW THE CREATION OF THE **FREE TRADE** ZONE.
THE DOCUMENTS SHOW THAT WILSON NOT ONLY LEAKED DETAILS TO RAMIREZ SO LIBREZONA COULD START BUYING UP LAND, BUT ALSO THAT WILSON WAS A SECRET **PARTNER** IN LIBREZONA.
AND AS FAR AS THE I.R.S. IS CONCERNED, **NOT A CENT** HAS BEEN REPORTED BY WILSON AS INCOME.
I HAVE WORD SENATOR WILSON WILL BE MAKING A **STATEMENT** TO RESPOND TO THESE ALLEGATIONS ANY MOMENT NOW, SO LET'S RETURN TO OUR CORRESPONDENT.
CLICK
BANG!
5
LIVE

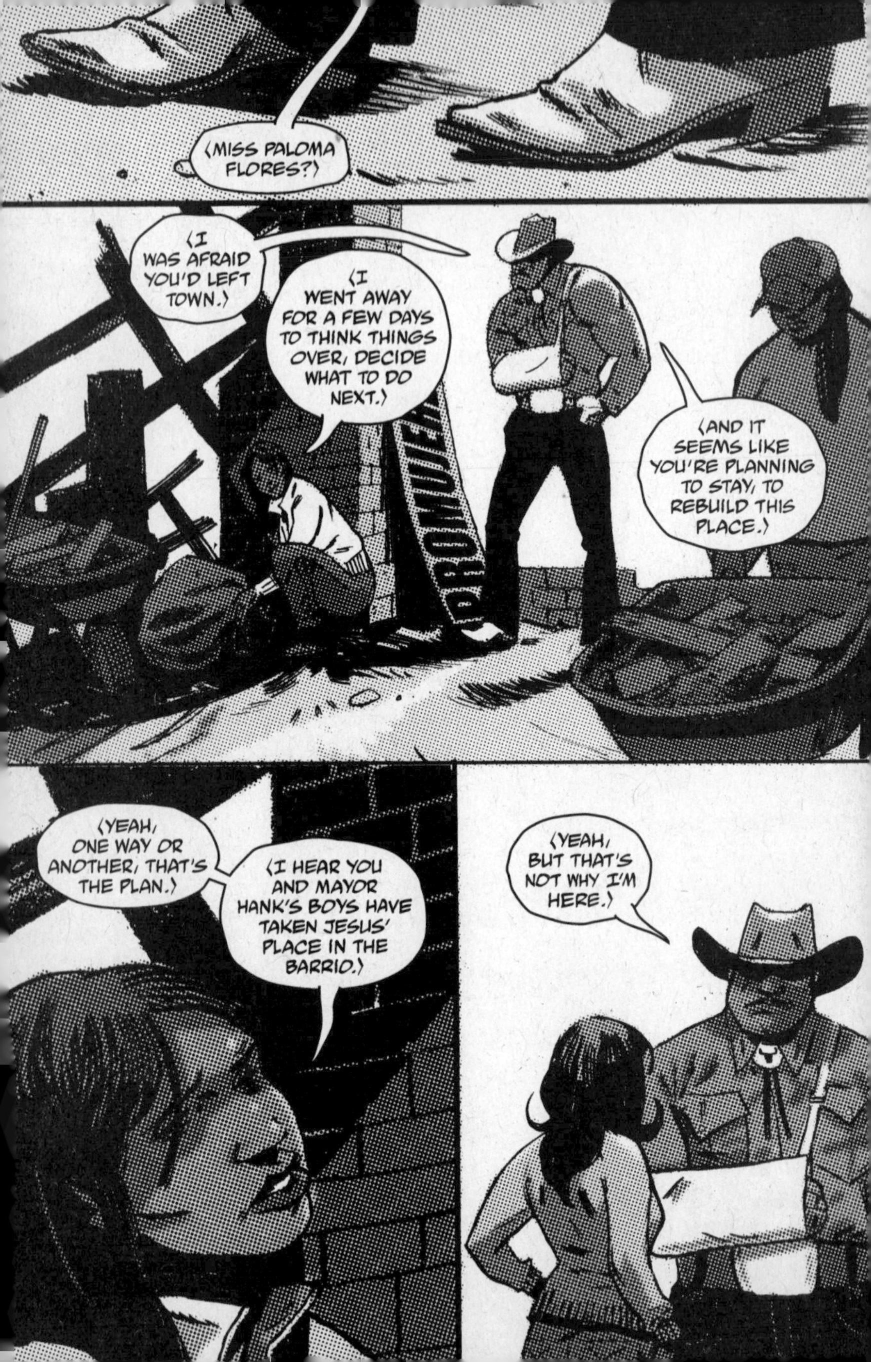
⟨MISS PALOMA FLORES?⟩
⟨I WAS AFRAID YOU'D LEFT TOWN.⟩
⟨I WENT AWAY FOR A FEW DAYS TO THINK THINGS OVER, DECIDE WHAT TO DO NEXT.⟩
⟨AND IT SEEMS LIKE YOU'RE PLANNING TO STAY, TO REBUILD THIS PLACE.⟩
⟨YEAH, ONE WAY OR ANOTHER, THAT'S THE PLAN.⟩
⟨I HEAR YOU AND MAYOR HANK'S BOYS HAVE TAKEN JESUS' PLACE IN THE BARRIO.⟩
⟨YEAH, BUT THAT'S NOT WHY I'M HERE.⟩

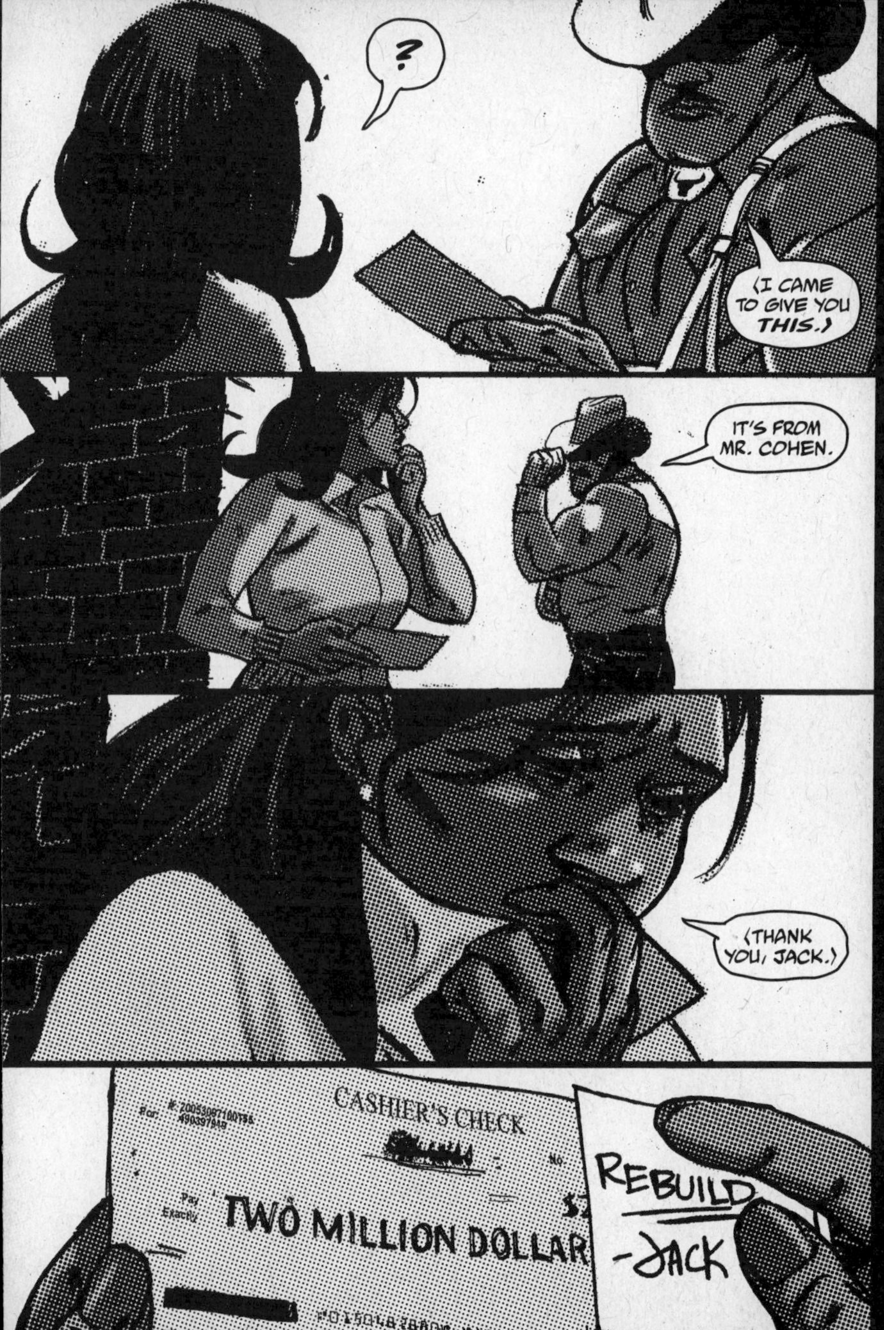
?
⟨I CAME TO GIVE YOU THIS.⟩
IT'S FROM MR. COHEN.
⟨THANK YOU, JACK.⟩
CASHIER'S CHECK
TWO MILLION DOLLAR
REBUILD
-JACK
THE END

DON'T MISS THESE OTHER VERTIGO CRIME BOOKS

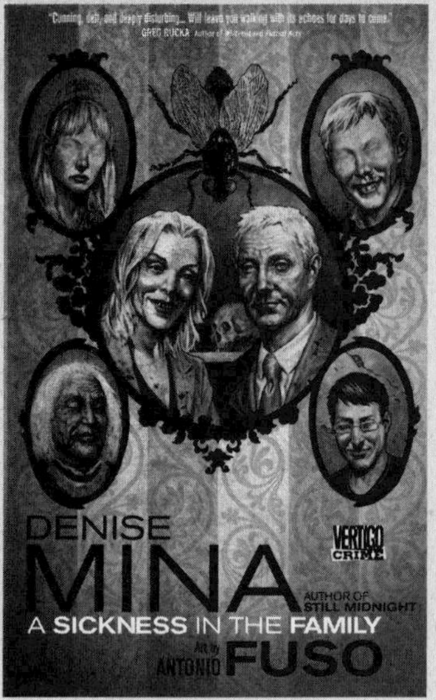
DENISE
MINA
AUTHOR OF STILL MIDNIGHT
A SICKNESS IN THE FAMILY
Art by ANTONIO FUSO
VERTIGO CRIME

A SICKNESS IN THE FAMILY

The Ushers seem like a perfectly normal family. Until they start dying. One by one. As secrets and resentments boil to the surface, it's clear that more than one Usher harbors a motive for killing off the others. But the truth turns out to be far more shocking than any of them could have imagined.

Written by **DENISE MINA**
(Author of *Still Midnight*)

Art by **ANTONIO FUSO**

FOGTOWN

It's San Francsico, 1953 and hard-boiled private œeye, Frank Grissel is caught up in a twisted case of sex, money, drugs and murder. And that's not all... because, like the city itself, Frank's not what he appears. Dig past the surface and there's a complex and tortured soul who realizes that exposing the truth of this case will mean revealing the long-buried truth about himself...

Written by **ANDERSON GABRYCH**

Art by **BRAD RADER**

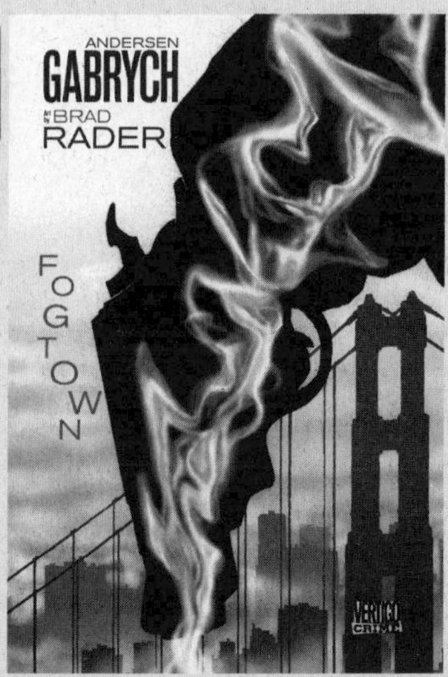
ANDERSEN
GABRYCH
BRAD
RADER
FOGTOWN
VERTIGO CRIME

MORE FROM VERTIGO CRIME

AVAILABLE NOW

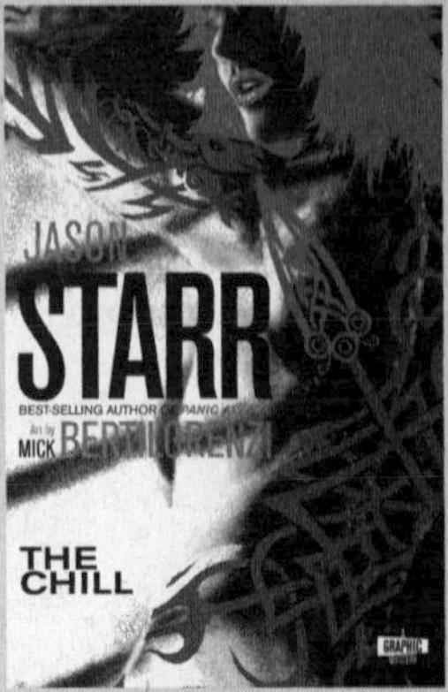
JASON
STARR
THE CHILL

THE CHILL

Written by **JASON STARR**
(Best-selling author of *Panic Attack* and *The Follower*)

Art by **MICK BERTILORENZI**

A modern thriller steeped in Celtic mythology — a broken-down cop tracks a seductive killer who possesses the supernatural power known as "the chill." Can he stop her before her next victim dies horribly... but with a smile on his face?

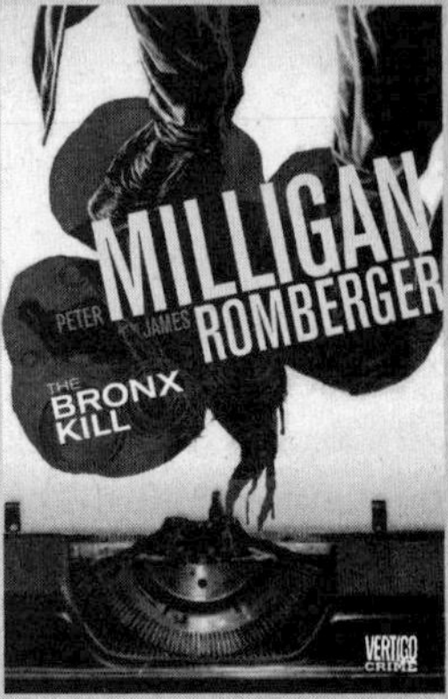
PETER MILLIGAN
JAMES ROMBERGER
THE BRONX KILL
VERTIGO CRIME

THE BRONX KILL

Written by **PETER MILLIGAN**
(GREEK STREET)

Art by **JAMES ROMBERGER**

A struggling writer is investigating his Irish cop roots for his next novel. When he returns home from a research trip, his wife is missing and finding her will lead him to a dark secret buried deep in his family's past.

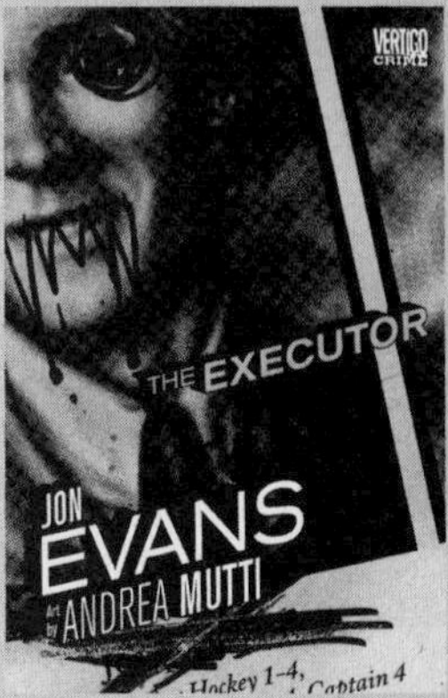
VERTIGO CRIME
THE EXECUTOR
JON EVANS
ANDREA MUTTI

THE EXECUTOR

Written by **JON EVANS**
(Author of *Dark Places* and *Invisible Armies*)

Art by **ANDREA MUTTI**

When a washed-up ex-hockey player is mysteriously named executor of an old girlfriend's will, he must return to the small town he left years earlier. There, he finds a deadly secret from his past that could hold the key to his girlfriend's murder... if it doesn't kill him first.

VERTIGO CRIME